Learn Visual C#®

A Computer Programm

Visual Studio 2019 Edition

16th Edition

By
Philip Conrod & Lou Tylee

©2019 Kidware Software LLC

PO Box 701
Maple Valley, WA 98038
http://www.kidwaresoftware.com

Kidware Software LLC
PO Box 701
Maple Valley, Washington 98038
1.425.413.1185
www.kidwaresoftware.com

Printed in the United States of America

ISBN-13: 978-1-951077-06-8 (Printed Edition)
ISBN-13: 978-1-951077-07-5 (Electronic Edition)

Cover Design by Neil Sauvageau
Cover Image by Vertigo3D
Illustrations by Kevin Brockschmidt

This guide was developed for the course, "Learn Visual C#," produced by Kidware Software, Maple Valley, Washington. It is not intended to be a complete reference to the Visual C# language. Please consult the Microsoft website for detailed reference information.

This guide refers to several software and hardware products by their trade names. These references are for informational purposes only and all trademarks are the property of their respective companies and owners.   Microsoft, Visual Studio, Small Basic, Visual Basic, Visual J#, and Visual C#, IntelliSense, Word, Excel, MSDN, and Windows are all trademark products of the Microsoft Corporation.   Java is a trademark product of the Oracle Corporation.

The example companies, organizations, products, domain names, e-mail addresses, logos, people, places, and events depicted are fictitious. No association with any real company, organization, product, domain name, e-mail address, logo, person, place, or event is intended or should be inferred.

This book expresses the author's views and opinions.   The information in this book is distributed on an "as is" basis, without and expresses, statutory, or implied warranties.

About The Authors

Philip Conrod has authored, co-authored and edited over two dozen computer programming books over the past thirty years. Philip holds a bachelor's degree in Computer Information Systems and a Master's certificate in the Essentials of Business Development from Regis University. Philip has served in various Information Technology leadership roles in companies like Sundstrand Aerospace, Safeco Insurance, FamilyLife, Kenworth Truck Company, and PACCAR. Philip last served as the Chief Information Officer (CIO) for Darigold for over a decade before returning to teaching and writing full-time. Today, Philip serves as the President & Publisher of Kidware Software LLC which is based in Maple Valley, Washington.

Lou Tylee holds BS and MS degrees in Mechanical Engineering and a PhD in Electrical Engineering. Lou has been programming computers since 1969 when he took his first Fortran course in college. He has written software to control suspensions for high speed ground vehicles, monitor nuclear power plants, lower noise levels in commercial jetliners, compute takeoff speeds for jetliners, locate and identify air and ground traffic and to let kids count bunnies, learn how to spell and do math problems. He has written several on-line texts teaching Visual Basic, Visual C# and Java to thousands of people. He taught computer programming courses for over 15 years at the University of Washington and currently teaches math and engineering courses at the Oregon Institute of Technology. Lou also works as a research engineer at a major Seattle aerospace firm. He is the proud father of five children, has six grandchildren and is married to an amazing woman. Lou and his family live in Seattle, Washington.

Acknowledgements

I want to thank my three wonderful daughters - Stephanie, Jessica and Chloe, who helped with various aspects of the book publishing process including software testing, book editing, creative design and many other more tedious tasks like finding errors and typos. I could not have accomplished this without all your hard work, love and support. I also want to thank my best friend, Jesus, who has always been there by my side giving me wisdom and guidance. Without you, this book would have never been printed or published.

I also want to thank my multi-talented co-author, Lou Tylee, for doing all the real hard work necessary to develop, test, debug, and keep current all the 'beginner-friendly' applications, games and base tutorial text found in this book. Lou has tirelessly poured his heart and soul into so many previous versions of this tutorial and there are so many beginners who have benefited from his work over the years. Lou is by far one of the best application developers and tutorial writers I have ever worked with.   Thank you, Lou, for collaborating with me on this book project.

Contents

1. Introduction to the Visual C# Environment

2. The Visual C# Language

3. Object-Oriented Programming (OOP)

4. Exploring the Visual C# Toolbox

\

5. More Exploration of the Visual C# Toolbox

6. Windows Application Design and Distribution

7. Sequential Files, Error-Handling and Debugging

8. Graphics Techniques with Visual C#

9. More Graphics Methods and Multimedia Effects

10. Other Windows Application Topics

11. Visual C# Database and Web Applications

More Computer Programming Tutorials By Kidware Software

Course Description

Learn Visual C# is an intense 11-week, self-paced overview of the Visual C# programming environment. Upon completion of the course, you will:

1. Understand the benefits of using Microsoft Visual C# as a Windows application development tool.
2. Understand the Visual C# event-driven programming concepts, terminology, and available controls.
3. Learn the fundamentals of designing, implementing, and distributing a wide variety of Visual C# Windows applications.

Learn Visual C# is presented using a combination of course notes and over 100 Visual C# examples and applications.

Course Prerequisites

To grasp the concepts presented in **Learn Visual C#**, you should possess a working knowledge of the Windows operating system. You should know how to use Windows Explorer to locate, copy, move and delete files. You should be familiar with the simple tasks of using menus, toolbars, resizing windows, and moving windows around.

You should have had some exposure to programming concepts. If you have never programmed a computer before, you'll have to put in a little preparation effort. Perhaps you might want to seriously consider our companion course, **Beginning Visual C#**, which is aimed at the person who has never programmed before.

Finally, and most obvious, you need to have Microsoft Visual C# which is part of Microsoft Visual Studio Community Edition. This is a free and separate product that must be downloaded from Microsoft

https://www.visualstudio.com/free-developer-offers/

Software Requirements

Visual Studio 2019 will install and run on the following operating systems:

•Windows 10 version 1507 or higher: Home, Professional, Education, and Enterprise (LTSB is not supported)
•Windows Server 2016: Standard and Datacenter
•Windows 8.1 (with Update 2919355): Basic, Professional, and Enterprise
•Windows Server 2012 R2 (with Update 2919355): Essentials, Standard, Datacenter
•Windows 7 SP1 (with latest Windows Updates): Home Premium, Professional, Enterprise, Ultimate

Hardware Requirements

•1.8 GHz or faster processor. Dual-core or better recommended
•2 GB of RAM; 4 GB of RAM recommended (2.5 GB minimum if running on a virtual machine)
•Hard disk space: 1GB to 40GB, depending on features installed
•Video card that supports a minimum display resolution of 720p (1280 by 720); Visual Studio will work best at a resolution of WXGA (1366 by 768) or higher

Installing and Using the Downloadable Solution Files

If you purchased this directly from our website you received an email with a special and individualized internet download link where you could download the compressed Program Solution Files.   If you purchased this book through a 3rd Party Book Store like Amazon.com, the solutions files for this tutorial are included in a compressed ZIP file that is available for download directly from our website (after registration) at:

http://www.kidwaresoftware.com/learnvcs2019-registration.html

Complete the online web form at the webpage above with your name, shipping address, email address, the exact title of this book, date of purchase, online or physical store name, and your order confirmation number from that store. We also ask you to include the last 4 digits of your credit card so we can match it to the credit card that was used to purchase this tutorial.   After we receive all this information we will email you a download link for the Source Code Solution Files associated with this book.

Warning: If you purchased this book "used" or "second hand" you are not licensed or entitled to download the Program Solution Files. However, you can purchase the Digital Download Version of this book at a highly discounted price which allows you access to the digital source code solutions files required for completing this tutorial.

Using Learn Visual C#

The course notes and code for **Learn Visual C#** are included in one or more ZIP file(s). Use your favorite 'unzipping' application to write all files to your computer. The course is included in the folder entitled **LearnVCS**. This folder contains two other folders: **VCS Notes** and **VCS Code**. There's a chance when you copy the files to your computer, they will be written as **'Read-Only.'** To correct this (in **Windows Explorer** or **My Computer**), right-click the **LearnVCS** folder and remove the check next to **Read only**. Make sure to choose the option to apply this change to all sub-folders and files.

The **VCS Code** folder includes all applications developed during the course. The applications are further divided into **Class** folders. Each class folder contains the Visual C# project folders. As an example, to open the Visual C# project named Example 1-1 discussed in Class 1, you would go to this directory:

C:\LearnVCS\VCS Code\Class 1\Example 1-1

How To Take the Course

Learn Visual C# is a self-paced course. The suggested approach is to do one chapter a week for eleven weeks. Each week's chapter should require about 4 to 10 hours of your time to grasp the concepts completely. Prior to doing a particular week's work, open the class notes file for that week and print it out. Then, work through the notes at your own pace. Try to do each example as they are encountered in the notes. If you need any help, all solved examples are included in the **VCS Code** folder.

After completing each week's notes, practice problems and homework exercise (sometimes, two) is given; covering many of the topics taught that in that class. Like the examples, try to work through the practice problems and homework exercise, or some variation thereof, on your own. Refer to the completed exercise in the **VCS Code** folder, if necessary. This is where you will learn to be a Visual C# programmer. You only learn how to build applications and write code by doing lots of it. The problems and exercises give you that opportunity. And, you learn coding by seeing lots of code. Programmers learn to program by seeing how other people do things. Feel free to 'borrow' code from the examples that you can adapt to your needs. I think you see my philosophy here. I don't think you can teach programming. I do, however, think you can teach people how to become programmers. This course includes numerous examples, problems, and exercises to help you toward that goal. We show you how to do lots of different things in the code examples. You will learn from the examples!

A Note on Visual C# Naming Conventions

Controls

The accepted standard for naming controls is to assign a three letter (lower case) prefix (identifying the type of control) followed by a descriptive name you assign. Some of the prefixes are:

Control	Prefix	Example
Form	frm	frmWatch
Button	btn	btnExit, btnStart
Label	lbl	lblStart, lblEnd
Text Box	txt	txtTime, txtName
Menu	mnu	mnuExit, mnuSave
Check Box	chk	chkChoice

Event Methods

Once a control is named, the standard for naming an event method associated with a control is

```
private void ControlName_Event(Arguments)
{

}
```

So, for a button control name **btnExample**, the event method for the **Click** event would be named **btnExample_Click**. And, since the earliest days of Visual Studio, if you double-click on a button control named **btnExample**, the event method appearing in the code window was:

```
private void btnExample_Click(object sender, EventArgs e)
{

}
```

This has changed with Visual Studio 2019.

In Visual Studio 2019, if you double-click on a button control named **btnExample**, the event method appearing in the code window is:

```
private void BtnExample_Click(object sender, EventArgs e)
{
```

```
    }
```

Note that the first letter of the control name is automatically capitalized. The folks at Microsoft have decided that the first letter of every method in Visual C# should be upper case (and there doesn't appear to be any way to turn off this "feature"). This creates a mismatch between the assigned control name (**btnExample**) and the name used in the event method (**BtnExample**). For our Visual C# tutorials, we needed to decide what to do about this new convention.

Our Naming Conventions

The mismatch between control name and event method name would quickly go away if we simply choose to apply a new control naming convention where the first letter of every control name is an upper case letter. We did not take this route – it would require a massive paradigm shift. And, it would require extensive rewriting of all legacy code written using the standard convention. We decided to continue use of the time-tested control naming convention, a three letter lower case prefix, followed by a describing name with mixed upper and lower case letters. This standard has been around forever and will probably remain so. With this decision, we had to choose what to do about event method names.

First, realize that the name of the event method associated with a control is completely arbitrary. You can give the method any name you want as long as it's properly connected to the correct event method using the Visual Studio properties window. So, we could continue to use our old standard of naming event methods, starting with a lower case letter. For a button control named **btnExample**, the **Click** event method would be

```
    private void btnExample_Click(object sender, EventArgs e)
    {

    }
```

Such a convention will work in Visual Studio 2019, but comes with problems.

The first problem in using the 'old standard' is that Visual Studio will flag each so named event method with an error message saying: 'Naming rule violation: These words must begin with upper case characters: btnExample_Click'. Again, the code will still work, but there will be all these annoying messages.

The second problem in using the 'old standard' in Visual Studio 2019 is that when building a project, if you double-click on a control to establish an event method, the first letter will be automatically capitalized. Then, you have to remember to change the case of that letter for every event method established. This would be a headache.

We have decided to live with this new naming convention where the first letter of every event method is capitalized, realizing there is a mismatch between the control names and associated event methods. So, in our tutorials, when we refer to the **Click** event method for a control named **btnExample**, that method's name in code will be **BtnExample_Click**. We recognize this is a change for programmers, but hopefully is something you can get used to. In our experience, it just took a few examples for the new convention to seem 'normal'.

Foreword By David B. Taylor, Former College Professor & Department Chair

Do you remember when you learned to ride a bike? The person holding you up let go and you were on your way. The exhilaration of that accomplishment, the freedom, and empowerment were indescribable and easily recalled to this day. Completing a computer program that you designed and built, either on your own or with a team, warrants the same degree of fulfilment and jubilation. Computer programming has a lot of parts so the better the explanation the more likely you are to succeed.

As a programmer, a long-time college professor, and as the former head of the Computer, Engineering, and Business Department, I have reviewed countless programming books for most of the popular programming languages. "Learn Visual C#" by Philip Conrod and Lou Tylee is my favorite.

The order in which the topics are presented is very easy for students to follow. The transitions from one topic to the next are so smooth it doesn't feel like steps but just a continuously smooth flow from start to finish.

Object-oriented programming (OOP) is often difficult to explain to new programmers and most books give it no consideration until the second half of the book. The authors have made OOP clear, logical, and astonishingly easy to understand and they have successfully presented it in the third chapter...it is absolute genius. Consequently, every topic after that is much clearer and relevant to students.

The examples in the book are interesting and easy to follow. I have worked through all of them line by line and found them easy to follow and replicate. Students quickly become frustrated with examples that contain errors so the fact that these work so well is critically important to the success of every student.

Topics included in "Learn Visual C#" are date, time, and financial calculations which are lacking in most first year programming books. I really appreciate the chapters that include business graphics for pie and bar charts and general graphics applied to multimedia.

The authors use code to access databases instead of the Visual Studio wizards. This gives the students a much better understanding of how databases work and how to program their interactions. Consequently, that also makes the eventual use of the database wizards less of a mystery and gives the student far more confidence in their application.

The useful topics in the examples and the well written explanations make this my favorite book for learning Visual C# programming so it is with absolute confidence that I recommend this book to you.

David B. Taylor, B.S.E.T., M.A.Ed., Ed.S.
Former Professor and Department Chair
Computer, Engineering, and Business
Seminole State College
Sanford, Florida

Forward by Alan Payne, A High School Computer Science Teacher

"What is "Learn Visual C#" and how it works.
These lessons are a highly organized and well-indexed set of lessons in the Visual C# programming environment. They are written for the initiated programmer - the college or university student seeking to advance their computer science repertoire on their own. The applications are practical, but the learning has far-reaching consequences in the student's computer science career.

While full solutions are provided, the projects are presented in an easy-to-follow set of lessons explaining the rational for the solution - the form layout, coding design and conventions, and specific code related to the problem. The learner may follow the tutorials at their own pace while focusing upon context relevant information. The finished product is the reward, but the adult student is fully engaged and enriched by the process. This kind of learning is often the focus of teacher training at the highest level. Every computer science teacher and self-taught learner knows what a great deal of work is required for projects to work in this manner, and with these tutorials, the work is done by an author who understands the adult need for streamlined learning.

Graduated Lessons for Every Project ... Lessons, examples, problems and projects. Graduated learning. Increasing and appropriate difficulty... Great results.

With these projects, there are lessons providing a comprehensive background on the programming topics to be covered. Once understood, concepts are easily applicable to a variety of applications. Then, specific examples are drawn out so that a learner can practice with the Visual C# form designer. Conventions relating to event-driven programming, naming controls and the scope of variables are explained. Then specific coding for the example is provided so that the user can see all the parts of the project come together for the finished product.

After the example is completed, then short problems challenge the user to repeat the process on their own, and finally, exercises provide a "summative" for the unit.

By presenting lessons in this graduated manner, adult students are fully engaged and appropriately challenged to become independent thinkers who can come up with their own project ideas and design their own forms and do their own coding. Once the process is learned, then student engagement is unlimited! I have seen even adult student literacy improve dramatically when students cannot get enough of what is being presented.

Indeed, lessons encourage accelerated learning - in the sense that they provide an enriched environment to learn computer science, but they also encourage accelerating learning because students cannot put the lessons away once they start! Computer Science provides this unique opportunity to challenge students, and it is a great testament to the authors that they are successful in achieving such levels of engagement with consistency.

How independent learners use the materials.

The style of presentation (lessons, examples, problems, exercises) encourages self-guided learning. Students may trust the order of presentation in order to have sufficient background information for every project. But the lessons are also highly indexed, so that students may pick and choose projects if limited by time.

Materials already condense what is available from MSDN so that students remember what they learn.

My history with the Kidware Software products.

I have used single license or shareware versions for over a decade to keep up my own learning as a Secondary School teacher of advanced Computer Science. As a learner who just wants to get down to business, these lessons match my learning style. I do not waste valuable time ensconced in language reference libraries for programming environments and help screens which can never be fully remembered! With every project, the pathway to learning is clear and immediate, though the topics in Computer Science remain current, relevant and challenging.

Some of the topics covered in these tutorials include:
- Data Types and Ranges
- Scope of Variables
- Naming Conventions
- Decision Making
- Looping
- Language Functions - String, Date, Numerical
- Arrays, Control Arrays
- Writing Your own Methods and Classes
- Windows Application Design and Distribution
- Sequential File Access, Error-Handling and Debugging techniques
- Graphics and Multimedia applications
- Visual C# Database and Web Applications

Any further advanced topics in post-secondary computing (advanced data structures such as Lists and Linked Lists, Stacks, Queues, Binary Trees, etc...) derive directly from those listed above. Nothing is forgotten. All can be extrapolated from the lessons provided.

Quick learning curve by Contextualized Learning

Having projects completed ahead of time encourages Contextualized Learning. Once a problem statement is understood, then the process of form-design, naming controls and coding is mastered for a given set of Visual C# controls. Then, it is much more likely that students create their own problems and solutions from scratch. This is the pattern of learning for any language!

Meet Different State and Provincial Curriculum Expectations and More

Different states and provinces have their own curriculum requirements for Computer Science. With the Kidware Software products, you have at your disposal a series of projects which will allow you to pick and choose from among those which best suit your learning needs. Students focus upon design stages and sound problem-solving techniques from a Computer Science perspective. In doing so, they become independent problem-solvers, and will exceed the curricular requirements of secondary and post-secondary schools everywhere.

Computer Science topics not explicitly covered in tutorials can be added at the learner's discretion. For example, recursive functions could be dealt with in a project which calculates factorials, permutations and combinations with a few text boxes and buttons on a form. Students learn to process information by collecting it in text boxes, and they learn to code command buttons. The language - whether it is Visual Basic, Visual C#, Visual C++, or Console Java, Java GUI, etc... is really up to the individual learner !

Lessons encourage your own programming extensions.

Once concepts are learned, it is difficult to NOT know what to do for your own projects.

Having my own projects in one language, such as Visual C#, I know that I could easily adapt them to other languages once I have studied the Kidware Software tutorials. I do not believe there is any other reference material out there which would cause me to make the same claim! In fact, I know there is not as I have spent over a decade looking!

Having used Kidware Software tutorials for the past decade, I have been successful at the expansion of my own learning of other platforms such as XNA for the Xbox, or the latest developer suites for tablets and phones. I thank Kidware Software and its authors for continuing to stand for what is right in the teaching methodologies which not only inspire, but propel the self-guided learner through what can be an intelligible landscape of opportunities."

Alan Payne, B.A.H. , B.Ed.
Computer Science Teacher
T.A. Blakelock High School

Oakville, Ontario
http://chatt.hdsb.ca/~paynea

1. Introduction to the Visual C# Environment

Preview

In this first class, we will do an overview of how to build a Windows application using Visual C# (pronounced **visual cee sharp**). You'll learn a new vocabulary, a new approach to programming, and ways to move around in the Visual C# environment. Once finished, you will have written your first Visual C# program.

Course Objectives

- Understand the benefits of using Microsoft Visual C# as an application tool
- Understand Visual C# event-driven programming concepts, object-oriented programming terminology, and available controls
- Learn the fundamentals of designing, implementing, and distributing a Visual C# Windows application
- Learn to use the Visual C# toolbox
- Learn to modify object properties and use of object methods
- Use menu and toolbar design tools
- Learn how to read and write sequential files
- Understand proper debugging and error-handling procedures
- Gain an understanding of graphic methods and simple animations
- Obtain an introduction to the Windows Application Programming Interface (API)
- Learn how to print text and graphics from a Visual C# application
- Gain skills to develop and implement an HTML-based help system
- Introduce database management using Visual C#

What is Visual C#?

Visual C# is part of a grand initiative by Microsoft. With Visual C#, you are able to quickly build Windows-based applications (the emphasis in this course), web-based applications and software for other devices, such as palm computers.

Windows applications built using Visual C# feature a Graphical User Interface (GUI). Users interact with a set of visual tools (buttons, text boxes, tool bars, menu items) to make an application do its required tasks. The applications have a familiar appearance to the user. As you develop as a Visual C# programmer, you will begin to look at Windows applications in a different light. You will recognize and understand how various elements of Word, Excel, Access and other applications work. You will develop a new vocabulary to describe the elements of Windows applications.

Visual C# Windows applications are **event-driven**, meaning nothing happens until an application is called upon to respond to some event (button pressing, menu selection, ...). Visual C# is governed by an event processor. As mentioned, nothing happens until an event is detected. Once an event is detected, a corresponding event method is located and the instructions provided by that method are executed. Those instructions are the actual code written by the programmer. In Visual C#, that code is written using the C# programming language. Once an event method is completed, program control is then returned to the event processor.

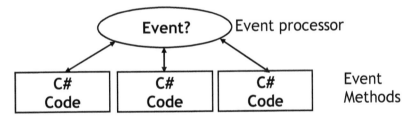

All Windows applications are event-driven. For example, nothing happens in Word until you click on a button, select a menu option, or type some text. Each of these actions is an event.

The event-driven nature of applications developed with Visual C# makes it very easy to work with. As you develop a Visual C# application, event methods can be built and tested individually, saving development time. And, often event methods are similar in their coding, allowing re-use (and lots of copy and paste).

Some Features of Visual C#

> ➢ All new, easy-to-use, powerful Integrated Development Environment (IDE)
> ➢ Full set of controls - you 'draw' the application
> ➢ Response to mouse and keyboard actions
> ➢ Clipboard and printer access
> ➢ Full array of mathematical, string handling, and graphics functions
> ➢ Can easily work with arrays of variables and objects
> ➢ Sequential file support
> ➢ Useful debugger and structured error-handling facilities
> ➢ Easy-to-use graphic tools
> ➢ Powerful database access tools
> ➢ Ability to develop both Windows and internet applications using similar techniques
> ➢ New common language runtime module makes distribution of applications a simple task

To use Visual C#, you (and your students) must be using Microsoft Windows. These notes were developed using Windows 10.

A Brief Look at Object-Oriented Programming (OOP)

Visual C# is fully **object-oriented**. For this particular course, we don't have to worry much about just what that means (many sizeable tomes have been written about OOP). What we need to know is that each application we write will be made up of **objects**. Just what is an object? It can be many things: a variable, a font, a graphics region, a rectangle, a printed document. The key thing to remember is that these objects represent reusable entities that are used to develop an application. This 'reusability' makes our job much easier as a programmer.

In Visual C#, there are three terms we need to be familiar with in working with object-oriented programming: **Namespace**, **Class** and **Object**. **Objects** are what are used to build our application. We will learn about many objects throughout this course. Objects are derived from **classes**. Think of classes as general descriptions of objects, which are then specific implementations of a class. For example, a class could be a general description of a car, where an object from that class would be a specific car, say a red 1965 Ford Mustang convertible (a nice object!). Lastly, a **namespace** is a grouping of different classes used in the .NET world. One namespace might have graphics classes, while another would have math functions. We will see several namespaces in our work. And, you'll start creating your very own objects in Class 3.

Structure of a Visual C# Windows Application

We want to get started building our first Visual C# Windows application. But, first we need to define some of the terminology we will be using. In Visual C#, a Windows **application** is defined as a **solution**. A solution is made up of one or more **projects**. Projects are groups of forms and code that make up some application. In most of our work in this course, our applications (solutions) will be made up of a single project. Because of this, we will usually use the terms application, solution and project synonymously.

As mentioned, a project (application) is made up of forms and code. Pictorially, this is:

Project

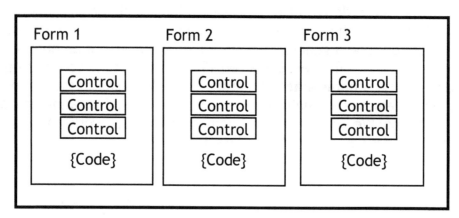

Application (Project) is made up of:

- ➢ **Forms** - Windows that you create for user interface
- ➢ **Controls** - Graphical features drawn on forms to allow user interaction (text boxes, labels, scroll bars, buttons, etc.) (Forms and Controls are **objects.**)
- ➢ **Properties** - Every characteristic of a form or control is specified by a property. Example properties include names, captions, size, color, position, and contents. Visual C# applies default properties. You can change properties when designing the application or even when an application is executing.
- ➢ **Methods** - Built-in methods that can be invoked to impart some action to a particular control or object.

> ➤ **Event Methods - Code** related to some object or control. This is the code that is executed when a certain event occurs. In our applications, this code will be written in the C# language (covered in detail in Chapter 2 of these notes).
>
> ➤ **General Methods - Code** not related to objects. This code must be invoked or called in the application.

The application displayed above has three forms. Visual C# uses a very specific directory structure for saving all of the components for a particular application. When you save a new project (solution), you will be asked for a **Name** and **Location** (directory). A folder named **Name** will be established in the selected **Location**. That folder will be used to store all solution files, project files, form files (**cs** extension) and other files needed by the project. Two subfolders will be established within the Name folder: **Bin** and **Obj**. The **Obj** folder contains files used for debugging your application as it is being developed. The **Bin\Debug** folder contains your compiled application (the actual executable code or **exe** file). Later, you will see that this folder is considered the 'application path' when ancillary data, graphics and sound files are needed by an application.

In a project folder, you will see these files (and possibly more):

Program.**cs**	Information on how things fit together
SolutionName.**sln**	Solution file for solution named SolutionName
SolutionName.**suo**	Solution options file
ProjectName.**csproj**	Project file – one for each project in solution
FormName.**resx**	Form resources file – one for each form
FormName.**cs**	Form code file – one for each form
FormName.Designer.**cs**	File holding design information for form
App.**ico**	Icon used to represent the application

Steps in Developing a Windows Application

The Visual C# Integrated Development Environment (IDE) makes building an application a straightforward process. There are three primary steps involved in building a Visual C# application:

1. **Draw** the user **interface** by placing controls on a Windows form
2. **Assign properties** to controls
3. **Write code** for control events (and perhaps write other methods)

These same steps are followed whether you are building a very simple application or one involving many controls and many lines of code.

The event-driven nature of Visual C# applications allows you to build your application in stages and test it at each stage. You can build one method, or part of a method, at a time and try it until it works as desired. This minimizes errors and gives you, the programmer, confidence as your application takes shape.

As you progress in your programming skills, always remember to take this sequential approach to building a Visual C# application. Build a little, test a little, modify a little and test again. You'll quickly have a completed application. This ability to quickly build something and try it makes working with Visual C# fun – not a quality found in some programming environments! Now, we'll start Visual C# and look at each step in the application development process.

Starting Visual C#

We assume you have Visual C# installed and operational on your computer. **Visual C#** is included as a part of **Microsoft Visual Studio**. Visual Studio includes not only Visual C#, but also Visual C++ and Visual Basic. All three languages use the same development environment.

To start Visual C#

> ➢ Click on the **Start** button on the Windows task bar.
> ➢ Click on **Visual Studio 2019**

Visual Studio will start and (among other things) a start page similar to this will appear:

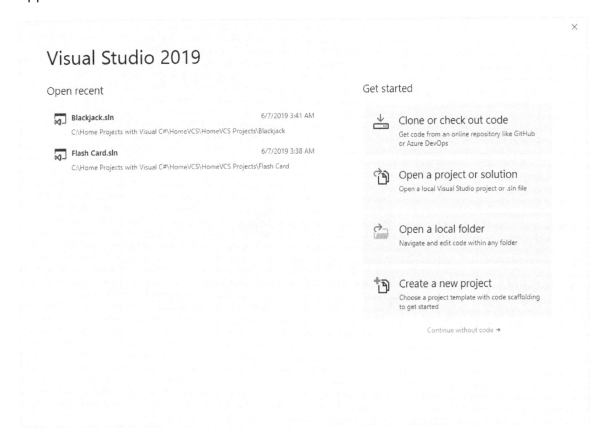

We want to create a project.

On the screen is a **Create a new project** link. Click that link and the following dialog box will appear:

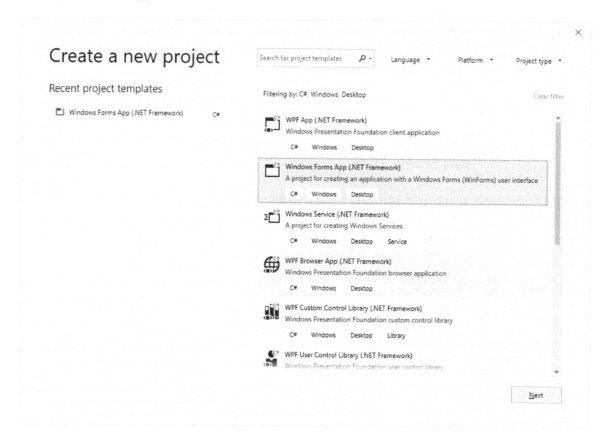

We want to build a Windows C# desktop application. In the **Language** drop-down box, choose **C#**. In the **Platform** drop-down box, choose **Windows**. In the **Project type** drop-down box, choose **Desktop**. Then, select the **Windows Forms App** template. Click **Next**. The selected options will be saved to your IDE environment, so you don't have to reselect them each time you create a new project.

This window appears

Configure your new project

Windows Forms App (.NET Framework)   C#   Windows   Desktop

Project name

    TestProject

Location

    C:\LearnVCS\VCS Code\Class 1\

Solution name ⓘ

    TestProject

☐ Place solution and project in the same directory

Framework

    .NET Framework 4.7.2

Back   Create

Assign a **Name** to your project (mine is named **TestProject**). **Location** should show the directory your project folder will be in. You can **Browse** to an existing location or create a new directory by checking the indicated box. For this course, we suggest saving each of your project folders in the same directory. For the course notes, all project folders are saved in the **\LearnVCS\VCS Code** folder, with additional folders for each individual class' projects. We suggest you save your projects in a folder you create.

Once done, click **Create** and the Visual C# development environment will appear. Your project will consist of a single Windows form.

Visual C# Integrated Development Environment (IDE)

The **Visual C# IDE** is where we build and test our application via implementation of the three steps of application development (draw controls, assign properties, write code). As you progress through this course, you will learn how easy-to-use and helpful the IDE is. There are many features in the IDE and many ways to use these features. Here, we will introduce the IDE and some of its features. You must realize, however, that its true utility will become apparent as you use it yourself to build your own applications.

Several windows appear when you start Visual C#. Each window can be viewed (made visible or active) by selecting menu options, depressing function keys or using the displayed toolbar. As you use the IDE, you will find the method you feel most comfortable with

The title bar area shows you the name of your project. When running your project you will also see one of two words in brackets: **Running** or **Debugging**. This shows the mode Visual C# is operating in. Visual C# operates in three modes.

> ➢ **Design** mode - used to build application (the mode if not **Running** or **Debugging**)
> ➢ **Running** mode - used to run the application
> ➢ **Debugging** mode - application halted and debugger is available; also referred to as **Break** mode

We focus here on the **design** mode. You should, however, always be aware of what mode you are working in.

Under the title bar is the **Menu**. This menu is dynamic, changing as you try to do different things in Visual C#. When you start working on a project, it should look like:

File   Edit   View   Project   Build   Debug   Format   Test   Analyze   Tools   Extensions   Window   Help

You will become familiar with each menu topic as you work through the course. Briefly, they are:

File	Use to open/close projects and files. Use to exit Visual C#
Edit	Used when writing code to do the usual editing tasks of cutting, pasting, copying and deleting text
View	Provides access to most of the windows in the IDE
Project	Allows you to add/delete components to your project
Build	Controls the compiling process
Debug	Comes in handy to help track down errors in your code (works when Visual C# is in **Debugging** mode)
Format	Used to modify appearance of your graphic interface.
Test	Allows you to compile and run your completed application (go to **Running** mode)
Analyze	Performs analytics on your code.
Tools	Allows custom configuration of the IDE. Be particularly aware of the **Options** choice under this menu item. This choice allows you to modify the IDE to meet any personal requirements.
Extensions	Allows customization of IDE
Window	Lets you change the layout of windows in the IDE
Help	Perhaps, the most important item in the Menu. Provides access to the Visual C# on-line documentation via help contents, index or search. Get used to this item!

The View menu also allows you to choose from a myriad of toolbars available in the Visual C# IDE. Toolbars provide quick access to many features. The **Standard** (default) toolbar appears below the menu:

If you forget what a toolbar button does, hover your mouse cursor over the button until a descriptive tooltip appears. We will discuss most of these toolbar functions in the remainder of the IDE information.

In the middle of the Visual C# IDE is the **Design Window**. This window is central to developing Visual C# applications. Various items are available by selecting tabs at the top of the window. The primary use is to draw your application on a form and, later, to write code. Forms are selected using the tab named **FormName.cs [Design]:**

The corresponding code for a form is found using the **FormName.cs** tab. The design window will also display help topics and other information you may choose.

The **Toolbox** is the selection menu for controls used in your application. It is active when a form is shown in the design window:

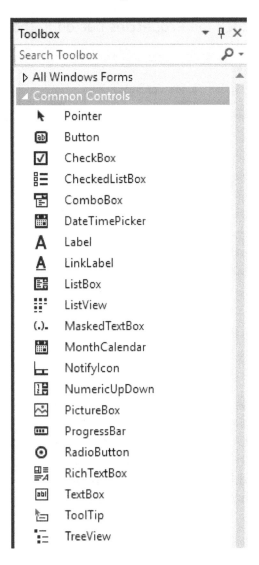

Many of these tools will look familiar to you. They are used in a wide variety of Windows applications you have used (the Visual C# IDE even uses them!) We will soon look at how to move a control from the toolbox to a form.

The **Properties Window** serves <u>two</u> purposes. Its primary purpose is to establish design mode (initial) property values for objects (controls). It can also be used to establish event methods for controls. Here, we just look at how to work with properties. To do this, click the **Properties** button in the task bar:

Properties
button

The drop-down box at the top of the window lists all objects in the current form. Under this box are the available properties for the active (currently selected) object. Two property views are available: **Alphabetic** and **Categorized** (selection is made using menu bar under drop-down box). Help with any property can be obtained by highlighting the property of interest and pressing **<F1>**. We will examine how to assign properties after placing some controls on a form.

The **Solution Explorer Window** displays a list of all forms and other files making up your application. To view a form in this window, simply double-click the file name. Or, highlight the file and press **<Shift>-<F7>**. Or, you can obtain a view of the form (**View Designer**) or code (**View Code**) windows (window containing the actual C# coding) from the Project window, using the toolbar near the top of the window. As we mentioned, there are many ways to do things using the Visual C# IDE.

The help facilities of Visual C# are vast and very useful. As you work more and more with Visual C#, you will become very dependent on these facilities. The on-line help feature is web-based (use the **Help** menu).

One other very useful source for help with Visual C# programming tasks is the Internet. Using a search engine such a Google will locate many helpful websites.

This completes our quick tour of the Visual C# IDE. After taking a look at how to save a project, we turn our attention to building our first application using these three steps:

- Draw the user interface (place controls on the form).
- Set control properties
- Write code

Saving a Visual C# Project

When a new project is created in Visual C#, it is automatically saved in the location you specify. If you are making lots of changes, you might occasionally like to save your work prior to running the project. Do this by clicking the **Save All** button in the Visual C# toolbar. Look for a button that looks like several floppy disks. (With writeable CD's so cheap, how much longer do you think people will know what a floppy disk looks like? – many new machines don't even have a floppy disk drive!)

 —**Save All**
Toolbar Button

Always make sure to save your project before running it or before leaving Visual C#.

Drawing the User Interface

The first step in developing a Visual C# Windows application is to draw the user interface on the form. Make sure the Form appears in the Design window. There are four ways to place controls on a form:

1. Click the tool (we use a button control) in the toolbox and hold the mouse button down. Drag the selected tool over the form. When the cursor pointer is at the desired upper left corner, release the mouse button and the default size control will appear. This is the classic "drag and drop" operation.

2. Double-click the tool in the toolbox and it is created with a default size on the form. You can then move it or resize it. Here is a button control placed on the form using this method:

3. Click the tool in the toolbox, then move the mouse pointer to the form window. The cursor changes to a crosshair. Place the crosshair at the upper left corner of where you want the control to be and click the left mouse button. The control will appear at the clicked point. Here is a default size button placed on the form using this technique:

4. Click the tool in the toolbox, then move the mouse pointer to the form window. The cursor changes to a crosshair. Place the crosshair at the upper left corner of where you want the control to be, press the left mouse button and hold it down while dragging the cursor toward the lower right corner. A rectangle will be drawn. When you release the mouse button, the control is drawn in the rectangle. A big button drawn using this method:

To **move** a control you have drawn, click the object in the form (a cross with arrows will appear). Now, drag the control to the new location. Release the mouse button.

To **resize** a control, click the control so that it is selected (active) and sizing handles appear. Use these handles to resize the object.

To delete a control, select that control so it is active (sizing handles will appear). Then, press **<Delete>** on the keyboard. Or, right-click the control. A menu will appear. Choose the **Delete** option. You can change your mind immediately after deleting a control by choosing the **Undo** option under the **Edit** menu.

Example 1-1

Stopwatch Application - Drawing Controls

1. Start a new project. The idea of this project is to start a timer, then stop the timer and compute the elapsed time (in seconds).

2. Place three buttons, three labels and three text boxes on the form. Move and size the controls and form so it looks something like this:

3. Save this project (saved in the **Example 1-1** folder in **LearnVCS\VCS Code\Class 1** folder). To save, simply click the **Save All** button in the toolbar.

Opening a Saved Visual C# Project

Every example, problem and exercise presented in this course has an accompanying Visual C# solution folder. This lets you see how we did things. These folders are saved in the **LearnVCS\VCS Code** directory, sorted by chapter number. You need to know how to open these projects. And, you need to know how to open any projects you may have saved.

Opening a previously saved Visual C# project is a simple task. Choose the **File** menu option in the Visual C# IDE and select **Open,** then **Project/Solution.** The **Open Project** dialog box will appear. Open the desired project folder and you see:

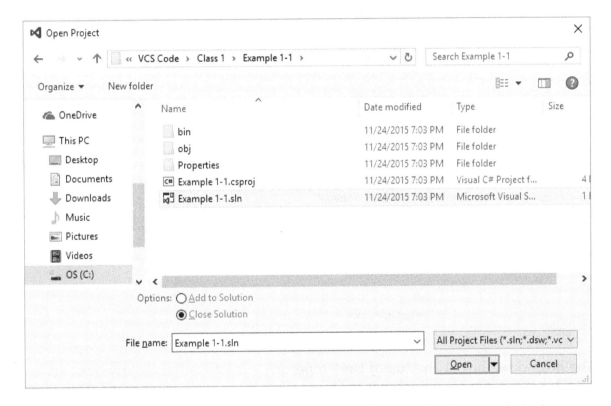

At this point, click on the **Solution** file and click **Open.** Or, double-click the **Solution** file. All the components of your project will be assembled and displayed. It's that easy!

Setting Properties of Controls at Design Time

Each form and control has **properties** assigned to it by default when you start up a new project. There are two ways to display the properties of an object. The first way is to click on the object (form or control) in the form window. Sizing handles will appear on that control. When a control has sizing handles, we say it is the **active** control. Now, click on the Properties window or the Properties window button in the tool bar. The second way is to first click on the Properties window. Then, select the object from the drop-down box at the top of the Properties window. When you do this, the selected object (control) will now be active (have sizing handles). Shown is the Properties window (make sure the **Properties** button, not the **Events** button is selected in the toolbar) for the stopwatch application (for the Form object):

Properties ——
button

The drop-down box at the top of the Properties Window is the **Object** box. It displays the name of each object in the application as well as its type. This display shows the **Form** object. The **Properties** list is directly below this box. In this list, you can scroll through the list of properties for the selected object. You select a property by clicking on it. Properties can be changed by typing a new value or choosing from a list of predefined settings (available as a drop down list). Properties can be viewed in two ways: **Alphabetic** (I always use this view) and **Categorized** (selected using the menu bar under the Object box). At the bottom of the Properties window is a short description of the selected property (a kind of dynamic help system).

A very important property for each control is its **Name**. The name is used by Visual C# to refer to a particular object or control in code. A convention has been established for naming Visual C# controls. This convention is to use a three letter (lower case) prefix (identifying the type of control) followed by a name you assign. A few of the prefixes are (we'll see more as we progress in the class):

Control	Prefix	Example
Form	frm	frmWatch
Button	btn	btnExit, btnStart
Label	lbl	lblStart, lblEnd
Text Box	txt	txtTime, txtName
Menu	mnu	mnuExit, mnuSave
Check box	chk	chkChoice

It is suggested to use a mixture of upper and lower case letters for better readability. But, be aware that Visual C# is a case-sensitive language, meaning the names **frmWatch** and **FRMWATCH** would <u>not</u> be the same name.

Control (object) names can be up to 40 characters long, must start with a letter, must contain only letters, numbers, and the underscore (_) character. Names are used in setting properties at run-time and also in establishing method names for control events. Use meaningful names that help you (or another programmer) understand the type and purpose of the respective controls.

Another set of important properties for each control are those that dictate position and size. There will be times you want to refer to (or change) these properties. There are four properties:

Left   Distance from left side of form to left edge of control, in pixels

Top   Distance from title bar of form to top edge of control, in pixels

Width   Width of control, in pixels

Height   Height of control, in pixels

Pictorially, these properties for a button control are:

Finding these properties in the Properties window is a bit tricky. To find the Left and Top properties, expand the **Location** property. The displayed X value is the Left property, while Y is the Top property. To find the Width and Height properties, expand the **Size** property – the width and height are displayed and can be modified.

Setting Properties at Run Time

In addition to setting properties at design time, you can set or modify properties while your application is running. To do this, you must write some code. The code format is:

    objectName.PropertyName = NewValue;

Such a format is referred to as dot notation. For example, to change the **BackColor** property of a button named **btnStart**, we'd type:

```
btnStart.BackColor = Color.Blue;
```

You've just seen your first line of code in Visual C#. Good naming conventions make it easy to understand what's going on here. The button named btnStart will now have a blue background. We won't learn much code in this first chapter (you'll learn a lot in Chapter 2), but you should see that the code that is used is straightforward and easy to understand.

How Names are Used in Control Events

The names you assign to controls are also used by Visual C# to set up a framework of event-driven methods for you to add code to. Hence, proper naming makes these methods easier to understand.

The format for each of these methods is:

```
private void ControlName_Event(Arguments)
{

}
```

where **Arguments** provides information needed by the method to do its work.

Visual C# provides the header line with its information and arguments and left and right curly braces (all code goes between these two braces) delineating the start and end of the method. Don't worry about how to provide any code right now. Just notice that with proper naming convention, it is easy to identify what tasks are associated with a particular event of a particular control.

Use of Form Name Property

When setting run-time properties or accessing events for the **Form** object, the **Name** property is not used in the same manner as it is for other controls. To set properties, rather than use the name property, the keyword **this** is used. Hence, to set a form property at run-time, use:

    this.PropertyName = Value;

We also need to distinguish between the form **Name** property and the **File Name** used within Visual C# to save the form file (which includes control descriptions and all code associated with a particular form). The Name property and File Name are two different entities. We have seen how the form Name property is used. A look at the Solution Explorer window for a sample application shows how the form File Name is used:

The name preceding the **cs** extension (**Form1**) is the form file name. Again, this is <u>not</u> the same as the name assigned in the Form Properties window.

To change the form file name, click the file in the Solution Explorer window to see the **File Properties** window (this is <u>not</u> the same as the Form Properties window):

In this window, you change the File Name by simply typing another name (with the **cs** extension). Visual C# will then automatically save the form file with this new name. This name is then used to refer to the form file. This is the name you would use if you want to load a particular form into a Visual C# solution or project.

<u>Example 1-2</u>

Stopwatch Application - Setting Properties

1. Continue with Example 1-1. Set properties of the form, three buttons, and three labels and three text boxes:

   Form1:
Name	frmStopWatch
FormBorderStyle	Fixed Single
StartPosition	CenterScreen
Text	Stopwatch Application

   button1:
Name	btnStart
Text	&Start Timing

   button2:
Name	btnEnd
Text	&End Timing

   button3:
Name	btnExit
Text	E&xit

   label1:
Text	Start Time

   label2:
Text	End Time

   label3:
Text	Elapsed Time (sec)

textBox1:
Name   txtStart

textBox2:
Name   txtEnd

textbox3:
Name   txtElapsed

In the **Text** properties of the three buttons, notice the ampersand (**&**). The ampersand precedes a button's **access key**. That is, in addition to clicking on a button to invoke its event, you can also press its access key (no need for a mouse). The access key is pressed in conjunction with the **Alt** key. Hence, to invoke 'Start Timing', you can either click the button or press **<Alt>+S**. Note in the button text on the form, the access keys appear with an underscore (_).

2. Your form should now look something like this:

3. Save this project (**Example 1-2** folder in **LearnVCS\VCS Code\Class 1** folder).

Writing Code

The last step in building a Visual C# application is to write code using the **C#** language. This is the most time consuming task in any Visual C# application. It is also the most fun and most rewarding task.

As controls are added to a form, Visual C# automatically builds a framework of all event methods. We simply add code to the event methods we want our application to respond to. And, if needed, we write general methods. For those who may have never programmed before, the code in these methods is simply a line by line list of instructions for the computer to follow. A useful feature when working with code is to put line numbers next to each line of code. To do this, select the **Tools** menu item in the IDE. Then, choose **Options**. In the left side of the window that appears, choose **Text Editor**. Choose the **General** tab under **C#**. Then, choose the **Line Numbers** option:

You will find the line numbers very useful as you write code. Any errors you make are identified by line number in the **Error List Window**. To view this window, choose the **View** menu option. Then select **Other Windows**, then **Error List**. The **Error List** window will appear:

Errors are listed under **Description**. The file the error occurs in is listed under **File**. And, the line number is listed under **Line**. You will use this window a lot while writing code.

Code is placed in the **Code Window**. Typing code in the code window is just like using any word processor. You can cut, copy, paste and delete text (use the **Edit** menu or the toolbar). Learn how to access the code window using the menu (**View**), toolbar, or by pressing <**F7**> (and there are still other ways) while the form is active. Here is the end of the Code window for the stopwatch application we are working on:

```
Example 1-2.cs    X   Example 1-2.cs [Design]
C# Example 1-2                    Example_1_1.frmStopWatch        txtStart
     1    using System;
     2    using System.Collections.Generic;
     3    using System.ComponentModel;
     4    using System.Data;
     5    using System.Drawing;
     6    using System.Text;
     7    using System.Windows.Forms;
     8
     9    namespace Example_1_1
    10    {
    11        public partial class frmStopWatch : Form
    12        {
    13            public frmStopWatch()
    14            {
    15                InitializeComponent();
    16            }
    17        }
    18    }
```

We see that our project is a **class** named **frmStopWatch**. Our application (an **object**) will be derived from this class. All code for the project will lie between the curly brackets associated with the header line (**public partial class frmStopWatch**). The initial code contains a **form constructor** (header is **public frmStopWatch**).

Working With Event Methods

There are two ways to establish event methods for controls – one directly from the form and one using the properties window. Let's look at both. Every control has a **default event method**. This is the method most often used by the control. For example, a button control's default event method is the Click event, since this is most often what we do to a button. To access a control's default event method, you simply double-click the control on the form. For example, if you double-click the button named **btnStart** in the stopwatch project, the bottom of the code window will display:

```
private void BtnStart_Click(object sender, EventArgs e)
{

}
```

Let's spend some time looking at this method – all event methods used in Visual C# look just like this. The time spent clarifying things now will be well worth it.

The assigned name for the event method is seen to be **BtnStart_Click**. Our naming convention tells us this is the method executed when the user clicks on the **btnStart** button (you will notice the IDE converts the first letter to upper case). The method has two arguments: **sender** and **e**. Sender tells the method what control caused the Click event to occur and e gives us some information about the event. Following the header line are a matched set of curly braces ({ }). The code for the event method will go between these two braces.

Though simple and quick, double-clicking a control to establish a control event method will not work if you are not interested in the default event. In that case, you need to use the properties window. Recall we mentioned that the properties window is not only used to establish properties, but also event methods. To establish an event method using the properties window, click on the **Events** button (appears as a lightning bolt) in the properties window toolbar:

Events button

The active control's events will be listed (the default event will be highlighted):

To establish an event method, scroll down the listed events and double-click the one of interest. The selected event method will appear in the code window.

There are several ways to locate a previously established method. One is to double-click the event name in the properties window, just as we did to create the method. Once you double-click the name, the code window will display the selected method. If the desired method is a default method, double-clicking the control on the form will take you to that method in the code window.

Another way to locate an event method is via the code window. At the top of the code window are three dropdown boxes, the **method list** is on the right. Selecting this box will provide a list of all methods in the code window. Find the event method of interest and select it. The selected event will appear in the code window:

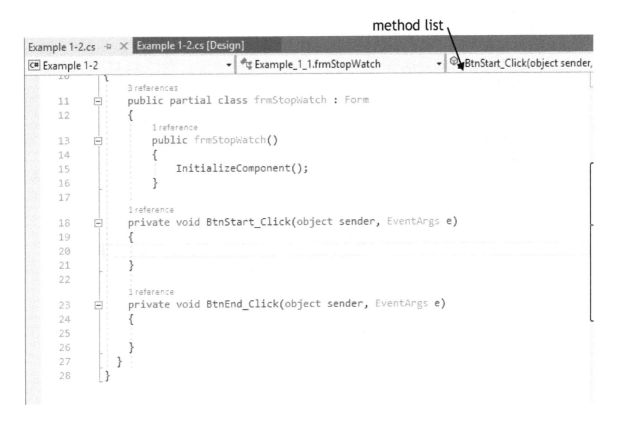

Deleting an existing event method can be tricky. Simply deleting the event method in the code window is not sufficient. When you add an event method to your application, Visual C# writes a line of code to connect the method to your control. That line of code remains after you delete the method. If you delete the method and try to run your application, an error will occur. In the Task Window will be a message saying your application does not contain a definition for a specific event method. Double-click the message and C# will take you to the offending statement (the one that connects the control and the method). Delete that line and your code will be fixed.

The preferred way to delete a method is to select the desired method using the properties window (make sure the control of interest is the active control). Once the event is selected, right-click the event method name and choose **Reset** from the pop-up menu. This process deletes the event from the code window <u>and</u> deletes the line of code connecting the method and control.

In the example in the class, we will just be giving you code to type in the code window. There are a few rules to pay attention to as you type Visual C# code (we will go over these rules again in the next class):

> ➢ Visual C# code requires perfection. All words must be spelled correctly.
> ➢ Visual C# is case-sensitive, meaning upper and lower case letters are considered to be different characters. When typing code, make sure you use upper and lower case letters properly
> ➢ Visual C# ignores any **"white space"** such as blanks. We will often use white space to make our code more readable.
> ➢ Curly **braces** are used for grouping. They mark the beginning and end of programming sections. Make sure your Visual C# programs have an equal number of left and right braces. We call the section of code between matching braces a **block**.
> ➢ It is good coding practice to **indent** code within a block. This makes code easier to follow. The Visual C# environment automatically indents code in blocks for you.
> ➢ Every Visual C# statement will end with a semicolon. A **statement** is a program expression that generates some result. Note that not all Visual C# expressions are statements (for example, the line defining the form constructor has no semicolon).

Variables

We're now ready to write code for our application. As just seen, as controls are added to the form, Visual C# builds a framework of event methods. We simply add code to the event methods we want our application to respond to. But before we do this, we need to discuss **variables**.

Variables are used by Visual C# to hold information needed by an application. Variables must be properly named. Rules used in naming variables:

> ➤ No more than 40 characters
> ➤ They may include letters, numbers, and underscore (_)
> ➤ The first character must be a letter which, by convention, is usually lower case
> ➤ You cannot use a reserved word (keywords used by Visual C#)

Use meaningful variable names that help you (or other programmers) understand the purpose of the information stored by the variable.

Examples of acceptable variable names:

startingTime	interest_Value	letter05
johnsAge	number_of_Days	timeOfDay

Visual C# Data Types

Each variable is used to store information of a particular **type**. Visual C# has a wide range of data types. You must always know the type of information stored in a particular variable.

bool (short for Boolean) variables can have one of two different values: **true** or **false** (reserved words in Visual C#). Boolean variables are helpful in making decisions. There is one possible point of confusion when working with Boolean values. Note some control properties are Boolean, for example, the Enabled property. When setting such a property at design time, the choices are **True** or **False** (using upper case letters). When setting Boolean values in code (either setting control properties or some other variable), the choices are **true** or **false** (using lower case letters). Be aware of this when writing code. A common error is to use upper case values, rather than the proper lower case values.

If a variable stores a whole number (no decimal), there are three data types available: **short**, **int** or **long**. Which type you select depends on the range of the value stored by the variable:

Data Type	Range
short	-32,678 to 32,767
int	-2,147,483,648 to 2,147,483,647
long	-9,223,372,036,854,775,808 to 9,223,372,036,854,775,807

We will almost always use the **int** type in our work.

If a variable stores a decimal number, there are two data types: **float** or **double**. The double uses twice as much storage as float, providing more precision and a wider range. Examples:

Data Type	Value
float	3.14
double	3.14159265359

Visual C# is a popular language for performing string manipulations. These manipulations are performed on variables of type **string**. A string variable is just that - a string (list) of various characters. In Visual C#, string variable values are enclosed in quotes. Examples of string variables:

   "Visual C#"   "012345"   "Title   Author"

Single character string variables have a special type, type **char**, for character type. Examples of character variables (enclosed in single quotes):

   'a'   '1'   'V'   '*'

Visual C# also has great facilities for handling dates and times. The **DateTime** variable type stores both dates and times. Using different formatting techniques (consult the Visual C# help system) allow us to display dates and times in any format desired. The **TimeSpan** variable type helps in doing date math; for example, the difference between two dates.

A last data type is type **Object**. That is, we can actually define a variable to represent any Visual C# object, like a button or form. We will see the utility of the Object type as we progress in the course.

Variable Declaration

Once we have decided on a variable name and the type of variable, we must tell our Visual C# application what that name and type are. We say, we must **explicitly declare** the variable.

There are many advantages to **explicitly** typing variables. Primarily, we insure all computations are properly done, mistyped variable names are easily spotted, and Visual C# will take care of insuring consistency in variable names. Because of these advantages, and because it is good programming practice, we will <u>always</u> explicitly type variables.

To **explicitly** type a variable, you must first determine its **scope**. Scope identifies how widely disseminated we want the variable value to be. We will use three levels of scope:

> ➤ Block level
> ➤ Method level
> ➤ Form level

Block level variables are only usable within a single block of code (will be discussed in more detail in Class 2).

The value of **method level** variables are only available within a method. Such variables are declared within a method, using the variable type as a declarer:

```
int myInt;
double myDouble;
string myString, yourString;
```

These declarations are usually placed after the opening left curly brace of a method.

Form level variables retain their value and are available to all methods within that form. Form level variables are declared in the code window right after the **Form constructor** generated automatically by Visual C#, outside of any other method:

```
Form1.cs*  -□  X  Form1.cs [Design]*
C# WindowsFormsApplication2     ▼   WindowsFormsApplication2.Fc ▼  InitializeComponent()
    1      ⊞using ...
   10
   11      ⊟namespace WindowsFormsApplication2
   12       {
   13      ⊟   public partial class Form1 : Form
   14          {
   15      ⊟     public Form1()
   16            {
   17               InitializeComponent();
   18            }
   19
   20            |
   21          }
   22       }
   23
```

Place form level variable declarations here, before any methods.

Form level variables are declared just like method level variables:

```
int myInt;
DateTime myDate;
```

Arrays

Visual C# has powerful facilities for handling arrays, which provide a way to store a large number of variables under the same name. Each variable, called an element, in an array must have the same data type, and they are distinguished from each other by an array index. In this class, we work with one-dimensional arrays, although multi-dimensional arrays are possible.

Arrays are declared in a manner similar to that used for regular variables. For example, to declare an integer array named **'item'**, with dimension **9**, we use:

```
int[] item = new int[9];
```

The index on an array variable begins at 0 and ends at the dimensioned value minus one. Hence, the **item** array in the above examples has **nine** elements, ranging from item[0] to item[8]. You use array variables just like any other variable - just remember to include its name and its index.

It is also possible to have arrays of controls. For example, to have 20 button types available use:

```
Button[] myButtons = new Button[20];
```

The utility of such a declaration will become apparent in later classes.

Constants

You can also define constants for use in Visual C#. The format for defining an **int** type constant named **numberOfUses** with a value **200** is:

```
const int numberOfUses = 200;
```

The scope of user-defined constants is established the same way a variables' scope is. That is, if defined within a method, they are local to the method. If defined in the top region of a form's code window, they are global to the form.

If you attempt to change the value of a defined constant, your program will stop with an error message.

Variable Initialization

By default, any declared numeric variables are initialized at zero. String variables are initialized at an empty string. If desired, Visual C# lets you initialize variables at the same time you declare them. Just insure that the type of initial value matches the variable type (i.e. don't assign a string value to an integer variable).

Examples of variable initialization:

```
int myInt = 23;
string myString = "Visual C#";
double myDouble = 7.28474746464;
bool isLeap = false;
```

You can even initialize arrays with this technique. With this technique, you can (optionally) delete the explicit dimension and let Visual C# figure it out by counting the number of elements used to initialize the array. An example is:

```
int[] item = new int[] {0, 1, 2, 3, 4, 5, 6, 7, 8, 9};
```

Visual C# will know this array has 10 elements (a dimension of 9).

Intellisense Feature

Yes, we're finally ready to start writing some code in the code window. You will see that typing code is just like using any word processor. The usual navigation and editing features are all there.

One feature that you will become comfortable with and amazed with is called **Intellisense**. As you type code, the Intellisense feature will, at times, provide assistance in completing lines of code. For example, once you type a control name and a dot (.), a drop-down list of possible properties and methods will appear. When we use methods, suggested values for arguments will be provided. Syntax errors will be identified. And, potential errors with running an application will be pointed out.

Intellisense is a very useful part of Visual C#. You should become acquainted with its use and how to select suggested values. We tell you about now so you won't be surprised when little boxes start popping up as you type code.

Let's finally complete the stopwatch application. We'll just give you the code. Don't worry about where it comes from for now. You'll learn a lot about coding as you venture forth in this course. Just type the code as given in the specified locations – you should see how easy it is to understand however.

Example 1-3

Stopwatch Application - Writing Code

All that's left to do is write code for the application. We write code for every event a response is needed for. In this application, there are three such events: clicking on each of the buttons.

1. Select 'View Code' from the project window to see the code window. Or, press <F7> while the form is active. Or, select **View** from the main menu, then **Code**.

2. Under the **Form constructor**, declare three form level variables. These lines go after the closing right curly brace ending the method:

```
DateTime startTime;
DateTime endTime;
TimeSpan elapsedTime;
```

This establishes **startTime**, **endTime**, and **elapsedTime** as variables with form level scope. At this point, the Code window should look like this:

```
 9    namespace Example_1_1
10    {
11        public partial class frmStopWatch : Form
12        {
13            public frmStopWatch()
14            {
15                InitializeComponent();
16            }
17            DateTime startTime;
18            DateTime endTime;
19            TimeSpan elapsedTime;
20
21    
22        }
23    }
```

3. Select the **btnStart** object in the Object box of the properties window. Click the **Events** button. Double-click the **Click** event. Or, try double-clicking the button control. Type the following code which begins the timing method. Note the header line and bounding braces are provided for you:

```
private void BtnStart_Click(object sender, EventArgs e)
{
  // Establish and print starting time
  startTime = DateTime.Now;
  txtStart.Text = startTime.ToLongTimeString();
  txtEnd.Text = "";
  txtElapsed.Text = "";
}
```

In this method, once the **Start Timing** button is clicked, we read the current time and print it in a text box (after proper formatting). We also blank out the other text boxes. In the code above (and in all code in these notes), any line beginning with a double slash (//) is a comment. You decide whether you want to type these lines or not. They are not needed for proper application operation.

4. Now, select the **btnEnd** object in the Object box of the properties window. Double-click the **Click** event. (Or, again just double-click the End Timing button.) Add this code:

```
private void BtnEnd_Click(object sender, EventArgs e)
{
  // Find the ending time, compute the elapsed time
  // Put both values in text boxes
  endTime = DateTime.Now;
  elapsedTime = endTime - startTime;
  txtEnd.Text = endTime.ToLongTimeString();
  txtElapsed.Text = elapsedTime.Seconds.ToString();
}
```

Here, when the **End Timing** button is clicked, we read the current time (**End Time**), compute the elapsed time, and put both values in their corresponding text boxes (with proper formatting).

5. Finally, select the **btnExit** object in the Object box of the properties
   window. Choose **Click** event. That button's Click event code:

```
private void BtnExit_Click(object sender, EventArgs e)
{
   this.Close();
}
```

This routine simply closes the form (identified by the keyword **this**) once the
Exit button is clicked. Did you notice as you typed in the code, how the
Intellisense feature of Visual C# worked

6. Run the application by clicking the **Start** button in the toolbar or pressing
   <F5>. Try it out. Here's a short run I made (I clicked **Start Timing**, then
   End Timing 28 seconds later):

If your application doesn't run, recheck to make sure the code is typed properly.
Save your application. This is saved in the **Example 1-3** folder in **LearnVCS\VCS
Code\Class 1** folder.

7. If you have the time, some other things you may try with the **Stopwatch Application**:

    A. Try changing the form color and the fonts used in the label boxes and buttons.

    B. Notice you can press the 'End Timing' button before the 'Start Timing' button. This shouldn't be so. Change the application so you can't do this. And make it such that you can't press the 'Start Timing' until 'End Timing' has been pressed. Hint: Look at the button **Enabled** property.

    C. Can you think of how you can continuously display the 'End Time' and 'Elapsed Time'? This is a little tricky because of the event-driven nature of Visual C#. Look at the **Timer** control. By setting the **Interval** property of this control to **1000** and the **Enabled** property to **True**, it will generate its own events (the **Tick** event) every one second. Put code similar to that in the **BtnEnd_Click** event in the Timer control's **Tick** event and see what happens. Also, see the exercise at the end of the class for help on this one. The Timer control will not appear on the form, but in a 'tray' below the form. This happens because the Timer control has no user interface.

Class Review

After completing this class, you should understand:

➢ The concept of an event-driven application
➢ What object-oriented programming (OOP) is about
➢ The parts of a Visual C# application (form, control, property, event, ...)
➢ The various windows of the Visual C# integrated development environment
➢ How to use the Visual C# on-line help system
➢ The three steps in building a Visual C# application
➢ Four ways to place controls on a form
➢ Methods to set properties for controls
➢ Proper control naming convention
➢ Proper variable naming and typing methods
➢ The concept of variable scope
➢ How to properly declare a variable
➢ How to define a constant
➢ How to add code and declarations using the code window
➢ Different ways of establishing and locating event methods in the code window
➢ Ways to use the Intellisense feature when typing code

Practice Problems 1*

Problem 1-1. Beep Problem. Build an application with a single button. When the button is clicked, make the computer beep. Use this method:

System.Media.SystemSounds.Beep.Play();

Problem 1-2. Text Problem. Build an application with a single button. When the button is clicked, change the button's **Text** property. This allows a button to be used for multiple purposes. If you want to change the button caption back when you click again, you'll need an **if** statement. We'll discuss this statement in the next class, but, if you're adventurous, look in on-line help to try it.

Problem 1-3. Enabled Problem. Build an application with two buttons. When you click one button, make it disabled (**Enabled** = **false**) and make the other button enabled (**Enabled** = **true**).

Problem 1-4. Date Problem. Build an application with a button. When the button is clicked, have the computer display the current date in a label control.

---

*Note: **Practice Problems** are given after each class to give you practice in writing code for your Visual C# applications. These are meant to be quick and, hopefully, short exercises. The Visual C# environment makes it easy to build and test quick applications – in fact, programmers develop such examples all the time to test some idea they might have. Use your imagination in working the problems – modify them in any way you want. You learn programming by doing programming! The more you program, the better programmer you will become. Our solutions to the **Practice Problems** are provided as an addenda to these notes.

Exercise 1*

Calendar/Time Display

Design a window that displays the current month, day, and year. Also, display the current time, updating it every second (look into the **Timer** control). Make the window look something like a calendar page. Play with control properties to make it pretty.

---

*Note: After completing each class' notes, a homework exercise (and, sometimes, more) is given, covering many of the topics taught. Try to work through the homework exercise on your own. This is how programming is learned – solving a particular problem. For reference, solutions to all **Exercises** are provided as an addenda to these notes. In our solutions, you may occasionally see something you don't recognize. When this happens, use the on-line help system to learn what's going on. This is another helpful skill – understanding other people's applications and code.

2. The Visual C# Language

Review and Preview

In the first class, we found there were three primary steps involved in developing a Windows application using Visual C#:

1. Draw the user interface
2. Assign properties to controls
3. Write code for events

In this class, we are primarily concerned with Step 3, writing code. We will become more familiar with moving around in the Code window and learn some of the elements of the C# language.

A Brief History of Visual C#

It's interesting to see just where the C# language fits in the history of some other computer languages. You will see just how new Visual C# is! In the early 1950's most computers were used for scientific and engineering calculations. The programming language of choice in those days was called **FORTRAN**. FORTRAN was the first modern language and is still in use to this day (after going through several updates). In the late 1950's, bankers and other business people got into the computer business using a language called **COBOL**. Within a few years after its development, COBOL became the most widely used data processing language. And, like FORTRAN, it is still being used today.

In the 1960's, two professors at Dartmouth College decided that "everyday" people needed to have a language they could use to learn programming. They developed **BASIC** (**B**eginner's **A**ll-Purpose **S**ymbolic **I**nstruction **C**ode). BASIC (and its many successors like Visual Basic) is probably the most widely used programming language. Many dismiss it as a "toy language," but BASIC was the first product developed by a company you may have heard of – Microsoft! And, BASIC has been used to develop thousands of commercial applications.

C# had its beginnings in 1972, when AT&T Bell Labs developed the **C** programming language. It was the first, new scientific type language since FORTRAN. If you've every seen a C program, you will notice many similarities between C# and C. Then, with object-oriented capabilities added, came **C++** in 1986 (also from Bell Labs). This was a big step.

In 2001, Microsoft introduced its .NET platform and a new language was introduced – C#. It represented a streamlined version of C and C++, with a little Java thrown in. This chapter provides an overview of the C# language used in the Visual C# environment. If you've ever used another programming language, you will see equivalent structures in the language of Visual C#.

Rules of C# Programming

Before starting our review of the C# language, let's review some of the rules of C# programming seen in the first class:

> ➤ C# code requires perfection. All words must be spelled correctly.
> ➤ C# is case-sensitive, meaning upper and lower case letters are considered to be different characters. When typing code, make sure you use upper and lower case letters properly.
> ➤ C# ignores any **"white space"** such as blanks. We will often use white space to make our code more readable.
> ➤ Curly **braces** are used for grouping. They mark the beginning and end of programming sections. Make sure your C# programs have an equal number of left and right braces. We call the section of code between matching braces a **block**.
> ➤ It is good coding practice to **indent** code within a block. This makes code easier to follow. The Visual C# environment automatically indents code in blocks for you.
> ➤ Every C# statement will end with a semicolon. A **statement** is a program expression that generates some. Note that not all C# expressions are statements (for example, the line defining the form constructor has no semicolon).

Visual C# Statements and Expressions

The simplest (and most common) statement in C# is the **assignment** statement. It consists of a variable name, followed by the assignment operator (=), followed by some sort of **expression**, followed by a semicolon (;). The expression on the right hand side is evaluated, then the variable on the left hand side of the assignment operator is **replaced** by that value of the expression.

Examples:

```
startTime = now;
explorer = "Captain Spaulding";
bitCount = byteCount * 8;
energy = mass * lightSpeed * lightSpeed;
netWorth = assets - liabilities;
```

The assignment statement stores information.

Statements normally take up a single line. Since C# ignores white space, statements can be **stacked** using a semicolon (;) to separate them. Example:

```
startTime = now; endTime = startTime + 10;
```

The above code is the same as if the second statement followed the first statement. The only place we tend to use stacking is for quick initialization of like variables.

If a statement is very long, it may be continued to the next line without any kind of continuation character. Again, this is because C# ignores white space. It keeps processing a statement until it finally sees a semicolon. Example:

```
months = Math.Log(final * intRate / deposit + 1)
/ Math.Log(1 + intRate);
```

This statement, though on two lines, will be recognized as a single line. We usually write each statement on a single line. Be aware that long lines of code in the notes many times wrap around to the next line (due to page margins).

Comment statements begin with the two slashes (//). For example:

```
// This is a comment
x = 2 * y // another way to write a comment
```

You, as a programmer, should decide how much to comment your code.
Consider such factors as reuse, your audience, and the legacy of your code. In
our notes and examples, we try to insert comment statements when necessary
to explain some detail. You can also have a multiple line comment. Begin the
comment with /* and end it with */. Example:

```
/*
  This is a very long
  comment over
  a few lines
*/
```

Type Casting

In each assignment statement, it is important that the type of data on both sides of the operator (=) is the same. That is, if the variable on the left side of the operator is an **int**, the result of the expression on the right side should be **int**.

C# (by default) will try to do any conversions for you. When it can't, an error message will be printed. In those cases, you need to explicitly **cast** the result. This means convert the right side to the same side as the left side. Assuming the desired type is **type**, the casting statement is:

```
leftSide = (type) rightSide;
```

You can cast from any basic type (decimal and integer numbers) to any other basic type. Be careful when casting from higher precision numbers to lower precision numbers. Problems arise when you are outside the range of numbers.

There are times we need to convert one data type to another. Visual C# offers a wealth of functions that perform these conversions. Some of these functions are:

Convert.ToBoolean(*Expression*)	Converts a numerical *Expression* to a **bool** data type (if *Expression* is nonzero, the result is true, otherwise the result is false)
Convert.ToChar(*Expression*)	Converts any valid single character string to a **char** data type
Convert.DateTime(*Expression*)	Converts any valid date or time *Expression* to a **DateTime** data type
Convert.ToSingle(*Expression*)	Converts an *Expression* to a **float** data type
Convert.ToDouble(*Expression*)	Converts an *Expression* to a **double** data type

Convert.ToInt16(*Expression*)	Converts an *Expression* to a **short** data type (any fractional part is rounded)
Convert.ToInt32(*Expression*)	Converts an *Expression* to an **int** data type (any fractional part is rounded)
Convert.ToInt64(*Expression*)	Converts an *Expression* to a **long** data type (any fractional part is rounded)

We will use many of these conversion functions as we write code for our applications and examples. The Intellisense feature of the code window will usually direct us to the function we need.

Visual C# Arithmetic Operators

Operators modify values of variables. The simplest **operators** carry out **arithmetic** operations. There are five **arithmetic operators** in C#.

Addition is done using the plus (+) sign and **subtraction** is done using the minus (-) sign. Simple examples are:

Operation	Example	Result
Addition	7 + 2	9
Addition	3.4 + 8.1	11.5
Subtraction	6 - 4	2
Subtraction	11.1 – 7.6	3.5

Multiplication is done using the asterisk (*) and **division** is done using the slash (/). Simple examples are:

Operation	Example	Result
Multiplication	8 * 4	32
Multiplication	2.3 * 12.2	28.06
Division	12 / 2	6
Division	45.26 / 6.2	7.3

The last operator is the **remainder** operator represented by a percent symbol (%). This operator divides the whole number on its left side by the whole number on its right side, ignores the main part of the answer, and just gives you the remainder. It may not be obvious now, but the remainder operator is used a lot in computer programming. Examples are:

Operation	Example	Division Result	Operation Result
Remainder	7 % 4	1 Remainder 3	3
Remainder	14 % 3	4 Remainder 2	2
Remainder	25 % 5	5 Remainder 0	0

The mathematical operators have the following **precedence** indicating the order they are evaluated without specific groupings:

1. Multiplication (*) and division (/)
2. Remainder (%)
3. Addition (+) and subtraction (-)

If multiplications and divisions or additions and subtractions are in the same expression, they are performed in left-to-right order. **Parentheses** around expressions are used to force some desired precedence.

Comparison and Logical Operators

There are six **comparison** operators in Visual C# used to compare the value of two expressions (the expressions must be of the same data type). These are the basis for making decisions:

Operator	Comparison
>	Greater than
<	Less than
>=	Greater than or equal to
<=	Less than or equal to
==	Equal to
!=	Not equal to

It should be obvious that the result of a comparison operation is a **bool** value (**true** or **false**). **Examples:**

a = 9.6, b = 8.1, a > b returns true
a = 14, b = 14, a < b returns false
a = 14, b = 14, a >= b returns true
a = 7, b = 11, a <= b returns true
a = 7, b = 7, a == b returns true
a = 7, b = 7, a != b returns false

Logical operators operate on **bool** data types, providing a Boolean result. They are also used in decision making. We will use three **logical** operators

Operator	Operation
!	Logical Not
&&	Logical And
||	Logical Or

The Not (!) operator simply negates a Boolean value. It is very useful for 'toggling' Boolean variables. Examples:

If a = true, then !a = false
If a = false, then !a = true

The And (**&&**) operator checks to see if two different bool data types are both true. If both are true, the operator returns a true. Otherwise, it returns a false value. Examples:

a = true, b = true, then a **&&** b = true
a = true, b = false, then a **&&** b = false
a = false, b = true, then a **&&** b = false
a = false, b = false, then a **&&** b = false

The Or (||) operator (typed as two "pipe" symbols) checks to see if either of two bool data types is true. If either is true, the operator returns a true. Otherwise, it returns a false value. Examples:

a = true, b = true, then a || b = true
a = true, b = false, then a || b = true
a = false, b = true, then a || b = true
a = false, b = false, then a || b = false

Logical operators follow arithmetic operators in precedence. Use of these operators will become obvious as we delve further into coding.

Concatenation Operators

To **concatentate** two string data types (tie them together), use the + symbol, the string concatenation operator:

```
currentTime = "The current time is" + "9:30";
textSample = "Hook this " + "to this";
```

Visual C# offers other concatenation operators that perform an operation on a variable and assign the resulting value back to the variable. Hence, the operation

```
a = a + 2;
```

Can be written using the addition concatenation operator (+=) as:

```
a += 2;
```

This says a is incremented by 2.

Other concatenation operators and their symbols are:

Operator Name	Operator Symbol	Operator Task
String	a += b;	a = a + b;
Addition	a += b;	a = a + b;
Subtraction	a -= b;	a = a - b;
Multiplication	a *= b;	a = a * b;
Division	a /= b;	a = a / b;

We often increment and decrement by one. There are operators for this also. The increment operator:

```
a++;      is equivalent to:   a = a + 1;
```

Similarly, the decrement operator:

```
a--;      is equivalent to:   a = a - 1;
```

Strings to Numbers to Strings

The **Text** property of all controls are string types. You will find you are constantly converting string types to numeric data types to do some math and then converting back to strings to display the information. Let's look at each of these operations.

To convert a string type to a numeric value, use one of the **Convert** methods seen in the Type Casting section. As an example, to convert the Text property of a text box control named txtExample to an **int** type, use:

```
Convert.ToInt32(txtExample.Text)
```

This result can then be used with the various mathematical operators. You need to be careful that the string you are converting to a number is a valid representation of a number. If it is not, an error will occur.

The **ToString** method can be used to convert a numeric variable to a string. This bit of code can be used to display the numeric variable **myNumber** in a text box control:

```
myNumber = 3.14159;
txtExample.Text = myNumber.ToString();
```

Some quantities do not support a **ToString** method. In such cases, you can use the **Convert.ToString** method. This code:

```
myNumber = 3.14159;
txtExample.Text = Convert.ToString(myNumber);
```

will also do a conversion.

If you need to control the number of decimal points (or other display features), you can use the **String.Format** method. This method has two arguments, the first is a **format string**, the second is the **number** to be formatted. The format string is enclosed in two curly braces and consists of the variable number (0 in this case, since we only have one variable – the method can also be used to format multiple variables), a colon followed by the letter f (floating point) and the number of decimals. Sounds complicated doesn't it? An example will clear things up. To format a floating point number (**myNumber**) to 2 decimal points, convert it to a string and display it in a text box (**txtExample**), we use:

```
txtExample.Text = String.Format("{0:f2}", myNumber);
```

This statement says take the first (the **0** term in the format string) floating point number **myNumber**, round it to 2 decimals (the **f2** term following the colon in the format string) and convert it to a string. If you apply this code to our sample number, the text box control in this example will display **3.14**.

You can also develop format strings to display numbers in scientific notation, as percentages, and as currency. You will see these in examples we build in this course. Consult Visual C# on-line help for more information.

Visual C# String Methods

In addition to methods for strings associated with controls, Visual C# offers a powerful set of methods to work with string type variables. You should become familiar with these methods.

To determine the number of characters in (or length of) a string variable, we use the **Length** property. Using **myString** as example:

```
myString = "Read Learn Visual C# ****!";
lenString = myString.Length;
```

lenString will have a value of **26**. The location of characters in the string is zero-based. That is, the individual characters for this string start at character 0 and end at character 25.

Many times, you need to extract single characters from string variables. To do this, you specify the array index of the desired character in the string. Recall, characters in a string start at character 0 and extend to the length of the string minus 1. To determine the character (**myChar**) at position **n** in a string **myString**, use:

```
myChar = myString[n];
```

For example:

```
myString = "Read Learn Visual C# ****!";
myChar = myString[5];
```

will return the **char** type variable 'L' in **myChar**.

You can also extract substrings of characters. The **Substring** method is used for this task. You specify the string, the starting position and the number of characters to extract. This example starts at character 2 and extracts 6 characters:

```
myString = "Read Learn Visual C# ****!";
midString = myString.Substring(2, 6);
```

The **midString** variable is equal to **"ad Lea"**

Perhaps, you just want a far left portion of a string. Use the **Substring** method with a starting position of 0. This example extracts the 3 left-most characters from a string:

```
myString = "Read Learn Visual C# ****!";
leftString = myString.Substring(0, 3);
```

The **leftString** variable is equal to **"Rea"**

Getting the far right portion of a string with the **Substring** method requires a bit of math using the Length property. If you want **r** characters from the right side of a string **myString**, use:

```
myString.Substring(myString.Length - r, r)
```

To get 8 characters at the end of our example, you would use:

```
myString = "Read Learn Visual C# ****!";
rightString = myString.Substring(myString.Length - 8, 8);
```

The **rightString** variable is equal to **"C# ****!"**

To locate a substring within a string variable, use the **IndexOf** method. Three pieces of information are needed: **string1** (the variable), **string2** (the substring to find), and a starting position in **string1** (optional). The method will work left-to-right and return the location of the first character of the substring (it will return -1 if the substring is not found). For our example:

```
myString = "Read Learn Visual C# ****!";
location = myString.IndexOf("ea", 3);
```

This says find the substring **"ea"** in **myString**, starting at character **3**. The returned **location** will have a value of **6**. If the starting location argument is omitted, 0 is assumed, so if:

```
myString = "Read Learn Visual C# ****!";
location = myString.IndexOf("ea");
```

location will have value of **1**.

Related to the **IndexOf** method is the **LastIndexOf** method. This method also identifies substrings using identical arguments, but works right-to-left, or in reverse. So, with our example string:

```
myString = "Read Learn Visual C# ****!";
location = myString.LastIndexOf("ea");
```

This says find the substring **"ea"** in **myString**, starting at the right and working left. The returned **location** will have a value of **6**. Note when we used **IndexOf** (without a starting location), the returned **location** was **2**.

Many times, you want to convert letters to upper case or vice versa. Visual C# provides two methods for this purpose: **ToUpper** and **ToLower**. The ToUpper method will convert all letters in a string variable to upper case, while the ToLower method will convert all letters to lower case. Any non-alphabetic characters are ignored in the conversion. And, if a letter is already in the desired case, it is left unmodified. For our example (modified a bit):

```
myString = "Read Learn Visual C# **** in 2019!";
a = myString.ToUpper();
b = myString.ToLower();
```

The first conversion using **ToUpper** will result in:

```
A = "READ LEARN VISUAL C# **** IN 2019!"
```

And the second conversion using **toLowerCase** will yield:

```
B = "read learn visual c# **** in 2019!"
```

There are a couple of ways to modify an existing string. If you want to replace a certain character within a string, use the **Replace** method. You specify the character you wish to replace and the replacing character. An example:

```
myString = "Read Learn Visual C# ****!";
myString = myString.Replace(' ', '*');
```

This will replace every space in myString with an asterisk. **myString** will become **"Read*Learn*Visual C#*****!"**.

To remove leading and trailing spaces from a string, use the **Trim** method. Its use is obvious:

```
myString = "    Read Learn Visual C# ****!      ";
myString = myString.Trim();
```

After this, **myString = "Read Learn Visual C# ****!"** – the spaces at the beginning and end are removed.

You can convert a string variable to an array of char type variables using the **ToCharArray** method. Here's an example:

```
myString = "Learn Visual C# ****!";
char[] myArray = myString.ToCharArray();
```

After this, the array **myArray** will have 20 elements, **myArray[0] = 'L'**, **myArray[1] = 'e'**, and so on, up to **myArray[19] = '!'**. Note you only need declare myArray, you do not need to create (size) it.

Every 'typeable' character has a numeric representation called a Unicode value. To determine the Unicode (**myCode**) value for a **char** type variable (named **myChar**), you simply cast the character to an **int** type:

```
myCode = (int) myChar;
```

For example:

```
myCode = (int) 'A';
```

returns the Unicode value (**myCode**) for the upper case A (65, by the way). To convert a Unicode value (**myValue**) to the corresponding character, cast the value to a **char** type::

```
myChar = (char) myCode;
```

For example:

```
myChar = (char) 49;
```

returns the character (**myChar**) represented by a Unicode value of 49 (a "1"). Unicode values are related to ASCII (pronounced "askey") codes you may have seen in other languages. I think you see that there's lots to learn about using string variables in Visual C#.

Dates and Times

Working with dates and times in computer applications is a common task. In Class 1, in Example 1-3, Problem 1-3 and Exercise 1, we used the **DateTime** and **TimeSpan** data types without much discussion. These particular data types are used to specify and determine dates, times and the difference betweens dates and times.

The **DateTime** data type is used to hold a date <u>and</u> a time. And, even though that's the case, you're usually only interested in the date <u>or</u> the time. To initialize a DateTime variable (**myDateTime**) to a specific date, use:

```
DateTime myDateTime = new DateTime(year, month, day);
```

where **year** is the desired year (**int** type), **month** the desired month (**int** type), and **day** the desired day (**int** type). The month 'numbers' run from 1 (January) to 12 (December), not 0 to 11. As an example, if you use:

```
DateTime myDateTime = new DateTime(1950, 7, 19);
```

then, display the result (after converting it to a string) in some control using:

```
myDateTime.ToString()
```

you would get:

```
7/19/1950 12:00:00 AM
```

This is my birthday, by the way. The time is set to a default value since only a date was specified.

Other **DateTime** formats are available. You will see some of them in further examples, problems and exercises in this course, or consult the on-line help facilities of Visual C#. Some examples using **myDateTime** are:

```
myDateTime.ToLongDateString();  // returns Wednesday, July
19, 1950
myDateTime.ToShortDateString();  // returns 7/19/1950
myDateTime.ToLongTimeString();  // returns 12:00:00 AM
myDateTime.ToShortDateString();  // returns 12:00 AM
```

Individual parts of a **DateTime** object can be retrieved. Examples include:

```
myDateTime.Month  // returns 7
myDateTime.Day  // returns 19
myDateTime.DayOfWeek  // returns DayOfWeek.Wednesday
```

Notice the **DayOfWeek** property yields a **DayOfWeek** object.

Visual C# also allows you to retrieve the current date and time using the **DateTime** data type. To place the current date in a variable use the **Today** property:

```
DateTime myToday = DateTime.Today;
```

The variable **myToday** will hold today's date with the default time. To place the current date and time in a variable, use the **Now** property:

```
DateTime myToday = DateTime.Now;
```

Doing that at this moment, I get:

```
myToday.ToString()  // returns 2/2/2005 12:51:55 PM
```

Many times, you want to know the difference between two dates and/or times, that is, determine some time span. The Visual C# **TimeSpan** data type does just that – it allows you to find the difference between any two **DateTime** variables. The syntax is simple. To compute the difference between two **DateTime** variables (**dateTime1** and **dateTime2**), use:

```
TimeSpan diff = dateTime1 - dateTime2;
```

The computed difference will be in the format:

```
days.hours:minutes:seconds
```

The **Days**, **Hours**, **Minutes** or **Seconds** property of the diff variable will provide each component of the time span. Note we used this in the Stopwatch application in Class 1.

As an example, let's use today's date (**myToday**) and the example date (**myDateTime**, my birthday) to see how long I've been alive. First, compute the difference between the two dates:

```
DateTime myToday = DateTime.Today;
DateTime myDateTime = new DateTime(1950, 7, 19);
TimeSpan diff = myToday - myDateTime;
```

Then, if we examine:

```
diff.ToString()
```

the result is:

```
19922.15:39:43.9750720
```

The tells me I've been alive 19922 days, 15 hours, 39 minutes, and 43.975 seconds. Looks like I should be getting ready to celebrate my 20,000 days birthday!!

We have only introduced the **DateTime** and **TimeSpan** data types. You will find them very useful as you progress in your programming studies. Do some research on your own to determine how best to use dates and times in applications you build.

Important: Recall Visual C# is an object-oriented language. The **DateTime** type is the first object we have encountered (besides the button, label and text box objects used in Class 1). We will see many more in this course. Note to get a DateTime type, we followed two steps. We first declared a variable (object) to be from the **DateTime class** using the standard statement:

```
DateTime myDateTime;
```

We then constructed the **DateTime object** using the **new** keyword and a **constructor** statement:

```
myDateTime = new DateTime(year, month, day);
```

(Actually, we combined the declaration and construction into one line of code, but you can see what's going on). Once constructed, we see the date has **properties** (day, month, year) and **methods**. These new terms will become very familiar as you progress in these notes.

Random Number Object

In writing games and learning software, we use a random number generator to introduce unpredictability. This insures different results each time you try a program. Visual C# has a few ways to generate random numbers. We will use one of them – a random generator of integers. The generator uses the Visual C# **Random** object.

To use the Random object (named **MyRandom** here), it is first declared and created using:

```
Random myRandom = new Random();
```

This statement is placed with the variable declaration statements.

Once created, when you need a random integer value, use the **Next** method of this Random object:

```
myRandom.Next(Limit)
```

This statement generates a random integer value that is greater than or equal to 0 and less than **Limit**. Note it is less than limit, not equal to. For example, the method:

```
myRandom.Next(5)
```

will generate random integers from 0 to 4. The possible values will be 0, 1, 2, 3 and 4.

As other examples, to roll a six-sided die, the number of spots would be computed using:

```
numberSpots = myRandom.Next(6) + 1;
```

To randomly choose a number between 100 and 200, use:

```
number = myRandom.Next(101) + 100;
```

Math Functions

A last set of functions we need are mathematical functions (yes, programming involves math!) Visual C# provides a set of functions that perform tasks such as square roots, trigonometric relationships, and exponential functions.

Each of the Visual C# math functions comes from the **Math** class of the .NET framework (an object-oriented programming concept). All this means is that each function name must be preceded by **Math.** (say Math-dot) to work properly. The functions and the returned values are:

Math Function	Value Returned
Math.Abs	Returns the absolute value of a specified number
Math.Acos	Returns a double value containing the angle whose cosine is the specified number
Math.Asin	Returns a double value containing the angle whose sine is the specified number
Math.Atan	Returns a double value containing the angle whose tangent is the specified number
Math.Cos	Returns a double value containing the cosine of the specified angle
Math.E	A constant, the natural logarithm base
Math.Exp	Returns a double value containing e (the base of natural logarithms) raised to the specified power
Math.Log	Returns a double value containing the natural logarithm of a specified number
Math.Log10	Returns a double value containing the base 10 logarithm of a specified number
Math.Max	Returns the larger of two numbers
Math.Min	Returns the smaller of two numbers
Math.PI	A constant that specifies the ratio of the circumference of a circle to its diameter
Math.Pow	Used to raise a number to a specified power – an exponentiation operator
Math.Round	Returns the number nearest the specified number of decimal points

Math.Sign	Returns an Integer value indicating the sign of a number
Math.Sin	Returns a Double value containing the sine of the specified angle
Math.Sqrt	Returns a double value specifying the square root of a number
Math.Tan	Returns a double value containing the tangent of an angle

Examples:

Math.Abs(-5.4) returns the absolute value of -5.4 (returns 5.4)
Math.Cos(2.3) returns the cosine of an angle of 2.3 radians
Math.Max(7, 10) returns the larger of the two numbers (returns 10)
Math.Sign(-3) returns the sign on -3 (returns a -1)
Math.Sqrt(4.5) returns the square root of 4.5

Example 2-1

Savings Account

1. Start a new project. The idea of this project is to determine how much you save by making monthly deposits into a savings account. For those interested, the mathematical formula used is:

$$F = D\ [\ (1 + I)^M - 1]\ /\ I$$

where

F - Final amount
D - Monthly deposit amount
I - Monthly interest rate
M - Number of months

2. Place 4 labels, 4 text boxes, and 2 buttons on the form. It should look something like this:

3. Set the properties of the form and each object.

Form1:
Name	frmSavings
FormBorderStyle	Fixed Single
Starting Position	CenterScreen
Text	Savings Account

label1:
Text	Monthly Deposit

label2:
Text	Yearly Interest

label3:
Text	Number of Months

label4:
Text	Final Balance

textBox1:
Name	txtDeposit

textBox2:
Name	txtInterest

textBox3:
Name	txtMonths

textBox4:
Name	txtFinal
BackColor	White
ReadOnly	True

button1:
    Name   btnCalculate
    Text   &Calculate

button2:
    Name   btnExit
    Text   E&xit

Now, your form should look like this:

4. Declare four variables under the **form constructor** in the Code window. This gives them form level scope, making them available to all the form methods:

```
double deposit;
double interest;
double months;
double final;
```

At this point, the Code window should look like this:

```
 9    namespace Example_2_1
10    {
11        public partial class frmSavings : Form
12        {
13            public frmSavings()
14            {
15                InitializeComponent();
16            }
17
18            double deposit;
19            double interest;
20            double months;
21            double final;
22
23
24
25        }
26    }
```

5. Write code for the **btnCalculate** button **Click** event (remember to select the **btnCalculate** object from the object box in the properties window, click the **Events** button and double-click the listed **Click** event – or, just double-click the button control):

```
private void BtnCalculate_Click(object sender, EventArgs
e)
{
   double intRate;
   // read values from text boxes
   deposit = Convert.ToDouble(txtDeposit.Text);
   interest = Convert.ToDouble(txtInterest.Text);
   intRate = interest / 1200;
   months = Convert.ToDouble(txtMonths.Text);
   // compute final value and put in text box
   final = deposit * (Math.Pow(1 + intRate, months) - 1) /
intRate;
   txtFinal.Text = String.Format("{0:f2}", final);
}
```

This code reads the three input values (monthly deposit, interest rate, number of months) from the text boxes, converts those string variables to number using the **Convert.ToDouble** method, converts the yearly interest percentage to monthly interest (**intRate**), computes the final balance using the provided formula, and puts that result in a text box (after converting it back to a string variable).

6. Now, write code for the **btnExit** button **Click** event.

```
private void BtnExit_Click(object sender, EventArgs e)
{
    this.Close();
}
```

7. Play with the program. Make sure it works properly. Here's a run I made:

Save the project (**Example 2-1** folder in the **LearnVCS\VCS Code\Class 2** folder).

Tab Stops and Tab Order

When you run Example 2-1, you should have noticed the cursor didn't necessarily start out at the top text box where you enter the Monthly Deposit. And, if you try to move from text box to text box using the **<Tab>** key, there may be no predictable order in how the cursor moves. To enter values, you have to make sure you first click in the text box. And, we never want to tab to the final value text box control since nothing is ever typed there. To make this process more orderly, we need to understand two properties of controls: **TabStop** and **TabIndex**.

When interacting with a Windows application, we can work with a single control at a time. That is, we can click on a single button or type in a single text box. We can't be doing two things at once. The control we are working with is known as the **active** control or we say the control has **focus**. In our savings account example, when the cursor is in a particular text box, we say that text box has focus. In a properly designed application, focus is shifted from one control to another (in a predictable, orderly fashion) using the **<Tab>** key.

To define an orderly Tab response, we do two things. First, for each control you want accessible via the **<Tab>** key, make sure its **TabStop** property is **True**. All non-accessible controls should have the TabStop property set to False. Second, the order in which the controls will be accessed (given focus) is set by the **TabIndex** property. The control with the lowest TabIndex property will be the first control with focus. Higher subsequent TabIndex properties will be followed with each touch of the **<Tab>** key. The process can be reversed using **<Tab>**in combination with the **<Shift>** key. Once the highest TabIndex property is found, the Tab process restarts at the lowest value.

There are two ways to set **TabIndex** values. You can set the property of each control using the Properties window. This is tedious especially when new controls are introduced to the form. The Visual C# IDE offers a great tool for setting the TabIndex property of all controls. To show how to use this tool requires a little example.

Start a new project in Visual C#. Add two text boxes and two buttons to the form. Make your form look something like this:

(By the way, this is something you can easily do with Visual C# – set up quick examples to try different things.) By default, each control will have a TabStop of True and some value of TabIndex. Run the application. Yes, I know there is no code, but that's OK. Press the **<Tab>** key and watch the focus move from control to control. Stop the application. Set button2's **TabStop** property to **False**. Rerun the application and notice (as expected) that button is now excluded from the tab sequence.

Now, we'll change the **TabIndex** properties. With the form selected (has resizing handles), choose the **View** menu option, and choose **Tab Order**. You should see this:

The little blue number on each control is its corresponding **TabIndex** property. To set (or reset) these values, simply click on each control in the sequence you want the Tab ordering to occur in. If you click on a control with a False TabStop property, the index value will be ignored in the Tab sequence. Reset the sequence and run the project again. Notice how easily the Tab sequence is modified. To turn off the tab order display, return to the TabIndex View menu and choose **TabOrder** again (make sure the form is active while doing this or that menu item does not appear in the View menu).

Example 2-2

Savings Account – Setting Tabs

1. We will modify our savings account example so it has orderly Tab sequencing. We want the focus to start in the text box requesting Monthly Deposit. Next in sequence will be the text boxes for Interest and Number of Months. We will delete the Tab stop for the Final Deposit box, since we can't type a number there. Next the focus should move to the Calculate button (when this button has focus, if you press **<Enter>** on the keyboard, it is the same as if you clicked on the button). We'll finally delete the tab stop for the Exit key to avoid accidental stopping of the program.

2. Open Example 2-1. Add these two property changes:

   txtFinal Text Box control:
        TabStop   False

   btnExit Button control:
        TabStop   False

3. Select the form and view the **Tab Order**. Set the values similar to those shown:

4. Now run the project and notice the nicer orderly flow as the Tab key is pressed. Save the project (**Example 2-2** folder in the **LearnVCS\VCS Code\Class 2** folder).

Improving a Visual C# Application

In the previous section, we noted a weakness in the savings application (unpredictable tab ordering) and fixed the problem, improving the performance of our application. This is something you, as a programmer, will do a lot of. You will build an application and while running it and testing it, will uncover weaknesses that need to be eliminated. These weaknesses could be actual errors in the application or just things that, if eliminated, make your application easier to use.

You will find, as you progress as a programmer, that you will spend much of your time improving your applications. You will always find ways to add features to an application and to make it more appealing to your user base. You should never be satisfied with your first solution to a problem. There will always be room for improvement. And Visual C# provides a perfect platform for adding improvements to an application. You can easily add features and test them to see if the desired performance enhancements are attained.

If you run the savings application a few more times, you can identify further weaknesses:

> ➤ For example, what happens if you input a zero interest? The program will show a final balance of **NaN** (not a number) because the formula that computes the final value will not work with zero interest.
> ➤ Notice you can type any characters you want in the text boxes when you should just be limited to numbers and a single decimal point – any other characters will cause the program to work incorrectly.
> ➤ As a convenience, it would be nice that when you hit the **<Enter>** key after typing a number, the focus would move to the next control.

We can (and will) address each of these points as we improve the savings application. But, to do so, requires learning more C# coding. We'll address the zero interest problem first. To solve this problem, we need to be able to make a decision. If the interest is zero, we'll do one computation. If it's not zero, we'll user another. One mechanism for making decisions with Visual C# is the **if** statement.

Visual C# Decisions - if Statements

The concept of an **if** statement for making a decision is very simple. We check to see if a particular **Boolean** condition is true. If so, we take a certain action. If not, we do something else. **if** statements are also called **branching** statements. **Branching** statements are used to cause certain actions within a program if a certain condition is met.

The simplest form for the Visual C# **if** statement is:

```
if (condition)
{
    [process this code]
}
```

Here, if **condition** is **true**, the code bounded by the two braces is executed. If condition is false, nothing happens and code execution continues after the closing right brace.

Example:

```
if (balance - check < 0)
{
  trouble = true;
  SendLettertoAccount();
}
```

In this case, if balance - check is less than zero, two lines of information are processed: trouble is set to true and a method sending a letter to the account holder is executed. Notice the indentation of the code between the two braces. The Visual C# environment automatically supplies this indentation. It makes understanding (and debugging) your code much easier. You can adjust the amount of indentation the IDE uses if you like.

What if you want to do one thing if a condition is true and another if it is false? Use an **if/else** block:

```
if (condition)
{
    [process this code]
}
else
{
    [process this code]
}
```

In this block, if condition is true, the code between the first two braces is executed. If condition is false, the code between the second set of braces is processed.

Example:

```
if (balance - check < 0)
{
   trouble = true;
   SendLettertoAccount();
}
else
{
   trouble = false;
}
```

Here, the same two lines are executed if you are overdrawn (balance - check < 0), but if you are not overdrawn (**else**), the trouble flag is turned off.

Lastly, we can test multiple conditions by adding the **else if** statement:

```
if (condition1)
{
    [process this code]
}
else if (condition2)
{
    [process this code]
}
else if (condition3)
{
    [process this code]
}
else
{
    [process this code]
}
```

In this block, if condition1 is true, the code between the if and first else if line is executed. If condition1 is false, condition2 is checked. If condition2 is true, the indicated code is executed. If condition2 is not true, condition3 is checked. Each subsequent condition in the structure is checked until a true condition is found, an else statement is reached or the last closing brace is reached.

Example:

```
if (balance - check < 0)
{
  trouble = true;
  SendLettertoAccount();
}
else if (balance - check == 0)
{
  trouble = false;
  SendWarningLetter();
}
else
{
  trouble = false;
}
```

Now, one more condition is added. If your balance equals the check amount [**else if** (balance - check == 0)], you're still not in trouble, but a warning is mailed.

In using branching statements, make sure you consider all viable possibilities in the if/else if structure. Also, be aware that each if and else if in a block is tested sequentially. The first time an if test is met, the code block associated with that condition is executed and the if block is exited. If a later condition is also true, it will never be considered.

Switch - Another Way to Branch

In addition to if/then/else type statements, the **switch** structure can be used when there are multiple selection possibilities. switch is used to make decisions based on the value of a single variable. The structure is:

```
switch (variable)
{
   case [variable has this value]:
      [process this code]
      break;
   case [variable has this value]:
      [process this code]
      break;
   case [variable has this value]:
      [process this code]
      break;
   default:
      [process this code]
      break;
}
```

The way this works is that the value of **variable** is examined. Each **case** statement is then sequentially examined until the value matches one of the specified cases. Once found, the corresponding code is executed. If no case match is found, the code in the default segment (if there) is executed. The **break** statements transfer program execution to the line following the closing right brace. These statements are optional, but will almost always be there. If a break is not executed, all code following the case processed will also be processed (until a break is seen or the end of the structure is reached). This is different behavior than **if** statements where only one 'case' could be executed.

As an example, say we've written this code using the **if** statement:

```
if (age == 5)
{
  category = "Kindergarten";
}
else if (age == 6)
{
  category = "First Grade";
}
else if (age == 7)
{
  category = "Second Grade";
}
else if (age == 8)
{
  category = "Third Grade";
}
else if (age == 9)
{
  category = "Fourth Grade";
}
else
{
  category = "Older Child";
}
```

This will work, but it is ugly code and difficult to maintain.

The corresponding code with **switch** is 'cleaner':

```
switch (age)
{
  case 5:
    category = "Kindergarten";
    break;
  case 6:
    category = "First Grade";
    break;
  case 7:
    category = "Second Grade";
    break;
  case 8:
    category = "Third Grade";
    break;
  case 9:
    category = "Fourth Grade";
    break;
  default:
    category = "Older Child";
    break;
}
```

Key Trapping

Recall in the savings example, there is nothing to prevent the user from typing in meaningless characters (for example, letters) into the text boxes expecting numerical data. We want to keep this from happening. Whenever getting input from a user using a text box control, we want to limit the available keys they can press. This process of intercepting and eliminating unacceptable keystrokes is called **key trapping.**

Key trapping is done in the **KeyPress** event method of a text box control. Such a method has the form (for a text box named **txtText**):

```
private void TxtText_KeyPress(object sender,
KeyPressEventArgs e)
{

}
```

What happens in this method is that every time a key is pressed in the corresponding text box, the **KeyPressEventArgs** class passes the key that has been pressed into the method via the **char** type **e.KeyChar** property. Recall the **char** type is used to represent a single character. We can thus examine this key. If it is an acceptable key, we set the **e.Handled** property to **false.** This tells Visual C# that this method has not been handled and the KeyPress should be allowed. If an unacceptable key is detected, we set **e.Handled** to **true.** This 'tricks' Visual C# into thinking the KeyPress event has already been handled and the pressed key is ignored.

We need some way of distinguishing what keys are pressed. The usual alphabetic, numeric and character keys are fairly simple to detect. To help detect non-readable keys, we can examine the key's corresponding Unicode value. Two values we will use are:

Definition	Value
Backspace	8
Carriage return (<Enter> key)	13

As an example, let's build a key trapping routine for our savings application example. We'll work with the **txtDeposit** control, knowing the KeyPress events for the other text box controls will be similar. There are several ways to build a key trapping routine. I suggest an if/else structure that, based on different values of **e.KeyChar**, takes different steps. If e.KeyChar represents a number, a decimal point or a backspace key (always include backspace or the user won't be able to edit the text box properly), we will allow the keypress (e.Handled = false). Otherwise, we will set e.Handled = true to ignore the keypress. The code to do this is:

```
if (e.KeyChar >= '0' && e.KeyChar <= '9')
{
  // number values
  e.Handled = false;
}
else if ((int) e.KeyChar == 8)
{
  // backspace
  e.Handled = false;
}
else if (e.KeyChar == '.')
{
  // decimal point
  e.Handled = false;
}
else
{
  // any other character
  e.Handled = true;
}
```

Note the use of single quotes to signify **char** types, the same type as e.KeyChar.

Note, this code does not eliminate one of the earlier identified problems. That is, there is nothing to keep the user from typing multiple decimal points. To solve this, we add some code to the 'decimal point' case:

```
else if (e.KeyChar == '.')
{
  // decimal point
  if (txtText.Text.IndexOf(".") == -1)
  {
    // no decimal yet
    e.Handled = false;
  }
  else
  {
    // has decimal
    e.Handled = true;
  }
}
```

In this new case, if there is no decimal point (determined using the **IndexOf** mthod), the keypress is allowed. If a decimal point is already there (**IndexOf** returns a positive value), the keypress is disallowed.

Control Focus

Earlier we saw that, in a running application, only one control can have user interaction at any one time. We say that control has **focus**. A text box with the cursor has focus – if the user begins typing, the typed characters go in that text box. If a button control has focus, that button can be 'clicked' by simply pressing the **<Enter>** key.

We also saw that the **<Tab>** key could be used to move from control to control, shifting the focus. Many times, you might like to move focus from one control to another in code, or programmatically. For example, in our savings example, once the user types in a Deposit Amount, it would be nice if focus would be moved to the Interest text box if the user presses **<Enter>**. We can do that with another 'else' structure in our KeyPress event.

To programmatically assign focus to a control, apply the **Focus** method to the control using this dot-notation:

    ControlName.**Focus**();

The **'else if'** to do this in our **txtDeposit** text box key trapping routine would be:

```
else if ((int) e.KeyChar == 13)
{
  // move focus
  txtInterest.Focus();
}
```

Here, if the <Enter> key is pressed (a Unicode value of 13), focus is shifted to the txtInterest text box control. We'll now put this code with our earlier code to add complete key trapping capabilities to our savings application.

Example 2-3

Savings Account - Key Trapping

1. We modify the Savings Account example to handle a zero interest value and to implement key trapping in the three text box **KeyPress** events. The key trapping implemented will only allow numbers, a single decimal point and the backspace. If **<Enter>** is pressed, focus is passed to the next control. For each text box control, the KeyPress event is <u>not</u> the control default event. Hence, to access the event, you <u>cannot</u> double-click the control. The KeyPress event must be selected from the properties window.

2. Modify the **btnCalculate Click** event code to accommodate a zero interest input. Note if interest is zero, the final value is just the deposited amount times the number of months. The modified routine is (new code shaded):

```
private void BtnCalculate_Click(object sender, EventArgs e)
{
  double intRate;
  // read values from text boxes
  deposit = Convert.ToDouble(txtDeposit.Text);
  interest = Convert.ToDouble(txtInterest.Text);
  intRate = interest / 1200;
  months = Convert.ToDouble(txtMonths.Text);
  // compute final value and put in text box
  if (interest == 0)
  {
    final = deposit * months;
  }
  else
  {
    final = deposit * (Math.Pow(1 + intRate, months) - 1) / intRate;
  }
  txtFinal.Text = String.Format("{0:f2}", final);
}
```

(In some of the statements above, the word processor may cause a line break where there really shouldn't be one. In all code in these notes, always look for such things.)

3. Add the following code to **txtDeposit** text box **KeyPress** event. Recall, you will have to select this event using the properties window. Double-clicking the control will bring up the TextChanged event (the default text box event); this is a case where the default event is not the desired one.

```
private void TxtDeposit_KeyPress(object sender,
KeyPressEventArgs e)
{
    // only allow numbers, a single decimal point, backspace
or enter
    if ((e.KeyChar >= '0' && e.KeyChar <= '9') || (int)
e.KeyChar == 8)
    {
        // acceptable keystrokes
        e.Handled = false;
    }
    else if ((int) e.KeyChar == 13)
    {
        // enter key - move to next box
        txtInterest.Focus();
    }
    else if (e.KeyChar == '.')
    {
        // check for existence of decimal point
        if (txtDeposit.Text.IndexOf(".") == -1)
        {
            e.Handled = false;
        }
        else
        {
            e.Handled = true;
        }
    }
    else
    {
        e.Handled = true;
    }
}
```

This code limits keystrokes to numbers, a single decimal point, the backspace key and moves focus to the **txtInterest** control if **<Enter>** is hit.

4. Add the following code to **txtInterest** text box **KeyPress** event (nearly same as above – use cut and paste – differences involve control names and where focus moves after **<Enter>**):

```csharp
private void TxtInterest_KeyPress(object sender,
KeyPressEventArgs e)
{
  // only allow numbers, a single decimal point, backspace
or enter
  if ((e.KeyChar >= '0' && e.KeyChar <= '9') || (int)
e.KeyChar == 8)
  {
    // acceptable keystrokes
    e.Handled = false;
  }
  else if ((int) e.KeyChar == 13)
  {
    // enter key - move to next box
    txtMonths.Focus();
  }
  else if (e.KeyChar == '.')
  {
    // check for existence of decimal point
    if (txtInterest.Text.IndexOf(".") == -1)
    {
      e.Handled = false;
    }
    else
    {
      e.Handled = true;
    }
  }
  else
  {
    e.Handled = true;
  }
}
```

This code limits keystrokes to numbers, a single decimal point, the backspace key and moves focus to the **txtMonth** control if **<Enter>** is hit.

5. Add the following code to **txtMonths** text box **KeyPress** event (nearly same as above – use cut and paste – differences involve control names, no decimal point allowed and where focus moves after **<Enter>**):

```
private void TxtMonths_KeyPress(object sender,
KeyPressEventArgs e)
{
  // only allow numbers, a single decimal point, backspace
or enter
  if ((e.KeyChar >= '0' && e.KeyChar <= '9') || (int)
e.KeyChar == 8)
  {
    // acceptable keystrokes
    e.Handled = false;
  }
  else if ((int) e.KeyChar == 13)
  {
    // enter key - move to calculate button
    btnCalculate.Focus();
  }
  else
  {
    e.Handled = true;
  }
}
```

This code limits keystrokes to numbers, the backspace key and moves focus to the **btnCalculate** control if **<Enter>** is hit. Notice we don't allow decimal points here – you can't enter a fractional month!

6. Rerun the application and test the key trapping performance. Here's I case I ran to test the zero interest possibility:

Save the application (**Example 2-3** folder in the **LearnVCS\VCS Code\Class 2** folder).

Visual C# Looping

Many applications require repetition of certain code segments. For example, you may want to roll a die (simulated die of course) until it shows a six. Or, you might generate financial results until a certain sum of returns has been achieved. This idea of repeating code is called iteration or **looping**.

In Visual C#, looping is done with one of two formats. The first is the **while** loop:

```
while (condition)
{
    [process this code]
}
```

In this structure, the code block in braces is repeated 'as long as' the Boolean expression condition is true. Note a while loop structure will not execute even once if the while condition is false the first time through. If we do enter the loop, it is assumed at some point condition will become false to allow exiting. Notice <u>there is no semicolon</u> after the while statement.

This brings up a very important point – if you use a loop, make sure you can get out of the loop!! It is especially important in the event-driven environment of Visual C# event-driven applications. As long as your code is operating in some loop, no events can be processed. You can also exit a loop using the **break** statement. This will get you out of a loop and transfer program control to the statement following the loop's closing brace. Of course, you need logic in a loop to decide when a break is appropriate.

You can also use a **continue** statement within a loop. When a continue is encountered, all further steps in the loop are skipped and program operation is transferred to the top of the loop.

Example:

```
counter = 1;
while (counter <= 1000)
{
   counter += 1;
}
```

This loop repeats as long as (**while**) the variable counter is less than or equal to 1000.

Another example:

```
roll = 0;
counter = 0;
while (counter < 10)
{
   // Roll a simulated die
   roll += 1;
   if (myRandom.Next(6) + 1 == 6)
   {
      counter += 1;
   }
}
```

This loop repeats **while** the counter variable is less than 10. The counter variable is incremented each time a simulated die rolls a 6. The roll variable tells you how many rolls of the die were needed to reach 10 sixes.

The second looping structure in Visual C# is a **do/while** structure:

```
do
{
   [process this code]
}
while (condition);
```

This loop repeats 'as long as' the Boolean expression condition is true. The loop is always executed at least once. Somewhere in the loop, condition must be changed to false to allow exiting. Notice <u>there is a semicolon</u> after the while statement.

Examples:

```
sum = 0;
do
{
   sum += 3;
}
while (sum <= 50);
```

In this example, we increment a sum by 3 until that sum exceeds 50 (or **while** the sum is less than or equal to 50).

Another example:

```
sum = 0;
counter = 0;
do
{
  // Roll a simulated die
  sum += myRandom.Next(6) + 1;
  counter += 1;
}
while (sum <= 30);
```

This loop rolls a simulated die **while** the sum of the rolls does not exceed 30. It also keeps track of the number of rolls (counter) needed to achieve this sum.

Again, make sure you can always get out of a loop! Infinite loops are never nice. Sometimes the only way out is rebooting your machine!

Visual C# Counting

With **while** and **do/while** structures, we usually didn't know, ahead of time, how many times we execute a loop or iterate. If you know how many times you need to iterate on some code, you want to use Visual C# **counting**. Counting is useful for adding items to a list or perhaps summing a known number of values to find an average.

Visual C# counting is accomplished using the **for** loop:

```
for (initialization; expression; update)
{
    [process this code]
}
```

The **initialization** step is executed <u>once</u> and is used to initialize a counter variable. The **expression** step is executed <u>before</u> each repetition of the loop. If expression is true, the code is executed; if false, the loop is exited. The **update** step is executed <u>after</u> each loop iteration. It is used to update the counter variable.

Example:

```
for (degrees = 0; degrees <= 360; degrees += 10)
{
  // convert to radians
  r = degrees * Math.PI / 180;
  a = Math.Sin(r);
  b = Math.Cos(r);
  c = Math.Tan(r);
}
```

In this example, we compute trigonometric functions for angles from 0 to 360 degrees in increments of 10 degrees. It is assumed that all variables have been properly declared.

Another Example:

```
for (countdown = 10; countdown <= 0; countdown--)
{
  timeTextField.setText(String.valueOf(countdown));
}
```

NASA called and asked us to format a text field control to count down from 10 to 0. The loop above accomplishes the task. Note the use of the **decrement** operator.

And, another Example:

```
double[] myValues = new double[100];
sum = 0;
for (int i = 0; i < 100; i++)
{
  sum += myValues[i];
}
average = sum / 100;
```

This code finds the average value of 100 numbers stored in the array **myValues**. It first sums each of the values in a **for** loop. That sum is then divided by the number of terms (100) to yield the average. Note the use of the **increment** operator. Also, notice the counter is declared in the initialization step. This is a common declaration in a loop or block of code. Such **loop** or **block level variables** lose their values once the loop is completed.

You may exit a for loop early using a **break** statement. This will transfer program control to the statement following the closing brace. Use of a **continue** statement will skip all statements remaining in the loop and return program control to the **for** statement.

Example 2-4

Savings Account - Decisions

As built, our savings account application is useful, but we can add more capability. For example, what if we know how much money we need in a number of months and the interest our deposits can earn. It would be nice if the program could calculate the needed month deposit. Or, what if we want to know how long it will take us to reach a goal, knowing how much we can deposit each month and the related interest. Here, we modify the Savings Account project to allow entering any three values and computing the fourth.

1. First, add a third button that will clear all of the text boxes. Assign the following properties:

Button3:
    Name   btnClear
    Text   Clear &Boxes

The form should look something like this when you're done:

2. Code the **btnClear** button **Click** event:

```
private void BtnClear_Click(object sender, EventArgs e)
{
  // blank out text boxes
  txtDeposit.Text = "";
  txtInterest.Text = "";
  txtMonths.Text = "";
  txtFinal.Text = "";
  txtDeposit.Focus();
}
```

This code simply blanks out the four text boxes when the **Clear** button is clicked. It then redirects focus to the txtDeposit text box.

3. We now need the capability to enter information into the Final Value text box. Related to this:

> Change the **ReadOnly** property of the **txtFinal** text box to False
> Change **TabStop** to **True**
> Reset the **Tab Order** so, the txtFinal text box is included
> Modify the **txtMonths KeyPress** event so focus is transferred to the **txtFinal** text box when **<Enter>** is pressed

4. Code the **KeyPress** event for the **txtFinal** object:

```
private void TxtFinal_KeyPress(object sender,
KeyPressEventArgs e)
{
  // only allow numbers, a single decimal point, backspace
or enter
  if ((e.KeyChar >= '0' && e.KeyChar <= '9') || (int)
e.KeyChar == 8)
  {
    // acceptable keystrokes
    e.Handled = false;
  }
  else if ((int) e.KeyChar == 13)
  {
    // enter key - move to calculate button
    btnCalculate.Focus();
  }
  else if (e.KeyChar == '.')
  {
    // check for existence of decimal point
    if (txtFinal.Text.IndexOf(".") == -1)
    {
      e.Handled = false;
    }
    else
    {
      e.Handled = true;
    }
  }
  else
  {
    e.Handled = true;
  }
}
```

Recall, we need this code because we can now enter information into the Final Balance text box. It is very similar to the other KeyPress events. This code limits keystrokes to numbers, a single decimal point, the backspace key and moves focus to the **btnCalculate** control if **<Enter>** is hit.

5. The modified code for the **Click** event of the **btnCalculate** button is:

```
private void BtnCalculate_Click(object sender, EventArgs
e)
{
  double intRate;
  double finalCompute, intChange;
  int intDirection;
  // Determine which box is blank
  // Compute that missing value and put in text box
  if (txtDeposit.Text.Trim() == "")
  {
    // Deposit missing
    // read other values from text boxes
    interest = Convert.ToDouble(txtInterest.Text);
    intRate = interest / 1200;
    months = Convert.ToDouble(txtMonths.Text);
    final = Convert.ToDouble(txtFinal.Text);
    if (interest == 0)
    {
      deposit = final / months;
    }
    else
    {
      deposit = final / ((Math.Pow(1 + intRate, months) -
1) / intRate);
    }
    txtDeposit.Text = String.Format("{0:f2}", deposit);
  }
  else if (txtInterest.Text.Trim() == "")
  {
    // Interest missing - requires iterative solution
    // read other values from text boxes
    deposit = Convert.ToDouble(txtDeposit.Text);
    months = Convert.ToDouble(txtMonths.Text);
    final = Convert.ToDouble(txtFinal.Text);
    // intChange is how much we change interest each step
    // intDirection is direction (+ or -) we change
interest
    interest = 0;
    intChange = 1;
    intDirection = 1;
    do
    {
      interest += intDirection * intChange;
      intRate = interest / 1200;
```

```csharp
      finalCompute = deposit * (Math.Pow(1 + intRate,
months) - 1) / intRate;
      if (intDirection == 1)
      {
        if (finalCompute > final)
        {
          intDirection = -1;
          intChange /= 10;
        }
      }
      else
      {
        if (finalCompute < final)
        {
          intDirection = 1;
          intChange /= 10;
        }
      }
    }
    while (Math.Abs(finalCompute -final) > 0.005);
    txtInterest.Text = String.Format("{0:f2}", interest);
  }
  else if (txtMonths.Text.Trim() == "")
  {
    // Months missing
    // read other values from text boxes
    deposit = Convert.ToDouble(txtDeposit.Text);
    interest = Convert.ToDouble(txtInterest.Text);
    intRate = interest / 1200;
    final = Convert.ToDouble(txtFinal.Text);
    if (interest == 0)
    {
      months = final / deposit;
    }
    else
    {
      months = Math.Log(final * intRate / deposit + 1) /
Math.Log(1 + intRate);
    }
    txtMonths.Text = String.Format("{0:f2}", months);
  }
  else if (txtFinal.Text.Trim() == "")
  {
    // Final value missing
    // read other values from text boxes
    deposit = Convert.ToDouble(txtDeposit.Text);
    interest = Convert.ToDouble(txtInterest.Text);
```

```
intRate = interest / 1200;
months = Convert.ToDouble(txtMonths.Text);
if (interest == 0)
{
  final = deposit * months;
}
else
{
  final = deposit * (Math.Pow(1 + intRate, months) -
1) / intRate;
}
txtFinal.Text = String.Format("{0:f2}", final);
}
}
```

This is nearly a complete rewrite of the existing method. In this code. we first read the text information from all four text boxes and based on which one is blank (the **Trim** function strips off leading and trailing blanks), compute the missing information and display it in the corresponding text box.

Let's look at the math involved in solving for missing information. Recall the equation given in Example 2-1:

$$F = D [(1 + I)^M - 1] / I$$

where F is the final amount, D the deposit, I the monthly interest, and M the number of months. This is the equation we've been using to solve for **Final** and we still use it here if the **Final** box is empty, unless the interest is zero. For zero interest, we use:

$$F = DM, \text{ if interest is zero}$$

See if you can find these equations in the code.

If the **Deposit** box is empty, we can easily solve the equation for D (the needed quantity):

$$D = F / \{[(1 + I)^M - 1] / I\}$$

If the interest is zero, this equation will not work. In that case, we use:

$$D = F/M, \text{ if interest is zero}$$

You should be able to find these equations in the code above.

Solving for missing **Months** information requires knowledge of logarithms. I'll just give you the equation:

$$M = \log (FI / D + 1) / \log (1 + I)$$

In this Visual C#, the logarithm (log) function is one of the math functions, **Math.Log**. Like the other cases, we need a separate equation for zero interest:

$$M = F/D, \text{ if interest is zero}$$

Again, see if you can find these equations in the code.

If the **Interest** value is missing, we need to resort to a widely used method for solving equations – we'll guess! But, we'll use a structured guessing method. Here's what we'll do. We'll start with a zero interest and increase it by one percent until the computed final amount is larger than the displayed final amount. At that point, we know the interest is too high so, we decrease the interest by a smaller amount (0.1 percent) until the computed final amount is less than the displayed final amount, meaning the interest is too low. We start increasing the interest again (this time by 0.01 percent). We'll repeat this process until the computed final amount is with 1 cent of the displayed amount. This kind of process is called **iteration** and is used often in computer programs. You should be able to see each step in the code – a good example of a do/while loop.

Don't be intimidated by the code in this example. I'll admit there's a lot of it! Upon study, though, you should see that it is just a straightforward list of instructions for the computer to follow based on input from the user.

6. Test and save your application (**Example 2-4** folder in the **LearnVCS\VCS Code\Class 2** folder). Here's a run I made (note the **Clear Boxes** button):

Try clearing one box at a time and make sure the deleted value returns once you click **Calculate**. I did this in the example above. That's why each number is formatted with two decimal places. Now, relax!.

Class Review

After completing this class, you should understand:

- ➢ Visual C# statements their use
- ➢ The C# assignment operator, mathematics operators, comparison and logic operators and concatenation operators
- ➢ The wide variety of built-in Visual C# methods, especially string methods, the random number generator, and mathematics methods
- ➢ How to set tabs and assign tab order to controls
- ➢ The **if/else if/else** structure used for branching and decisions
- ➢ The **switch** decision structure
- ➢ How key trapping can be used to eliminate unwanted keystrokes from text box controls
- ➢ The concept of control focus and how to assign focus in code
- ➢ How the **while** and **do/while** structures are used for iterative procedures
- ➢ How the **for** loop is used for counting

Practice Problems 2

Problem 2-1. Random Number Problem. Build an application where each time a button is clicked, a random number from 1 to 100 is displayed.

Problem 2-2. Price Problem. The neighborhood children built a lemonade stand. The hotter it is, the more they can charge. Build an application that produces the selling price, based on temperature:

Temperature	Price
<50	Don't bother
50 - 60	20 Cents
61 - 70	25 Cents
71 - 80	30 Cents
81 - 85	40 Cents
86 - 90	50 Cents
91 - 95	55 Cents
96 - 100	65 Cents
>100	75 Cents

Problem 2-3. Odd Integers Problem. Build an application that adds consecutive odd integers (starting with one) until the sum exceeds a target value. Display the sum and how many integers were added.

Problem 2-4. Pennies Problem. Here's an old problem. Today, I'll give you a penny. Tomorrow, I'll give you two pennies. I'll keep doubling the amount I'll give you each day. How much will you have at the end of a week? Use a **long** integer type to keep track.

Problem 2-5. Code Problem. Build an application with a text box and two buttons. Type a word or words in the text box. Click one of the buttons. Subtract one from the Unicode value of each character in the typed word(s), then redisplay it. This is a simple encoding technique. When you click the other button, reverse the process to decode the word. This is good practice using string methods.

Exercise 2-1

Computing a Mean and Standard Deviation

Develop an application that allows the user to input a sequence of numbers. When done inputting the numbers, the program should compute the mean of that sequence and the standard deviation. If N numbers are input, with the ith number represented by x_i, the formula for the mean ($\bar{x}$) is:

$$\bar{x} = \left(\sum_{i=1}^{N} x_i \right) / N$$

and to compute the standard deviation (s), take the square root of this equation:

$$s^2 = \left[N \sum_{i=1}^{N} x_i^2 - \left(\sum_{i=1}^{N} x_i \right)^2 \right] / [N(N-1)]$$

The Greek sigmas in the above equations simply indicate that you add up all the N corresponding elements next to the sigma. If the standard deviation equation scares you, just write code to find the average value – you should have no trouble with that one.

Exercise 2-2

Flash Card Addition Problems

Write an application that generates random addition problems. Provide some kind of feedback and scoring system as the problems are answered.

3. Object Oriented Programming (OOP)

Review and Preview

Visual C# is object-oriented, where objects are reusable entities of code. In the first two chapters, we have used several "built-in" objects: button controls, label controls, text box controls, DateTime objects and Random objects. Having these reusable objects available makes our programming life much simpler, reducing the need to write and rewrite code.

In this class, we learn the terminology of object-oriented programming (OOP), learn to create our own objects and learn to extend existing objects to customize them for our use (the idea of inheritance).

Introduction to Object-Oriented Programming (OOP)

We say Visual C# is an **object-oriented** language. In the first two classes, we have used some of the built-in objects included with Visual C#. We have used button objects, text box objects and label objects. We see that objects have **properties** (Name, Text, BackColor) and **methods** (Focus, PerformClick). We have used date time objects and random number objects where we were introduced to the ideas of **declaring** an object and **constructing** an object.

We have seen that objects are just things that have attributes (properties) with possible actions (methods). As you progress in your programming education, you may want to include your own objects in applications you build. But, it's tough to decide when you need (if ever) an object. A general rule is that you might want to consider using an object when you are working with some entity that fits the structure of having properties and methods and has some **re-use potential**.

The big advantage to objects (as seen with the ones we've used already) is that they can be used over and over again. This re-use can be multiple copies (**instances**) of a single object within a particular application or can be the re-use of a particular object in several different applications (like the controls of Visual C#).

The most common object is some entity with several describing features (**properties**). Such objects in other languages are called **structured variables**. One could be a line object using the end points, line thickness and line color as properties. Or, a person could be an object, with name, address, phone number as properties.

You could extend these simple objects (properties only) by adding **methods**. Methods allow an object to do something. With our simple line object example, we could add methods to draw a line, erase a line, color a line, and dot a line. In the person object example, we could have methods to sort, search or print the person objects.

I realize this explanation of when to use your own objects is rather vague. And, it has to be. Only through experience can you decide when you might need an object. As we progress through the remainder of this course, we will use more and more objects. This will show you how objects can be employed in Visual C#. And, don't feel bad if you never use a custom object. The great power of Visual C# is that you can do many things just using the built-in objects! In this class, we'll look at how to add an object to a Visual C# application, discussing properties, constructors and methods. And we'll look at how to modify an existing object (a Visual C# control) to meet some custom needs.

A word of warning – we are jumping a bit ahead presenting OOP material early in this course. Some of the material introduced here (such as methods and argument lists) is covered more deeply later in the course. If anything is unclear, do a little research on our own if you need further explanation – or just accept what we say for now and it should become clearer as you progress in your programming education.

Objects in Visual C#

Let's review some of the vocabulary of object-oriented programming. These are terms you've seen before in working with the built-in objects of Visual C#. A **class** provides a general description of an **object**. All objects are created from this class description. The first step in creating an object is adding a class to a Visual C# project. Every application we build in this course is a class itself. Note the top line of every application has the keyword **Class**.

The **class** provides a framework for describing three primary components:

> ➢ **Properties** – attributes describing the objects
> ➢ **Constructors** – methods that initialize the object
> ➢ **Methods** – procedures describing things an object can do

Once a class is defined, an object can be created or **instantiated** from the class. This simply means we use the class description to create a copy of the object we can work with. Once the instance is created, we **construct** the finished object for our use.

One last important term to define, related to OOP, is **inheritance**. This is a capability that allows one object to 'borrow' properties and methods from another object. This prevents the classic 'reinventing the wheel' situation. Inheritance is one of the most powerful features of OOP. In this chapter, we will see how to use inheritance in a simple example and how we can create our own control that inherits from an existing control.

Adding a Class to a Visual C# Project

The first step in creating our own object is to define the class from which the object will be created. This step (and all following steps) is best illustrated by example. In the example here, we will be creating **Widget** objects that have two properties: a **color** and a **size**. Start a new project in Visual C# – name the project **Widget Class**. Place a text box control on the form. Set these properties:

Form1:

Name	frmWidget
FormBorderStyle	Fixed Single
Starting Position	CenterScreen
Text	Widget Class Example

textBox1:

Name	txtWidget
Font Size	10
Multiline	True
ScrollBars	Vertical

Use **WidgetExample.cs** to save the form file. Your finished form should resemble this:

We need to add a class to this project to allow the definition of our **Widget** objects. We could add the class in the existing form file. However, doing so would defeat a primary advantage of objects that being re-use. Hence, we will create a separate file to hold our class. To do this, go to **Solution Explorer**, right-click the project name (**Widget Class**), choose **Add**, then **Add Class**. The following window will appear:

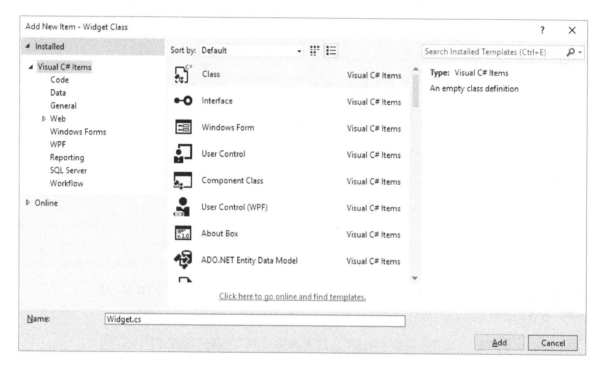

Type **Widget.cs** in the **Name** box and make sure the **Class** template is selected. Click **Add** to open the newly created class file.

A file named **Widget.cs** will now be seen in the Solution Explorer window and that file will open. All our code (to define properties, constructors and methods) will be written in the **class Widget** code block:

```
class Widget
{

}
```

All code needed to define properties, constructors and methods for this class will be within the curly braces.

Declaring and Constructing an Object

We now have a class we can use to create Widget objects. Yes, it's a very simple class, but it will work. There are two steps in creating an object from a class – **declare** the object, then **construct** the object. Note these are the same steps we've used with the built-in Visual C# objects.

Return to the example project. The **Widget** object will be created in the **WidgetExample.cs** file (the file describing **frmWidget**). Open that file and double-click the form to navigate to its **Load** procedure in the code window:

```
private void frmWidget_Load(object sender, EventArgs e)
{

}
```

All the code we write in this example will be in this **frmWidget_Load** procedure.

To declare a **Widget** object named **myWidget**, type this line of code in this procedure:

```
Widget myWidget;
```

Now, to construct this object, type this line of code:

```
myWidget = new Widget()
```

This line just says "give me a new widget." Note as soon as you type the keyword **new**, the Intellisense feature pops up suggesting possible object types. Notice **Widget** is one of the selections! This is due to the existence of the Widget class in the project.

Our Widget object is now complete, ready for use. There's not much we can do with it obviously – it has no properties or methods, but it does exist! You may wonder how we can construct a Widget object if we have not defined a constructor. The line above uses the **default** constructor automatically included with every class. The default constructor simply creates an object with no defined properties.

Adding Properties to a Class

There are two ways to define properties within a class description: creating direct **public variables** or creating **accessor methods**. We look at the first way here. Our Widget class will have two properties: **WidgetColor** (a **string** type) and **WidgetSize** (an **int** type). Class properties can be any type of variable or object – yes, properties can actually be other objects!

To define these properties in our class, go to the **Widget.cs** file and add the shaded lines to the file:

```
class Widget
{
  public string WidgetColor;
  public int WidgetSize;
}
```

The keyword **public** is used so the properties are available outside the class when the object is created.

Now, return to the **WidgetExample.cs** file so we can provide some definition to these properties in our instance of the object. In the **frmWidget_Load** method, add this shaded code to define and print the properties:

```
private void FrmWidget_Load(object sender, EventArgs e)
{
  Widget myWidget;
  myWidget = new Widget();
  myWidget.WidgetColor = "red";
  myWidget.WidgetSize = 15;
  txtWidget.Text = "Color is " + myWidget.WidgetColor;
  txtWidget.Text += "\r\nSize is " +
myWidget.WidgetSize.ToString();
}
```

Note, to refer to an object property, you use this format:

```
objectName.PropertyName
```

You should have seen that when typing in the properties, the Intellisense feature recognized the existence of your Widget class, providing a drop-down list of available properties. Also note, in setting the text box property, the four character "escape sequence" \r\n represents a 'carriage return' that puts each property on a separate line.

Run the example project. You should see this:

We've created and defined our first object! There's nothing to keep you from creating as many widgets as you want. Make sure your work is saved as we take a sidebar.

How Visual C# Puts Controls on a Form

A thought may have come to you by now. You might be asking, if controls are objects, why don't we ever write code to declare and construct controls, including definition of all their properties? The answer is that we do write such code; well, actually, the Visual C# development environment writes it for us. When we move a control from the toolbox onto a form and establish properties using the Properties window, code mimicking all these steps is written for us. All of this code resides in a hidden area of our project. Let's take a look.

Start a new project and put a single button control on the form. Here's my form:

Now, go to the **Solution Explorer** window and click on the **Show All Files** button to display all files in the project. Expand the element next to **Form1.cs**:

Open the **Form1.Designer.cs** file. This is the file where Visual C# writes the code to create the form.

Let's see how the single button is declared and constructed, then positioned on the form. The code window should appear as:

```
22
23 ⊞   Windows Form Designer generated code
56
57       private System.Windows.Forms.Button button1;
58 ⌐   }
59 ⌐ }
60
```

Expand the **Windows Form Designer generated code** line. This line should appear:

```
this.button1 = new System.Windows.Forms.Button();
```

This line is equivalent to a statement declaring **button1** to be a member of the **Button** class. It also constructs an instance of the button.

Another place in the code shows these lines:

```
//
// button1
//
this.button1.Location = new System.Drawing.Point(106, 38);
this.button1.Name = "button1";
this.button1.Size = new System.Drawing.Size(75, 23);
this.button1.TabIndex = 0;
this.button1.Text = "button1";
this.button1.UseVisualStyleBackColor = true;
```

This code sets several properties (including **Location** and **Size**). The button control is placed on the form using this line of code (under the **Form1** section):

```
this.Controls.Add(this.button1);
```

We see to add a control to the form, we need to follow four steps: (1) declare the control, (2) construct the control, (3) set control properties, and (4) add control to form. If there are events, we would also need to connect event handlers. For now, we'll let the IDE handle these tasks – later, in Chapter 10, we'll see how to add controls using code. Now, back to our Widget example. Open that example.

Another Way to Add Properties to a Class

We mentioned there are two ways to add properties to a class. We will look at the second method, creating **accessor methods**, here. The rationale behind this second method is to allow validation and/or modification of properties, giving you complete control over the property. The Visual C# controls use such methods to **get** and **set** properties.

For each property to be established using a method, first determine the property name (**Name**) and type (**type**). A **private** variable **name** (not the same as **Name**, since a lower case letter is used) is used to represent the local value of the property. Then type lines similar to these inside the boundaries of your class:

```
private type name;
public type Name
{
  get
  {
    return nameLocal;
  }
  set
  {
    nameLocal = value;
  }
```

There are two methods in this code: a **get** method (called a getter method) to determine the current property value and a **set** method (called a setter method) to establish a new property value. The keyword **value** in the set method is used to establish the property value.

With such methods, a **property** for an object (**objectName**) is accessed using:

```
property = objectName.Name;
```

And is set using:

```
objectName.Name = property;
```

Note a user cannot directly access the variable representing the property value.

The use of this technique is best illustrated with example. For our **Widget** class, the **WidgetColor** property can be established using:

```
private string widgetColor;
public string WidgetColor
{
  get
  {
   return widgetColor;
  }
  set
  {
    widgetColor = value;
  }
}
```

In this snippet, **widgetColor** is now a local variable representing the Widget color. This variable cannot be accessed directly. The **get** method is used to determine the widget color, while the **set** method is used to provide a color value.

For the **WidgetSize** property in our **Widget** class, we can use:

```
private int widgetSize;
public int WidgetSize
{
  get
  {
   return widgetSize;
  }
  set
  {
    widgetSize = value;
  }
}
```

Go to the **Widget.cs** file, remove the property variable declarations and add the accessor methods. The file should appear as:

```
class Widget
{
  private string widgetColor;
  public string WidgetColor
  {
    get
    {
      return widgetColor;
    }
    set
    {
      widgetColor = value;
    }
  }
  private int widgetSize;
  public int WidgetSize
  {
    get
    {
      return widgetSize;
    }
    set
    {
      widgetSize = value;
    }
  }
}
```

Now, return to the **WidgetExample.cs** file and run the project. You will see the same results in the output window. As written, this new code offers no advantage to directly reading and writing the property value. The real advantage to using methods rather than public variables is that property values can be validated and modified. Let see how to do such a validation.

Validating Class Properties

Validation of class properties is done in the **set** method (the **get** method can be used to modify properties before returning values). In this method, we can examine the value provided by the user and see if it meets the validation criteria (in range, positive, non-zero, etc.).

For our **Widget** example, let's assume there are only three color possibilities: red, white, or blue and that the size must be between 5 and 40. Return to the example and open the code window for **Widget.cs**. Modify the accessor methods as follows (changes are shaded):

```csharp
private string widgetColor;
public string WidgetColor
{
  get
  {
    return widgetColor;
  }
  set
  {
    switch (value.ToUpper())
    {
      case "RED":
        widgetColor = value;
        break;
      case "WHITE":
        widgetColor = value;
        break;
      case "BLUE":
        widgetColor = value;
        break;
      default:
        System.Windows.Forms.MessageBox.Show("Bad widget color!");
        return;
    }
    widgetColor = value;
  }
}
```

```
private int widgetSize;
public int WidgetSize
{
  get
  {
    return widgetSize;
  }
  set
  {
    if (value >= 5 && value <= 40)
    {
      widgetSize = value;
    }
    else
    {
      System.Windows.Forms.MessageBox.Show("Bad widget
size!");
    }
  }
}
```

Notice how the validation works – a message box will appear if a bad value is selected.

Return to the **WidgetExample.cs** code and make the shaded change (use a bad color):

```
private void FrmWidget_Load(object sender, EventArgs e)
{
  Widget myWidget;
  myWidget = new Widget();
  myWidget.WidgetColor = "green";
  myWidget.WidgetSize = 15;
  txtWidget.Text = "Color is " + myWidget.WidgetColor;
  txtWidget.Text += "\r\nSize is " +
myWidget.WidgetSize.ToString();
}
```

Rerun the application and this message box announcing a bad color property should appear:

Reset the color property to a proper value, change the size property to a bad value and make sure its validation also works.

We suggest that, except in very simple classes, you always use the accessor approach to setting and getting properties. This approach, though a little more complicated, allows the most flexibility in your application. Using the accessor approach, you can also make properties read-only and write-only. Consult the Visual C# on-line help system for information on doing this.

Adding Constructors to a Class

Once an object is declared, it must be created using a **constructor**. A constructor is a method (with the same name as the class) that provides a way to initialize an object. Each class automatically includes an implied default constructor.

We can add our own default constructor to establish initial object properties. One way to establish initial properties for our **Widget** class is:

```
public Widget()
{
  widgetColor = "red";
  widgetSize = 12;
}
```

This will work, but the properties would not be checked in the validation code just written. To validate initial properties, use this code instead:

```
public Widget()
{
  this.WidgetColor = "red";
  this.WidgetSize = 12;
}
```

Where the keyword **this** refers to the current object. Type the above code after the opening brace declaring the **Widget** class example. Then, return to the **WidgetExample.cs** code, delete the two lines setting the color and size, and then rerun the application. You should see (in the text box) that the color is now red and the size is 12.

You can also define **overloaded constructors**. Such constructors have the same name, but have different argument lists, providing the potential for multiple ways to initialize an object. We will see overloaded constructors with the built-in Visual C# objects. In our Widget example, say we wanted to allow the user to specify the initial color and size at the same time the object is created. A constructor that does this task is:

```
public Widget(string c, int s)
{
  this.WidgetColor = c;
  this.WidgetSize = s;
}
```

Type the above code below the default constructor, **Widget()**, in the **Widget.cs** code..

Return to the **WidgetExample.cs** code and modify the constructor line so it looks like the shaded line:

```
private void frmWidget_Load(object sender, EventArgs e)
{
  Widget myWidget;
  myWidget = new Widget("blue", 22);
  txtWidget.Text = "Color is " + myWidget.WidgetColor;
  txtWidget.Text += "\r\nSize is " +
myWidget.WidgetSize.ToString();
}
```

Notice when you type the new constructor it appears as one of two overloaded choices in the editor Intellisense window. This code now uses the new overloaded constructor, setting the color to blue and the size to 22. Run the application to make sure it works.

A class can have any number of constructors. The only limitation is that no two constructors can have matching argument lists (same number and type of arguments).

Adding Methods to a Class

Class **methods** allow objects to perform certain tasks. Class methods are written like any Visual C# general method. Like constructors, a class can have overloaded methods, similar to the overloaded methods we have seen with the built-in objects of Visual C#.

To add a method to a class description, first select a name and a type of information the method will return (if there is any returned value). The framework for a method named **MyMethod** that returns a **type** value is:

```
public type MyMethod()
{

}
```

This code is usually placed following the accessor methods in a class description.

In our **Widget** example, say we want a method that describes the color and size of the widget. Such a method would look like this:

```
public string DescribeWidget()
{
   return ("My widget is colored " + widgetColor + "\r\nMy
widget size is " + widgetSize.ToString());
}
```

Type the above code near the end of the **Widget.cs** file in our example.

To use an object's method in code, use the following syntax:

```
objectName.MethodName(Arguments);
```

In this syntax, **objectName** is the name of the object, **MethodName** the name of the method and **Arguments** is a comma-delimited list of any arguments needed by the method.

To try the **DescribeWidget** method in our example, return to the
WidgetExample.cs code and modify the shaded line as shown:

```
private void FrmWidget_Load(object sender, EventArgs e)
{
  Widget myWidget;
  myWidget = new Widget("blue", 22);
  txtWidget.Text = myWidget.DescribeWidget();
}
```

In this code, we now use the method to describe widget color and size. Note the
method has been added to the Intellisense menu. Run the application to check
that the method works as expected. The output window should appear as:

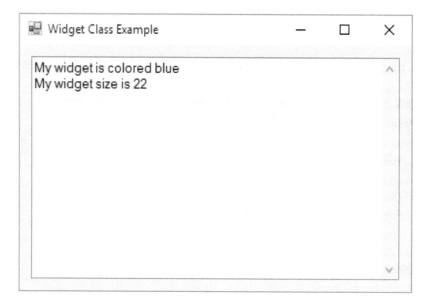

Let's try another method. This method (**CompareWidget**, in **Widget.cs**) compares a widget's size to a standard widget (which has size 20):

```
public string CompareWidget()
{
  int diff;
  diff = widgetSize - 20;
  if (diff > 0)
  {
    return ("My widget is " + diff.ToString() + " units
larger than a standard widget.");
  }
  else
  {
    return ("My widget is " + Math.Abs(diff).ToString() +
" units smaller than a standard widget.");
  }
}
```

Type the **CompareWidget** method into **Widget.cs**, then modify **WidgetExample.cs** as (shaded line is new):

```
private void FrmWidget_Load(object sender, EventArgs e)
{
  Widget myWidget;
  myWidget = new Widget("blue", 22);
  txtWidget.Text = myWidget.DescribeWidget();
  txtWidget.Text += "\r\n" + myWidget.CompareWidget();
}
```

Run the application to see this new output window:

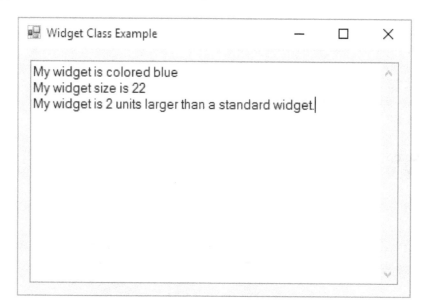

Methods can also have arguments and overload other methods. Suppose in our example, we want to input the size of a widget (**s**, an integer type) we would like to compare our widget to. This method does the job:

```
public string CompareWidget(int s)
{
  int diff;
  diff = widgetSize - s;
  if (diff > 0)
  {
    return ("My widget is " + diff.ToString() + " units
larger than your widget.");
  }
  else
  {
    return ("My widget is " + Math.Abs(diff).ToString() +
" units smaller than your widget.");
  }
}
```

Note this method has the same name as our previous method (**CompareWidget**), but the different argument list differentiates this overloaded version from the previous version.

Type the overloaded version of **CompareWidget** into the **Widget.cs** class code. Then, modify the **WidgetExample.cs** code to use this method (shaded line is new):

```
private void FrmWidget_Load(object sender, EventArgs e)
{
  Widget myWidget;
  myWidget = new Widget("blue", 22);
  txtWidget.Text = myWidget.DescribeWidget();
  txtWidget.Text += "\r\n" + myWidget.CompareWidget();
  txtWidget.Text += "\r\n" + myWidget.CompareWidget(15);
}
```

Note when adding **CompareWidget** to the code, the Intellisense feature presents the two overloaded versions. Run the modified application and you should see:

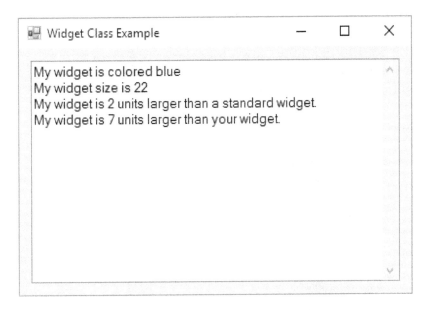

Inheritance

The people you built the Widget class for are so happy with it, they've decided they now want to develop an 'armed' widget. This new widget will be just like the old widget (have a color and size), but will also have arms. This means this new class (**ArmedWidget**) will have one additional property – the number of arms.

To build the **ArmedWidget** class, we could start from scratch – develop a class with three properties, a method that describes the armed widget and a method that compares the armed widget. Or, we could take advantage of a very powerful concept in object-oriented programming, **inheritance**. Inheritance is the idea that you can base one class on another existing class, adding properties and/or methods as needed. This saves lots of work.

Let's see how inheritance works with our widget. Return to the **Widget Class** project we've been using. Add another class to the project (right-click the project name in Solution Explorer and choose **Add Class**), naming it **ArmedWidget** (hence adding a file named **ArmedWidget.cs**). Use this code for the class (modifications to the added file are shaded):

```
class ArmedWidget : Widget
{
  private int widgetArms;
  public int WidgetArms
  {
    get
    {
      return widgetArms;
    }
    set
    {
      widgetArms = value;
    }
  }
}
```

The key line in the Class description is:

```
class ArmedWidget : Widget
```

The shaded portion makes all the properties and methods of the **Widget** class available to our new class (**ArmedWidget**). The remaining code simply adds the unvalidated property **WidgetArms**. We could, of course, add validation to this property if desired.

Now, return to the **WidgetExample.cs** code file. We will modify the code to create and define an **ArmedWidget** object. The modifications are shaded:

```
private void FrmWidget_Load(object sender, EventArgs e)
{
  Widget myWidget;
  myWidget = new Widget("blue", 22);
  txtWidget.Text = myWidget.DescribeWidget();
  txtWidget.Text += "\r\n" + myWidget.CompareWidget();
  txtWidget.Text += "\r\n" + myWidget.CompareWidget(15);
  ArmedWidget myArmedWidget;
  myArmedWidget = new ArmedWidget();
  myArmedWidget.WidgetColor = "white";
  myArmedWidget.WidgetSize = 33;
  myArmedWidget.WidgetArms = 11;
  txtWidget.Text += "\r\n\r\n" +
myArmedWidget.DescribeWidget();
  txtWidget.Text += "\r\nMy armed widget has " +
myArmedWidget.WidgetArms.ToString() + " arms.";
  txtWidget.Text += "\r\n" +
myArmedWidget.CompareWidget();
  txtWidget.Text += "\r\n" +
myArmedWidget.CompareWidget(15);
}
```

Notice that when you type this new code, the Intellisense feature recognizes the inherited properties and methods of the new class.

Run the application to see:

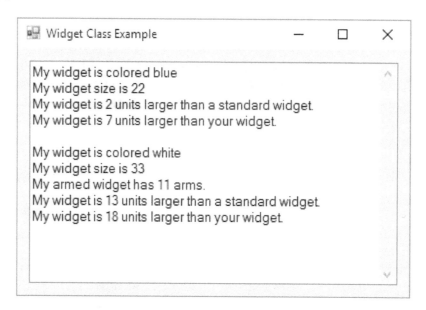

You see the descriptions of both the old 'standard' widget and the new, improved 'armed' widget.

You may have noticed a couple of drawbacks to this inherited class. First, the method used to describe the widget (**DescribeWidget**) only provides color and size information. We added an extra line of code to define the number of arms. It would be nice if this information could be part of the **DescribeWidget** method. That process is called **overriding** methods. Second, we need to know how to use the constructors developed for the **Widget** class in our new **ArmedWidget** class. Let's attack both drawbacks.

If your new class is to use a method that has the same name (and same argument list) as a method in the base class (the class you inherit from), two things must happen. First, the base class method must be **overridable**. This simply means it is defined using the **virtual** keyword in its original definition. This requires a little thinking ahead when defining a class. That is, you must decide if a class inheriting the base class might redefine any method. Then, to use an overridable method in the new class, you redefine the method using the **override** keyword. An example will make this clear.

Return to the **Widget.cs** class file. We will make the **DescribeWidget** function overridable. Add the shaded keyword to its definition:

```
public virtual string DescribeWidget()
{
   return ("My widget is colored " + widgetColor + "\r\nMy
widget size is " + widgetSize.ToString());
}
```

Now, go to the **ArmedWidget.cs** file and add this method to the class definition:

```
public override string DescribeWidget()
{
   return ("My armed widget is colored " + this.WidgetColor
+ "\r\nMy armed widget size is " +
this.WidgetSize.ToString() + " and has " +
widgetArms.ToString() + " arms.");
}
```

Some comments about this method. This now adds a method **DescribeWidget** to the **ArmedWidget** class, allowing the number of arms to be included in the description. It **overrides** the method in the Widget class. Since widgetArms is a local variable in the class, it is referred to by its name. The color property is not local to the ArmedWidget class. Note, to refer to properties inherited from the base class, you use the syntax:

```
this.PropertyName
```

Hence, in this example, we use:

```
this.WidgetColor
```

to refer to the inherited color property.

Now, rerun the application and the output window should display:

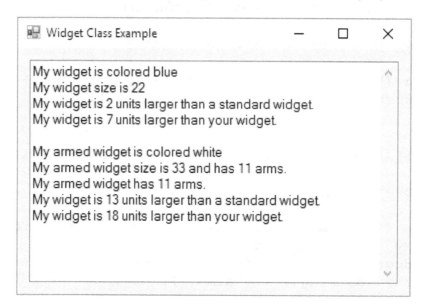

The armed widget description now includes the number of arms (making the line of code following the **DescribeWidget** method invocation redundant). Any method in the base class can be overridden using the same approach followed here.

Before leaving this example, let's see how constructors in base classes can be used in the new class. Any base class constructor can be called using this syntax:

```
base()
```

where there may or not be an argument list. Recall the default constructor in the **Widget** class created a red widget that was 12 units in size. To use this constructor in the **ArmedWidget** class (while at the same time, setting the number of arms to 4), add this constructor to that class code file:

```
public ArmedWidget() : base()
{
   this.WidgetArms = 4;
}
```

This constructor will first invoke the Widget constructor, then add the new property value.

Now, return to the **WidgetExample.cs** code and delete the three lines defining properties for the ArmedWidget and the line printing out the number of arms (since that information is now in the **DescribeWidget** method). Run the modified application and note in the output window:

As expected, the new default armed widget is red, size 12, and has 4 arms.

We're done playing with our widget example. The information you've learned should help when you want to implement custom objects in your applications. The final version of our Widget Class example is saved in the **Widget Class** folder in the **LearnVCS\VCS Code\Class 3** folder.

Let's leave our 'make-believe' widget world and do a real-world OOP example. We'll modify the savings account example we did in Class 2 using a **Savings** object.

Example 3-1

Savings Account

In Example 2-4, we completed a Savings Account calculator that would compute one of these values: monthly deposit, yearly interest, number of months or final amount, given the other three values. In this example, we will do the same computations, using OOP, rather than the 'sequential' process followed in Example 2-4.

1. Load the finished project in Example 2-4. Add a **Savings** class file (**Savings.cs**) from which to create Savings objects. The class will have four public properties: **Deposit**, **Interest**, **Months**, and **Final**, all **double** types. The class will have four methods:

ComputeFinal	Computes **Final** (a **double** type), given **Deposit**, **Interest** and **Months**
ComputeDeposit	Computes **Deposit** (a **double** type), given **Interest**, **Months** and **Final**
ComputeInterest	Computes **Interest** (a **double** Type), given **Deposit**, **Months** and **Final**
ComputeMonths	Computes **Months** (a **double** type), given **Deposit**, **Interest** and **Final**

The code is:

```
class Savings
{
  public double Deposit, Interest, Months, Final;
  private double intRate;

  public double ComputeFinal()
  {
    // Final missing
    intRate = this.Interest / 1200.0;
    if (this.Interest == 0)
    {
      // zero interest case
      return (this.Deposit * this.Months);
    }
    else
    {
      return (this.Deposit * (Math.Pow(1 + intRate,
this.Months) - 1) / intRate);
    }
  }

  public double ComputeDeposit()
  {
    // Deposit missing
    intRate = this.Interest / 1200;
    if (this.Interest == 0)
    {
      return (this.Final / this.Months);
    }
    else
    {
      return(this.Final / ((Math.Pow(1 + intRate,
this.Months) - 1) / intRate));
    }
  }

  public double ComputeInterest()
  {
    // Interest missing - requires iterative solution
    // intChange is how much we change interest each step
    // intDirection is direction (+ or -) we change
interest
    double interest = 0;
    double intChange = 1;
    int intDirection = 1;
```

```csharp
    double finalCompute;
    do
    {
      interest += intDirection * intChange;
      intRate = interest / 1200;
      finalCompute = this.Deposit * (Math.Pow(1 + intRate,
this.Months) - 1) / intRate;
      if (intDirection == 1)
      {
        if (finalCompute > this.Final)
        {
          intDirection = -1;
          intChange /= 10;
        }
      }
      else
      {
        if (finalCompute < this.Final)
        {
          intDirection = 1;
          intChange /= 10;
        }
      }
    }
    while (Math.Abs(finalCompute - this.Final) > 0.005);
    return (interest);
  }

  public double ComputeMonths()
  {
    // Months missing
    // read other values from text boxes
    intRate = this.Interest / 1200;
    if (this.Interest == 0)
    {
      return (this.Final / this.Deposit);
    }
    else
    {
      return (Math.Log(this.Final * intRate / this.Deposit
+ 1) / Math.Log(1 + intRate));
    }
  }
}
```

2. Return to the Savings account form. Modify the code in the **btnCalculate** button **Click** event to use the newly formed class (all new code):

```
private void BtnCalculate_Click(object sender, EventArgs
e)
{
  // create and construct Savings object
  Savings savingsAccount;
  savingsAccount = new Savings();
  // Determine which box is blank
  // Compute that missing value and put in text box
  if (txtDeposit.Text.Trim() == "")
  {
    // read needed properties from text boxes
    savingsAccount.Interest =
Convert.ToDouble(txtInterest.Text);
    savingsAccount.Months =
Convert.ToDouble(txtMonths.Text);
    savingsAccount.Final =
Convert.ToDouble(txtFinal.Text);
    txtDeposit.Text = String.Format("{0:f2}",
savingsAccount.ComputeDeposit());
  }
  else if (txtInterest.Text.Trim() == "")
  {
    // read needed properties from text boxes
    savingsAccount.Deposit =
Convert.ToDouble(txtDeposit.Text);
    savingsAccount.Months =
Convert.ToDouble(txtMonths.Text);
    savingsAccount.Final =
Convert.ToDouble(txtFinal.Text);
    txtInterest.Text = String.Format("{0:f2}",
savingsAccount.ComputeInterest());
  }
  else if (txtMonths.Text.Trim() == "")
  {
    // read needed properties from text boxes
    savingsAccount.Deposit =
Convert.ToDouble(txtDeposit.Text);
    savingsAccount.Interest =
Convert.ToDouble(txtInterest.Text);
    savingsAccount.Final =
Convert.ToDouble(txtFinal.Text);
    txtMonths.Text = String.Format("{0:f2}",
savingsAccount.ComputeMonths());
  }
```

```
    else if (txtFinal.Text.Trim() == "")
    {
      // read needed properties from text boxes
      savingsAccount.Deposit =
Convert.ToDouble(txtDeposit.Text);
      savingsAccount.Interest =
Convert.ToDouble(txtInterest.Text);
      savingsAccount.Months =
Convert.ToDouble(txtMonths.Text);
      txtFinal.Text = String.Format("{0:f2}",
savingsAccount.ComputeFinal());
    }
}
```

This code creates a **savingsAccount** object from the **Savings** class. It then determines which text box is empty, reads the needed property values (monthly deposit, interest rate, number of months, and/or final amount) from the text boxes, establishes the object properties, and computes the missing information using the corresponding method and puts that result in a text box.

Compare this OOP code with the more 'sequential' code used in Example 2-4, where we established variables (deposit, interest, months, final) and computed the missing value using formulas within the event procedure. The two approaches are not that different. The advantage to the OOP approach is that the Savings class can be re-used in other applications and it would be very simple to model other savings account objects within this application.

3. Delete the form level variable declarations – these variables have been replaced by the object properties.

4. Play with the program. Make sure it works properly. Here's a run I made:

Save the project (**Example 3-1** folder in the **LearnVCS\VCS Code\Class 3** folder).

Inheriting from Visual C# Controls

We saw in the Widget example that we could create new, enhanced widgets from an existing widget class. We can do the same with the existing Visual C# controls. That is, we can design our own controls, based on the standard controls, with custom features. (Actually, you can design controls that aren't based on existing controls, but that's beyond the scope of this discussion.)

Inheriting from existing controls allow us to:

> ➤ Establish new default values for properties.
> ➤ Introduce new properties.
> ➤ Establish commonly used event methods.

As an example, note whenever a text box is used for numeric input (like the Savings Account example), we need to validate the key strokes to make sure only numeric input is provided. Wouldn't it be nice to have a text box control with this validation "built-in?" To demonstrate inheritance from Visual C# controls, we will build just this control – a **numeric text box**.

Our numeric text box control will be built in several stages to demonstrate each step. Once done, we will have a control that anyone can add to their Visual C# toolbox and use in their applications. The specifications for our numeric text box are:

> ➤ Yellow background color
> ➤ Blue foreground color
> ➤ Size 10, Arial font
> ➤ Allows numeric digits (0-9)
> ➤ Allows a backspace
> ➤ Allows a single decimal point (optional)
> ➤ Allows a negative sign (optional)
> ➤ Ignores all other keystrokes

Note some specifications address setting and defining properties while others (keystroke validation) require establishing a common control event method. Let's start with setting properties.

Building a Custom Control

As a start, we'll build a text box control with the desired background color (Yellow), foreground color (Blue), and font (Size 10, Arial). Start a new Visual C# project. In the **New Project** window, choose **Visual C#, Windows, Desktop**. Select **Windows Forms Control Library**, then click **Next.**

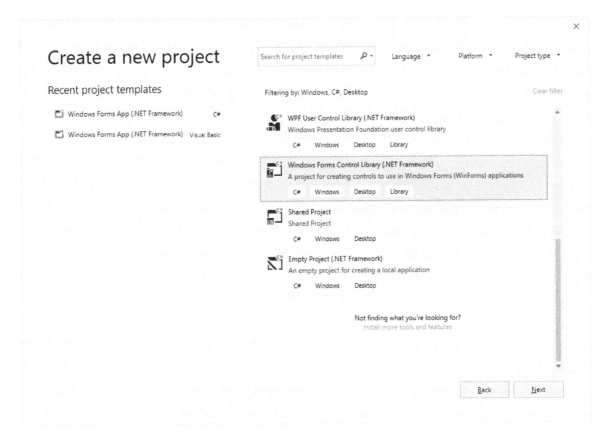

Name the project **NumericTextBox** (put the project in a folder of your choice –
here we use **LearnVCS\VCS Code\Class 3**):

Click **Create.**

By default, when you create a new Windows Control Library project, a new blank user control, and associated code, will be created as a starting point and saved as a file named **UserControl1.cs**. Rename this file **NumericTextBox.cs**. Go to the **Solution Explorer** window, click the **Show All Files** button and delete the **NumericTextBox.Designer.cs** file.

We do not need this file since our control has no separate interface (it uses the TextBox interface).

Open the code window in the **NumericTextBox.cs** file and make the shaded changes:

```
namespace NumericTextBox
{
  public partial class NumericTextBox :
System.Windows.Forms.TextBox
  {
    public NumericTextBox()
    {
      // InitializeComponent();
    }
  }
}
```

This says we are creating a class named **NumericTextBox** that inherits from the **TextBox** control. Since there is no other code, this new control will act and behave just like a normal text box. Nothing will change until we add properties and methods of our own.

We want our numeric text box to have a default background color of yellow, a default foreground color of blue and a default font of size 10, Arial. These default properties are established in the default constructor for the control. Modify the **NumericTextBox** class code with the shaded lines to implement such an initialization:

```
public partial class NumericTextBox :
System.Windows.Forms.TextBox
{
  public NumericTextBox()
  {
    this.BackColor = Color.Yellow;
    this.ForeColor = Color.Blue;
    this.Font = new Font("Arial", 10);
  }
}
```

I've deleted the **InitializeComponent()** line that was commented out.

Let's create the control and try it out. First, save the project in a desired location. Select **Build** from the Visual C# menu, and click **Build NumericTextBox**. If you made no errors, a **DLL** (dynamic link library) for the new control will be found in the **Bin\Debug** folder for the **NumericTextBox** project. The file will be named **NumericTextBox.dll**. If you'd like, check to see that it truly is there.

To try out the new control, start a <u>new</u> Windows application (make sure you have saved the NumericTextBox project). We need to add the **NumericTextBox** control to the toolbox. To do this, follow these steps:

> ➢ Choose **Tools** from the menu.
> ➢ Select **Choose Toolbox Items**.
> ➢ When the **Choose Toolbox Items** window appears, click the **.NET Framework Components** tab.
> ➢ Click the **Browse** button. Navigate to the directory (the **Bin\Debug** folder of the **NumericTextBox** project) containing the **NumericTextBox.dll** file. Select that file.

At this point, you should see:

Make sure there is a check mark next to the **NumericTextBox** control, and click **OK**.

Scroll down on the toolbox and you should now see:

New control

Give it a try. Place the **NumericTextBox** control on your form and you should see (after making the control a bit wider and setting the **Text** property to something):

Note the default colors and font are apparent. Save this Windows project – we will be returning to it.

Adding New Properties to a Control

Many times, when creating new controls, you also want to define new properties for the control. To make the **NumericTextBox** control as general as possible, we want the user to be able to determine if they want decimal inputs and/or negative inputs.

We will define two Boolean (**bool** type) properties to allow these selections. If the property **HasDecimal** is **True**, a decimal point is allowed in the input; if **False**, no decimal point is allowed. If the property **HasNegative** is **True**, a minus sign is allowed; if **False**, no minus sign entry is allowed. Let's modify the **NumericTextBox** class to allow setting and retrieving the values of these properties.

Return to the **NumericTextBox** project. Open the code window. Define two local **bool** type variables to represent the **HasDecimal** and **HasNegative** properties. And, establish the **get** and **set** methods. Add this code to the class to get/set the properties:

```
private bool hasDecimal;
public bool HasDecimal
{
  get
  {
    return hasDecimal;
  }
  set
  {
    hasDecimal = value;
  }
}
private bool hasNegative;
public bool HasNegative
{
  get
  {
    return hasNegative;
  }
  set
  {
    hasNegative = value;
  }
}
```

We also need to initialize the two new properties in the constructor code (add the two shaded lines):

```
public NumericTextBox()
{
    this.BackColor = Color.Blue;
    this.ForeColor = Color.Yellow;
    this.Font = new Font("Arial", 14);
    this.HasDecimal = true;
    this.HasNegative = false;
}
```

You could rebuild the control at this point and try it, but you won't notice any difference in behavior. Why? Well, for one thing, we aren't doing anything with the two new properties (**HasDecimal** and **HasNegative**). We use them next when writing the code that limits acceptable keystrokes. And, if we add the new control to a form and go to the properties window, the two new properties don't even appear! Let's fix that.

To add new properties to the property window for a new control, you first decide what **category** the properties should be listed under (for most of this course, we have used an alphabetical, rather than categorized, view of properties). The choices for category are:

Appearance
Behavior
Configurations
Data
Design
Focus
Layout
Misc
Window Style

Then, preface the property declaration line with this code:

```
[Category("category")]
```

With this addition, the new properties will appear in the properties window for the new control.

Modify the property declaration lines in the **NumericTextBox** class code as follows (shaded code is new):

```
[Category("Behavior")] public bool HasDecimal

[Category("Behavior")] public bool HasNegative
```

Rebuild the control (select **Build** from menu, then **Build Solution**).

Return to a Windows application where you added the NumericTextBox control to a form to look at default properties. Look in the properties window for the **NumericTextBox** and you should now see the two new properties and their default values displayed:

New properties →

Now, let's write some code that uses these new properties while limiting allowable keystrokes.

Adding Control Event Methods

The major impetus for building this new control is to limit keystrokes to only those that can be used for numeric inputs: numbers, decimal (optional based on **HasDecimal** property), negative sign (optional based on **HasNegative** property) and backspace (needed for proper editing).

As in previous work with text boxes to limit keystrokes, we use the **KeyPress** event method. We want to override the **KeyPress** event inherited from the text box control. To do this, we override the control method that raises the **KeyPress** event. That method is named **OnKeyPress** (each control has a set of methods, named **OnEventName**, that raise an event). Such methods are very similar to the event methods <u>without</u> the sender argument. The example will clear this up.

The code to limit keystrokes in our numeric text box is essentially the same code used in each text box in the Savings Account example. Type this code in the **NumericTextBox** class (you must type each line as listed).

```
protected override void
OnKeyPress(System.Windows.Forms.KeyPressEventArgs e)
{
  // check pressed key
  if ((e.KeyChar >= '0' && e.KeyChar <= '9') || (int)
e.KeyChar == 8)
  {
    // allow numbers or backspace
    e.Handled = false;
  }
  else if (e.KeyChar == '.')
  {
    // allow decimal if HasDecimal is True
    if (hasDecimal)
    {
      // allow only one
      if (this.Text.IndexOf(".") == -1)
      {
        e.Handled = false;
      }
      else
      {
        e.Handled = true;
      }
    }
    else
    {
      e.Handled = true;
```

```
        }
     }
   else if (e.KeyChar == '-')
   {
      // allow single negative sign in first position only
if HasNegative is True
      if (hasNegative)
      {
         if (this.Text.IndexOf("-") != -1 ||
this.SelectionStart != 0)
         {
            e.Handled = true;
         }
         else
         {
            e.Handled = false;
         }
      }
      else
      {
         e.Handled = true;
      }
   }
   else
   {
      // no other keys allowed
      e.Handled = true;
   }
}
```

Let's go through this code step-by-step to understand just what's going on. The
first line overrides the **OnKeyPress** method of the standard TextBox control.
Note the single argument. We then examine **e.KeyChar** (the pressed key) to see
if it is acceptable (e.Handled = false) or not acceptable (e.Handled = true).
Checking for a number or backspace is straightforward. Note in checking for a
decimal point, we check two conditions – first, we make sure hasDecimal is
True; second, we make sure there is not a decimal point there already.
Similarly, in checking for a negative sign, we make sure hasNegative is True and
make sure we are typing the first character in the text box.

Rebuild the **NumericTextBox** control. Then, return to the Windows application with the NumericTextBox on the form. Run the application and test the performance of the code. By default, you should only be able to type a positive (no negative sign) decimal number. Here's one I did:

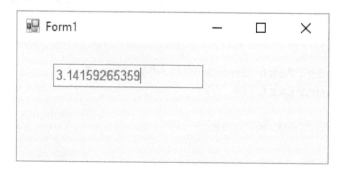

Note you can't type anything but numbers and a single decimal point.

Now, stop the application, change **HasDecimal** to **False** and **HasNegative** to **True**. Now, you should only be able to type integer values (no decimal) with or without a negative sign. Here's one I did:

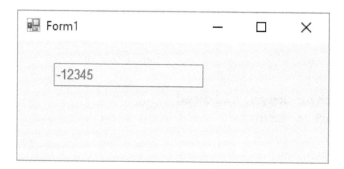

This completes our look at inheriting from existing controls. The final result is saved in the **NumericTextBox** folder in the **LearnVCS\VCS Code\Class 3** folder. With these newfound skills, you can probably think of several ways you might modify existing Visual C# controls to fit your needs.

Example 3-2

Savings Account (Revisited)

1. Let's modify the Savings Account example (Example 3-1) to use the new numeric text box control to show how things are simplified. Open Example 3-1. Replace each text box with a numeric text box control. Change the **Font** on each label to **Arial, Size 10** to match the text boxes. The form should look something like this:

2. Set the properties of the new controls.

   numericTextBox1:
   Name   txtDeposit

   numericTextBox2:
   Name   txtInterest

   numericTextBox3:
   Name   txtMonths
   HasDecimal   False

   numericTextBox4:
   Name   txtFinal

3. Re-establish proper tab ordering among the controls. Eliminate the **KeyPress** event procedures for each of the text box controls. They are no longer needed.

4. That's all the needed changes. Play with the program. Make sure it works properly. Here's a run I made:

Save the project (**Example 3-2** folder in the **LearnVCS\VCS Code\Class 3** folder). To open this project from the class folder, the **NumericTextBox** project must be built and the resulting **dll** file located in the **LearnVCS\VCS Code\Class 3\NumericTextBox\Bin\Debug** folder.

One bit of functionality we've lost is the detection of pressing the <Enter> key which would move the focus from one control to the other. See if you can add this functionality. You need some way to determine which control is next in line for focus.

Class Review

After completing this class, you should understand:

- ➢ Creating classes and objects.
- ➢ Setting and validating object properties.
- ➢ Creating class methods.
- ➢ Creating object constructors.
- ➢ How inheritance is used with classes.
- ➢ Extending Visual C# controls using inheritance
- ➢ Adding properties to controls
- ➢ Overriding control methods.
- ➢ Adding new controls to toolbox.

Practice Problems 3

Problem 3-1. Mortgage Problem. The two lines of Visual C# code that compute the monthly payment on a mortgage are:

```
multiplier = (double) (Math.Pow((1 + interest / (12 * 100)),
12 * years));
payment = loan * interest * multiplier / (12 * 100 *
(multiplier - 1));
```

where:

loan	Loan amount
interest	Yearly interest percentage
years	Number of years of payments
multiplier	Interest multiplier
payment	Computed monthly payment

(The 12 * 100 value in these equations converts yearly interest to a monthly rate.) Use this code to build a class that computes the monthly payment, given the other three variables. Also, compute the total of payments over the life of the mortgage.

Problem 3-2. Accelerated Mortgage Problem. Rather than make monthly payments on a mortgage, say you make a specified number of payments spread evenly throughout the year (for example, bi-weekly payments). The two lines of Visual C# code that compute the periodic payment on such an "accelerated mortgage" are:

```
multiplier = (double) (Math.Pow((1 + interest /
(numberPayments * 100)), numberPayments * years));
payment = loan * interest * multiplier / (numberPayments *
100 * (multiplier - 1));
```

where:

loan	Loan amount
interest	Yearly interest percentage
years	Number of years of payments
numberPayments	Number of payments each year
multiplier	Interest multiplier
payment	Computed monthly payment

Modify Problem 3-1 to allow computation of such an accelerated mortgage. Have your new mortgage class inherit from the class developed in Problem 3-1. Use this class to compute the periodic payment, given the other four variables. Also, compute the total of payments over the life of the mortgage.

Problem 3-3. Flashing Label Problem. Create a label control that looks like a text box (3D border, white background) with the option of flashing its Text property.

Exercise 3

Mailing List

Build an application that accepts a person's name, address, city, state and zip for use in a mailing list. Use a class to describe each person and develop a new text control that can accept just letters, just numbers or both.

4. Exploring the Visual C# Toolbox

Review and Preview

We have now learned the three steps in developing a Windows application, have been introduced to the Visual C# language and seen some object-oriented programming concepts.

In this class, we begin a journey where we look at each tool in the Visual C# toolbox. We will revisit some tools we already know and learn a lot of new tools. Examples of how to use each control will be presented.

Method Overloading

As we delve further into Visual C#, we will begin to use many of its built-in methods for dialog boxes, drawing graphics, and other tasks. Before using these methods (we will use the **MessageBox** method soon), you need be aware of an object-oriented concept known as **overloading**. We were briefly introduced to this idea in the last chapter.

Overloading lets a method vary its behavior based on its input arguments. Visual C# will have multiple methods with the same name, but with different argument lists. The different argument lists may have different numbers of arguments and different types of arguments.

What are the implications of overloading? What this means to us is that when using a Visual C# method, there will be several different ways to use that method. In these notes, we will show you a few ways, but not all. You are encouraged to use on-line help to investigate all ways to use a method.

Another implication is that, when typing code for a method, the Intellisense feature of the Visual C# IDE will appear with a drop-down list of all implementations of a particular method. As you type in your implementation, Intellisense adjusts to the particular form of the method it "thinks" you are using. Suggestions are made for possible arguments – it's like magic! Sometimes, Intellisense guesses right, sometimes not. You must insure the implementation is the one you desire. If, after typing in a method use, Intellisense does not recognize it as proper usage, it will be flagged with an error indication (underlined) and you are given some direction for correcting the error.

Overloading is a powerful feature of Visual C#. You will quickly become accustomed to using multiple definitions of methods and how Intellisense interacts with you, the programmer.

MessageBox Dialog

One of the most often used methods in Visual C# is the **MessageBox** object. This object lets you display messages to your user and receive feedback for further information. It can be used to display error messages, describe potential problems or just to show the result of some computation. The **MessageBox** object is versatile, with the ability to display any message, an optional icon, and a selected set of Button buttons. The user responds by clicking a button in the message box

You've seen message boxes if you've ever used a Windows application. Think of all the examples you've seen. For example, message boxes are used to ask you if you wish to save a file before exiting and to warn you if a disk drive is not ready. For example, if while writing these notes in Microsoft Word, I attempt to exit, I see this message box:

In this message box, the different parts that you control have been labeled. You will see how you can format a message box any way you desire.

To use the **MessageBox** object, you decide what the **Text** of the message should be, what **Caption** you desire, what **Icon** and **Buttons** are appropriate, and which **DefaultButton** you want. To display the message box in code, you use the MessageBox **Show** method.

The MessageBox object is **overloaded** with several ways to implement the **Show** method. Some of the more common ways are:

```
MessageBox.Show(Text);
MessageBox.Show(Text, Caption);
MessageBox.Show(Text, Caption, Buttons);
MessageBox.Show(Text, Caption, Buttons, Icon);
MessageBox.Show(Text, Caption, Buttons, Icon,
DefaultButton);
```

In these implementations, if **DefaultButton** is omitted, the first button is default. If **Icon** is omitted, no icon is displayed. If **Buttons** is omitted, an 'OK' button is displayed. And, if **Caption** is omitted, no caption is displayed.

You decide what you want for the message box **Text** and **Caption** information (string data types). The other arguments are defined by Visual C# predefined constants. The **Buttons** constants are defined by the **MessageBoxButtons** constants:

Member	Description
AbortRetryIgnore	Displays Abort, Retry and Ignore buttons
OK	Displays an OK button
OKCancel	Displays OK and Cancel buttons
RetryCancel	Displays Retry and Cancel buttons
YesNo	Displays Yes and No buttons
YesNoCancel	Displays Yes, No and Cancel buttons

The syntax for specifying a choice of buttons is the usual dot-notation:

MessageBoxButtons.Member

So, to display an OK and Cancel button, the constant is:

MessageBoxButtons.OKCancel

You don't have to remember this, however. When typing the code, the Intellisense feature will provide a drop-down list of button choices when you reach that argument! Again, like magic! This will happen for all the arguments in the MessageBox object.

The displayed Icon is established by the **MessageBoxIcon** constants:

Member	Description
IconAsterisk	Displays an information icon
IconInformation	Displays an information icon
IconError	Displays an error icon (white X in red circle)
IconHand	Displays an error icon
IconNone	Display no icon
IconStop	Displays an error icon
IconExclamation	Displays an exclamation point icon
IconWarning	Displays an exclamation point icon
IconQuestion	Displays a question mark icon

To specify an icon, the syntax is:

MessageBoxIcon.Member

Note there are eight different members of the **MessageBoxIcon** constants, but only four icons (information, error, exclamation, question) available. This is because the current Windows operating system only offers four icons. Future implementations may offer more.

When a message box is displayed, one of the displayed buttons will have focus or be the default button. If the user presses <Enter>, this button is selected. You specify which button is default using the **MessageBoxDefaultButton** constants:

Member	Description
Button1	First button in message box is default
Button2	Second button in message box is default
Button3	Third button in message box is default

To specify a default button, the syntax is:

MessageBoxDefaultButton.Member

The specified default button is relative to the displayed buttons, left to right. So, if you have Yes, No and Cancel buttons displayed and the second button is selected as default, the No button will have focus (be default).

When you invoke the Show method of the MessageBox object, the method returns a value from the **DialogResult** constants. The available members are:

Member	Description
Abort	The Abort button was selected
Cancel	The Cancel button was selected
Ignore	The Ignore button was selected
No	The No button was selected
OK	The OK button was selected
Retry	The Retry button was selected
Yes	The Yes button was selected

MessageBox **Example**:

This little code snippet (the first line is very long):

```
if (MessageBox.Show("This is an example of a message box",
"Message Box Example", MessageBoxButtons.OKCancel,
MessageBoxIcon.Information,
MessageBoxDefaultButton.Button1) == DialogResult.OK)
{
   // everything is OK
}
else
{
   // cancel was pressed
}
```

displays this message box:

Of course, you would need to add code for the different tasks depending on whether OK or Cancel is clicked by the user.

Another MessageBox **Example:**

Many times, you just want to display a quick message to the user with no need for feedback (just an OK button). This code does the job:

```
MessageBox.Show("Quick message for you.", "Hey You!");
```

The resulting message box:

Notice there is no icon and the OK button (default if no button specified) is shown. Also, notice in the code, there is no need to read the returned value – we know what it is! You will find a lot of uses for this simple form of the message box (with perhaps some kind of icon) as you progress in Visual C#.

We now start our study of the Visual C# toolbox, looking at important properties, methods and events for many controls. We start this study with the most important 'control,' the form.

Form Object

The **Form** is the object where the user interface is drawn. It is central to the development of Visual C# applications. The form is known as a **container** object, since it 'holds' other controls. One implication of this distinction is that controls placed on the form will share **BackColor**, **ForeColor** and **Font** properties. To change this, select the desired control (after it is placed on the form) and change the desired properties. Another feature of a container control is that when its Enabled property is False, all controls in the container are disabled. Likewise, when the container control Visible property is False, all controls in the container are not visible.

Here, we present some of the more widely used **Properties**, **Methods** and **Events** for the form. Recall **properties** described the appearance and value of a control, **methods** are actions you can impose on controls and **events** occur when something is done to the control (usually by a user). This is not an exhaustive list – consult on-line help for such a list. You may not recognize all of these terms now. They will be clearer as you progress in the course. The same is true for the remaining controls presented in this chapter.

Form **Properties:**

Name	Gets or sets the name of the form (three letter prefix for form name is **frm**).
AcceptButton	Gets or sets the button on the form that is clicked when the user presses the \<Enter\> key.
BackColor	Get or sets the form background color.
CancelButton	Gets or sets the button control that is clicked when the user presses the \<Esc\> key.
ControlBox	Gets or sets a value indicating whether a control box is displayed in the caption bar of the form.

Form **Properties** (continued)

Enabled	If False, all controls on form are disabled.
Font	Gets or sets font name, style, size.
ForeColor	Gets or sets color of text or graphics.
FormBorderStyle	Sets the form border to be fixed or sizeable.
Height	Height of form in pixels.
Help	Gets or sets a value indicating whether a Help button should be displayed in the caption box of the form.
Icon	Gets or sets the icon for the form.
Left	Distance from left of screen to left edge of form, in pixels.
MaximizeButton	Gets or sets a value indicating whether the maximize button is displayed in the caption bar of the form.
MinimizeButton	Gets or sets a value indicating whether the minimize button is displayed in the caption bar of the form.
StartPosition	Gets or sets the starting position of the form when the application is running.
Text	Gets or sets the form window title.
Top	Distance from top of screen to top edge of form, in pixels.
Width	Width of form in pixels.

Form **Methods:**

Close	Closes the form.
Focus	Sets focus to the form.
Hide	Hides the form.
Refresh	Forces the form to immediately repaint itself.
Show	Makes the form display by setting the Visible property to True.

The normal syntax for invoking a method is to type the control name, a dot, then the method name. For form methods, the name to use is **this**. This is a Visual C# keyword used to refer to a form. Hence, to close a form, use:

```
this.Close();
```

Form **Events**:

Activated	Occurs when the form is activated in code or by the user.
Click	Occurs when the form is clicked by the user.
FormClosing	Occurs when the form is closing.
DoubleClick	Occurs when the form is double clicked.
Load	Occurs before a form is displayed for the first time (the Form object **default** event).
Paint	Occurs when the form is redrawn.

Typical use of **Form** object (for each control in this, and following chapters, we will provide information for how that control is typically used):

➢ Set the **Name** and **Text** properties
➢ Set the **StartPosition** property (in this course, this property will almost always be set to **CenterScreen**)
➢ Set the **FormBorderStyle** to some value. In this course, we will mostly use **FixedSingle** forms. You can have resizable forms in Visual C# (and there are useful properties that help with this task), but we will not use resizable forms in this course.
➢ Write any needed initialization code in the form's **Load** event. To access this event, double-click the form or select it using the properties window.

Button Control

In Toolbox:

On Form (Default Properties):

We've seen the **Button** control before. It is probably the most widely used Visual C# control. It is used to begin, interrupt, or end a particular process. Here, we provide some of the more widely used properties, methods and events for the button control.

Button **Properties:**

Name	Gets or sets the name of the button (three letter prefix for button name is **btn**).
BackColor	Get or sets the button background color.
Enabled	If False, button is visible, but cannot accept clicks.
Font	Gets or sets font name, style, size.
ForeColor	Gets or sets color of text or graphics.
Image	Gets or sets the image that is displayed on a button control.
Text	Gets or sets string displayed on button.
TextAlign	Gets or sets the alignment of the text on the button control.

Button **Methods:**

Focus	Sets focus to the button.
PerformClick	Generates a Click event for a button.

Button **Events:**

Click	Event triggered when button is selected either by clicking on it or by pressing the access key (the Button control **default** event).

Typical use of **Button** control:

> ➢ Set the **Name** and **Text** property.
> ➢ Write code in the button's **Click** event.
> ➢ You may also want to change the **Font**, **Backcolor** and **Forecolor** properties.

Label Control

In Toolbox:

A Label

On Form (Default Properties):

label1

A **Label** control is used to display text that a user can't edit directly. We've seen, though, in previous examples, that the text of a label box can be changed at run-time in response to events.

Label **Properties:**

Name	Gets or sets the name of the label (three letter prefix for label name is **lbl**).
AutoSize	Gets or sets a value indicating whether the label is automatically resized to display its entire contents.
BackColor	Get or sets the label background color.
BorderStyle	Gets or sets the border style for the label.
Font	Gets or sets font name, style, size.
ForeColor	Gets or sets color of text or graphics.
Text	Gets or sets string displayed on label.
TextAlign	Gets or sets the alignment of text in the label.

Note, by default, the label control has no resizing handles. To resize the label, set AutoSize to False.

Label **Methods:**

Refresh	Forces an update of the label control contents.

Label **Events:**

Click	Event triggered when user clicks on a label (the Label control's **default** event).
DblClick	Event triggered when user double-clicks on a label.

Typical use of **Label** control for static, unchanging display:

> ➤ Set the **Name** (though not really necessary for static display) and **Text**
>   property.
> ➤ You may also want to change the **Font**, **Backcolor** and **Forecolor**
>   properties.

Typical use of **Label** control for changing display:

> ➤ Set the **Name** property. Initialize **Text** to desired string.
> ➤ Set **AutoSize** to **False**, resize control and select desired value for
>   **TextAlign.**
> ➤ Assign **Text** property (String type) in code where needed.
> ➤ You may also want to change the **Font**, **Backcolor** and **Forecolor**
>   properties.

TextBox Control

In Toolbox:

On Form (Default Properties):

A **TextBox** control is used to display information entered at design time, by a user at run-time, or assigned within code. The displayed text may be edited.

TextBox **Properties:**

Name	Gets or sets the name of the text box (three letter prefix for text box name is **txt**).
AutoSize	Gets or sets a value indicating whether the height of the text box automatically adjusts when the font assigned to the control is changed.
BackColor	Get or sets the text box background color.
BorderStyle	Gets or sets the border style for the text box.
Font	Gets or sets font name, style, size.
ForeColor	Gets or sets color of text or graphics.
HideSelection	Gets or sets a value indicating whether the selected text in the text box control remains highlighted when the control loses focus.
Lines	Gets or sets the lines of text in a text box control.
MaxLength	Gets or sets the maximum number of characters the user can type into the text box control.
MultiLine	Gets or sets a value indicating whether this is a multiline text box control.
PasswordChar	Gets or sets the character used to mask characters of a password in a single-line TextBox control.
ReadOnly	Gets or sets a value indicating whether text in the text box is read-only.
ScrollBars	Gets or sets which scroll bars should appear in a multiline TextBox control.

TextBox **Properties** (continued)

SelectedText	Gets or sets a value indicating the currently selected text in the control.
SelectionLength	Gets or sets the number of characters selected in the text box.
SelectionStart	Gets or sets the starting point of text selected in the text box.
Tag	Stores a string expression.
Text	Gets or sets the current text in the text box.
TextAlign	Gets or sets the alignment of text in the text box.
TextLength	Gets length of text in text box.

TextBox **Methods:**

AppendText	Appends text to the current text of text box.
Clear	Clears all text in text box.
Copy	Copies selected text to clipboard.
Cut	Moves selected text to clipboard.
Focus	Places the cursor in a specified text box.
Paste	Replaces the current selection in the text box with the contents of the Clipboard.
SelectAll	Selects all text in text box.
Undo	Undoes the last edit operation in the text box.

TextBox **Events:**

Click	Occurs when the user clicks the text box.
Enter	Occurs when the control receives focus.
KeyDown	Occurs when a key is pressed down while the control has focus.
KeyPress	Occurs when a key is pressed while the control has focus – used for key trapping.
Leave	Triggered when the user leaves the text box. This is a good place to examine the contents of a text box after editing.
TextChanged	Occurs when the Text property value has changed (the TextBox control **default** event).

Typical use of **TextBox** control as display control:

> ➢ Set the **Name** property. Initialize **Text** property to desired string.
> ➢ Set **ReadOnly** property to **True**.
> ➢ If displaying more than one line, set **MultiLine** property to **True**.
> ➢ Assign **Text** property in code where needed.
> ➢ You may also want to change the **Font**, **Backcolor** and **Forecolor** properties.

Typical use of **TextBox** control as input device:

> ➢ Set the **Name** property. Initialize **Text** property to desired string.
> ➢ If it is possible to input multiple lines, set **MultiLine** property to **True**.
> ➢ In code, give **Focus** to control when needed. Provide key trapping code in **KeyPress** event. Read **Text** property when **Leave** event occurs.
> ➢ You may also want to change the **Font**, **Backcolor** and **Forecolor** properties.

Use of the TextBox control should be minimized if possible. Whenever you give a user the option to type something, it makes your job as a programmer more difficult. You need to validate the information they type to make sure it will work with your code (recall the **Savings Account** example in the last class, where we need key trapping to insure only numbers were being entered). There are many controls in Visual C# that are 'point and click,' that is, the user can make a choice simply by clicking with the mouse. We'll look at such controls through the course. Whenever these 'point and click' controls can be used to replace a text box, do it!

Example 4-1

Password Validation

1. Start a new project. The idea of this project is to ask the user to input a password. If correct, a message box appears to validate the user. If incorrect, other options are provided.

2. Place a two buttons, a label box, and a text box on your form so it looks something like this:

3. Set the properties of the form and each object (we do the buttons first so their names are available for the form properties).

button1:

Name	btnValid
Text	&Accept

button2:

Name	btnExit
Text	E&xit

Form1:

Name	frmPassword
AcceptButton	btnValid
CancelButton	btnExit
FormBorderStyle	FixedSingle
StartPosition	CenterScreen
Text	Password Validation

label1:

AutoSize	False
BorderStyle	Fixed3D
Font Size	10
Font Style	Bold
Text	Please Enter Your Password:
TextAlign	MiddleCenter

textBox1:

Name	txtPassword
Font Size	14
PasswordChar	*
Tag	[Whatever you choose as a password]
Text	[Blank]

Your form should now look like this:

4. Use the following code in the **btnValid Click** event.

```
private void BtnValid_Click(object sender, EventArgs e)
{
   // This method checks the input password
   DialogResult response;
   if (txtPassword.Text ==
Convert.ToString(txtPassword.Tag))
   {
      // If correct, display message box
      MessageBox.Show("You've passed security!", "Access
Granted", MessageBoxButtons.OK,
MessageBoxIcon.Exclamation);
   }
   else
   {
      // If incorrect, give option to try again
      response = MessageBox.Show("Incorrect password",
"Access Denied", MessageBoxButtons.RetryCancel,
MessageBoxIcon.Error);
      if (response == DialogResult.Retry)
      {
         txtPassword.SelectionStart = 0;
         txtPassword.SelectionLength =
txtPassword.Text.Length;
      }
      else
      {
         this.Close();
      }
   }
   txtPassword.Focus();
}
```

This code checks the input password to see if it matches the stored value. If so, it prints an acceptance message. If incorrect, it displays a message box to that effect and asks the user if they want to try again. If Yes (Retry), another try is granted. If No (Cancel), the program is ended. Notice the use of **SelectionLength** and **SelectionStart** to highlight an incorrect entry. This allows the user to type right over the incorrect response.

5. Use the following code in the **frmPassword Load** event (double-click the form to reach this event).

```
private void FrmPassword_Load(object sender, EventArgs e)
{
  // make sure focus starts in text box
  this.Show();
  txtPassword.Focus();
}
```

6. Use the following code in the **btnExit_ Click** event.

```
private void BtnExit_Click(object sender, EventArgs e)
{
  this.Close();
}
```

7. Try running the program. Here's a run I made (notice the echo character):

Try both options. Input the correct password (note it is case sensitive) to see:

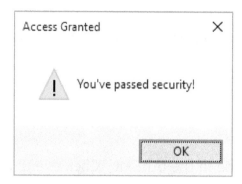

Input the incorrect password to see:

Save your project (saved in **Example 4-1** folder in the **LearnVCS\VCS Code\Class 4** folder).

If you have time, define a constant, tryMax = 3, and modify the code to allow the user to have just tryMax attempts to get the correct password. After the final try, inform the user you are logging him/her off. You'll also need a variable that counts the number of tries.

CheckBox Control

In Toolbox:

On Form (Default Properties):

As mentioned earlier, Visual C# features many 'point and click' controls that let the user make a choice simply by clicking with the mouse. These controls are attractive, familiar and minimize the possibility of errors in your application. We will see many such controls. The first, the **CheckBox** control, is examined here.

The **CheckBox** control provides a way to make choices from a list of potential candidates. Some, all, or none of the choices in a group may be selected. Check boxes are used in all Windows applications (even the Visual C# IDE). Examples of their use would be to turn options on and off in an application or to select from a 'shopping' list.

CheckBox **Properties:**

Name	Gets or sets the name of the check box (three letter prefix for check box name is **chk**).
AutoSize	Gets or sets a value indicating whether the label is automatically resized to display its entire contents.
BackColor	Get or sets the check box background color.
Checked	Gets or sets a value indicating whether the check box is in the checked state.
Font	Gets or sets font name, style, size.
ForeColor	Gets or sets color of text or graphics.
Text	Gets or sets string displayed next to check box.
TextAlign	Gets or sets the alignment of text of the check box.

CheckBox **Methods:**

Focus	Moves focus to this check box.

CheckBox **Events:**

CheckedChanged	Occurs when the value of the Checked property changes, whether in code or when a check box is clicked (CheckBox **default** event).
Click	Triggered when a check box is clicked. **Checked** property is automatically changed by Visual C#.

When a check box is clicked, if there is no check mark there (Checked = False), Visual C# will place a check there and change the Checked property to True. If clicked and a check mark is there (Checked = True), then the check mark will disappear and the Checked property will be changed to False. The check box can also be configured to have three states: checked, unchecked or indeterminate. Consult on-line help if you require such behavior.

Typical use of **CheckBox** control:

> ➤ Set the **Name** and **Text** property. Initialize the **Checked** property.
> ➤ Monitor **Click** or **CheckChanged** event to determine when button is clicked. At any time, read **Checked** property to determine check box state.
> ➤ You may also want to change the **Font**, **Backcolor** and **Forecolor** properties.

RadioButton Control

In Toolbox:

On Form (Default Properties):

RadioButton controls provide the capability to make a "mutually exclusive" choice among a group of potential candidate choices. This simply means, radio buttons work as a group, only one of which can be selected. Radio buttons are seen in all Windows applications. They are called radio buttons because they work like a tuner on a car radio – you can only listen to one station at a time! Examples for radio button groups would be twelve buttons for selection of a month in a year, a group of buttons to let you select a color or buttons to select the difficulty in a game.

A first point to consider is how do you define a 'group' of radio buttons that work together? Any radio buttons placed on the form will act as a group. That is, if any radio button on a form is 'selected', all other buttons will be automatically 'unselected.' What if you need to make two independent choices; that is, you need two independent groups of radio buttons? To do this requires one of two grouping controls in Visual C#: the **GroupBox** control or the **Panel** control. Radio buttons placed on either of these controls are independent from other radio buttons. We will discuss the grouping controls after the RadioButton control. For now, we'll just be concerned with how to develop and use a single group of radio buttons.

RadioButton **Properties:**

Name	Gets or sets the name of the radio button (three letter prefix for radio button name is **rdo**).
AutoSize	Gets or sets a value indicating whether the label is automatically resized to display its entire contents.
BackColor	Get or sets the radio button background color.
Checked	Gets or sets a value indicating whether the radio button is checked.
Font	Gets or sets font name, style, size.
ForeColor	Gets or sets color of text or graphics.
TextAlign	Gets or sets the alignment of text of the radio button.

RadioButton **Methods:**

Focus	Moves focus to this radio button.
PerformClick	Generates a Click event for the button, simulating a click by a user.

RadioButton **Events:**

CheckedChanged	Occurs when the value of the Checked property changes, whether in code or when a radio button is clicked (the RadioButton control **default** event).
Click	Triggered when a button is clicked. **Checked** property is automatically changed by Visual C#.

When a radio button is clicked, it's Checked property is automatically set to True by Visual C#. And, all other radio buttons in that button's group will have a Checked property of False. Only one button in the group can be checked.

Typical use of **RadioButton** control:

> ➢ Establish a group of radio buttons.
> ➢ For each button in the group, set the **Name** (give each button a similar name to identify them with the group) and **Text** property. You might also change the **Font**, **BackColor** and **Forecolor** properties.
> ➢ Initialize the **Checked** property of one button to **True**.
> ➢ Monitor the **Click** or **CheckChanged** event of each radio button in the group to determine when a button is clicked. The 'last clicked' button in the group will always have a **Checked** property of **True**.

GroupBox Control

In Toolbox:

On Form (Default Properties):

We've seen that both radio buttons and check boxes usually work as a group. Many times, there are logical groupings of controls. For example, you may have a scroll device setting the value of a displayed number. The **GroupBox** control provides a convenient way of grouping related controls in a Visual C# application. And, in the case of radio buttons, group boxes affect how such buttons operate.

To place controls in a group box, you first draw the GroupBox control on the form. Then, the associated controls must be placed in the group box. This allows you to move the group box and controls together. There are several ways to place controls in a group box:

> ➢ Place controls directly in the group box using any of the usual methods.
> ➢ Draw controls outside the group box and drag them in.
> ➢ Copy and paste controls into the group box (prior to the paste operation, make sure the group box is selected).

To insure controls are properly place in a group box, try moving it and make sure the associated controls move with it. To remove a control from the group box, simple drag it out of the control.

Like the Form object, the group box is a **container** control, since it 'holds' other controls. Hence, controls placed in a group box will share **BackColor**, **ForeColor** and **Font** properties. To change this, select the desired control (after it is placed on the group box) and change the desired properties. Another feature of a group box control is that when its Enabled property is False, all controls in the group box are disabled. Likewise, when the group box control Visible property is False, all controls in the group box are not visible.

As mentioned, group boxes affect how radio buttons work. Radio buttons within a GroupBox control work as a **group**, independently of radio buttons in other GroupBox controls. Radio buttons on the form, and not in group boxes, work as another independent group. That is, the form is itself a group box by default. We'll see this in the next example.

GroupBox **Properties:**

Name	Gets or sets the name of the group box (three letter prefix for group box name is **grp**).
BackColor	Get or sets the group box background color.
Enabled	Gets or sets a value indicating whether the group box is enabled. If False, all controls in the group box are disabled.
Font	Gets or sets font name, style, size.
ForeColor	Gets or sets color of text.
Text	Gets or sets string displayed in title region of group box.
Visible	If False, hides the group box (and all its controls).

The GroupBox control has some methods and events, but these are rarely used. We are more concerned with the methods and events associated with the controls in the group box.

Typical use of **GroupBox** control:

➢ Set **Name** and **Text** property (perhaps changing **Font**, **BackColor** and **ForeColor** properties).
➢ Place desired controls in group box. Monitor events of controls in group box using usual techniques.

Panel Control

In Toolbox:

On Form (Default Properties):

The **Panel** control is another Visual C# grouping control. It is nearly identical to the **GroupBox** control in behavior. The Panel control lacks a Text property (titling information), but has optional scrolling capabilities. Controls are placed in a Panel control in the same manner they are placed in the GroupBox. And, radio buttons in the Panel control act as an independent group. Panel controls can also be used to display graphics (lines, curves, shapes, animations). We will look at those capabilities in later chapters.

Panel **Properties:**

Name	Gets or sets the name of the panel (three letter prefix for panel name is **pnl**).
AutoScroll	Gets or sets a value indicating whether the panel will allow the user to scroll to any controls placed outside of its visible boundaries.
BackColor	Get or sets the panel background color.
BorderStyle	Get or set the panel border style.
Enabled	Gets or sets a value indicating whether the panel is enabled. If False, all controls in the panel are disabled.
Visible	If False, hides the panel (and all its controls).

Like the GroupBox control, the Panel control has some methods and events, but these are rarely used (we will see a few Panel events in later graphics chapters). We usually only are concerned with the methods and events associated with the controls in the panel.

Typical use of **Panel** control:

> ➢ Set **Name** property.
> ➢ Place desired controls in panel control.
> ➢ Monitor events of controls in panel using usual techniques.

Handling Multiple Events in a Single Method

In the few applications we've built in this course, each event method handles a single event. Now that we are grouping controls like check boxes and radio buttons, it would be nice if a single method could handle multiple events. For example, if we have 4 radio buttons in a group, when one button is clicked, it would be preferable to have a single method where we decide which button was clicked, as opposed to having to monitor 4 separate event methods. Let's see how to do this.

We use this radio button example to illustrate. Assume we have four radio buttons (**radioButton1**, **radioButton2**, **radioButton3**, **radioButton4**) that we want to share the same **CheckedChanged** event method. To make this method sharing possible, we use the properties window to establish events. First, we select **radioButton1**, go to the properties window and click the **Events** button. The **CheckedChanged** event will be highlighted since it is the default event for the radio button control:

Usually, at this point, we would double-click the event and the Visual C# environment would build an event method named **radioButton1_CheckedChanged**. The name assigned to this method by Visual C# is <u>arbitrary</u>. We can assign any name we want and it would still handle the **CheckedChanged** event for **radioButton1**. To use a different name, we type the name next to the event in the properties window. Since the method will now handling multiple events, we would want to use a name to represent a group of radio buttons, not just a single button. A name like **group1_CheckedChanged** might be more appropriate - we will use that in this example.

Once you type a name for an event in the properties window and press <Enter>, the code window will open in the new method. For this example, we would see:

```
private void Group1_CheckedChanged(object sender,
EventArgs e)
{

}
```

Right now, this method only handles the **CheckedChanged** event for **radioButton1**.

To have another control share this method, we again use the properties window. Next, we would choose **radioButton2** in the properties window, then display its events and click the drop-down box that appears to the right of the **CheckedChanged** event. One of the choices will be the **group1_CheckedChanged** event method. By simply choosing this existing method, it will now be the method called for the **CheckedChanged** event for **radioButton2**. We then repeat this process for each control we want to share the same event method. **Hint:** a quick way to do this is to "group select" every control on the form that is to share an event method. Then using event selection in the properties window, choose the shared method.

With this process, we can attach any existing event of any control to any method we want! It is best to append like events of like controls. It is possible to process dissimilar events of dissimilar controls with a single event method, but you need to be careful.

If we have a single method responding to events from multiple controls, how do we determine which particular event from which particular control invoked the method. In our example with a single method handling the **CheckedChanged** event for 4 radio buttons, how do we know which of the 4 buttons is invoking the method? The **sender** argument of the event method provides the answer.

Each event method has a **sender** argument (the first argument of two) which identifies the control whose event caused the method to be invoked. With a little Visual C# coding, we can identify the **Name** property (or any other needed property) of the sending control. For our radio button example, that code is:

```
RadioButton rdoExample;
string buttonName;
// Determine which button was clicked
rdoExample = (RadioButton) sender;
buttonName = rdoExample.Name;
```

In this code, we define a variable (**rdoExample**) to be the type of the control attached to the method (a **RadioButton** in this case). Then, we assign this variable to **sender** (after casting sender to the proper control type). Once this variable is established, we can determine any property we want to identify the button. In the above example, we find the radio button's **Name** property. With this information, we now know which particular button was selected and we can process any code associated with this radio button. Notice a shortcut way to identify the Name property (without declaring any variables) is to use:

```
((RadioButton) sender).Name
```

Control Arrays

When using controls that work in groups, like check boxes and radio buttons, it is sometimes desirable to have some way to quickly process every control in that group. A concept of use in this case is that of a **control array**.

In Chapter 2, we learned about variable arrays - variables referred by name and index to allow quick processing of large amounts of data. The same idea applies here. We can define an array of controls, using the same statements used to declare a variable array. For example, to declare an array of 20 buttons, use:

```
Button[] myButtons = new Button[20];
```

This array declaration is placed according to desired scope, just like variables. For form level scope, place the statement at the top of the form code (after the **Form** constructor). For method level scope, place it in the respective method. Once the array has been declared, each element of the 'control array' can be referred to by its name (**myButton**) and index. An example will clarify the advantage of such an approach.

Say we have 10 check boxes (chkBox00, chkBox01, chkBox02, chkBox03, chkBox04, chkBox05, chkBox06, chkBox07, chkBox08, chkBox09) on a form and we need to examine each check box's Checked property. If that property is true, we need to process 30 lines of additional code. For one check box, that code would be:

```
if (chkBox00.Checked)
{
  [do these 30 lines of code]
}
```

We would need to repeat this 9 more times (for the nine remaining check boxes), yielding a total of 32 x 10 = 320 lines of code. And, if we needed to add a few lines to the code being processed, we would need to add these lines in 10 different places - a real maintenance headache. Let's try using an array of check boxes to minimize this headache.

Here's the solution. Define an array of 10 check box controls and assign the array values to existing controls:

```
CheckBox[] myCheck = new CheckBox[10];
myCheck[0] = chkBox00;
myCheck[1] = chkBox01;
myCheck[2] = chkBox02;
myCheck[3] = chkBox03;
myCheck[4] = chkBox04;
myCheck[5] = chkBox05;
myCheck[6] = chkBox06;
myCheck[7] = chkBox07;
myCheck[8] = chkBox08;
myCheck[9] = chkBox09;
```

Again, make sure the declaration statement is properly located for proper scope. Having made these assignments, the code for examining the Checked property of each has been reduced to these few lines:

```
for (int i = 0; i < 10; i++)
{
  if (myCheck[i].Checked)
  {
    [do these 30 lines of code]
  }
}
```

The 320 lines of code have been reduced to about 45 (including all the declarations) and code maintenance is now much easier.

Obviously, it is not necessary to use control arrays, but they do have their advantages. You will start to see such arrays in the course examples and problems, so you should understand their use.

Example 4-2

Pizza Order

1. Start a new project. We'll build a form where a pizza order can be entered by simply clicking on check boxes and radio buttons. The pizza we build will be described by a Pizza class. Since this is the first example built using classes and objects, study it carefully to understand how OOP is used.

2. Draw three group boxes. In the first, draw three radio buttons, in the second, draw two radio buttons, and in the third, draw six check boxes. Draw two radio buttons on the form. Add two buttons. Make things look something like this.

3. Set the properties of the form and each control.

Form1:

Name	frmPizza
FormBorderStyle	FixedSingle
StartPosition	CenterScreen
Text	Pizza Order

groupBox1:

Text	Size

groupBox2:

Text	Crust Type

groupBox3

Text	Toppings

radioButton1:

Name	rdoSmall
Checked	True
Text	Small

radioButton2:

Name	rdoMedium
Text	Medium

radioButton3:

Name	rdoLarge
Text	Large

radioButton4:
    Name   rdoThin
    Checked   True
    Text   Thin Crust

radioButton5:
    Name   rdoThick
    Text   Thick Crust

radioButton6:
    Name   rdoIn
    Checked   True
    Text   Eat In

radioButton7:
    Name   rdoOut
    Text   Take Out

checkBox1:
    Name   chkCheese
    Text   Extra Cheese

checkBox2:
    Name   chkMushrooms
    Text   Mushrooms

checkBox3:
    Name   chkOlives
    Text   Black Olives

checkBox4:
    Name   chkOnions
    Text   Onions

checkBox5:
    Name   chkPeppers
    Text   Green Peppers

checkBox6:
    Name   chkTomatoes
    Text   Tomatoes

button1:
     Name   btnBuild
     Text   &Build Pizza

button2:
     Name   btnExit
     Text   E&xit

The form should look like this now:

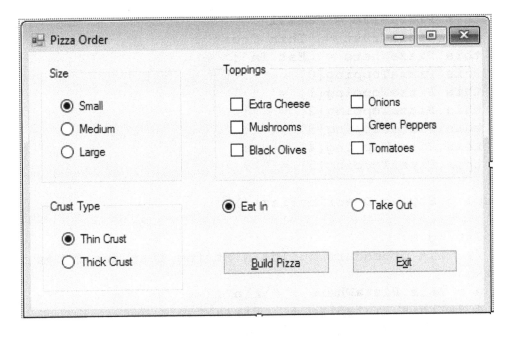

4. Add a class to your project named **Pizza.cs**. Use this code for the class:

```
class Pizza
{
  public String PizzaSize;
  public String PizzaCrust;
  public String PizzaWhere;
  public String[] PizzaTopping = new String[6];
  public Pizza()
  {
    this.PizzaSize = "Small";
    this.PizzaCrust = "Thin Crust";
    this.PizzaWhere = "Eat In";
    this.PizzaTopping[0] = "";
    this.PizzaTopping[1] = "";
    this.PizzaTopping[2] = "";
    this.PizzaTopping[3] = "";
    this.PizzaTopping[4] = "";
    this.PizzaTopping[5] = "";
  }
  public String DescribePizza()
  {
    String s;
    // This procedure builds a string that describes the
pizza
    s = this.PizzaWhere + "\r\n";
    s += this.PizzaSize + " Pizza\r\n";
    s += this.PizzaCrust + "\r\n";
    // Check each topping using the array we set up
    for (int i = 0; i < 6; i++)
    {
      if (!this.PizzaTopping[i].Equals(""))
      {
        s += this.PizzaTopping[i] + "\r\n";
      }
    }
    return (s);
  }
}
```

The Pizza class has several properties: **PizzaSize, PizzaCrust, PizzaWhere** and **PIzzaTopping** (an array). A method **DescribePizza** forms a string variable that describes the pizza. In this method, a string is established by concatenating the pizza size, crust type, and eating location (recall \r\n is a sqeuence representing a 'carriage return' that puts each piece of ordering information on a separate line). Next, the code cycles through the six toppings and adds any non-blank information to the string.

5. Form level scope variable declarations:

```
Pizza myPizza;
CheckBox[] topping = new CheckBox[6];
bool loading = true;
```

This makes the **myPizza** object global to the form. The array of check box controls will help us determine which toppings are selected. As mentioned in the notes, it is common to use 'control arrays' when working with check boxes and radio buttons. The **loading** variable is used often in Visual C# to avoid triggering event procedures while the form is being created.

6. Use this code in the **frmPizza Load** procedure. This constructs the initial pizza object.

```
private void FrmPizza_Load(object sender, EventArgs e)
{
  myPizza = new Pizza();
  // Define an array of topping check boxes
  topping[0] = chkCheese;
  topping[1] = chkMushrooms;
  topping[2] = chkOlives;
  topping[3] = chkOnions;
  topping[4] = chkPeppers;
  topping[5] = chkTomatoes;
  loading = false;
}
```

Here, the myPizza object is constructed.. The topping variables are set to their respective check boxes. The loading variable is set to false once this procedure is executed.

7. Use this code to define single **CheckedChanged** events for each of the three groups of radio buttons. If necessary, review the process to do this: assign the method name when creating the method for the first button in the group. Then, for subsequent buttons, select the method name from the events list in the properties window for the particular control.

```csharp
private void RdoSize_CheckedChanged(object sender,
EventArgs e)
{
  if (!loading)
  {
    myPizza.PizzaSize = ((RadioButton) sender).Text;
  }
}


private void RdoCrust_CheckedChanged(object sender,
EventArgs e)
{
  if (!loading)
  {
    myPizza.PizzaCrust = ((RadioButton) sender).Text;
  }
}


private void RdoWhere_CheckedChanged(object sender,
EventArgs e)
{
  if (!loading)
  {
    myPizza.PizzaWhere = ((RadioButton) sender).Text;
  }
}
```

In each of these routines, when a radio button's Checked property changes, the value of the corresponding button's Text is loaded into the respective pizza object property. Note if loading is true, none of these procedures is executed. This is needed because, when the form is being built by Visual C#, the Pizza object does not exist yet and an error would occur when attempting to set a property.

8. Use this code in the **btnBuild Click** event.

```
private void BtnBuild_Click(object sender, EventArgs e)
{
  // This method builds a message box that displays your
pizza type
  for (int i = 0; i < 6; i++)
  {
    if (topping[i].Checked)
    {
      myPizza.PizzaTopping[i] = topping[i].Text;
    }
    else
    {
      myPizza.PizzaTopping[i] = "";
    }
  }
  MessageBox.Show(myPizza.DescribePizza() , "Your Pizza",
MessageBoxButtons.OK);
}
```

This cycles through the six topping check boxes (defined by our Topping array) and sets the MyPizza object properties. The code then displays the pizza order in a message box (using the object DescribePizza method).

9. Use this code in the **btnExit Click** event.

```
private void BtnExit_Click(object sender, EventArgs e)
{
  this.Close();
}
```

10. Get the application working. Notice how the different selection buttons work in their individual groups. Here's some choices in my run (my favorite pizza):

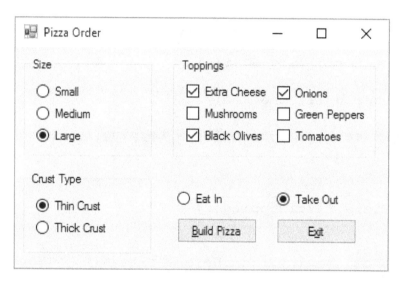

Then, when I click **Build Pizza**, I see:

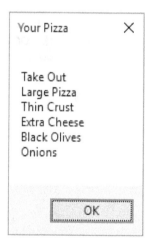

Save your project (saved in **Example 4-2** folder in the **LearnVCS\VCS Code\Class 4 folder).**

If you have time, try these modifications:

A. Add a new program button that resets the order form to the initial default values. You'll have to reinitialize the pizza object, reset all check boxes to unchecked, and reset all three radio button groups to their default values.

B. Modify the Pizza class code so that if no toppings are selected, the message "Cheese Only" appears on the order form. You'll need to figure out a way to see if no check boxes were checked.

ListBox Control

In Toolbox:

On Form (Default Properties):

Check boxes are useful controls for selecting items from a list. But, what if your list has 100 items? Do you want 100 check boxes? No, but fortunately, there is a tool that solves this problem. A **Listbox** control displays a list of items (with as many items as you like) from which the user can select one or more items. If the number of items exceeds the number that can be displayed, a scroll bar is automatically added. Both single item and multiple item selections are supported.

ListBox **Properties:**

Name	Gets or sets the name of the list box (three letter prefix for list box name is **lst**).
BackColor	Get or sets the list box background color.
Font	Gets or sets font name, style, size.
ForeColor	Gets or sets color of text.
Items	Gets the Items object of the list box.
SelectedIndex	Gets or sets the zero-based index of the currently selected item in a list box.
SelectedIndices	Zero-based array of indices of all currently selected items in the list box.
SelectedItem	Gets or sets the currently selected item in the list box.
SelectedItems	SelectedItems object of the list box.
SelectionMode	Gets or sets the method in which items are selected in list box (allows single or multiple selections).

ListBox **Properties** (continued)

Sorted	Gets or sets a value indicating whether the items in list box are sorted alphabetically.
Text	Text of currently selected item in list box.
TopIndex	Gets or sets the index of the first visible item in list box.

ListBox **Methods:**

ClearSelected	Unselects all items in the list box.
FindString	Finds the first item in the list box that starts with the specified string.
GetSelected	Returns a value indicating whether the specified item is selected.
SetSelected	Selects or clears the selection for the specified item in a list box.

ListBox **Events:**

SelectedIndexChanged	Occurs when the SelectedIndex property has changed (list box control **default** event).

Some further discussion is needed to use the list box **Items** object, **SelectedItems** object and **SelectionMode** property. The **Items** object has its own properties to specify the items in the list box. It also has its own methods for adding and deleting items in the list box. The **Items** object is a zero-based array of the items in the list and **Count** (a property of **Items**) is the number of items in the list. Hence, the first item in a list box named **lstExample** is:

```
lstExample.Items[0]
```

The last item in the list is:

```
lstExample.Items[lstExample.Items.Count - 1]
```

The minus one is needed because of the zero-based array.

To add items in design mode, choose the **Items** property, then click the ellipsis next to the (**Collections**) word that appears. An editor window will open allowing you to enter one item per line. Click **OK** when done.

To add an item to a list box in code, use the **Add** method, to delete an item, use the **Remove** or **RemoveAt** method and to clear a list box use the **Clear** method. For our example list box, the respective commands are:

Add Item:	`lstExample.Items.Add`(ItemToAdd);
Delete Item:	`lstExample.Items.Remove`(ItemToRemove);
	`lstExample.Items.RemoveAt`(IndexofItemToRemove);
Clear list box:	`lstExample.Items.Clear`();

List boxes normally list string data types, though other types are possible. Note, when removing items, that indices for subsequent items in the list change following a removal.

In a similar fashion, the **SelectedItems** object has its own properties to specify the currently selected items in the list box Of particular use is **Count** which tells you how many items are selected. This value, in conjunction with the SelectedIndices array, identifies the set of selected items.

The **SelectionMode** property specifies whether you want single item selection or multiple selections. When the property is **SelectionMode.One**, you can select only one item (works like a group of option buttons). When the SelectionMode property is set to **SelectionMode.MultiExtended**, pressing <Shift> and clicking the mouse or pressing <Shift>and one of the arrow keys extends the selection from the previously selected item to the current item. Pressing <Ctrl>and clicking the mouse selects or deselects an item in the list. When the property is set to **SelectionMode.MultiSimple**, a mouse click or pressing the spacebar selects or deselects an item in the list.

The **CheckedListBox** is a nearly identical control in Visual C#. The only difference is, with the CheckedListBox, a check mark appears before selected items. Other than that, performance is identical to the ListBox control.

Typical use of **ListBox** control:

> ➤ Set **Name** property, **SelectionMode** property and populate **Items** object (usually in **Form_Load** method).
> ➤ Monitor **SelectedIndexChanged** event for individual selections.
> ➤ Use **SelectedIndex** and **SelectIndices** properties to determine selected items.

ComboBox Control

In Toolbox:

On Form (Default Properties):

We saw that the **ListBox** control is equivalent to a group of check boxes (allowing multiple selections in a long list of items). The equivalent control for a long list of radio buttons is the **ComboBox** control. The ComboBox allows the selection of a single item from a list. And, in some cases, the user can type in an alternate response.

ComboBox **Properties:**

ComboBox properties are nearly identical to those of the ListBox, with the deletion of the **SelectionMode** property and the addition of a **DropDownStyle** property.

Name	Gets or sets the name of the combo box (three letter prefix for combo box name is **cbo**).
BackColor	Get or sets the combo box background color.
DropDownStyle	Specifies one of three combo box styles.
Font	Gets or sets font name, style, size.
ForeColor	Gets or sets color of text.
Items	Gets the Items object of the combo box.
MaxDropDownItems	Maximum number of items to show in dropdown portion.
SelectedIndex	Gets or sets the zero-based index of the currently selected item in list box portion.
SelectedItem	Gets or sets the currently selected item in the list box portion.
SelectedText	Gets or sets the text that is selected in the editable portion of combo box.
Sorted	Gets or sets a value indicating whether the items in list box portion are sorted alphabetically.
Text	String value displayed in combo box.

ComboBox **Events**:

KeyPress	Occurs when a key is pressed while the combo box has focus.
SelectedIndexChanged	Occurs when the SelectedIndex property has changed (the combo box control **default** event).

The **Items** object for the ComboBox control is identical to that of the ListBox control. You add and remove items in the same manner and values are read with the same properties.

The **DropDownStyle** property has three different values. The values and their description are:

Value	Description
DropDown	Text portion is editable; drop-down list portion.
DropDownList	Text portion is not editable; drop-down list portion.
Simple	The text portion is editable. The list portion is always visible. With this value, you'll want to resize the control to set the list box portion height.

Typical use of **ComboBox** control:

➢ Set **Name** property, **DropDownStyle** property and populate **Items** object (usually in form **Load** method).
➢ Monitor **SelectedIndexChanged** event for individual selections.
➢ Read **SelectedText** property to identify choice.

Example 4-3

Flight Planner

1. Start a new project. In this example, you select a destination city, a seat location, and a meal preference for airline passengers.

2. Place a list box, two combo boxes, three labels and two buttons on the form. The form should appear similar to this:

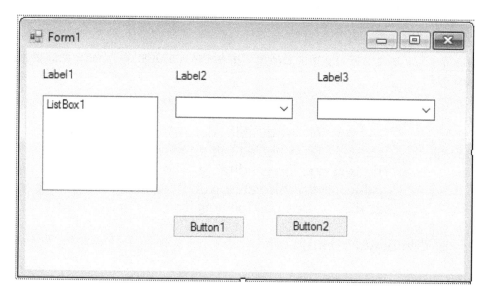

3. Set the form and object properties:

Form1:
Name	frmPlanner
FormBorderStyle	FixedSingle
StartPosition	CenterScreen
Text	Flight Planner

listBox1:
Name	lstCities
Sorted	True

comboBox1:
Name	cboSeat
DropDownStyle	DropdownList

comboBox2:
    Name   cboMeal
    DropDownStyle   Simple
    Text   [Blank]

(You may need to resize this control after setting properties).

label1:
    Text   Destination City

label2:
    Text   Seat Location

label3:
    Text   Meal Preference

button1:
    Name   btnAssign
    Text   &Assign

button2:
    Name   btnExit
    Text   E&xit

Now, the form should look like this:

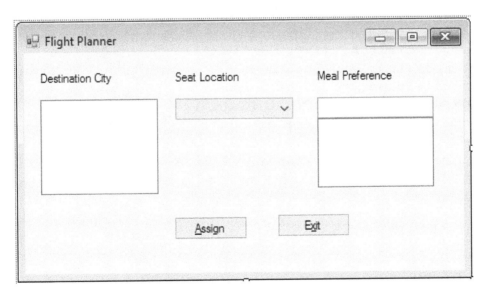

4. Use this code in the **frmPlanner Load** method:

```
private void FrmPlanner_Load(object sender, EventArgs e)
{
  // Add city names to list box
  lstCities.Items.Clear();
  lstCities.Items.Add("San Diego");
  lstCities.Items.Add("Los Angeles");
  lstCities.Items.Add("Orange County");
  lstCities.Items.Add("Ontario");
  lstCities.Items.Add("Bakersfield");
  lstCities.Items.Add("Oakland");
  lstCities.Items.Add("Sacramento");
  lstCities.Items.Add("San Jose");
  lstCities.Items.Add("San Francisco");
  lstCities.Items.Add("Eureka");
  lstCities.Items.Add("Eugene");
  lstCities.Items.Add("Portland");
  lstCities.Items.Add("Spokane");
  lstCities.Items.Add("Seattle");
  lstCities.SelectedIndex = 0;
  // Add seat types to first combo box
  cboSeat.Items.Add("Aisle");
  cboSeat.Items.Add("Middle");
  cboSeat.Items.Add("Window");
  cboSeat.SelectedIndex = 0;
  // Add meal types to second combo box
  cboMeal.Items.Add("Chicken");
  cboMeal.Items.Add("Mystery Meat");
  cboMeal.Items.Add("Kosher");
  cboMeal.Items.Add("Vegetarian");
  cboMeal.Items.Add("Fruit Plate");
  cboMeal.Text = "No Preference";
}
```

This code simply initializes the list box and the list box portions of the two combo boxes.

5. Use this code in the **btnAssign Click** event:

```
private void BtnAssign_Click(object sender, EventArgs e)
{
  // Build message box that gives your assignment
  string message;
  message = "Destination: " + lstCities.Text + "\r\n";
  message += "Seat Location: " + cboSeat.Text + "\r\n";
  message += "Meal: " + cboMeal.Text + "\r\n";
  MessageBox.Show(message, "Your Assignment",
MessageBoxButtons.OK, MessageBoxIcon.Information);
}
```

When the **Assign** button is clicked, this code forms a message box message by concatenating the selected city (from the list box **lstCities**), seat choice (from **cboSeat**), and the meal preference (from **cboMeal**).

6. Use this code in the **btnExit Click** event:

```
private void BtnExit_Click(object sender, EventArgs e)
{
  this.Close();
}
```

7. Run the application. Here's my screen with choices I made:

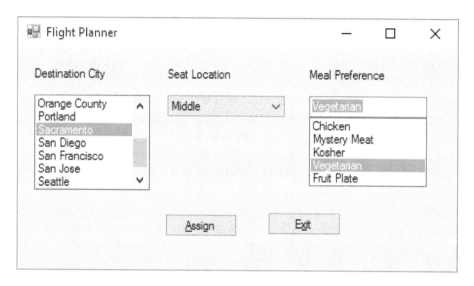

And, after clicking **Assign**, I see:

Save the project (saved in **Example 4-3** folder in **LearnVCS\VCS Code\Class 4** folder).

Class Review

After completing this class, you should understand:

> ➤ How to use the MessageBox dialog assigning messages, icons and buttons
> ➤ Useful properties, events, and methods for the form, button, text box, label, check box, and radio button controls
> ➤ Where the above listed controls can and should be used
> ➤ How GroupBox and Panel controls are used to group controls, particularly radio buttons
> ➤ How several events can be handled by a single event method
> ➤ The concept of 'control arrays' and how to use them
> ➤ How to use list box and combo box controls

Practice Problems 4

Problem 4-1. Message Box Problem. Build an application that lets you see what various message boxes look like. Allow selection of icon, buttons displayed, default button, and input message. Provide feedback on button clicked on displayed message box.

Problem 4-2. Tray Problem. Here's a sheet of cardboard (**L** units long and **W** units wide). A square cut **X** units long is made in each corner:

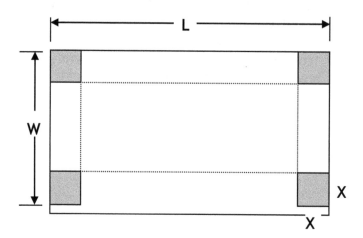

If you cut out the four shaded corners and fold the resulting sides up along the dotted lines, a tray is formed. Build an application that lets a user input the length (L) and width (W). Have the application decide what value X should be such that the tray has the largest volume possible. Use the NumericTextBox class developed in Chapter 3 for input.

Problem 4-3. List Box Problem. Build an application with two list boxes. Select items from one box. Click a button to move selected items to the other list box. If you then double-click an item in the second list box, have it return to the first box.

Problem 4-4. Combo Box Problem. Build an application with a Simple style combo box. Populate with some kind of information. If the user decides to type in their own selection (that is, they don't choose one of the listed items), add that new item to the list box portion of the combo box.

Exercise 4

Customer Database Input Screen

A new sports store wants you to develop an input screen for its customer database. The required input information is:

1. Name
2. Age
3. City of Residence
4. Sex (Male or Female)
5. Activities (Running, Walking, Biking, Swimming, Skiing and/or In-Line Skating)
6. Athletic Level (Extreme, Advanced, Intermediate, or Beginner)

Set up the screen so that only the Name and Age (use text boxes) and, perhaps, City (use a combo box) need to be typed; all other inputs should be set with check boxes and radio buttons. When a screen of information is complete, display the summarized profile in a message box. Use object-oriented programming to describe the customer. This profile message box should resemble this:

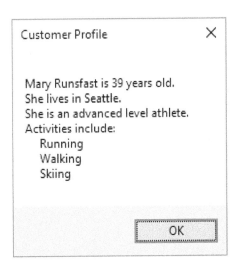

5. More Exploration of the Visual C# Toolbox

Review and Preview

In this class, we continue looking at tools in the Visual C# toolbox. We will look at some input tools, scroll bars, picture boxes and controls that allow direct interaction with drives, directories, and files.

In the examples, you should start trying to do as much of the building and programming of the applications you can with minimal reference to the notes. This will help you build your programming skills.

Control Z Order

As you build Windows applications using Visual C#, you will notice that whenever controls occupy the same space on a form, one control is on top of the other. The relative location of controls on a form is established by what is called the **Z Order**.

As each control is placed on the form, it is assigned a Z Order value. Controls placed last will lie over controls placed earlier. While designing an application, the Z Order can be changed by right-clicking the control of interest. A menu will appear. Selecting **BringToFront** will bring that control 'in front' of all other controls. Conversely, selecting **SendToBack** will send that control 'behind' all other controls.

A control's Z Order can also be changed in code. Why would you want to do this? Perhaps, you have two controls on the form in exactly the same location, one that should be accessible for one particular operation and the other accessible for another operation. To place one control in front of the other, you need to change the Z Order. The **BringToFront** and **SendToBack** methods accomplish this task. For a control named **controlExample**, the code to accomplish this is:

```
controlExample.BringToFront();
```

Or

```
controlName.SendToBack();
```

Now, let's continue our look at the Visual C# toolbox, looking first at more controls that allow 'point and click' selections.

NumericUpDown Control

In Toolbox:

On Form (Default Properties):

The **NumericUpDown** Control is used to obtain a numeric input. It looks like a text box control with two small arrows. Clicking the arrows changes the displayed value, which ranges from a specified minimum to a specified maximum. The user can even type in a value, if desired. Such controls are useful for supplying a date in a month or are used as volume controls in some Windows multimedia applications.

NumericUpDown **Properties:**

Name	Gets or sets the name of the numeric updown (three letter prefix for numeric updown name is **nud**).
BackColor	Get or sets the numeric updown background color.
BorderStyle	Gets or sets the border style for the updown control.
Font	Gets or sets font name, style, size.
ForeColor	Gets or sets color of text or graphics.
Increment	Gets or sets the value to increment or decrement the updown control when the up or down buttons are clicked.
Maximum	Gets or sets the maximum value for the updown control.
Minimum	Gets or sets the minimum value for the updown control.
ReadOnly	Gets or sets a value indicating whether the text may be changed by the use of the up or down buttons only.
TextAlign	Gets or sets the alignment of text in the numeric updown.
Value	Gets or sets the value assigned to the updown control.

NumericUpDown **Methods:**

DownButton   Decrements the value of the updown control.
UpButton   Increments the value of the updown control.

NumericUpDown **Events:**

Leave   Occurs when the updown control loses focus.
ValueChanged   Occurs when the Value property has been changed in
                        some way (numeric updown control **default** event).

The **Value** property can be changed by clicking either of the arrows or,
optionally by typing a value. If using the arrows, the value will always lie
between **Minimum** and **Maximum**. If the user can type in a value, you have no
control over what value is typed. However, once the control loses focus, the
typed value will be compared to Minimum and Maximum and any adjustments
made. Hence, if you allow typed values, only check the Value property in the
Leave event.

Typical use of **NumericUpDown** control:

➤ Set the **Name, Minimum** and **Maximum** properties. Initialize **Value**
  property. Decide on value for **ReadOnly.**
➤ Monitor **ValueChanged** (or **Leave**) event for changes in Value.
➤ You may also want to change the **Font, Backcolor** and **Forecolor**
  properties.

DomainUpDown Control

In Toolbox:

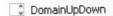

On Form (Default Properties):

The **DomainUpDown** control is similar in appearance to the NumericUpDown control. The difference is that the DomainUpDown control displays a list of string items (rather than numbers) as potential choices. It is much like a single line ComboBox control with no dropdown list. You will see it shares many of the properties of the ComboBox. The DomainUpDown control is usually reserved for relatively small lists. Examples of use are selecting a state in the United States for an address book, selecting a month for a calendar input or selecting a name from a short list.

DomainUpDown **Properties:**

Name	Gets or sets the name of the domain updown (three letter prefix for domain updown name is **dud**).
BackColor	Get or sets the domain updown background color.
Font	Gets or sets font name, style, size.
ForeColor	Gets or sets color of text.
Items	Gets the Items object of the domain updown.
ReadOnly	Gets or sets a value indicating whether the text may be changed by the use of the up or down buttons only.
SelectedIndex	Gets or sets the zero-based index of the currently selected item.
SelectedItem	Gets or sets the selected item based on the index value of the selected item.
Sorted	Gets or sets a value indicating whether items are sorted alphabetically.
Text	Gets or sets the text displayed in the updown control.
TextAlign	Gets or sets the alignment of the text in the updown control.
Wrap	Gets or sets a value indicating whether the list of items continues to the first or last item if the user continues past the end of the list.

DomainUpDown **Methods**:

DownButton	Displays the next item in the control.
UpButton	Displays the previous item in the control.

DomainUpDown **Events**:

KeyPress	Occurs when a key is pressed while the domain updown has focus.
Leave	Occurs when the control loses focus.
SelectedItemChanged	Occurs when the SelectedItem property has changed (the domain updown control **default** event).
TextChanged	Occurs when the Text property has changed.

Like the ListBox and ComboBox controls, the Items object provides details on what is in the control and how to add/delete information from the control. The first item in a updown control named **dudExample** is:

```
dudExample.Items.Item[0]
```

The last item in the list is:

```
dudExample.Items.Item[dudExample.Items.Count - 1]
```

Items can be added at design time or in code. To add an item in design mode, click the Items property, then the ellipsis that appears. A dialog control will display allowing one entry per line. Click OK when done.

To add an item in code, use the **Add** method, to delete an item, use the **Remove** or **RemoveAt** method and to clear it use the **Clear** method. For our example:

Add Item:	`dudExample.Items.Add`(StringToAdd)
Delete Item:	`dudExample.Items.Remove`(ItemToRemove)
	`DudExample.Items.RemoveAt`(IndexOfItemToRemove)
Clear list box:	`dudExample.Items.Clear`

Typical use of **DomainUpDown** control:

> - Set **Name** property, decide whether **ReadOnly** should be True and populate **Items** object (usually in form **Load** method).
> - Monitor **SelectedItemChanged** (or **TextChanged**) event for individual selections.
> - Read **Text** property to identify choice.
> - As usual, you may also want to change the **Font**, **Backcolor** and **Forecolor** properties.

Example 5-1

Date Input Device

1. Start a new project. In this project, we'll use a NumericUpDown control, in conjunction with a DomainUpDown control, to select a month and day of the year.

2. Place a NumericUpDown control, a DomainUpDown control and a Label control on the form. The form should resemble this:

3. Set these properties:

Form1:

Name	frmDate
FormBorderStyle	FixedSingle
StartPosition	CenterScreen
Text	Date Input

domainUpDown1:

Name	dudMonth
BackColor	White
Font Size	14
ReadOnly	True
Text	December
Wrap	True

numericUpDown1:

Name	nudDay
BackColor	White
Font Size	14
Maximum	31
Minimum	1
ReadOnly	True
TextAlign	Center
Value	1

label1:

Name	lblDate
Font Size	12
Text	[Blank]

When done, the form should look like this:

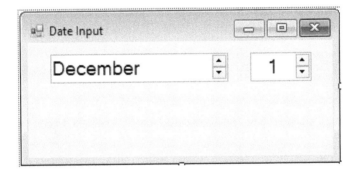

The label control cannot be seen.

4. Use this code in the **frmDate Load** method to populate the control with the month names:

```
private void FrmDate_Load(object sender, EventArgs e)
{
  dudMonth.Items.Add("January");
  dudMonth.Items.Add("February");
  dudMonth.Items.Add("March");
  dudMonth.Items.Add("April");
  dudMonth.Items.Add("May");
  dudMonth.Items.Add("June");
  dudMonth.Items.Add("July");
  dudMonth.Items.Add("August");
  dudMonth.Items.Add("September");
  dudMonth.Items.Add("October");
  dudMonth.Items.Add("November");
  dudMonth.Items.Add("December");
  dudMonth.SelectedIndex = 0;
}
```

5. Use this code in the **dudMonth SelectedItemChanged** event to update date if month changes:

```
private void DudMonth_SelectedItemChanged(object sender,
EventArgs e)
{
  lblDate.Text = dudMonth.Text + " " +
nudDay.Value.ToString();
}
```

6. Use this code in the **nudDay ValueChanged** event to update date if day changes:

```
private void NudDay_ValueChanged(object sender, EventArgs
e)
{
   lblDate.Text = dudMonth.Text + " " +
nudDay.Value.ToString();
}
```

7. Run the program. Here's some selections I made:

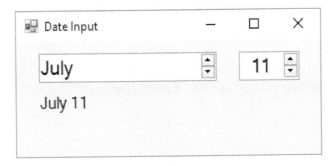

Scroll through the month names. Notice how the **Wrap** property allows the list to return to January after December. Scroll through the day values, noticing how the displayed date changes. Save the project (saved in **Example 5-1** folder in the **LearnVCS\VCS Code\Class 5** folder).

Do you notice that you could enter April 31 as a date, even though it's not a legal value? Can you think of how to modify this example to make sure you don't exceed the number of days in any particular month? And, how would you handle February – you need to know if it's a leap year.

Horizontal and Vertical ScrollBar Controls

Horizontal ScrollBar In Toolbox:

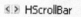

Horizontal ScrollBar On Form (Default Properties):

Vertical ScrollBar In Toolbox:

Vertical ScrollBar On Form (Default Properties):

The NumericUpDown control is useful for relatively small ranges of numeric input. It wouldn't work well for large number ranges – you'd spend a lot of time clicking those little arrows. For large ranges of numbers, we use horizontal (**HScrollBar**) and vertical (**VScrollBar**) scroll bar controls.   Scroll bars are widely used in Windows applications. Scroll bars provide an intuitive way to move through a list of information and make great input devices. Here, we use a scroll bar to obtain a whole number (**Integer** data type).

Both types of scroll bars are comprised of three areas that can be clicked, or dragged, to change the scroll bar value. Those areas are:

End arrow ——————

Scroll box (thumb)

Bar area

Clicking an **end arrow** increments the **scroll box** a small amount, clicking the **bar area** increments the scroll box a large amount, and dragging the scroll box (thumb) provides continuous motion. Using the properties of scroll bars, we can completely specify how one works. The scroll box position is the only output information from a scroll bar.

ScrollBar **Properties** (apply to both horizontal and vertical controls):

Name	Gets or sets the name of the scroll bar (three letter prefix for horizontal scroll bar is **hsb**, for vertical scroll bar **vsb**).
LargeChange	Increment added to or subtracted from the scroll bar Value property when the bar area is clicked.
Maximum	The maximum value of the horizontal scroll bar at the far right and the maximum value of the vertical scroll bar at the bottom.
Minimum	The minimum value of the horizontal scroll bar at the left and the vertical scroll bar at the top
SmallChange	The increment added to or subtracted from the scroll bar Value property when either of the scroll arrows is clicked.
Value	The current position of the scroll box (thumb) within the scroll bar. If you set this in code, Visual C# moves the scroll box to the proper position.

Location of properties for **horizontal** scroll bar:

LargeChange

SmallChange

Minimum

SmallChange

Value

Maximum

LargeChange

Location of properties for **vertical** scroll bar:

A couple of important notes about scroll bar properties:

1. Notice the vertical scroll bar has its Minimum at the top and its Maximum at the bottom. This may be counter-intuitive in some applications. That is, users may expect things to 'go up' as they increase. You can give this appearance of going up by defining another variable that varies 'negatively' with the scroll bar Value property.

2. If you ever change the **Value**, **Minimum**, or **Maximum** properties in code, make sure Value is at all times between Minimum and Maximum or the program will stop with an error message.

ScrollBar **Events:**

Scroll	Occurs when the scroll box has been moved by either a mouse or keyboard action (**default** scroll bar event).
ValueChanged	Occurs whenever the scroll bar **Value** property changes, either in code or via a mouse action.

Typical use of **HScrollBar** and **VScrollBar** controls:

➢ Decide whether horizontal or vertical scroll bar fits your needs best.
➢ Set the **Name, Minimum, Maximum, SmallChange, LargeChange** properties. Initialize **Value** property.
➢ Monitor **Scroll** or **ValueChanged** event for changes in Value.

A Note on the **Maximum** Property:

For some reason, if **LargeChange** is not equal to one, the **Maximum** value cannot be achieved by clicking the end arrows, the bar area or moving the scroll box. It can only be achieved by setting the **Value** property in code. The maximum achievable **Value,** via mouse operations, is given by the relation:

Achievable Maximum = Maximum – LargeChange + 1

What does this mean? To meet an "achievable maximum," you need to set the scroll bar Maximum property using this equation:

Maximum = Achievable Maximum + LargeChange - 1

For example, if you want a scroll bar to be able to reach 100 (with a LargeChange property of 10), you need to set **Maximum** to **109**, not 100! Very strange, I'll admit ...

TrackBar Control

In Toolbox:

On Form (Default Properties):

The **TrackBar** control is similar to the scroll bar control with a different interface. It is used to establish numeric input (usually a fairly small range). It can be oriented either horizontally or vertically.

TrackBar **Properties:**

Name	Gets or sets the name of the track bar (three letter prefix is **trk**).
LargeChange	Increment added to or subtracted from the track bar Value property when the user clicks the track bar or presses the <**PageUp**> or <**PageDn**> keys.
Maximum	The maximum value of the horizontal track bar at the far right and the maximum value of the vertical track bar at the top (this is different than the scroll bar).
Minimum	The minimum value of the horizontal track bar at the left and the vertical track bar at the bottom.
Orientation	Specifies a vertical or horizontal orientation for the control
SmallChange	The increment added to or subtracted from the track bar Value property when user presses left or right cursor control keys (horizontal orientation); when user presses up or down cursor control keys (vertical orientation).
TickFrequency	Determines how many tick marks appear on the track bar.
TickStyle	Determines how and where ticks appear.
Value	The current position of the pointer within the track bar. If you set this in code, Visual C# moves the pointer to the proper position.

A couple of important notes about track bar properties:

1. Notice the vertical track bar has its Maximum at the top. This is different than the vertical scroll bar control.

2. If you ever change the **Value**, **Minimum**, or **Maximum** properties in code, make sure Value is at all times between Minimum and Maximum or the program will stop with an error message.

3. The track bar **Maximum** property can be achieved in code or via mouse operations. It does not exhibit the odd behavior noted with the scroll bar control.

TrackBar **Events:**

Scroll	Occurs when the track bar pointer has been moved by either a mouse or keyboard action (**default** event for the track bar control).
ValueChanged	Occurs whenever the track bar **Value** property changes, either in code or via a mouse action.

Typical use of **TrackBar** control:

➢ Decide whether horizontal or vertical track bar fits your needs best.
➢ Set the **Name, Minimum, Maximum, SmallChange, LargeChange** properties. Initialize **Value** property.
➢ Monitor **Scroll** or **ValueChanged** event for changes in Value.

Example 5-2

Temperature Conversion

1. Start a new project. In this project, we convert temperatures in degrees Fahrenheit (set using a horizontal scroll bar) to degrees Celsius. The formula for converting Fahrenheit (F) to Celsius (C) is:

$$C = (F - 32) * 5 / 9$$

Temperatures will be adjusted and displayed in tenths of degrees.

2. Place a horizontal scroll bar, two labels and two text boxes on the form. Place two more labels (right behind each other, with **AutoSize** set to **False** so they can be resized) behind the scroll bar (we'll use these for special effects). It should resemble this:

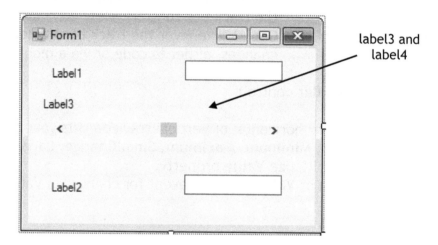

label3 and label4

3. Set the properties of the form and each control:

Form1:
Name	frmTemp
FormBorderStyle	FixedSingle
StartPosition	CenterScreen
Text	Temperature Conversion

label1:
Font	Bold, Size 10
Text	Fahrenheit

textBox1:
Name	txtTempF
BackColor	White
Font	Bold, Size 10
ReadOnly	True
Text	32.0
TextAlign	Center

label2:
Font	Bold, Size 10
Text	Celsius

textBox2:
Name	txtTempC
BackColor	White
Font	Bold, Size 10
ReadOnly	True
Text	0.0
TextAlign	Center

Label3:
Name	lblBlue
AutoSize	False
BackColor	Blue
Text	[blank]

label4:

Name	lblRed
AutoSize	False
BackColor	Red
Text	[blank]

hScrollBar1:

Name	hsbTemp
LargeChange	10
Maximum	1209
Minimum	-600
SmallChange	1
Value	320

Note the scroll bar properties (Value, Minimum, Maximum, SmallChange, LargeChange) are in tenths of degrees. The initial temperatures are initialized at 32.0 F (Value = 320 tenths of degrees) and 0.0 C, known values. We want an "achievable maximum" of 120.0 degrees or a value of 1200. Why, then, is Maximum = 1209 and not 1200? Recall the formula for the actual Maximum to use is:

$$\text{Maximum} = \text{Achievable Maximum} + \text{LargeChange} - 1$$

Or, using our numbers:

$$\text{Maximum} = 1200 + 10 - 1 = 1209$$

When done, the form should look like this:

4. Form level scope declarations:

```
bool isHot;
```

5. Use this code in the **hsbTemp Scroll** event.

```
private void HsbTemp_Scroll(object sender, ScrollEventArgs
e)
{
  double tempF, tempC;
  // Read F and convert to C - divide by 10 needed since
Value is tenths of degrees
  tempF = Convert.ToDouble(hsbTemp.Value) / 10;
  // check to see if changed from hot to cold or vice
versa
  if (isHot && tempF < 70)
  {
    // changed to cold
    isHot = false;
    lblBlue.BringToFront();
    hsbTemp.BringToFront();
  }
  else if (!isHot && tempF >= 70)
  {
    // changed to hot
    isHot = true;
    lblRed.BringToFront();
    hsbTemp.BringToFront();
  }
  txtTempF.Text = String.Format("{0:f1}", tempF);
  tempC = (tempF - 32) * 5 / 9;
  txtTempC.Text = String.Format("{0:f1}", tempC);
}
```

This code determines the scroll bar Value as it changes, takes that value as Fahrenheit temperature, computes Celsius temperature, and displays both values. A blue label is used for cold temperatures, a red label for warm temperatures.

6. Give the program a try. Make sure it provides correct information at obvious
   points. For example, 32.0 F better always be the same as 0.0 C! What
   happens around 70 F? Here's a run I made:

Save the project (saved in **Example 5-2** folder in the **LearnVCS\VCS Code\Class
5** folder).

Can you find a point where Fahrenheit temperature equals Celsius temperature?
If you don't know this off the top of your head, it's obvious you've never lived in
extremely cold climates. I've actually witnessed one of those bank temperature
signs flashing degrees F and degrees C and seeing the same number! Ever
wonder why body temperature is that odd figure of 98.6 degrees F? Can your
new application give you some insight to an answer to this question?

PictureBox Control

In Toolbox:

On Form (Default Properties):

Visual C# has powerful features for graphics. The **PictureBox** control is a primary tool for exploiting these features. The picture box control can display graphics files (in a variety of formats), can host many graphics functions and can be used for detailed animations. Here, we concentrate on using the control to display a graphics file.

PictureBox **Properties:**

Name	Gets or sets the name of the picture box (three letter prefix for picture box name is **pic**).
BackColor	Get or sets the picture box background color.
BorderStyle	Indicates the border style for the picture box.
Height	Height of picture box in pixels.
Image	Establishes the graphics file to display in the picture box.
Left	Distance from left edge of form to left edge of picture box, in pixels.
SizeMode	Indicates how the image is displayed.
Top	Distance bottom of form title bar area to top edge of picture box, in pixels.
Width	Width of picture box in pixels.

PictureBox **Events:**

Click	Triggered when a picture box is clicked (the picture box control **default** event).

The **Image** property specifies the graphics file to display. It can be established in design mode or at run-time. Five types of graphics files can be viewed in a picture box:

File Type	Description
Bitmap	An image represented by pixels and stored as a collection of bits in which each bit corresponds to one pixel. This is the format commonly used by scanners and paintbrush programs. Bitmap filenames have a **.bmp** extension.
Icon	A special type of bitmap file of maximum 32 x 32 size. Icon filenames have an **.ico** extension. We'll create icon files in Class 5
Metafile	A file that stores an image as a collection of graphical objects (lines, circles, polygons) rather than pixels. Metafiles preserve an image more accurately than bitmaps when resized. Many graphics files available for download from the internet are metafiles. Metafile filenames have a **.wmf** extension.
JPEG	JPEG (Joint Photographic Experts Group) is a compressed bitmap format which supports 8 and 24 bit color. It is popular on the Internet and is a common format for digital cameras. JPEG filenames have a **.jpg** extension.
GIF	GIF (Graphic Interchange Format) is a compressed bitmap format originally developed by CompuServe. It supports up to 256 colors and is also popular on the Internet. GIF filenames have a **.gif** extension.

Setting the Image property in design mode requires a few steps. Let's do an example to illustrate the process. Start a new project and put a picture box control on the form. Mine looks like this:

Graphics files used at design-time are saved as program **Resources**. Once these resources are established, they can be used to set the **Image** property. The process to follow is to display the **Properties** window for the picture box control and select the **Image** property. An ellipsis (...) will appear. Click the ellipsis. A **Select Resource** window will appear. Make sure the **Project resource file** radio button is selected and click the button marked **Import** - a file open window will appear. Move (as shown) to the **\LearnVCS\VCS Code\Class 5\Example 5-3** folder and you will see some sample files listed:

We have included one of each file type. There is a bitmap picture of a beany (**beany.bmp**), a metafile of an answering machine (**answer.wmf**), a copy of the KIDware logo (**kidware.gif**) and a picture from my Mexico vacation (**mexico.jpg**). Notice there is no icon file (ico extension). By default, icon files are not displayed. To see the icon file (a CD-ROM), click the drop-down box next to **Files of type** and choose **All Files**. All files (including the **ico** file and even non-graphics files will be displayed). Hence, if you need an icon file in a picture box, you must take an extra step to select it. Select all five graphics files and click **Open**.

You should now see the **Select Resource** window, with all five files now added to the program resources. Individual images are selected using this window:

Select the beany graphic (a bitmap) and click the **OK** button.

It will be displayed in the picture box on our form:

To set the **Image** property at run-time, you use the **FromFile** method associated with the **Image** object. As an example, to load the file **c:\sample\myfile.bmp** into a picture box name **picExample**, the proper code is:

```
picExample.Image = Image.FromFile("c:\sample\myfile.bmp");
```

The argument in the **Image.FromFile** method must be a legal, complete path and file name, or your program will stop with an error message.

To clear an image from a picture box control at run-time, simply set the corresponding Image property to **null** (a C# keyword). This disassociates the Image property from the last loaded image. For our example, the code is:

```
picExample.Image = null;
```

The **SizeMode** property dictates how a particular image will be displayed. There are four possible values for this property: **Normal**, **CenterImage**, **StretchImage**, **AutoSize**. The effect of each value is:

SizeMode	Effect
Normal	Image appears in original size. If picture box is larger than image, there will be blank space. If picture box is smaller than image, the image will be cropped.
CenterImage	Image appears in original size, centered in picture box. If picture box is larger than image, there will be blank space. If picture box is smaller than image, image is cropped.
StretchImage	Image will 'fill' picture box. If image is smaller than picture box, it will expand. If image is larger than picture box, it will scale down. Bitmap and icon files do not scale nicely. Metafiles, JPEG and GIF files do scale nicely.
AutoSize	Reverse of StretchImage - picture box will change its dimensions to match the original size of the image. Be forewarned – metafiles are usually very large!
Zoom	Similar to StretchImage. The image will adjust to fit within the picture box, however its actual height to width ratio is maintained.

Notice picture box dimensions remain fixed for **Normal**, **CenterImage**, **StretchImage**, and **Zoom SizeMode** values. With **AutoSize**, the picture box will grow in size. This may cause problems at run-time if your form is not large enough to 'contain' the picture box.

Typical use of **PictureBox** control for displaying images:

> ➤ Set the **Name** and **SizeMode** property (most often, **StretchImage**).
> ➤ Set **Image** property, either in design mode or at run-time.

OpenFileDialog Control

In Toolbox:

Below Form (Default Properties):

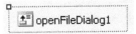

Note that to set the **Image** property of the picture box control using the **FromFile** method, you need the path and filename for the image file. How can you get this from a user? One possibility would be to use a text box control, asking the user to type in the desired information? This is just asking for trouble. Even the simplest of paths is difficult to type, remembering drive names, proper folder names, file names and extensions, and where all the slashes go. And then you, the programmer, must verify that the information typed contains a valid path and valid file name.

I think you see that asking a user to type a path and file name is a bad idea. We want a 'point and click' type interface to get a file name. Every Windows application provides such an interface for opening files. [Click on the **Open File** toolbar button in Visual C# and an 'Open File' dialog box will appear.] Visual C# lets us use this same interface in our applications via the **OpenFileDialog** control. This control is one of a suite of dialog controls we can add to our applications. There are also dialog controls to save files, change fonts, change colors, and perform printing operations. We'll look at other dialog controls as we work through the course.

What we learn here is not just limited to opening image files for the picture box control. There are many times in application development where we will need a file name from a user. Applications often require data files, initialization files, configuration files, sound files and other graphic files. The **OpenFileDialog** control will also be useful in these cases.

OpenFileDialog **Properties:**

Name	Gets or sets the name of the open file dialog (I usually name this control **dlgOpen**).
AddExtension	Gets or sets a value indicating whether the dialog box automatically adds an extension to a file name if the user omits the extension.
CheckFileExists	Gets or sets a value indicating whether the dialog box displays a warning if the user specifies a file name that does not exist.
CheckPathExists	Gets or sets a value indicating whether the dialog box displays a warning if the user specifies a path that does not exist.
DefaultExt	Gets or sets the default file extension.
FileName	Gets or sets a string containing the file name selected in the file dialog box.
Filter	Gets or sets the current file name filter string, which determines the choices that appear in "Files of type" box.
FilterIndex	Gets or sets the index of the filter currently selected in the file dialog box.
InitialDirectory	Gets or sets the initial directory displayed by the file dialog box.
Title	Gets or sets the file dialog box title.

OpenFileDialog **Methods:**

ShowDialog	Displays the dialog box. Returned value indicates which button was clicked by user (**OK** or **Cancel**).

To use the **OpenFileDialog** control, we add it to our application the same as any control. Since the OpenFileDialog control has no immediate user interface (you control when it appears), the control does not appear on the form at design time. Such Visual C# controls (the **Timer** control seen briefly back in Chapter 1 was a similar control) appear in a 'tray' below the form in the IDE Design window. Once added, we set a few properties. Then, we write code to make the dialog box appear when desired. The user then makes selections and closes the dialog box. At this point, we use the provided information for our tasks.

The **ShowDialog** method is used to display the **OpenFileDialog** control. For a control named **dlgOpen**, the appropriate code is:

```
rtnValue = dlgOpen.ShowDialog();
```

And the displayed dialog box is similar to:

The user selects a file using the dialog control (or types a name in the **File name** box). The file type is selected form the **Files of type** box (values here set with the **Filter** property). Once selected, the **Open** button is clicked. **Cancel** can be clicked to cancel the open operation. The ShowDialog method returns (in **rtnValue** in the above example code) the clicked button. It returns **DialogResult.OK** if Open is clicked and returns **DialogResult.Cancel** if Cancel is clicked. The nice thing about this control is that it can validate the file name before it is returned to the application. The **FileName** property contains the complete path to the selected file.

Typical use of **OpenFileDialog** control:

> ➢ Set the **Name, Filter**, and **Title** properties.
> ➢ Use **ShowDialog** method to display dialog box.
> ➢ Read **FileName** property to determine selected file

Example 5-3

Picture Box Playground

1. Start a new project. In this project, we will use a **OpenFileDialog** control to select image files. The selected file will be displayed in five different picture box controls (one for each setting of the **SizeMode** property).

2. Place five labels on a form. Place a picture box control under each of the labels. Place another label, a text box and a button control under these controls. Finally, place the OpenFileDialog control in the 'tray' under the form. The form (which will be rather wide) should look like this:

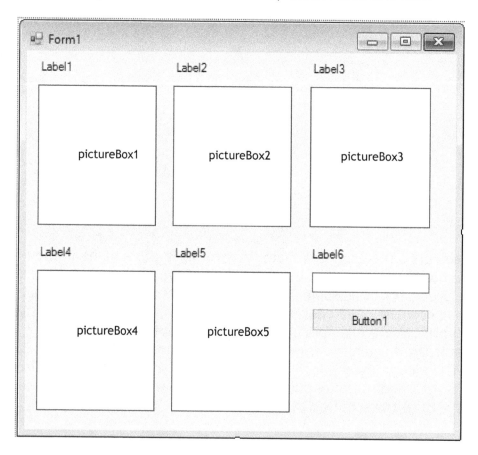

Other controls in tray:

　　　　📇 openFileDialog1

3. Set the properties of the form and each control:

Form1:
Name	frmPlayground
Text	Picture Box Playground

label1:
Text	Normal:

label2:
Text	CenterImage:

label3:
Text	AutoSize:

label4:
Text	StretchImage:

label5:
Text	Zoom:

pictureBox1:
Name	picNormal
BackColor	White
BorderStyle	FixedSingle
SizeMode	Normal

pictureBox2:
Name	picCenter
BackColor	White
BorderStyle	FixedSingle
SizeMode	CenterImage

pictureBox3:
Name	picAuto
BackColor	White
BorderStyle	FixedSingle
SizeMode	AutoSize

pictureBox4:

Name	picStretch
BackColor	White
BorderStyle	FixedSingle
SizeMode	StretchImage

pictureBox5:

Name	picZoom
BackColor	White
BorderStyle	FixedSingle
SizeMode	Zoom

label6:

Text	Size:

textBox1:

Name	txtSize
TextAlign	Center

button1:

Name	btnImage
Text	&Select Image

openFileDialog1:

Name	dlgOpen
FileName	[blank]
Filter	Bitmaps (*.bmp)|*.bmp|Icons (*.ico)|*.ico|Metafiles (*.wmf)|*.wmf|JPEG (*.jpg)|*.jpg|GIF (*.gif)|*.gif [Type this line carefully! – consult on-line help as reference]
Title	Open Image File

When done, the form should look like this:

Other controls in tray:

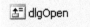

4. Form level scope declarations:

```
int wSave, hSave;
```

5. Use this code in the **frmPlayground Load** event to initialize positions and save size:

```
private void FrmPlayground_Load(object sender, EventArgs e)
{
  // start form in upper left corner
  this.Left = 0;
  this.Top = 0;
  // save form width/height for initialization
  wSave = this.Width;
  hSave = this.Height;
}
```

6. Use this code in the **BtnImage Click** event:

```
private void btnImage_Click(object sender, EventArgs e)
{
  // reset autosize picture box and form to initial size
  picAuto.Width = picNormal.Width;
  picAuto.Height = picNormal.Height;
  this.Width = wSave;
  this.Height = hSave;
  // display open dialog box
  if (dlgOpen.ShowDialog() == DialogResult.OK)
  {
    picNormal.Image = Image.FromFile(dlgOpen.FileName);
    picCenter.Image = Image.FromFile(dlgOpen.FileName);
    picAuto.Image = Image.FromFile(dlgOpen.FileName);
    picStretch.Image = Image.FromFile(dlgOpen.FileName);
    picZoom.Image = Image.FromFile(dlgOpen.FileName);
    txtSize.Text = picAuto.Width.ToString() + " x " +
picAuto.Height.ToString();
  }
}
```

This code reads the selected file and displays it in each of the picture box controls.

7. Save the application (saved in **Example 5-3** folder in the **LearnVCS\VCS Code\Class 5** folder). Run the application and open different types of image files (we've included one of each type in the project folder). Here's a beany in bitmap format:

Notice how the different SizeMode properties affect the display. Images in the AutoSize mode may be very large requiring resizing of the form.

Legacy Controls

In the **Picture Box Playground** example just developed, every time we want to change the image, it is necessary to bring up the open file dialog box. What would be nice is to have the capability of the dialog box built into the form providing a clickable list of image files, directories and drives. As each file name was clicked, the corresponding image would be displayed in each of the picture boxes. Controls to build such a built-in dialog box exist, but they are not part of Visual C# - they are part of Visual Basic, another programming language, but we can still use them like any other control. (One caveat - since the controls discussed in this section are from Visual Basic, you must be using Visual Studio, making sure Visual Basic is included in your installation. If Visual Basic is not part of your current Visual Studio installation, you will have to do a reinstall. If you are using a stand-alone Visual C# product, you cannot complete the remaining example.)

We will be using three controls. The **DriveListBox** control is a dropdown box that allows selection of drives. The **DirListBox** control is a list box allowing folder selection. And, the **FileListBox** control is a list box allowing file selection. Using these three controls on a form allows a 'built-in' replication of the open file dialog box. And, the nice thing about these controls is you can use as many (or as few) as you like. For example, if you just want to present your user a selection of files in a single directory they could not change, you just use the FileListBox control. The **OpenFileDialog** control does not allow such a limitation.

The controls we are using are referred to as **legacy** controls. These are controls that existed in previous versions of a product and have been eliminated in current versions. For the most part, elimination of these **legacy controls** is a good thing, providing a more up-to-date product. But the three controls discussed here have real utility - we wish they had not been eliminated.

So, are we just left with our 'wishing and hoping' these controls were back? Unfortunately, no. Visual C# still has some of these legacy controls (as part of the **Microsoft.Visual Basic.Compatibility.VB6** namespace), but they must be added to the toolbox. To do this, click the **Tools** menu item and select **Choose Toolbox Items.** When the dialog box appears, select **.NET Framework Components.** Place check marks next to: **DriveListBox, DirListBox** and **FileListBox.** Click **OK** and the controls will appear in the toolbox and become available for use (on-line help is available for documentation).

You may see other legacy controls in the Customize Toolbox dialog box. You can decide if you need any other such controls. Be aware, however, that using legacy controls could be dangerous. Microsoft may decide to drop support for such controls at any time. Our hope is that controls similar to the drive, directory and file list tools are added with the next version of Visual Studio – their utility calls out for their inclusion.

DriveListBox Controls

In Toolbox:

 DriveListBox

On Form (Default Properties):

The **DriveListBox** control allows a user to select a valid disk drive at run-time. It displays the available drives in a drop-down combo box. No code is needed to load a drive list box with valid drives; the control does this for us. We use the box to get the current drive identification.

DriveListBox **Properties:**

Name	Gets or sets the name of the drive list box (three letter prefix for drive list box name is **drv**).
BackColor	Get or sets the drive list box background color.
Drive	Contains the name of the currently selected drive.
DropDownStyle	Gets or sets a value specifying the style of the drive list box.
Font	Gets or sets font name, style, size.
ForeColor	Gets or sets color of text.

DriveListBox **Events:**

SelectedValueChanged	Triggered whenever the user or program changes the drive selection.

This control is always used in conjunction with the DirListBox and FileListBox controls – we rarely look at the **Drive** property.

Typical use of **DriveListBox** control:

> ➤ Set the **Name** property.
> ➤ Use **SelectedValueChanged** event to update displayed directories.

DirListBox Control

In Toolbox:

 DirListBox

On Form (Default Properties):

The **DirListBox** control displays an ordered, hierarchical list of the user's disk directories and subdirectories. The directory structure is displayed in a list box. Like, the drive list box, little coding is needed to use the directory list box – the control does most of the work for us.

DirListBox **Properties:**

Name	Gets or sets the name of the directory list box (three letter prefix for directory list box name is **dir**).
BackColor	Get or sets the directory list box background color.
BorderStyle	Establishes the border for directory list box.
Font	Gets or sets font name, style, size.
ForeColor	Gets or sets color of text.
Path	Gets or sets the current directory path.

DirListBox **Events:**

Change	Triggered when the directory selection is changed.

Typical use of **DirListBox** control:

> ➢ Set the **Name** property.
> ➢ Use **Change** event to update displayed files.
> ➢ Read **Path** property for current path.

FileListBox Control

In Toolbox:

 FileListBox

On Form (Default Properties):

The **FileListBox** control locates and lists files in the directory specified by its **Path** property at run-time. You may select the types of files you want to display in the file list box. You will notice most of its properties are very similar to those of the list box control studied in Class 3.

FileListBox **Properties:**

Name	Gets or sets the name of the file list box (three letter prefix for file list box name is **fil**).
BackColor	Get or sets the file list box background color.
FileName	Contains the currently selected file name.
Font	Gets or sets font name, style, size.
ForeColor	Gets or sets color of text.
Items	Gets the Items object of the file list box.
Path	Contains the current path directory.
Pattern	Contains a string that determines which files will be displayed. It supports the use of * and ? wildcard characters. For example, using *.dat only displays files with the .dat extension.
SelectedIndex	Gets or sets the zero-based index of the currently selected item in a list box.
SelectionMode	Gets or sets the method in which items are selected in file list box (allows single or multiple selections).

FileListBox **Events:**

    SelectedIndexChanged   Occurs when the SelectedIndex property
                                   has changed (**default** event for this
                                   control).

If needed, the number of items in the list is provided by the **Items.Count** property. The individual items in the list are found by examining elements of the **Items.Item** zero-based array.

Typical use of **FileListBox** control:

> ➤ Set **Name** and Pattern properties.
> ➤ Monitor **SelectedIndexChanged** event for individual selections.
> ➤ Use **Path** and **FileName** properties to form complete path to selected file.

Synchronizing the Drive, Directory, and File List Box Controls

The drive, directory and file list boxes are controls that can be used independently of each other. As such, there are no common properties or linking mechanisms. When used with each other to obtain a file name, their operation must be synchronized to insure the displayed information is always consistent.

When the drive selection is changed (drive list box **SelectedValueChanged** event), you need to update the directory list box path. For example, if the drive list box is named **drvExample** and the directory list box is **dirExample**, use the code:

```
dirExample.Path = drvExample.Drive;
```

When the directory selection is changed (directory list box **Change** event), you must update the names displayed in the file list box. With a file list box named **filExample**, this code is:

```
filExample.Path = dirExample.Path;
```

Once all of the selections have been made and you want the file name, you need to form a text string that specifies the complete path to the file. This string concatenates the **Path** and **FileName** information from the file list box. This should be an easy task, except for one problem. The problem involves the backslash (\) character. If you are at the root directory of your drive, the path name ends with a backslash. If you are not at the root directory, there is no backslash at the end of the path name and you have to add one before tacking on the file name.

Example code for concatenating the available information into a proper file name (**yourFile**):

```
string yourName;
string yourPath = filExample.Path;

if (yourPath[yourPath.Length - 1] == '\\')
{
  yourFile = yourPath + filExample.FileName;
}
else
{
  yourFile = yourPath + "\\" + filExample.FileName;
}
```

This code checks the last character in the Path property to see if it is a backslash [we need to use two characters (\\) to represent a backslash to distinguish it from C# escape characters]. Note we only have to use properties of the file list box. The drive and directory box properties are only used to create changes in the file list box via code.

Example 5-4

Image Viewer

1. Start a new project. In this application, we search our computer's file structure for graphics files and display the results of our search in an picture box control.

2. First, place a group box control on the form. In this group box, place a drive list box, directory list box, file list box, a text box and three labels. Make sure you have added the three legacy list box controls to your toolbox using instructions provided earlier. Add a second group box. In that group box, place a picture box control and four radio buttons. The form should look like this:

3. Set properties of the form and each control.

Form1:
Name	frmImage
FormBorderStyle	FixedSingle
StartPosition	CenterScreen
Text	Image Viewer

groupBox1:
Name	grpFile
BackColor	Red
Text	[Blank]

txtBox1:
Name	txtImage
BackColor	Yellow
MultiLine	True

label1:
ForeColor	Yellow
Text	Files:

driveListBox1:
Name	drvImage

label2:
ForeColor	Yellow
Text	Directories:

dirListBox1:
Name	dirImage

label3:
ForeColor	Yellow
Text	Drives:

fileListBox1:
Name	filImage
Pattern	*.bmp;*.ico;*.wmf;*.gif;*.jpg
	[type this line with <u>no</u> spaces]

groupBox2:
Name	grpImage
BackColor	Blue
Text	[Blank]

pictureBox1:
Name	picImage
BackColor	White
BorderStyle	FixedSingle

radioButton1:
Name	rdoNormal
ForeColor	Yellow
Text	Normal

radioButton2:
Name	rdoCenter
ForeColor	Yellow
Text	Center

radioButton3:
Name	rdoStretch
ForeColor	Yellow
Text	Stretch

radioButton4:
Name	rdoZoom
ForeColor	Yellow
Text	Zoom

My finished form is this:

4. Use this code in the **frmImage Load** method (initializes Stretch size mode):

```
private void FrmImage_Load(object sender, EventArgs e)
{
  // initialize stretch mode
  rdoStretch.PerformClick();
}
```

5. Use this code in the **drvImage SelectedValueChanged** method.

```
private void DrvImage_SelectedValueChanged(object sender,
EventArgs e)
{
  // If drive changes, update directory
  dirImage.Path = drvImage.Drive;
}
```

When a new drive is selected, this code forces the directory list box to display directories on that drive.

6. Use this code in the **DirImage Change** method.

```
private void dirImage_Change(object sender, EventArgs e)
{
  // If directory changes, update file path
  filImage.Path = dirImage.Path;
}
```

Likewise, when a new directory is chosen, we want to see the files on that directory.

7. Use this code for the **FilImage SelectedIndexChanged** event.

```
private void filImage_SelectedIndexChanged(object sender,
EventArgs e)
{
  // Get complete path to file name and open graphics
  string imageName;
  string imagePath = filImage.Path;
  if (imagePath[imagePath.Length - 1] == '\\')
  {
    imageName = imagePath + filImage.FileName;
  }
  else
  {
    imageName = imagePath + "\\" + filImage.FileName;
  }
  txtImage.Text = imageName;
  picImage.Image = Image.FromFile(imageName);
}
```

This code forms the file name (**ImageName**) by concatenating the directory path with the file name. It then displays the complete name and loads the image into the picture box.

8. Lastly, code the four radio button **CheckedChanged** events to change the display size mode:

```
private void RdoNormal_CheckedChanged(object sender,
EventArgs e)
{
   picImage.SizeMode = PictureBoxSizeMode.Normal;
}

private void RdoCenter_CheckedChanged(object sender,
EventArgs e)
{
   picImage.SizeMode = PictureBoxSizeMode.CenterImage;
}

private void RdoStretch_CheckedChanged(object sender,
EventArgs e)
{
   picImage.SizeMode = PictureBoxSizeMode.StretchImage;
}

private void RdoZoom_CheckedChanged(object sender,
EventArgs e)
{
   picImage.SizeMode = PictureBoxSizeMode.Zoom;
}
```

9. Save your project (saved in **Example 5-4** folder in **LearnVCS\VCS Code\Class 5** folder). Run and try the application. Find bitmaps, icons, metafiles, gif files, and JPEGs (an example of each is included in the project folder). Here's how the form should look when displaying the example JPEG file (a photo from my Mexican vacation):

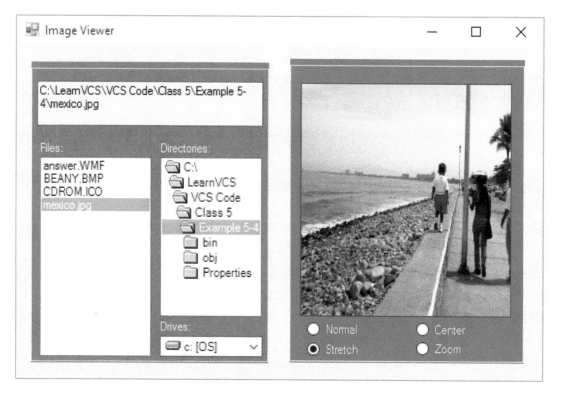

Note the picture is distorted a bit. Click the **Zoom** mode and you'll see the height to width ratio is correct.

Class Review

After completing this class, you should understand:

> - The concept of Z Order for a control
> - Useful properties, events, methods and typical uses for the numeric updown and domain updown controls
> - Properties, events, methods, and uses for the horizontal and vertical scroll bar controls
> - The five types of graphics files that can be displayed by the picture box control
> - How the picture box SizeMode property affects Image display
> - How to load image files at both design time and run time
> - How to use the file open common dialog box to obtain file names for opening files
> - How the legacy drive, directory, and file list controls work and when they could be used

Practice Problems 5

Problem 5-1. Tic-Tac-Toe Problem. Build a simple Tic-Tac-Toe game. Use 'skinny' label controls for the grid and picture box controls for markers (use different pictures to distinguish players). Click the picture box controls to add the markers. Can you write logic to detect a win?

Problem 5-2. Number Guess Problem. Build a game where the user guesses a number between 1 and 100. Use a scroll bar for entering the guess and change the extreme limits (**Minimum** and **Maximum** properties) with each guess to help the user adjust their guess.

Problem 5-3. File Times Problem. Using the drive, directory and file list controls, write an application that lists all files in a directory. For every file, find what time the file was created (use the **FileInfo** object from the **System.IO** namespace). Determine the most popular hours of the day for creating files.

Exercise 5

Student Database Input Screen

You did so well with last chapter's assignment that, now, a school wants you to develop the beginning structure of an input screen for its students. The required input information is:

1. Student Name
2. Student Grade (1 through 6)
3. Student Sex (Male or Female)
4. Student Date of Birth (Month, Day, Year)
5. Student Picture (Assume they can be loaded as jpeg files)

Set up the screen so that only the Name needs to be typed; all other inputs should be set with option buttons, scroll bars, and common dialog boxes. When a screen of information is complete, display the summarized profile in a message box. This profile message box should resemble this:

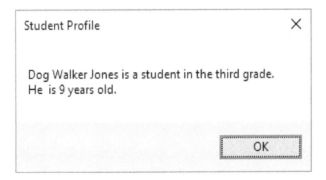

Note the student's age must be computed from the input birth date - watch out for pitfalls in doing the computation. The student's picture does not appear in the profile, only on the input screen.

6. Windows Application Design and Distribution

Review and Preview

We've finished looking at many of the Visual C# controls and have been introduced to most of the C# language features. In this class, we learn how to enhance our application design using tabbed controls, general methods and menus. And, we learn how to distribute the finished product to our user base.

Application Design Considerations

Before beginning the actual process of building your application by drawing the Visual C# interface, setting the control properties, and writing the C# code, many things should be considered to make your application useful. A first consideration should be to determine what processes and functions you want your application to perform. What are the inputs and outputs? Develop a framework or flow chart of all your application's processes.

Decide what controls you need. Do the built-in Visual C# controls and methods meet your needs? Do you need to develop some controls or methods of your own? You can design and build your own controls using Visual C#, but that topic is beyond the scope of this course. The skills gained in this course, however, will be invaluable if you want to tackle such a task.

Design your user interface. What do you want your form to look like? Consider appearance and ease of use. Make the interface consistent with other Windows applications. Familiarity is good in program design.

Write your code. Make your code readable and traceable - future code modifiers (including yourself) will thank you. Consider developing reusable code – classes and objects with utility outside your current development. This will save you time in future developments.

Make your code 'user-friendly.' Make operation of your application obvious to the user. Step the user through its use. Try to anticipate all possible ways a user can mess up in using your application. It's fairly easy to write an application that works properly when the user does everything correctly. It's difficult to write an application that can handle all the possible wrong things a user can do and still not bomb out.

Debug your code completely before distributing it. There's nothing worse than having a user call you to point out flaws in your application. A good way to find all the bugs is to let several people try the code - a mini beta-testing program.

TabControl Control

In Toolbox:

On Form (Default Properties):

The **TabControl** control provides an easy way to present several dialogs or screens of information on a single form. This is the same interface seen in many commercial Windows applications. The tab control provides a group of tabs, each of which acts as a container (works just like a group box or panel) for other controls. In particular, groups of radio buttons within a tab 'page' operate as an independent group. Only one tab can be active at a time. Using this control is easy. Just build each tab container as a separate group: add controls, set properties, and write code like you do for any application. Navigation from one tab to the next is simple: just click on the corresponding tab.

TabControl **Properties:**

Name	Gets or sets the name of the tab control (three letter prefix for control name is **tab**).
BackColor	Get or sets the tab control background color.
BorderStyle	Gets or sets the border style for the tab control.
Font	Gets or sets font name, style, size.
ForeColor	Gets or sets color of text or graphics.
ItemSize	Size structure determining tab size.
SelectedIndex	Gets or sets the currently displayed tab index.
SizeMode	Determines how tabs are sized.
TabPages	Collection describing each tab page.

TabControl **Events:**

> **SelectedIndexChanged**   Occurs when the **SelectedIndex** property changes (**default** event).

The most important property for the tab control is **TabPages**. It is used to design each tab (known as a **TabPage**). Choosing the **TabPages** property in the Properties window and clicking the ellipsis that appears will display the **TabPage Collection Editor**. With this editor, you can add, delete, insert and move tab pages. To add a tab page, click the **Add** button. A name and index will be assigned to a tab. There are two tabs added initially so the editor appears like this:

Add as many tab pages as you like. The tab page 'array' is zero-based; hence, if you have N tabs, the first is index 0, the last index N – 1.

You can change any property you desire in the **Properties** area:

TabPage **Properties**:

Name	Gets or sets the name of the tab page (three letter prefix for control name is **tab**).
BackColor	Get or sets the tab page background color.
BorderStyle	Gets or sets the border style for the tab page.
Font	Gets or sets font name, style, size.
ForeColor	Gets or sets color of text or graphics.
Text	Titling information appearing on tab.

When done, click **OK** to leave the TabPage Collection Editor. Note the properties are in a Categorized (not Alphabetic) view.

The next step is to add controls to each 'page' of the tab control. This is straightforward. Simply display the desired tab page by clicking on the tab. Then place controls on the tab page, treating the page like a group box or panel control. Make sure your controls become 'attached' to the tab page. You can still place controls on the form that are not associated with any tab. As the programmer, you need to know which tab is active (**SelectedIndex** property). And, you need to keep track of which controls are available with each tab page.

Typical use of **TabControl** control:

➢ Set the **Name** property and size appropriately.
➢ Establish each tab page using the **TabPage Collection Editor**.
➢ Add controls to tabs and form.
➢ Write code for the various events associated with controls on the tab control and form.

Example 6-1

Shopping Cart

1. Start a new project. We will build a tab control based application that provides a good start for a simple 'on-line' commerce system. Products will be described by simple objects. One tab will be used to enter a mailing address and add items to a shopping cart. Other tabs will display a mailing label and display the current contents of the shopping cart. We'll build each tab page individually.

2. Add a class to the project named **Product.cs**. Use this code (properties only and a constructor):

```
class Product
{
  public string Description;
  public double Cost;
  public int NumberOrdered;
  public Product(String d, double c)
  {
    this.Description = d;
    this.Cost = c;
  }
}
```

3. Return to the form in the newly started project. Add a tab control to the form. Set these properties:

Form1:
      Name   frmShopping
      FormBorderStyle   FixedSingle
      StartPosition   CenterScreen
      Text   Shopping Cart

tabControl1:
      Name   tabShopping

Your form should look like this:

Order Form:

1. We build the **Order Form** tab first. Using the **Tab Pages** property of the tab control, set these properties for the first tab:

   tabPage1:
Name	tabOrder
Text	Order Form

2. Place two labels, a text box, a domain updown control and three button controls on the tab page so they look something like this:

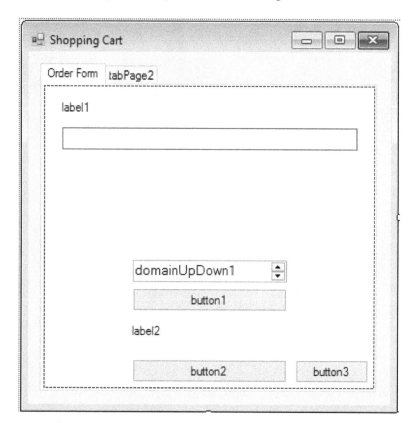

3. Set the properties of controls:

label1:

Font	Bold, Size 10
Text	Order Address

textBox1:

Name	txtOrder
Font Size	10
MultiLine	True
Text	[Blank]

domainUpDown1:

Name	dudOrder
BackColor	Light Yellow
Font Size	10
Text	[Blank]
Wrap	True

label2:

Name	lblOrdered
AutoSize	False
BackColor	White
BorderStyle	Fixed3D
Text	Items Ordered: 0
TextAlign	MiddleCenter

button1:

Name	btnAdd
Text	&Add to Order

button2:

Name	btnNew
Text	&New Order

button3:

Name	btnExit
Text	E&xit

This first tab page should look something like this when you're done:

We'll now add code for this tab page.

4. Form level scope variable declarations:

```
int itemsOrdered;
// we have ten products in a zero-based array
const int numberProducts = 10;
Product[] myProduct = new Product[numberProducts];
```

5. Use this code in **frmShopping Load** method:

```
private void FrmShopping_Load(object sender, EventArgs e)
{
  // define products and cost
  myProduct[0] = new Product("Tricycle",  50);
  myProduct[1] = new Product("Skateboard", 60);
  myProduct[2] = new Product("In-Line Skates", 100);
  myProduct[3] = new Product("Magic Set", 15);
  myProduct[4] = new Product("Video Game", 45);
  myProduct[5] = new Product("Helmet", 25);
  myProduct[6] = new Product("Building Kit", 35);
  myProduct[7] = new Product("Artist Set", 40);
  myProduct[8] = new Product("Doll Baby", 25);
  myProduct[9] = new Product("Bicycle", 150);
  for (int i = 0; i < numberProducts; i++)
  {
     dudOrder.Items.Add(myProduct[i].Description);
  }
  dudOrder.SelectedIndex = 0;
}
```

This code initializes the available products.

6. Use this code in the **btnAdd Click** method:

```
private void BtnAdd_Click(object sender, EventArgs e)
{
  // increment selected product by one
  // products are base 0 array
  myProduct[dudOrder.SelectedIndex].NumberOrdered++;
  itemsOrdered++;
  lblOrdered.Text = "Items Ordered: " +
itemsOrdered.ToString();
}
```

This code adds a selected item to the shopping cart.

7. Use this code in the **btnNew Click** method:

```
private void BtnNew_Click(object sender, EventArgs e)
{
  // clear form
  txtOrder.Text = "";
  itemsOrdered = 0;
  lblOrdered.Text = "Items Ordered: 0";
  for (int i = 0; i < numberProducts; i++)
  {
    myProduct[i].NumberOrdered = 0;
  }
  dudOrder.SelectedIndex = 0;
  lstProducts.Items.Clear();
  lblCost.Text = "Total Cost";
  txtLabel.Text = "";
}
```

This code clears the form for a new order.

8. Use this code in the **BtnExit Click** method which stops the application:

```
private void btnExit_Click(object sender, EventArgs e)
{
  this.Close();
}
```

9. Save your work (saved in **Example 6-1** folder in the **LearnVCS\VCS Code\Class 6** folder). Try running the incomplete application to eliminate any errors that may be there. Try out the controls.

Shopping Cart:

1. We now build the tab page that will display the **Shopping Cart**. Using the **Tab Pages** property of the tab control, set these properties for the second tab:

   tabPage2:
Name	tabCart
Text	Shopping Cart

Add a list box control and a label control. The tab page should look like this:

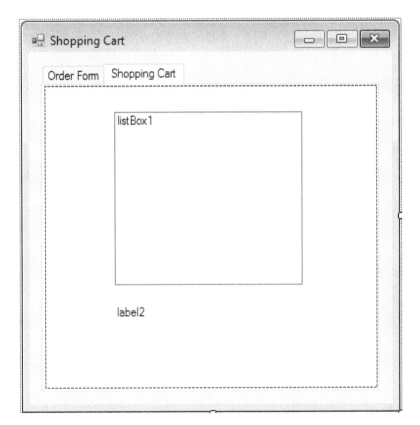

2. Set the properties of the controls:

listBox1:

Name	lstProducts
Items	[Blank]
Font Size	10

label2:

Name	lblCost
AutoSize	False
BackColor	Light Yellow
BorderStyle	Fixed3D
Font	Bold, Size 10
Text	Total Cost
TextAlign	MiddleLeft

When done, this is my second tab page:

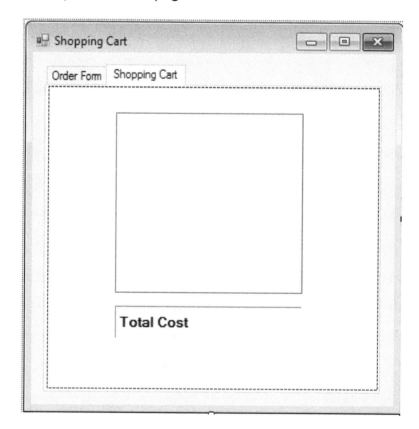

3. When the Shopping Cart tab is clicked, we want to display the ordered items. Use this code in the **tabShopping SelectedIndexChanged** method:

```csharp
private void TabShopping_SelectedIndexChanged(object
sender, EventArgs e)
{
  switch (tabShopping.SelectedIndex)
  {
    case 1:
      // shopping cart tab
      if (itemsOrdered == 0)
      {
        MessageBox.Show("No items have been ordered.",
"Error", MessageBoxButtons.OK, MessageBoxIcon.Error);
        tabShopping.SelectedIndex = 0;
      }
      else
      {
        double totalCost;
        // load in ordered items
        totalCost = 0;
        lstProducts.Items.Clear();
        for (int i = 0; i < numberProducts; i++)
        {
          if (myProduct[i].NumberOrdered != 0)
          {

lstProducts.Items.Add(myProduct[i].NumberOrdered.ToString(
) + " " + myProduct[i].Description);
            totalCost += myProduct[i].NumberOrdered *
myProduct[i].Cost;
          }
        }
        lblCost.Text = "Total Cost: $" +
String.Format("{0:f2}", totalCost);
      }
      break;
  }
}
```

This code brings up the window that displays the shopping cart (if any items have been ordered.

Mailing Label:

1. Last, we build the tab page that will display the **Mailing Label**. Using the **Tab Pages** property of the tab control, establish a third tab page with these properties:

    tabPage3:
Name	tabLabel
Text	Mailing Label

2. Add a text box control to the tab page. Set these properties:

    textBox1:
Name	txtLabel
Font Size	10
MultiLine	True
Text	[Blank]

When done, this is my third tab page:

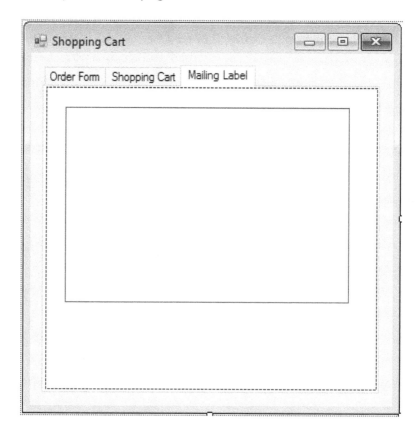

3. When the Mailing Label tab is clicked, we want to display the label. Add the shaded code to the **tabShopping SelectedIndexChanged** method:

```
private void TabShopping_SelectedIndexChanged(object
sender, EventArgs e)
{
   switch (tabShopping.SelectedIndex)
   {
     case 1:
       // shopping cart tab
       if (itemsOrdered == 0)
       {
         MessageBox.Show("No items have been ordered.",
"Error", MessageBoxButtons.OK, MessageBoxIcon.Error);
         tabShopping.SelectedIndex = 0;
       }
       else
       {
         double totalCost;
         // load in ordered items
         totalCost = 0;
         lstProducts.Items.Clear();
         for (int i = 0; i < numberProducts; i++)
         {
           if (myProduct[i].NumberOrdered != 0)
           {

lstProducts.Items.Add(myProduct[i].NumberOrdered.ToString(
) + " " + myProduct[i].Description);
             totalCost += myProduct[i].NumberOrdered *
myProduct[i].Cost;
           }
         }
         lblCost.Text = "Total Cost: $" +
String.Format("{0:f2}", totalCost);
       }
       break;
     case 2:
       // mailing label tab
       if (txtOrder.Text == "")
       {
         MessageBox.Show("Address is blank.", "Error",
MessageBoxButtons.OK, MessageBoxIcon.Error);
         tabShopping.SelectedIndex = 0;
         txtOrder.Focus();
       }
       else
```

```
        {
        string address = txtOrder.Text;
        string lf = "\r\n";
        // form label
        txtLabel.Text = "My Company" + lf + "My Address" +
lf + "My City, State, Zip" + lf + lf + lf;
        txtLabel.Text += address;
        txtLabel.SelectionLength = 0;
        }
    break;
  }
}
```

Completed Application

The application is, at long last, complete. Run it. Notice how the shopping cart works and how the different tabs work together. Here's a run I made, first entering an order:

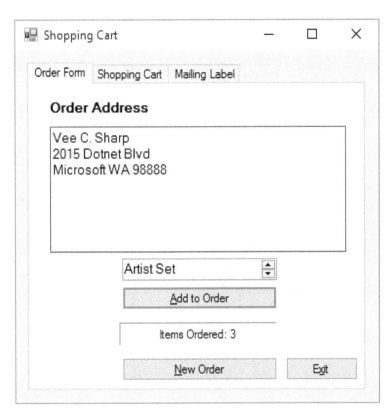

With such an order, the shopping cart appears as (click **Shopping Cart** tab):

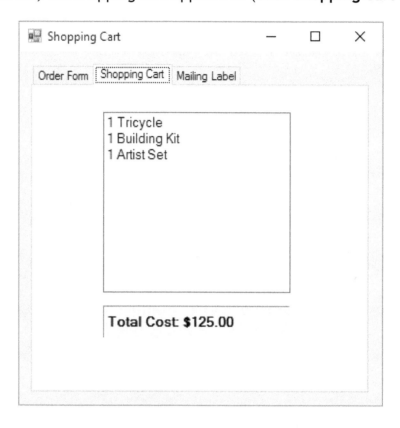

And, the mailing label is (click **Mailing Label** tab):

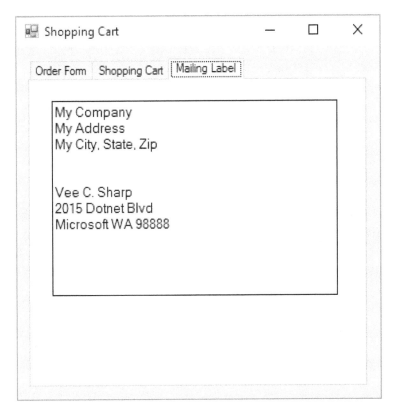

As mentioned, this is a start to an e-commerce type system. If you're interested in such projects, you can expand this to meet your needs. Save the project (saved in **Example 6-1** folder in the **LearnVCS\VCS Code\Class 6** folder).

Using General Methods in Applications

So far in this class, with few exceptions, the only methods we have studied are the event methods associated with the various controls. Most applications have tasks not related to controls that require some code to perform these tasks. Such tasks are usually coded in a general **method** (essentially the same as a function in other languages). A method performs a specific task, returning some value.

Using general methods can help divide a complex application into more manageable units of code. This helps meet the earlier stated goals of readability and reusability. As you build applications, it will be obvious where such a method is needed. Look for areas in your application where code is repeated in different places. It would be best (shorter code and easier maintenance) to put this repeated code in a method. And, look for places in your application where you want to do some long, detailed task - this is another great use for a general method. It makes your code much easier to follow.

The form for a general method named **MyMethod** is:

```
public type MyMethod(arguments) // definition header
{
  [Method code]
  return(returnedValue);
}
```

The definition header names the **method**, specifies its **type** (the type of the returned value - if no value is returned, use the keyword **void**) and defines any input **arguments** passed to the method. The keyword **public** indicates the method can be called from anywhere in the project. If this is replaced by **private**, the method will have form level scope.

Arguments are a comma-delimited list of variables passed to the method. If there are arguments, we need to take care in how they are declared in the header statement. In particular, we need to be concerned with:

> Number of arguments
> Order of arguments
> Type of arguments

We will address each point separately.

The **number** of arguments is dictated by how many variables the method needs to do its job. You need a variable for each piece of input information. You then place these variables in a particular **order** for the argument list.

Each variable in the argument list will be a particular **data type**. This must be known for each variable. In Visual C#, all variables are passed by value, meaning their value cannot be changed in the method. Variables are declared in the argument list using standard notation:

```
type variableName
```

The variable name (variableName) is treated as a local variable in the method.

Arrays can also be used as input arguments. To declare an array as an argument, use:

```
type[] arrayName
```

The brackets indicate an array is being passed.

To use a general method, simply refer to it, by name, in code (with appropriate arguments). Wherever it is used, it will be replaced by the computed value. A function can be used to return a value:

```
rtnValue = MyMethod(arguments);
```

or in an expression:

```
thisNumber = 7 * MyMethod(arguments) / anotherNumber;
```

Let's build a quick example that converts Fahrenheit temperatures to Celsius (remember the example in Class 4?) Here's such a function:

```
public double DegFTodegC(double tempF)
{
   double tempC;
   tempC = (tempF - 32) * 5 / 9;
   return(tempC);
}
```

The method is named **DegFTodegC**. It has a single argument, **tempF**, of type **double**. It returns a **double** data type. This code segment converts 45.7 degrees Fahrenheit to the corresponding Celsius value:

```
double t;
   .

   .

t = DegFTodegC(45.7);
```

After this, **t** will have a value of **7.61 degrees** C.

To put a general method in a Visual C# application, simply type it among the event methods associated with controls. I usually put general methods below the last event method. Just make sure it is <u>before</u> the final closing brace for the Visual C# class defining the project. Type the header, the opening left brace, the code and the closing right brace.

Example 6-2

Average Value

1. Start a new project. This will be an application where a user inputs a list of numbers. Once complete, the average value of the input numbers is computed using a general method. This example illustrates the use of arrays in argument lists.

2. On the form, add a label, two text boxes, three button controls and a listbox control. Make your form look similar to this:

3. Set the properties of the form and controls:

Form1:

Name	frmAverage
FormBorderStyle	FixedSingle
StartPosition	CenterForm
Text	Average Value

label1:

Text	Enter Number

textBox1:

Name	txtValue
Text	[Blank]

textBox2:

Name	txtAverage
BackColor	White
ReadOnly	True
Text	[Blank]
TextAlign	Center

listBox1:

Name	lstValue

button1:

Name	btnAccept
Text	Add to &List

button2:

Name	btnClear
Text	&Clear List

button3:

Name	btnCompute
Text	Compute &Average

The finished form appears as:

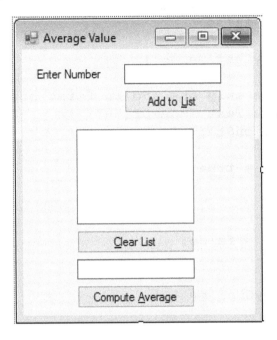

4. Here is the code for a method that computes an average. The numbers it averages are in the 0-based array **values**. There are **numberValues** elements in the array:

```
public double Average(int numberValues, double[] values)
{
  // find average
  double sum = 0.0;
   for (int i = 0; i < numberValues; i++)
   {
     sum += values[i];
  }
  return(sum / numberValues);
}
```

Type this after the form constructor. Notice how the array (values) is passed into the method.

5. Use this code in the **txtValue KeyPress** event for key trapping:

```
private void TxtValue_KeyPress(object sender,
KeyPressEventArgs e)
{
  // only allow numbers, a single decimal point, negative
sign, backspace  or enter
  if ((e.KeyChar >= '0' && e.KeyChar <= '9') || (int)
e.KeyChar == 8)
```

```
  {
    // number or backspace
    e.Handled = false;
  }
  else if (e.KeyChar == '-')
  {
    // make sure only one and in first position
    if (txtValue.Text.IndexOf("-") != -1 ||
txtValue.SelectionStart != 0)
    {
      e.Handled = true;
    }
    else
    {
      e.Handled = false;
    }
  }
  else if (e.KeyChar == '.')
  {
    // allow only one
    if (txtValue.Text.IndexOf(".") == -1)
    {
      e.Handled = false;
    }
    else
    {
      e.Handled = true;
    }
  }
  else if ((int) e.KeyChar == 13)
  {
    // enter key - click on accept button
    btnAccept.PerformClick();
    e.Handled = false;
  }
  else
  {
    e.Handled = true;
  }
}
```

6. Use this code in the **btnClear Click** event - it clears the list box for another average:

```
private void BtnClear_Click(object sender, EventArgs e)
{
  // resets form for another average
  lstValue.Items.Clear();
  txtAverage.Text = "";
  txtValue.Text = "";
  txtValue.Focus();
}
```

7. Use this code for the **btnAccept Click** event:

```
private void BtnAccept_Click(object sender, EventArgs e)
{
  // accept typed value unless it is a blank
  if (txtValue.Text == "")
  {
    return;
  }
  if (lstValue.Items.Count == 100)
  {
    MessageBox.Show("Maximum of 100 items has been
reached.", "Error", MessageBoxButtons.OK,
MessageBoxIcon.Error);
    return;
  }
  lstValue.Items.Add(txtValue.Text);
  txtValue.Text = "";
  txtValue.Focus();
}
```

This adds the value to the list box.

8. Use this code for the **btnCompute Click** event:

```
private void BtnCompute_Click(object sender, EventArgs e)
{
  double[] myValues = new Double[100];
  double myAverage;
  if (lstValue.Items.Count != 0)
  {
    // load values in array and compute average
    for (int i = 0; i < lstValue.Items.Count; i++)
    {
      myValues[i] = Convert.ToDouble(lstValue.Items[i]);
    }
    myAverage = Average(lstValue.Items.Count, myValues);
    txtAverage.Text = String.Format("{0:f2}", myAverage);
  }
  txtValue.Focus();
}
```

This takes the values from the list box and finds the average value.

9. Save the application (saved in **Example 6-2** folder in **LearnVCS\VCS Code\Class 6** folder). Run the application and try different values. This averaging function might come in handy for some task you may have. Here's a run I made averaging the first 10 integers:

Returning Multiple Values from General Methods

You may have noticed a general method can only return a single value (or no value). What if you need to **compute** and **return multiple values**? Can a method still be used? There are two possible approaches to this situation, depending on the types of information being returned.

If the returned values are of different types, you would need to add form level variables for all additional computed values. Then, these values would be available where needed in the project. This works, but is not ideal since it tends to destroy the "portability" of a method. This portability is destroyed because you need to make sure users of your method know what the form level variables are and make sure they include the needed declarations in their project.

If the returned values are all of the same type, there is a better solution that maintains the portability of methods. In this situation, simply return an array of output values. With such an approach, no form level variables are needed and the users don't need to add any extra declarations. They just need to use the method.

An example of this second approach should make things clearer. Assume you are a carpet layer and always need the perimeter and area for a rectangle. We'll build a method that helps you with the computations. We need, for inputs, the length and width of the rectangle. The output information will be an array with the perimeter and area. Here is the method that does the job:

```
public double[] RectangleInfo(double length, double width)
{
  double[] info = new double[2];
  info[0] = 2 * (length + width); // perimeter
  info[1] = length * width; // area
  return(info);
}
```

The method is named **RectangleInfo**. It has two arguments, both of type **double**. The two arguments are **length** and **width**. Notice how the computed perimeter and area are placed in the **info** array returned by the method. Make sure the type in the header statement indicates an array is returned (**double[]** in this case).

This code segment will call our method:

```
double l;
double w;
double[] carpet = new double[2];
       .
       .
       .
l = 6.2;
w = 2.3;
carpet = RectangleInfo(l, w);
```

Once this code is executed, the variable **carpet[0]** will have the perimeter of a rectangle of length 6.2 and width 2.3 (17.0). The variable **carpet[1]** will have the area of the same rectangle (14.26). Notice there is no reason for the variables in the calling argument sequence to have the same names assigned in the method declaration. The location of each variable in the calling sequence defines which variable is which (that's why order of arguments is important).

Example 6-3

Circle Geometry

1. Start a new project. This will be a simple application that illustrates use of a method that returns an array. The method will compute the area and circumference of a circle, given its diameter.

2. Return to the application form and add three labels, three text boxes and a button control. Make your form look similar to this:

3. Set the properties of the form and controls:

Form1:

Name	frmCircle
FormBorderStyle	FixedSingle
StartPosition	CenterForm
Text	Circle Geometry

label1:

Text	Enter Diameter

label2:

Text	Computed Circumference

label3:

Text	Computed Area

textBox1:

Name	txtDiameter
Text	[Blank]

textBox2:

Name	txtCircumference
BackColor	Light Yellow
ReadOnly	True
Text	[Blank]
TextAlign	Center

textBox3:

Name	txtArea
BackColor	Light Yellow
ReadOnly	True
Text	[Blank]
TextAlign	Center

button1:

Name	btnCompute
Text	&Compute

The finished form appears as:

4. Add a general method (**CircleGeometry**) that computes the circumference and area of a circle:

```
public double[] CircleGeometry(double diameter)
{
   double [] geometry = new double[2];
   geometry[0] = Math.PI * diameter; // circumference
   geometry[1] = Math.PI * diameter * diameter / 4; // area
   return(geometry);
}
```

Notice the variable **diameter** is input and an array (**geometry**) contains the outputs. **geometry[0]** holds the circumference and **geometry[1]** holds the area.

5. Use this code in the **txtDiameter KeyPress** event for key trapping:

```csharp
private void TxtDiameter_KeyPress(object sender,
KeyPressEventArgs e)
{
  // only allow numbers, a single decimal point, negative
sign, backspace  or enter
  if ((e.KeyChar >= '0' && e.KeyChar <= '9') || (int)
e.KeyChar == 8)
  {
    // number or backspace
    e.Handled = false;
  }
  else if (e.KeyChar == '.')
  {
    // allow only one
    if (txtDiameter.Text.IndexOf(".") == -1)
    {
      e.Handled = false;
    }
    else
    {
      e.Handled = true;
    }
  }
  else if ((int) e.KeyChar == 13)
  {
    // enter key - click on compute button
    btnCompute.PerformClick();
    e.Handled = false;
  }
  else
  {
    e.Handled = true;
  }
}
```

6. Use this code in the **btnCompute Click** to compute the values using the general method in the code module:

```
private void BtnCompute_Click(object sender, EventArgs e)
{
  // check for valid number
  if (txtDiameter.Text == "")
  {
    return;
  }
  double[] info = new double[2];
  double d = Convert.ToDouble(txtDiameter.Text);
  info = CircleGeometry(d);
  txtCircumference.Text = String.Format("{0:f2}",
info[0]);
  txtArea.Text = String.Format("{0:f2}", info[1]);
}
```

7. Save the application (saved in **Example 6-3** folder in **LearnVCS\VCS Code\Class 6** folder). Run the application and try some different diameters. Here's my try:

MenuStrip Control

In Toolbox:

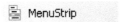

Below Form (Default Properties):

As the applications you build become more and more detailed, with more features for the user, you will need some way to organize those features. A **menu** provides such organization. Menus are a part of most applications. They provide ways to navigate within an application and access desired features. Menus are easily incorporated into Visual C# programs using the **MenuStrip Control**.

The **MenuStrip** control has many features. It provides a quick and easy way to add menus, menu items and submenu elements to your Visual C# application. And it also has an editor to make any changes, deletions or additions you need. Modifications to the menu structure are also possible at run-time.

A good way to think about elements of a menu structure is to consider them as a hierarchical list of button-type controls that only appear when pulled down from the menu. Each element in the menu structure is an object of type **ToolStripMenuItem**. When you click on a menu item, some action is taken. Like buttons, menu items are named, have properties and a **Click** event. The best way to learn to use the MenuStrip control is to build an example menu. The menu structure we will build is:

File	Edit	Format
New	Cut	Bold
Open	Copy	Italic
Save	Paste	Underline
————		Size
Exit		10
		15
		20

The underscored characters in this structure are access keys, just like those on button controls. The level of indentation indicates position of a menu item within the hierarchy. For example, **New** is a sub-element of the **File** menu. The line under **Save** in the **File** menu is a separator bar (separates menu items).

With this structure, at run-time, the menu would display:

<u>F</u>ile   **<u>E</u>dit**   **F<u>o</u>rmat**

The sub-menus appear when one of these 'top' level menu items is selected. Note the **Size** sub-menu under **Format** has another level of hierarchy. It is good practice to not use more than two levels in menus. Each menu element will have a **Click** event associated with it.

When designing your menus, follow formats used by standard Windows applications. For example, if your application works with files, the first heading should be **File** and the last element in the sub-menu under **File** should be **Exit**. If your application uses editing features (cutting, pasting, copying), there should be an **Edit** heading. Use the same access and shortcut keys (keys that let you immediately invoke the menu item without navigating the menu structure) you see in other applications. By doing this, you insure your user will be comfortable with your application. Of course, there will be times your application has unique features that do not fit a 'standard' menu item. In such cases, choose headings that accurately describe such unique features.

We're ready to use the **MenuStrip** control. For this little example, we'll start a new project with a blank form. Drag the **MenuStrip** control to the form. The control will be placed in the 'tray' area below the form. Set a single property for the menu control – **Name** it **mnuMain**. Click on the form and make sure its **MainMenuStrip** property now reads **mnuMain**. If it doesn't, make the change. This property sets which MenuStrip control is used by the form to establish its menu structure.

Now, select the menu control (make it the active control) and your form will display the first menu element:

In the displayed box, type the first main heading (**&File** in this case). This establishes the first property (**Text**) for the menu element. Once done typing this heading, you can move to the properties window and set any other properties. What I usually do, though, is type all the **Text** properties, building the menu structure. Then, I return to each item and assign properties. You choose which method you like best: set properties as you go or build structure, then set properties. We'll talk more about properties after building the menu structure.

After typing the first heading, the form will look like this:

At this point, the menu control will let you type either the first sub-menu heading under the File heading or move to the next heading. If you press **<Enter>** after typing an entry, the cursor will stay within the menu structure (go to a sub-heading).

Type the first sub-menu heading of **&New**:

The menu control suggests locations for the next heading.

I think you see how the MenuStrip control works. It's really easy. Just type headings (**Text** properties) where they belong in the menu hierarchy. At any time, you can click on an "already entered" value to change it. Or, a right-click on any element allows adding or deleting elements. Once you've built a few menu structures, you will see how easy and intuitive this control is to use. The best hint I can give is just click where you want to type and magical boxes will appear. Click on the form or any other control to stop menu editing.

Separator bars are used in menu structures to delineate like groups of menu items. There are two ways to enter a 'separator bar' in a menu. First, you can simply type a **Text** property of a single hyphen (-). Or, right-click on the element below the desired separator bar location and choose **Insert Separator**.

After typing the remaining elements of our example menu (with just the captions), the form will look like this:

Our menu framework is built, but we must still set properties. Each element in the menu structure has several properties that must be established:

Property	Description
Name	Each menu item must have a name, even separator bars! The prefix **mnu** is used to name menu items. Sub-menu item names usually refer back to main menu headings. For example, if the menu item **New** is under the main heading **File** (name **mnuFile**) menu, use the name **mnuFileNew**
Checked	If True, a check mark appears next to the menu item.
Enabled	If True, the menu item can be selected. If False, the menu item is grayed and cannot be selected.
Shortcut	Used to assign shortcut keystrokes to any item in a menu structure. The shortcut keystroke will appear to the right of the menu item.
Text	Caption appearing on menu item, including assignment of any access keys (these captions are what the user sees).
Visible	Controls whether the menu item appears in the structure.

We've set the **Text** properties already. At this point, you need to go back and select each menu item and set desired properties. To do this, make the appropriate menu item active by clicking on it. Once active, move to the properties window (I press <F4>) and assign whatever properties you want. Do this for each menu item. Yes, I realize there's a lot to do, but then a menu structure does a lot for your application.

For our example menu structure, I used these properties:

Text	Name	Shortcut
&File	mnuFile	None
&New	mnuFileNew	None
&Open	mnuFileOpen	None
&Save	mnuFileSave	None
-	mnuFileBar	None
E&xit	mnuFileExit	None
&Edit	mnuEdit	None
Cu&t	mnuEditCut	CtrlX
&Copy	mnuEditCopy	CtrlC
&Paste	mnuEditPaste	CtrlV
F&ormat	mnuFmt	None
&Bold	mnuFmtBold	CtrlB
&Italic	mnuFmtItalic	CtrlI
&Underline	mnuFmtUnderline	CtrlU
&Size	mnuFmtSize	None
&10	mnuFmtSize10	None
1&5	mnuFmtSize15	None
&20	mnuFmtSize20	None

In particular, notice how the naming convention makes it easy to identify the purpose of each menu item. Notice, too, we have to name the separator bar. And, open the menu structure to see how the shortcut keys are listed.

I also assigned a **Checked** property of **True** to the **10** element under the **Size** sub-menu. This indicates the size of the default font in the application using this structure. Be aware you need to control when this checkmark appears and disappears. It does not work like the check in the check box control. That is, it will not automatically appear when a menu item is clicked.

You might think we're finally done, but we're not. We still need to write code for each menu item's **Click** event (the **default** event). Yes, even more work is needed. The Click event method for a menu item is found in the same manner any other event method is located. Select the menu item in the properties window, click the **Events** button, and double-click the listed Click event. The event framework will appear and code can be entered. Alternately, double-click the desired menu item and the event method will appear.

ContextMenuStrip Control

In Toolbox:

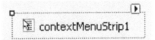

Below Form (Default Properties):

contextMenuStrip1

There is another type of menu you can add to an application – a context menu. This is a menu that appears when you right-click a control. It lets you customize features for a particular control. Perhaps, you want to allow a user to change a color or font. The **ContextMenuStrip** control makes it easy to add such menus to any control. There are two simple steps: design the menu and assign it to the control.

For each context menu you need, you add a ContextMenuStrip control to your application and set the **Name** property. The context menu control appears in the tray area below the form since there is no user interface. The menu is then designed using exactly the same steps followed for the main menu control. Select the ContextMenuStrip control and the structure will appear on the form. Fill in the desired headings. The difference here is that you are only designing a single menu listing (with sub-headings).

Once your menu is designed, assigning **Name** (still use **mnu** prefix), **Text**, **Checked** and other properties, and writing code for the **Click** events, you assign it to the control by setting the control's **ContextMenuStrip** property. Run the application, right-click the control and the menu appears. It's that simple! Be aware that some controls (for example, the text box) have default context menus. Setting the ContextMenuStrip property for such a control will override the default menu with your custom menu.

Font Object

Each Visual C# control with a **Text** property (or some other 'text-related' property) also has a **Font** property, allowing us to select how the text will appear. Changing the font at design time is a simple task. You simply click **Font** in the properties window and click the ellipsis (...) that appears. A **Font** dialog box appears allowing you to make selections determining font name, font style (bold, italic, underline) and font size.

With the introduction of menus to an application, we might want to let our user change the font for a particular control at run-time. To do this, we introduce the idea of the **Font** object. The font object (part of the **Drawing** namespace) is simply the structure used by Visual C# to define all characteristics of a particular font (name, size, effects).

To change a font at run-time, we assign the **Font** property of the corresponding control to a **new** instance of a Font object using the **Font** constructor. The syntax is:

    controlName.**Font** = **new Font**(FontName, FontSize, FontStyle);

In this line of code, **FontName** is a string variable defining the name of the font and **FontSize** is an integer value defining the font size in points. These are the same values you choose using the Font dialog at design-time.

The **FontStyle** argument is a Visual C# constant defining the style of the font. It has five possible values:

Value	Description
Regular	Regular text
Bold	Bold text
Italic	Italic text
Strikeout	Text with a line through the middle
Underline	Underlined text

The basic (no effects) font is defined by **FontStyle.Regular**. To add any effects, use the corresponding constant. If the font has more than one effect, combine them using a 'bitwise' Or operator (|). For example, if you want an underlined, bold font, the **FontStyle** argument in the Font constructor would be:

```
FontStyle.Underline | FontStyle.Bold
```

Let's look at a couple of examples. To change a button control (**btnExample**) font to Arial, Bold, Size 24, use:

```
btnExample.Font = new Font("Arial", 24, FontStyle.Bold);
```

or, to change the font in a text box (**txtExample**) to Courier New, Italic, Underline, Size 12, use:

```
txtExample.Font = new Font("Courier New", 12,
FontStyle.Italic | FontStyle.Underline);
```

You can also define a variable to be of type **Font**. Declare the variable according to the usual scope considerations. Then, assign a font to that variable for use in other controls:

```
Font myFont;
   .
   .
myFont = new Font("Courier New", 12, FontStyle.Regular);
thisControl.Font = myFont;
thatControl.Font = myFont;
```

When you declare and create an object, you should dispose of the object when you are done with it. This conserves system resources. To dispose of the font object created above, use its **Dispose** method:

```
myFont.Dispose();
```

FontDialog Control

In Toolbox:

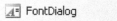

Below Form (Default Properties):

Remember the Font dialog box that appears when you set a control Font property at design-time? That same dialog box is available for use in your Visual C# applications whenever you want to allow the user to change fonts. The **FontDialog** control provides display of the Font dialog box, allowing the user to choose font and font color.

FontDialog **Properties:**

Name	Gets or sets the name of the font dialog (I usually name this control **dlgFont**).
Color	Indicates selected font color.
Font	Indicates selected font.
MaxSize	Maximum font size (in points) user can select.
MinSize	Maximum font size (in points) user can select.
ShowColor	Indicates whether dialog box displays Color choice (default value is False).
ShowEffects	Indicates where the dialog box allows the user to specify strikethrough and underline.

FontDialog **Methods:**

ShowDialog	Displays the dialog box. Returned value indicates which button was clicked by user (**OK** or **Cancel**).

To use the **FontDialog** control, we add it to our application the same as any control. It will appear in the tray below the form. Once added, we set a few properties. Then, we write code to make the dialog box appear when desired. The user then makes selections and closes the dialog box. At this point, we use the provided information for our tasks.

The **ShowDialog** method is used to display the **FontDialog** control. For a control named **dlgFont**, the appropriate code is:

```
dlgFont.ShowDialog();
```

And the displayed dialog box is:

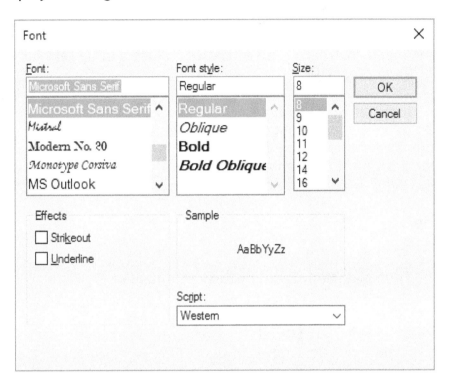

The user selects a font by making relevant choices. Once complete, the **OK** button is clicked. At this point, the **Font** property is available for use (as is **Color**, if available). **Cancel** can be clicked to cancel the font change. The ShowDialog method returns the clicked button. It returns **DialogResult.OK** if OK is clicked and returns **DialogResult.Cancel** if Cancel is clicked.

Typical use of **FontDialog** control:

> ➤ Set the **Name** property. Decide if **Color** should be a choice.
> ➤ Use **ShowDialog** method to display dialog box.
> ➤ Use **Font** property (and perhaps **Color**) to change control **Font** (and perhaps **ForeColor**) property.

Example 6-4

Note Editor

1. Start a new project. We will use this application the rest of this class. We will build a note editor with a menu structure that allows us to control the appearance of the text in the editor box.

2. Add a main menu control to the application. Place a large text box on a form. Set these properties:

Form1:
Name	frmEdit
FormBorderStyle	FixedSingle
StartPosition	CenterForm
Text	Note Editor

menuStrip1:
Name	mnuMain

Make sure the Form **MainMenuStrip** property is **mnuMain**.

text1:
Name	txtEdit
MultiLine	True
ScrollBars	Vertical
Text	[Blank]

The form should look something like this with controls (no menu yet):

Other controls in tray:

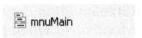

3. We want to add this menu structure to the Note Editor:

File   Format
    New   Bold
    ─────   Italic
    Exit   Underline
                      Size
                          Small
                          Medium
                          Large

Note the identified access keys. Use the MenuStrip control to enter this
structure and the following Text, Name, and Shortcut properties for each item:

Text	Name	Shortcut
&File	mnuFile	[None]
&New	mnuFileNew	[None]
-	mnuFileBar	[None]
E&xit	mnuFileExit	[None]
F&ormat	mnuFmt	[None]
& Bold	mnuFmt Bold	CtrlB
&Italic	mnuFmtItalic	CtrlI
&Underline	mnuFmtUnderline	CtrlU
&Size	mnuFmtSize	[None]
&Small	mnuFmtSizeSmall	CtrlS
&Medium	mnuFmtSizeMedium	CtrlM
&Large	mnuFmtSizeLarge	CtrlL

The **Checked** property of the **Small** item (Name **mnuFmtSizeSmall**) under the
Size sub-menu should also be **True** to indicate the initial font size. When done,
look through your menu structure in design mode to make sure it looks correct.
With a menu, the form will appear like:

4. Declare a variable and a constant with form level scope:

```
int fontSize = 8;
string fontName = "MS Sans Serif";
```

5. Add a general method called **ChangeFont**, with no arguments. This generates the **Font** object for the text box based on user menu choices:

```
public void ChangeFont()
{
  // Put together font based on menu selections
  FontStyle newFont;
  newFont = FontStyle.Regular;
  if (mnuFmtBold.Checked)
  {
    newFont = newFont | FontStyle.Bold;
  }
  if (mnuFmtItalic.Checked)
  {
    newFont = newFont | FontStyle.Italic;
  }
  if (mnuFmtUnderline.Checked)
  {
    newFont = newFont | FontStyle.Underline;
  }
  txtEdit.Font = new Font(fontName, fontSize, newFont);
}
```

6. Each menu item that performs an action requires code for its **Click** event. The only menu items that do <u>not</u> have events are the menu and sub-menu headings, namely File, Format, and Size. All others need code. Use the following code for each menu item **Click** event. (This may look like a lot of typing, but you should be able to use a lot of cut and paste.)

If **mnuFileNew** is clicked, the program checks to see if the user really wants a new file and, if so (the default response), clears out the text box:

```
private void MnuFileNew_Click(object sender, EventArgs e)
{
  // If user wants new file, clear out text
  if (MessageBox.Show("Are you sure you want to start a
new file?", "New File", MessageBoxButtons.YesNo,
MessageBoxIcon.Question) == DialogResult.Yes)
  {
    txtEdit.Text = "";
  }
}
```

If **mnuFileExit** is clicked, the program checks to see if the user really wants to exit. If not (the default response), the user is returned to the program:

```
private void MnuFileExit_Click(object sender, EventArgs e)
{
  // Make sure user really wants to exit
  if (MessageBox.Show("Are you sure you want to exit the
note editor?", "Exit Editor", MessageBoxButtons.YesNo,
MessageBoxIcon.Question, MessageBoxDefaultButton.Button2)
== DialogResult.No)
  {
    return;
  }
  else
  {
    this.Close();
  }
}
```

If **mnuFmtBold** is clicked, the program toggles the current bold status:

```
private void MnuFmtBold_Click(object sender, EventArgs e)
{
  // Toggle bold font status
  mnuFmtBold.Checked = !mnuFmtBold.Checked;
  ChangeFont();
}
```

If **mnuFmtItalic** is clicked, the program toggles the current italic status:

```
private void MnuFmtItalic_Click(object sender, EventArgs
e)
{
  // Toggle italic font status
  mnuFmtItalic.Checked = !mnuFmtItalic.Checked;
  ChangeFont();
}
```

If **mnuFmtUnderline** is clicked, the program toggles the current underline status:

```
private void MnuFmtUnderline_Click(object sender,
EventArgs e)
{
  // Toggle underline font status
  mnuFmtUnderline.Checked = !mnuFmtUnderline.Checked;
  ChangeFont();
}
```

If either of the three size sub-menus is clicked (we use one method for all three Click events), indicate the appropriate check mark location and change the font size:

```csharp
private void MnuSize_Click(object sender, EventArgs e)
{
  //determine which size was clicked
  string sizeClick = ((ToolStripMenuItem) sender).Text;
  mnuFmtSizeSmall.Checked = false;
  mnuFmtSizeMedium.Checked = false;
  mnuFmtSizeLarge.Checked = false;
  switch (sizeClick)
  {
    case "&Small":
      fontSize = 8;
      mnuFmtSizeSmall.Checked = true;
      break;
    case "&Medium":
      fontSize = 12;
      mnuFmtSizeMedium.Checked = true;
      break;
    case "&Large":
      fontSize = 18;
      mnuFmtSizeLarge.Checked = true;
      break;
  }
  ChangeFont();
}
```

7. Save your application (saved in **Example 6-4** folder in **LearnVCS\VN Code\Class 6** folder). We will use it again in Class 7 where we'll learn how to save and open text files created with the Note Editor. Test out all the options. Notice how the toggling of the check marks works. Try the shortcut keys. Here's some text I wrote – note the appearance of the scroll bar since the text exceeds the size allotted to the text box:

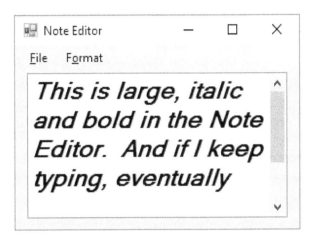

Notice whatever formatting is selected is applied to all text in the control. You cannot selectively format text in a text box control. In Class 10, we look at another control, the rich text control that does allow selective formatting.

Distribution of a Visual C# Windows Application

I bet you're ready to show your friends and colleagues some of the applications you have built using Visual C#. Just give them a copy of all your project files, ask them to buy and install Visual C# and learn how to open and run a project. Then, have them open your project and run the application. I think you'll agree this is asking a lot of your friends, colleagues, and, ultimately, your user base. We need to know how to run an application **without** Visual C#.

To run an application without Visual C#, you need to create an **executable** version of the application. So, how is an executable created? A little secret ... Visual C# builds an executable version of an application every time we run the application! In every project folder is a sub-folder named **Bin\Debug**. The executable file is in that folder. Open the Bin/Debug folder for any project you have built and you'll see a file with your project name of type **Application**. For example, using Windows Explorer to open the Bin\Debug folder for Example 6-4 shows:

The file named **Example 6-4.exe** (of size 12 KB) is the executable version of the application. If I make sure Visual C# is not running and double-click this file, the following appears:

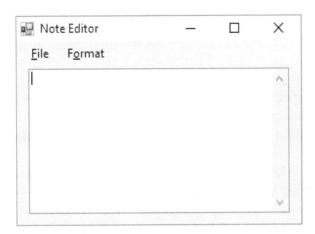

Voila! The Note Editor application is running outside of the Visual C# IDE!

So distributing a Visual C# application is as simple as giving your user a copy of the executable file, having them place it in a folder on their computer and double-clicking the file to run it? Maybe. This worked on my computer (and will work on yours) because I have a very important set of files known as the **.NET Framework** installed (they are installed when Visual C# is installed). Every Visual C# application needs the .NET Framework to be installed on the hosting computer. The .NET Framework is central to Microsoft's .NET initiative. It is an attempt to solve the problem of first determining what language (and version) an application was developed in and making sure the proper run-time files were installed. The .NET Framework supports all Visual Studio languages, so it is the only runtime software need by Visual Studio applications.

The next question is: how do you know if your user has the .NET Framework installed on his or her computer? And, if they don't, how can you get it installed? These are difficult questions. For now, it is best to assume your user does not have the .NET Framework on their computer.

So, in addition to our application's executable file, we also need to give a potential user the Microsoft .NET Framework files and inform them how to install and register these files on their computer. Things are getting complicated. Further complications for application distribution are inclusion and installation of ancillary data files, graphics files and configuration files. Fortunately, Visual C# offers help in distributing, or **deploying**, applications.

Visual C# uses **Setup Wizard** for deploying applications. **Setup Wizard** will identify all files needed by your application and bundle these files into a **Setup** program. You distribute this program to your user base (usually on a CD-ROM). Your user then runs the resulting **Setup** program. This program will:

> ➢ Install the application (and all needed files) on the user's computer.
> ➢ Add an entry to the user's **Start/Programs** menu to allow execution of your application.
> ➢ Add an icon to the user's desktop to allow execution of your application.

We'll soon look at use of Setup Wizard to build a deployment package for a Visual C# application. First, let's quickly look at the topic of icons.

Application Icons

Notice there is an icon file that looks like a little, blank Windows form associated with the application executable. And, notice that whenever you design a form in the Visual C# IDE (and run it), a small icon appears in the upper left hand corner of the form. Icons are used in several places in Visual C# applications: to represent files in Windows Explorer, to represent programs in the Programs menu, to represent programs on the desktop and to identify an application removal tool. Icons are used throughout applications. The default icons are ugly! We need the capability to change them.

Changing the icon connected to a form is simple. The idea is to assign a unique icon to indicate the form's function. To assign an icon, click on the form's **Icon** property in the properties window. Click on the ellipsis (...) and a window that allows selection of icon files will appear. The icon file you load must have the **.ico** filename extension and format.

A different icon can be assigned to the application. This will be the icon that appears next to the executable file's name in Windows Explorer, in the Programs menu and on the desktop. To choose this icon, first make sure the project file is highlighted in the **Solution Explorer** window of the IDE. Choose the **View** menu item and select **Property Pages**. Select the **Application** page and this window will appear:

The icon is selected in the **Icon** drop-down box. You can either choose an icon already listed or click the ellipsis (...) that allows you to select an icon using a dialog box. Once you choose an icon, two things will happen. The icon will appear on the property pages and the icon file will be added to your project's folder. This will be seen in the Solution Explorer window.

The Internet and other sources offer a wealth of icon files from which you can choose an icon to assign to your form(s) and applications. But, it's also fun to design your own icon to add that personal touch.

It is possible to create your own icon using Visual Studio. To create an icon for a particular project, in **Solution Explorer**, right-click the project name, choose **Add**, then **New Item**. This window will appear:

As shown, expand **Visual C# Items** and choose **General**. Then, pick **Icon File**. Name your icon and click **Add**.

A generic icon will open:

The icon is very large. Let's make a few changes to make it visible and editable. First, resize the image to 32 x 32 pixels. Then, use the magnifying tool to make the image as large as possible. Finally, add a grid to the graphic. When done, I see:

At this point, we can add any detail we need by setting pixels to particular colors. Consult on-line help for the exact steps needed. Once done, the icon will be saved in your project file and can be used by your project. The icon file (**Icon1.ico** in this case) is also listed in **Solution Explorer**:

Setup Wizard

As mentioned earlier, to allow someone else to install and run your Visual C# application requires more than just a simple transfer of the executable file. Visual C# provides **Setup Wizard** that simplifies this task of application **deployment**.

Note: **Setup Wizard** must be a part of your Visual Studio installation. To download and install **Setup Wizard**, use the following link:

Download Setup Wizard

Setup Wizard will build a **Setup** program that lets the user install the application (and other needed files) on their computer. At the same time, **Program** menu entries, desktop icons and application removal programs are placed on the user's computer.

The best way to illustrate use of **Setup Wizard** is through an example. In these notes, we will build a Setup program for our **Note Editor** example. Follow the example closely to see all steps involved. All results of this example will be found in the **Example 6-5** and **Note Editor** folders of the **LearnVCS\VCS Code\Class 6** folder. Let's start.

Open the **Note Editor** project (**Example 6-4**). Attach an icon to the **Titles** form (one possible icon, **NOTE.ICO**, is included in the project folder). The form should look like this with its new icon:

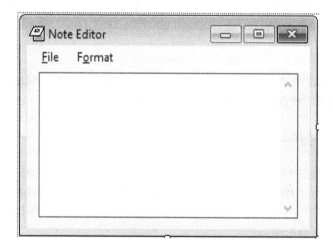

Assign this same icon to the application using the steps mentioned earlier:

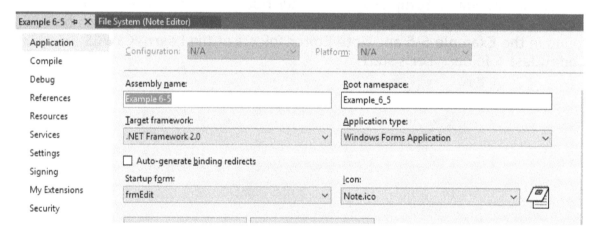

Setup Wizard is a separate project you add to your application solution. Choose the **File** menu option, then **New** then **Project**. In the window that appears, select **Setup Wizard** and click **Next**:

This window appears:

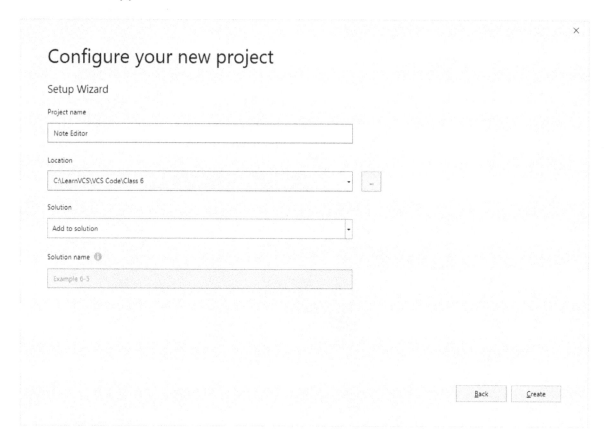

Under **Solution**, choose **Add to Solution**. **Name** the project **Note Editor** and click **Create**. Notice I have put the project folder in the **LearnVCS\VCS Code\Class 6** folder.

The **Setup Wizard** will begin with Step 1 of 5.

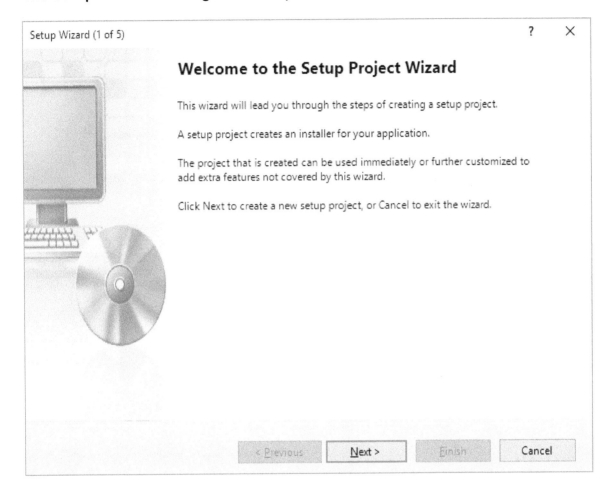

Continue from step to step, providing the requested information. Here, just click **Next**.

Step 2.

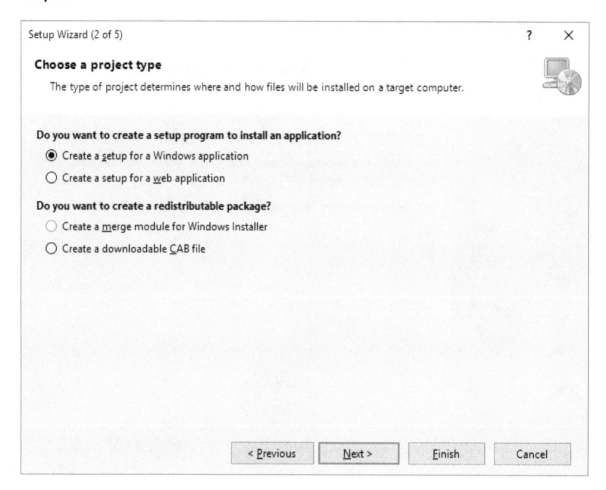

Choose **Create a setup for a Windows application.** Click **Next.**

Step 3.

Here you choose the files to install. The main one is the executable file (known here as the **primary output file**). Place a check next to **Primary ouput from Example 6-5** and click **Next**.

Step 4.

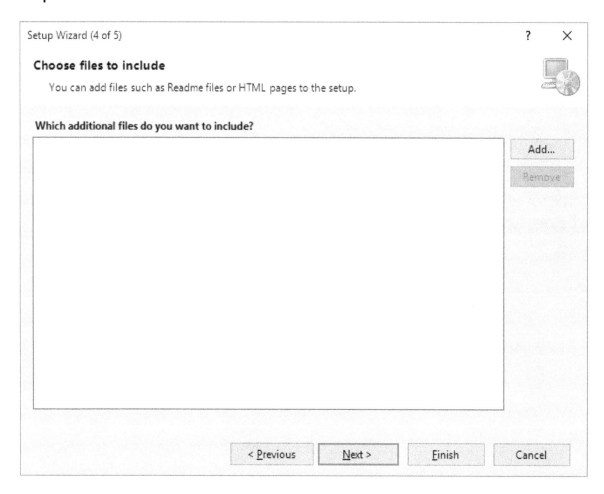

Here you can also additional files with your deployment package. You could specify ReadMe files, configuration files, help files, data files, sound files, graphic files or any other files your application needs. Our simple application needs no such files, so we just move to the next step. If you did need to add a file, click the **Add Files** button to select the desired file.

Move to the next step (click **Next**).

Step 5.

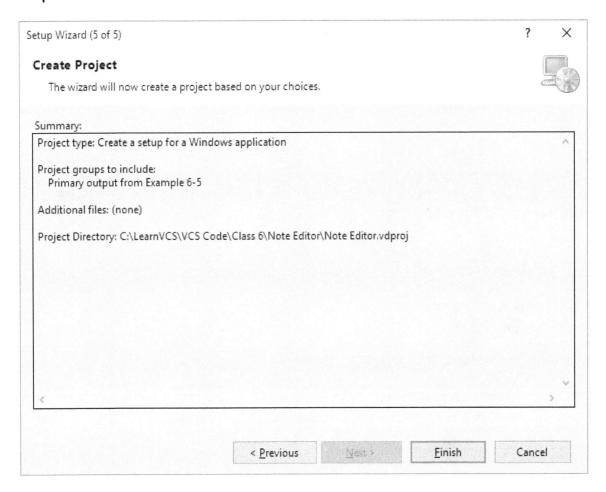

Click **Finish** to see the resulting **File System:**

We also want shortcuts to start the program both on the **Desktop** and the **Programs Menu.** First, we do the **Desktop** shortcut. To do this, open the **Application Folder** to see:

Right-click **Primary output from ...** and choose **Create Shortcut to Primary output ....** Cut the resulting shortcut from the **Application Folder** and paste it into the **User's Desktop** folder:

Rename the shortcut **Note Editor** to yield

Lastly, we want to change the icon associated with the shortcut. This is a little tricky. The steps are:

> ➢ Highlight the shortcut and choose the **Icon** property in the Properties window
> ➢ Choose **Browse.**
> ➢ When the **Icon** dialog box appears, click **Browse.** You will see

As shown, look in the **Application Folder** and click **Add File.**

> Locate and select the icon file (there is one in the **LearnVCS\VCS Code\Class 6\Example 6-5** folder), then click **OK**. The **Icon** window will appear:

Select the desired icon and click **OK**.

Next, follow nearly identical steps to put a shortcut in the **User's Programs Menu** folder. The **Setup Wizard** has completed its job.

Debug Versus Release Configurations

When you create an executable (run your application) in Visual C#, it is created using the default **debug configuration**. We have been using this configuration for every application studied thus far. You use the debug configuration while designing, testing and debugging your application. An application built in debug mode has lots of symbolic references included for debug purposes and the code is not optimized for best performance.

When you have fully tested your application, are sure it is error free and ready for deployment, we suggest switching to **release configuration**. To do this, select the **Build** menu option and choose **Configuration Manager** (this option is only available when a setup project is being used. This window will appear:

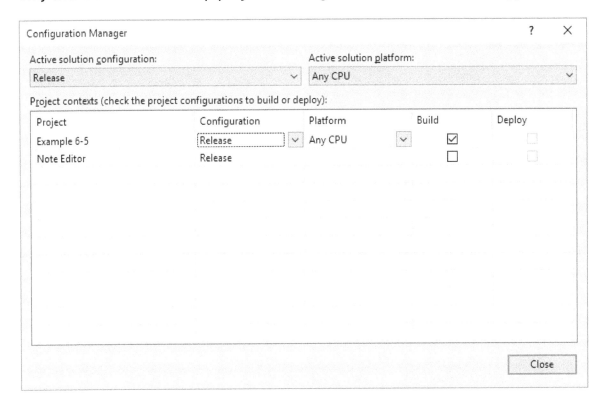

Under **Active solution configuration**, choose **Release**. Click **Close**. Next, in the **Solution Explorer**, right click the project name (not the setup project) and choose **Build**.

The **release** configuration of an application is fully optimized and contains no symbolic debugging information. Such an application will usually be smaller in size, have the fastest speed and provide the best performance. This is the configuration that should be part of a deployment package. If you ever need to make significant changes to a project, you probably want to change back to **Debug** configuration while testing your changes.

Building the Setup Program

Now, let's build the **Setup** program. In the Solution Explorer window, right-click the **Note Editor** project and choose **Build** from the menu. After a short time, the **Setup** program and an msi (Microsoft Installer) file will be written. They will be located in the executable folder of the **Note Editor** project folder (**LearnVCS\VCS Code\Class 6\Note Editor\Release**). The **Setup** program is small. A look at the resulting directory shows:

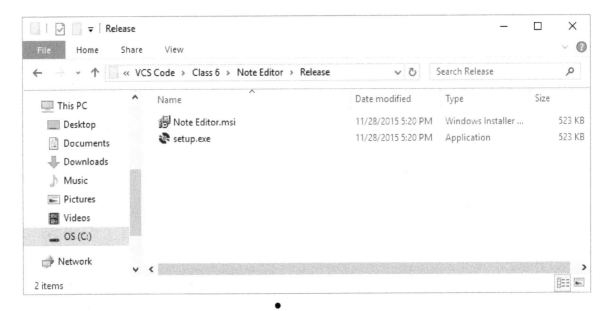

Use some media (zip disk, CD-ROM or downloaded files) to distribute these files your user base. Provide the user with the simple instruction to run the **Setup.exe** program and installation will occur.

Installing a Visual C# Application

To install the program, simply run the **Setup.exe** program. These are the same brief instructions you need to provide a user. Users have become very familiar with installing software and running Setup type programs. Let's try the example just created and see what a nice installation interface is provided. Double-click the **Setup.exe** program from Example 6-5 and this introduction window should appear:

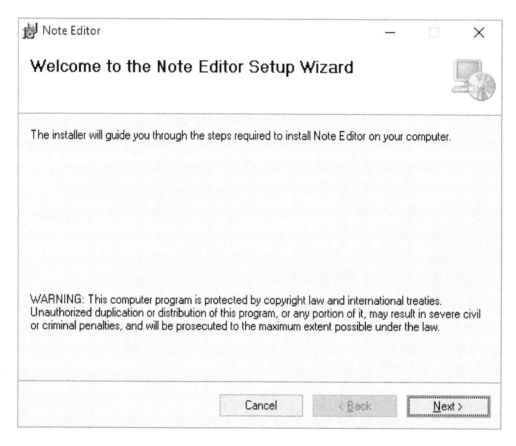

Click **Next** and you will be asked where you want the application installed.

After a few clicks, installation is complete and you will see:

After installing, look on your desktop. There should be an icon named **Note Editor**. Double-click that icon and the program will run. Similarly, the program can be accessed by clicking **Start** on your taskbar, then choosing **All Apps**. Click the **Note Editor** entry and the program runs. I think you'll agree the installer does a nice job.

Class Review

After completing this class, you should understand:

> ➢ How to work with tab controls in a Visual C# application
> ➢ How to use general methods in a Visual C# application
> ➢ How to insert a menu structure into a Visual C# application using the MenuStrip control
> ➢ How to use the ContextMenuStrip control to add menus to controls
> ➢ The concept of a Font object and use of the FontDialog control
> ➢ How to design an icon using Icon Editor and how to assign an icon to a Visual C# application
> ➢ Use of the Setup Wizard to create a deployment package (Setup program) for a Visual C# application

Practice Problems 6

Problem 6-1. Tab Control Problem. Build an application with three tabs on a tab control. On each tab, have radio buttons that set the background color of the corresponding tab page.

Problem 6-2. Note Editor About Box Problem. Most applications have a **Help** menu heading. When you click on this heading, at the bottom of the menu is an **About** item. Choosing this item causes a dialog box to appear that provides the user with copyright and other application information. Prepare such an About box (use a message box) for the Note Editor we build in this chapter (Example 6-4). Implement the About box in the application.

Problem 6-3. Normal Numbers Problem. There are other ways to generate random numbers in Visual C#. One is the **NextDouble** method (associated with the **Random** object) that returns a double type number between 0 and 1. These numbers produce what is known as a uniform distribution. This means all numbers come up with equal probabilities. Statisticians often need a 'bell-shaped curve' to do their work. This curve is what is used in schools when they 'grade on a curve.' Such a 'probability distribution' is spread about a mean with some values very likely (near the mean) and some not very likely (far from the mean). Such distributions (called normal distributions) have a specified mean and a specified standard deviation (measure of how far spread out possible values are). One way to simulate a single 'normally distributed' number, using the 'uniformly distributed' random number generator, is to sum twelve random numbers (from the **NextDouble** method) and subtract six from the sum. That value is approximately 'normal' with a mean of zero and a standard deviation of one. See if such an approximation really works by first writing a general method that computes a single 'normally distributed number.' Then, write general methods to compute the mean (average) and standard deviation of an array of values (the equations are found back in Exercise 2-1). See if the described approximation is good by computing a large number of 'normally approximate' numbers.

Problem 6-4. Context Menu Problem. Build an application with a single button control. When you click on the button, have a font dialog box appear, allowing you to change the font and color of the displayed text. When you right-click the button, have a context menu appear allowing you to change the background color of the button.

Exercise 6

US/World Capitals Quiz

Develop an application that quizzes a user on states and capitals in the United States and/or capitals of world countries. Or, if desired, quiz a user on any matching pairs of items - for example, words and meanings, books and authors, or inventions and inventors. Use a menu structure that allows the user to decide whether they want to name states (countries) or capitals and whether they want multiple choice or type-in answers. Thoroughly test your application. Design an icon for your program using the Image Editor or some other program. Create an executable file. Create a **Setup** program using the Setup Wizard. Try installing and removing the program from your computer. Or, give it to someone else and let him or her enjoy your nifty little program.

7. Sequential Files, Error-Handling and Debugging

Review and Preview

In this class, we expand our Visual C# knowledge from past classes and examine a few new topics. We first study reading and writing sequential disk files. We then look at handling errors in programs, using both run-time error trapping and debugging techniques.

Sequential Files

In many applications, it is helpful to have the capability to read and write information to a disk file. This information could be some computed data or perhaps information needed by your Visual C# project. Visual C# supports several file formats. We will look at the most common format: **sequential files**.

A sequential file is a line-by-line list of data that can be viewed with any text editor. Sequential access easily works with files that have lines with mixed information of different lengths. Hence, sequential files can include both variables and text data. When using sequential files, it is helpful, but not necessary, to know the order data was written to the file to allow easy retrieval.

The ability to read and generate sequential files is a very powerful capability of Visual C#. This single capability is the genesis of many applications I've developed. Let's examine a few possible applications where we could use such files. One possibility is to use sequential files to provide initialization information for a project. Such a file is called a **configuration** or **initialization file** and almost all applications use such files. Here is the idea:

In this diagram, the configuration file (a sequential file) contains information that can be used to initialize different parameters (control properties, variable values) within the Visual C# application. The file is opened when the application begins, the file values are read and the various parameters established.

Similarly, when we exit an application, we could have it write out current parameter values to an output configuration file:

This output file could then become an input file the next time the application is executed. We will look at how to implement such a configuration file in a Visual C# application.

Many data-intensive, or not-so intensive, Windows applications provide file export capabilities. For example, you can save data from a Microsoft Excel spreadsheet to an external file. The usual format for such an exported data file is a **CSV** (comma separated variables) sequential file. You can write a Visual C# application that reads this exported file and performs some kind of analysis or further processing of the data:

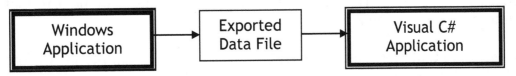

In the above example, the results of the Visual C# program could be displayed using Windows controls (text boxes, list boxes, picture boxes) or the program could also write another sequential file that could be used by some other application (say Microsoft Access or Microsoft Word). This task is actually more common than you might think. Many applications support exporting data. And, many applications support importing data from other sources. A big problem is that the output file from one application might not be an acceptable input file to another application. Visual C# to the rescue:

In this diagram, Application 1 writes an exported data file that is read by the Visual C# application. This application writes a data file in an input format required by Application 2.

You will find that you can use Visual C# to read a sequential file in any format and, likewise, write a file in any format. As we said, the ability to read and generate sequential files is a very powerful capability of Visual C#.

Sequential File Output (Variables)

We will first look at **writing** values of **variables** to sequential files. The initial step in accessing any sequential file (either for input or output) is to open the file, knowing the name of the file. Visual C# uses the **StreamWriter** class to open a file for output. This class uses the Visual C# **IO** (input/output) namespace, so for any application using file input and output, you will need to add this line to the code:

```
using System.IO;
```

You will see similar **using** statements at the very top of the code window. These statements load in needed system utilities. Type it there. If you omit the line and try to use any file input/output functions you will receive an error message something like:

```
The type or namespace name 'StreamWriter' could not be
found (are you missing a using directive or an assembly
reference?)
```

The constructor for opening a sequential file (**myFile**) for output is:

```
StreamWriter outputFile = new StreamWriter(myFile);
```

where **myFile** is the name (a **string**) of the file to open and **outputFile** is the returned StreamWriter object used to write variables to disk. The filename must be a complete path to the file. As you type this line, the Intellisense feature of the IDE will help you fill in the arguments.

A word of warning - when you open a file using the **StreamWriter** class, if the file already exists, it will be erased immediately! So, make sure you really want to overwrite the file. Using the **SaveFileDialog** control (discussed in this chapter) can prevent accidental overwriting. Just be careful. You can open and add to an existing sequential file by opening it using this overloaded version of the constructor:

```
StreamWriter outputFile = new StreamWriter(myFile, true);
```

The second argument (**true**) is a **bool** type specifying you want to add information. If the file doesn't exist or can't be found, it will be created as an empty file.

When done writing to a sequential file, it must be closed using the **Close** method. For our example, the syntax is:

```
outputFile.Close();
```

Once a file is closed, it is saved on the disk under the path (if used) and filename used to open the file.

Information (variables or text) is written to a sequential file in an appended fashion. Separate Visual C# statements are required for each appending. There are two different ways to write variables to a sequential file. You choose which method you want based on your particular application.

The first method uses the **Write** method. For a file opened as **outputFile**, the syntax is to print a variable named **myVariable** is:

```
outputFile.Write(myVariable);
```

This statement will append the specified variable to the current line in the sequential file. If you only use **Write** for output, everything will be written in one very long line. And, if no other characters (**delimiters**) are entered to separate variables, they will all be concatenated together.

Example using **Write** method:

```
int a;
string b;
double c, e;
bool d;
StreamWriter outputFile = new
StreamWriter("c:\\junk\\testout.txt");
outputFile.Write(a);
outputFile.Write(b);
outputFile.Write(c);
outputFile.Write(d);
outputFile.Write(e);
outputFile.Close();
```

After this code runs, the file **c:\junk\testOut.txt** will have a single line with all five variables (a, b, c, d, e) concatenated together. This, of course, assumes proper values have been assigned to each of the variables.

The other way to write variables to a sequential file is **WriteLine**, the companion to **Write**. Its syntax is:

```
outputFile.WriteLine(myVariable);
```

This method works identically to the **Write** method with the exception that a 'carriage return' is added, moving down a line in the file once the write is complete. It can be used to insert blank lines by omitting the variable.

Example using **WriteLine** method:

```
int a;
string b;
double c, e;
bool d;
StreamWriter outputFile = new
StreamWriter("c:\\junk\\testout.txt");
outputFile.WriteLine(a);
outputFile.WriteLine(b);
outputFile.WriteLine(c);
outputFile.WriteLine(d);
outputFile.WriteLine(e);
outputFile.Close();
```

After this code runs, the file **c:\junk\testout.txt** will have five lines, each of the variables (a, b, c, d, e) on a separate line.

Application Path

We have seen the **StreamWriter** object needs a path to the file to be opened. Ma ny times, the file we want to open (for either writing or reading) is located in the same directory as the application executable file (the **Bin\Debug** folder for our projects, but could be different when users install an application). How do we know what directory that is? Visual C# maintains a parameter that has the location of an application's executable file. That path is a string data type defined by:

```
Application.StartupPath
```

When a user installs an application on their own machine (using a Setup program like that developed in Class 5), this same parameter will hold the executable location.

As an example, to use this parameter to open a file (for writing) named **testOut.txt** and store it in the current application directory, we would use the statement:

```
StreamWriter outputFile = new
StreamWriter(Application.StartupPath + "\\testOut.txt");
```

Note an additional backslash (\\) must be appended to the path, before adding the file name. We will use the **Application.StartupPath** parameter whenever we need to open or save files within the application directory (data files or initialization files are examples).

Example 7-1

Writing Variables to Sequential Files

1. Start a new project. We will build a simple application that writes data to sequential files using each of the two methods for doing such writing. The **Application.StartupPath** parameter will be used to save the file. Add a label control to the form in your new project.

2. Set the properties of the form and each control:

Form1:

Name	frmWrite
FormBorderStyle	FixedSingle
StartPosition	CenterScreen
Text	Sequential File Output

label1:

Name	lblPath
AutoSize	False
BackColor	White
Text	[Blank]

The form should look something like this:

3. Add this line at the top of the code window with the other **using** statements:

```
using System.IO;
```

4. Use this code in the **frmWrite Load** event:

```csharp
private void FrmWrite_Load(object sender, EventArgs e)
{
  // variables
  int v1 = 5;
  String v2 = "Visual C# 2019 is fun";
  double v3 = 1.23;
  int v4 = -4;
  bool v5 = true;
  String v6 = "Another string type";

  lblPath.Text = Application.StartupPath;

  // open and write file for Write method
  StreamWriter outputFile1 = new
StreamWriter(Application.StartupPath + "\\test1.txt");
  outputFile1.Write(v1);
  outputFile1.Write(v2);
  outputFile1.Write(v3);
  outputFile1.Write(v4);
  outputFile1.Write(v5);
  outputFile1.Write(v6);
  outputFile1.Close();

  // open and write file for WriteLine method
  StreamWriter outputFile2 = new
StreamWriter(Application.StartupPath + "\\test2.txt");
  outputFile2.WriteLine(v1);
  outputFile2.WriteLine(v2);
  outputFile2.WriteLine(v3);
  outputFile2.WriteLine(v4);
  outputFile2.WriteLine(v5);
  outputFile2.WriteLine(v6);
  outputFile2.Close();
}
```

This code writes six variables of different types to two different sequential files (using the two different printing methods).

5. Save the application (saved in **Example 7-1** folder in **LearnVCS\VCS Code\Class 7** folder) and run it. Two files will be written to the folder containing the Example 7-1 executable file (the application path). That folder will be displayed in the label control:

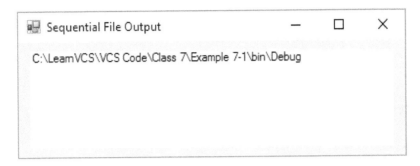

In that folder will be two files: test1.txt (written using **Write** function) and test2.txt (written using **WriteLine** function) Open each file using Windows Notepad and notice how each file is different. Pay particular attention to how variables of different types are represented. My files look like this:

test1.txt (uses Write)

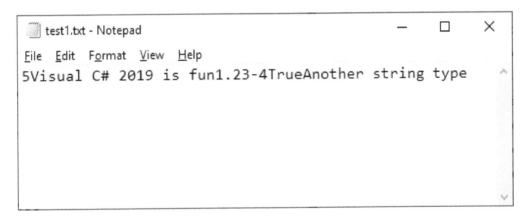

Notice how the variables are just "glommed" together. To read these variables back into an application would require a bit of tricky programming. Later, we discuss the use of delimiters to separate variables, so individual variables can be easily identified.

test2.txt (uses WriteLine)

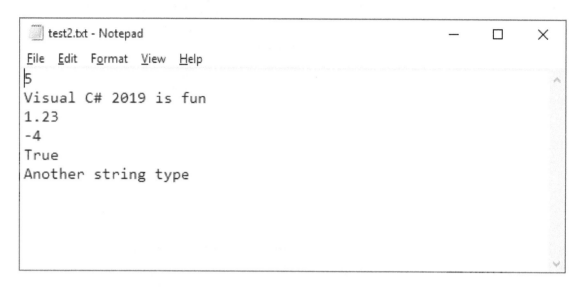

Having each variable on a separate line makes each variable easily identifiable. This is the preferred way of writing variables to disk.

Sequential File Input (Variables)

In the previous section, we saw that if the **Write** method is used to write variables to disk, you obtain one long concatenated line. We need to use special techniques (parsing) to recover variable values from such a line. We discuss those methods next. In this section, we discuss reading variables written to a file using the WriteLine method, a single variable on each line. To **read variables** from a sequential file, we essentially reverse the write procedure. First, open the file using a **StreamReader**:

```
StreamReader inputFile = new StreamReader(myFile);
```

where **inputFile** is the returned file object and **myFile** is a valid path to the file.

If the file you are trying to open does not exist, an error will occur. A way to minimize errors is to use the **OpenFileDialog** control to insure the file exists before trying to open it.

When all values have been read from the sequential file, it is closed using:

```
inputFile.Close();
```

Variables are read from a sequential file in the same order they were written. Hence, to read in variables from a sequential file, you need to know:

> How many variables are in the file
> The order the variables were written to the file
> The type of each variable in the file

If you developed the structure of the sequential file (say for a configuration file), you obviously know all of this information. And, if it is a file you generated from another source (spreadsheet, database), the information should be known. If the file is from an unknown source, you may have to do a little detective work. Open the file in a text editor and look at the data. See if you can figure out what is in the file.

Many times, you may know the order and type of variables in a sequential file, but the number of variables may vary. For example, you may export monthly sales data from a spreadsheet. One month may have 30 variables, the next 31 variables, and February would have 28 or 29. In such a case, you can read from the file until you reach an end-of-file condition. To determine whether we have reached the end of the file, we call the **Peek** method of the **StreamReader** object. The Peek method reads the next character in the file without changing the place that we are currently reading. If we have reached the end of the file, Peek returns -1.

Variables are read from a sequential file using the **ReadLine** method. The syntax for our example file is:

```
myVariableString = inputFile.ReadLine();
```

where **myVariableString** is the **string** representation of the variable being read. To retrieve the variable value from this string, we need to convert the string to the proper type. Conversions for **int**, **double** and **bool** variables are:

```
myintVariable = Convert.ToInt32(myVariableString);
mydoubleVariable = Convert.ToDouble(myVariableString);
myboolVariable = Convert.ToBoolean(myVariableString);
```

Example using **ReadLine** method:

```
int a;
string b;
double c, e;
bool d;
StreamReader inputFile = new StreamReader("testout.txt");
a = Convert.ToInt32(inputFile.ReadLine());
b = inputFile.ReadLine();
c = Convert.ToDouble(inputFile.ReadLine());
d = Convert.ToBoolean(inputFile.ReadLine());
e = Convert.ToDouble(inputFile.ReadLine());
inputFile.Close();
```

This code opens the file **testout.txt** (in the **Bin\Debug** folder) and sequentially reads five variables. Notice how the **ReadLine** method is used directly in the conversions. Also notice, the string variable **b** (obviously) requires no conversion.

Example 7-2

Reading Variables from Sequential Files

1. Start a new project. We will build an application that opens and reads in the data file written using WriteLine in Example 7-1. As a first step, copy that file (test2.txt) into the **Bin\Debug** folder in your new project's folder (you may have to create the folder first). We want these files to be in our application path, so we can use the **Application.StartupPath** parameter to open them.

2. Add a list control and a button control to the form so it looks like this:

3. Set the properties of the form and each control:

Form1:

Name	frmRead
FormBorderStyle	FixedSingle
StartPosition	CenterScreen
Text	Sequential File Input

listBox1:

Name	lstInput

button1:

Name	btnRead
Text	&Read Data

The form should look something like this:

4. Add this line at the top of the code window with the other **using** statements:

   ```
   using System.IO;
   ```

5. Use this code in the **btnRead Click** event:

   ```csharp
   private void BtnRead_Click(object sender, EventArgs e)
   {
     int v1;
     string v2;
     double v3;
     int v4;
     bool v5;
     string v6;
     // open file
     lstInput.Items.Clear();
     StreamReader inputFile = new
   StreamReader(Application.StartupPath + "\\test2.txt");
     v1 = Convert.ToInt32(inputFile.ReadLine());
     v2 = inputFile.ReadLine();
     v3 = Convert.ToDouble(inputFile.ReadLine());
     v4 = Convert.ToInt32(inputFile.ReadLine());
     v5 = Convert.ToBoolean(inputFile.ReadLine());
     v6 = inputFile.ReadLine();
     lstInput.Items.Add("v1 = " + v1.ToString());
     lstInput.Items.Add("v2 = " + v2.ToString());
     lstInput.Items.Add("v3 = " + v3.ToString());
     lstInput.Items.Add("v4 = " + v4.ToString());
     lstInput.Items.Add("v5 = " + v5.ToString());
     lstInput.Items.Add("v6 = " + v6.ToString());
     inputFile.Close();
   }
   ```

This code opens the file, then reads and converts the six variables. The variable values are written in the list box control.

6. Save the application (saved in **Example 7-2** folder in **LearnVCS\VCS Code\Class 7** folder). Run the application - you may get this error message when you click **Read Data:**

Remember that the project expects the input file to be in the application path. If you forgot to copy that file (from our previous example's directory) into this example's **Bin\Debug** directory, do that now. Copy **test2.text** (from Example 7-1) into the **Bin\Debug** folder for Example 7-2. Then, try running again.

With successful running, you should see:

Notice how each of the six variables was read in and properly converted.

Parsing Data Lines

In Example 7-1, we saw that variables written to sequential files using the **Write** method are concatenated in one long line. Many times, data files you receive from other applications will also have several variables in one line. How can we read variables in such formats? One possible correction for this problem is to restructure the file so each variable is on a single line and it can be read using techniques like those in Example 7-2. But, many times this is not possible. If the file is coming from a source you have no control over, you need to work with what you are given. But, there's still hope. You can do anything with Visual C#!

The approach we take is called **parsing** a line. We read in a single line as a long string. Then, we successively remove substrings from this longer line that represent each variable. To do this, we still need to know how many variables are in a line, their types and their location in the line. The location can be specified by some kind of delimiter (a quote, a space, a slash) or by an exact position within the line. All of this can be done with the Visual C# string functions (you may want to review these - they are in Class 2). Though here we are concerned with lines read from a sequential file, note these techniques can be applied to any string data type in Visual C#.

The first thing we need to do is open the file with the lines to be parsed and read in each line as a string. This is <u>exactly</u> what we did in reading variables written to a file using the **WriteLine** method. The file is opened using **StreamReader** objects. Once the file (**inputFile**) is opened a line is read using the **ReadLine** method:

```
myLine = inputFile.ReadLine();
```

Once we have the line (**myLine**) to parse, what we do with it depends on what we know. The basic idea is to determine the bounding character positions of each variable within the line. Character location is zero-based, hence the first character in a string is character 0. If the first position is **fp** and the last position is **lp**, the substring representation of this variable (**variableString**) can be found using the Visual C# **Substring** method:

```
variableString = myLine.Substring(fp, lp - fp + 1);
```

Recall this says return the **substring** in **myLine** that starts at position **fp** and is **lp - fp + 1** characters long. Once we have extracted **variableString**, we convert it to the proper data type.

So, how do you determine the starting and ending positions for a variable in a line? The easiest case is when you are told by those providing the file what 'columns' bound certain data. This is common in engineering data files. Otherwise, you must know what 'delimits' variables. You can search for these delimiters using the **IndexOf** and **LastIndexOf** methods. A common delimiter is just a lot of space between each variable (you may have trouble retrieving strings containing space). Other delimiters include slashes, commas, pound signs and even exclamation points. The power of Visual C# allows you to locate any delimiters and extract the needed information

As variables are extracted from the input data line, we sometimes shorten the line (excluding the extracted substring) before looking for the next variable To do this, we use again use the **Substring** method. If **lp** was the last position of the substring removed from left side of **myLine**, we shorten this line using:

```
myLine = myLine.Substring(lp + 1, myLine.Length - lp -
1).Trim();
```

This removes the first lp characters from the left side of myLine. The Trim method removes any leading and/or trailing spaces and myLine is replaced by the shortened line. Notice by shortening the string in this manner, the first position for finding each extracted substring will always be 0 (**fp** = 0).

Example 7-3

Parsing Data Lines

1. Start a new project. We will build an application that opens and reads in the single line data file written with the Write function in Example 7-1. We will then parse that line to extract all the variables. As a first step, copy the **test1.txt** file into the **Bin\Debug** folder in your new project's folder (you may have to create the folder first). We want the file to be in our application path, so we can use the **Application.StartupPath** parameter to open it.

2. Add a list control and a button control to the form so it looks like this:

3. Set the properties of the form and each control:

Form1:

Name	frmParse
FormBorderStyle	FixedSingle
StartPosition	CenterScreen
Text	Parsing Lines

ListBox1:

Name	lstInput

Button1:

Name	btnRead
Text	&Read Data

The form should look something like this:

4. Add this line at the top of the code window with the other **using** statements:

    ```
    using System.IO;
    ```

5. Use this code in the **btnRead Click** event:

    ```
    private void BtnRead_Click(object sender, EventArgs e)
    {
        int v1;
        string v2;
        double v3;
        int v4;
        bool v5;
        string v6;
        string myLine = "";

        // open file
        StreamReader inputFile = new
    StreamReader(Application.StartupPath + "\\test1.txt");
        myLine = inputFile.ReadLine();
        inputFile.Close();

        v1 = Convert.ToInt32(myLine.Substring(0, 1));
        v2 = myLine.Substring(1, 16);
        v3 = Convert.ToDouble(myLine.Substring(22, 4));
        v4 = Convert.ToInt32(myLine.Substring(26, 2));
        v5 = Convert.ToBoolean(myLine.Substring(28, 4));
        v6 = myLine.Substring(32, 19);
        lstInput.Items.Add("v1 = " + v1.ToString());
        lstInput.Items.Add("v2 = " + v2.ToString());
        lstInput.Items.Add("v3 = " + v3.ToString());
        lstInput.Items.Add("v4 = " + v4.ToString());
        lstInput.Items.Add("v5 = " + v5.ToString());
        lstInput.Items.Add("v6 = " + v6.ToString());
    }
    ```

This code opens the file and reads the single line as a string data type. It then extracts each variable from that line. It uses position within the data line to extract the variables. You should be able to figure out this code. Look at the single data line (test1.txt) and see how I determined the arguments used in the Substring methods.

6. Save the application (saved in **Example 7-3** folder in **LearnVCS\VCS Code\Class 7** folder). Run the application. . If you get a 'file not found,' error, make sure the data file is in your **Bin\Debug** folder. The six variables should all display correctly in the list box:

Reading Tokenized Lines

Parsing a data line using character positions is tedious and assumes the variables are always the same length – not necessarily a good assumption. It would be preferable if multiple variable values in a single line were separated by some kind of delimiter. Then, these delimiters could be used to identify where variables start and end. Let's try that. Open **test1.txt** in a text editor and place exclamation points (!) between each of the variables. My file looks like this:

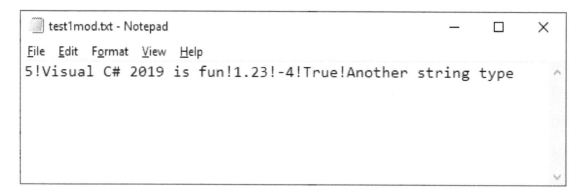

Resave the file as **test1mod.txt**. We could have also added these exclamation points when we originally wrote the file to disk by inserting **Write** statements (writing exclamation points) between each Write statement printing a variable.

The exclamation points (delimiters) now define starting and ending positions for each variable. By locating successive delimiters, we can retrieve the variables. The approach for a data line named **myLine** is:

1. Locate the first exclamation point (position **ep**) in the input line:

   ```
   ep = myLine.IndexOf("!");
   ```

   If there is no exclamation point, **ep = -1**.

2. Extract the variable string (**myString**) using:

   ```
   myString = myLine.Substring(0, ep);
   ```

3. Convert **myString** to the proper variable type.
4. Shorten the data line by eliminating the first variable and its exclamation point:

```
myLine = myLine.Substring(ep + 1, myLine.Length - ep -
1).Trim();
```

Repeat each of these steps until all that remains is the last variable.

Example 7-4

Reading Tokenized Lines

1. Using the steps just developed, we modify Example 7-3 to read in the modified text file (**test1mod.txt**). Make sure that file is in the **Bin\Debug** folder of Example 7-3. We will use **Application.StartupPath** to access the file. Open Example 7-3.

2. Modify the **btnRead_Click** code as shaded (we essentially replace the 'hard-coded' string positions with the locations of exclamation points):

```
private void BtnRead_Click(object sender, EventArgs e)
{
    int v1;
    string v2;
    double v3;
    int v4;
    bool v5;
    string v6;
    string myLine = "";
    int ep;

    // open file
    StreamReader inputFile = new
StreamReader(Application.StartupPath + "\\test1mod.txt");
    myLine = inputFile.ReadLine();
    inputFile.Close();

    ep = myLine.IndexOf("!");
    v1 = Convert.ToInt32(myLine.Substring(0, ep));
    myLine = myLine.Substring(ep + 1, myLine.Length - ep -
1).Trim();

    ep = myLine.IndexOf("!");
    v2 = myLine.Substring(0, ep);
    myLine = myLine.Substring(ep + 1, myLine.Length - ep -
1).Trim();

    ep = myLine.IndexOf("!");
    v3 = Convert.ToDouble(myLine.Substring(0, ep));
    myLine = myLine.Substring(ep + 1, myLine.Length - ep -
1).Trim();

    ep = myLine.IndexOf("!");
    v4 = Convert.ToInt32(myLine.Substring(0, ep));
```

```
   myLine = myLine.Substring(ep + 1, myLine.Length - ep -
1).Trim();

  ep = myLine.IndexOf("!");
  v5 = Convert.ToBoolean(myLine.Substring(0, ep));
  myLine = myLine.Substring(ep + 1, myLine.Length - ep -
1).Trim();

  // last variable is just what's left of line
  v6 = myLine;
```

```
  lstInput.Items.Add("v1 = " + v1.ToString());
  lstInput.Items.Add("v2 = " + v2.ToString());
  lstInput.Items.Add("v3 = " + v3.ToString());
  lstInput.Items.Add("v4 = " + v4.ToString());
  lstInput.Items.Add("v5 = " + v5.ToString());
  lstInput.Items.Add("v6 = " + v6.ToString());
  inputFile.Close();
}
```

This code simply finds delimiters (exclamation points) bounding the six variables. The variable **ep** is used to identify delimiter location. Once a variable is found, it is extracted, the data line is shortened and the next variable found. Notice there are no specific numbers in the method arguments. This makes your job easier, especially when variables may have different lengths in different files. You still need to know how many variables and what type of variables are in each line, but the coding is simpler.

7. Save the application (saved in **Example 7-4** folder in **LearnVCS\VCS Code\Class 7** folder). Run the application. If you get a 'file not found,' error, make sure the data file is in your **Bin\Debug** folder. The six variables should all display correctly in the list box:

Building Data Lines

Code similar to that used to parse, or break up, a line of data can also be used to build a line of data that can then be used in a control such as a text area or written to a sequential file. A primary application for such lines is to write precisely formatted data files. It allows left justification, centering and right justification of values. It also allows positioning data in any 'column' desired.

You might think you could just directly modify the contents of some string variable to accomplish this task. Unfortunately, string variables in Visual C# are **immutable** – they cannot be modified directly. We take another approach. We will build the data line as an array of characters. Then, we will convert that array to a string for output. We will build a couple of general methods that help in building data lines.

A first step in building data lines is to choose the maximum number of characters that will be in each line. This length is usually established by the width of a displaying control or the width of a printed page (we'll look at this in Chapter 10). Once this maximum width is selected, each line is initialized as a blank string of that length. We will use a general method to initialize such a string to all blank spaces. The method (**BlankLine**) is:

```
public string BlankLine(int n)
{
  string s = "";
  for (int i = 0; i < n; i++)
  {
    s += " ";
  }
  return (s);
}
```

The method simply concatenates **n** spaces to form a returned string variable **s**. Hence, to initialize a string variable **myLine** to **n** spaces, you use:

```
myLine = BlankLine(n);
```

Once the blank line is established, the spaces are replaced with specified substrings at specific locations. We create a general method (**MidLine**) to accomplish this task:

```
public string MidLine(string string1, string string2, int p)
{
  string s = "";
  // convert big string to character array
  char[] sArray = string2.ToCharArray();
  // put string1 in string2
  for (int i = p; i < p + string1.Length; i++)
  {
    sArray[i] = string1[i - p];
  }
  // put array in string variable
  for (int i = 0; i < string2.Length; i++)
  {
    s += sArray[i].ToString();
  }
  return (s);
}
```

This method takes the contents of **string1** and places it in **string2**, starting at position **p**. The result is returned in the string **s**. Hence, to left justify **mySubString** in **myLine** at position **lp**, and return the result in **myLine**, use:

```
myLine = MidLine(mySubString, myLine, lp);
```

When doing these replacements, always make sure you are within the bounding length of the myLine string variable. Once all desired substrings have been placed in a data line, it can be printed in a sequential file or used for other purposes.

So, to build a line of variable data (**myLine**), we decide what variables we want in each line and where we want to position them. We then successively convert each variable to a string and place it in a string variable using the **MidLine** method. When this string is complete, if it is for a sequential file, it is printed to the file (**outputFile**) using the **WriteLine** method:

```
outputFile.WriteLine(myLine);
```

We don't have to use the newly constructed line in a data file. It could also be added to the **Text** property of any control. In such a case, if you want the new line on its own separate line, be sure to append the proper line feed character (\r\n).

We saw how to left justify a substring in a data line represented by a character array. We can also center justify and right justify. To right justify **mySubString** in **myLine** at location **rp**, use:

```
myLine = MidLine(mySubString, myLine, rp + 1 -
mySubString.Length);
```

And to center **mySubString** in **myLine**, use:

```
myLine = MidLine(mySubString, myLine, (int) (0.5 *
(myLine.Length - mySubString.Length)));
```

Of course, to center justify a substring, the substring must be shorter than the line it is being centered in. To see how both of these replacements work, just go through an example and you'll see the logic.

Most of what is presented here works best with fixed width fonts (each character is the same width). I usually use **Courier New**. You will have to experiment if using proportional fonts to obtain desired results.

Example 7-5

Building Data Lines

1. Start a new project. We will build an application that lets a user enter a minimum and maximum circle diameter. The program then computes perimeter and area for twenty circles between those two input values. We will use the **CircleGeometry** method developed in Example 6-3 for the computations. The computed results are displayed in tabular form.

2. Place two labels, three text box controls and a button control on your form so it looks like this:

3. Set the properties of the form and each control:

Form1:
Name	frmCircle
FormBorderStyle	FixedSingle
StartPosition	CenterScreen
Text	Circle Geometries

label1:
Text	Minimum Diameter

textBox1:
Name	txtMinimum
Text	[Blank]

label2:
Text	Maximum Diameter

textBox2:
Name	txtMaximum
Text	[Blank]

button1:
Name	btnCompute
Text	&Compute Geometries

textBox3:
Name	txtOutput
BackColor	White
Font	Courier New, Size 10
MultiLine	True
ReadOnly	True
ScrollBars	Vertical
TabStop	False
Text	[Blank]

The finished form should look something like this:

I set the width of the big text box so that it would hold 36 characters across. How? At design time, set the **Text** property to something 36 characters wide and increase the text box width until it fits!

4. Add the two general methods developed earlier (**BlankLine** and **MidLine**) for building the data lines:

```
public string BlankLine(int n)
{
  string s = "";
  for (int i = 0; i < n; i++)
  {
s += " ";
  }
  return (s);
}
```

```csharp
public string MidLine(string string1, string string2, int
p)
{
  string s = "";
  // convert big string to character array
  char[] sArray = string2.ToCharArray();
  // put string1 in string2
  for (int i = p; i < p + string1.Length; i++)
  {
    sArray[i] = string1[i - p];
  }
  // put array in string variable
  for (int i = 0; i < string2.Length; i++)
  {
    s += sArray[i].ToString();
  }
  return (s);
}
```

5. Add the **CircleGeometry** general method from Example 6-3:

```csharp
public double[] CircleGeometry(double diameter)
{
  double [] geometry = new double[2];
  geometry[0] = Math.PI * diameter; // circumference
  geometry[1] = Math.PI * diameter * diameter / 4; // area
  return(geometry);
}
```

6. Use this code in the **btnCompute Click** event:

```csharp
private void BtnCompute_Click(object sender, EventArgs e)
{
  double d, delta;
  double[] values = new double[2];
  string myLine;
  string mySubString;
  const int numberValues = 20;
  const int lineWidth = 36;
  // read min/max and increment
  double dMin = Convert.ToDouble(txtMinimum.Text);
  double dMax = Convert.ToDouble(txtMaximum.Text);
  if (dMin >= dMax)
  {
    MessageBox.Show("Maximum must be less than minimum.",
"Error", MessageBoxButtons.OK, MessageBoxIcon.Error);
    txtMinimum.Focus();
```

```
      return;
   }
   delta = (dMax - dMin) / numberValues;
   // center header
   myLine = BlankLine(lineWidth);
   mySubString = "Circle Geometries";
   myLine = MidLine(mySubString, myLine, (int) (0.5 *
(lineWidth - mySubString.Length)));
   txtOutput.Text = myLine + "\r\n";
   txtOutput.Text += "Diameter     Perimeter
Area\r\n";
   for (d = dMin; d <= dMax; d += delta)
   {
     values = CircleGeometry(d);
     // right justify three values with two decimals
     myLine = BlankLine(lineWidth);
     mySubString = String.Format("{0:f2}", d);
     myLine = MidLine(mySubString, myLine, 8 -
mySubString.Length);
     mySubString = String.Format("{0:f2}", values[0]);
     myLine = MidLine(mySubString, myLine, 22 -
mySubString.Length);
     mySubString = String.Format("{0:f2}", values[1]);
     myLine = MidLine(mySubString, myLine, 36 -
mySubString.Length);
     txtOutput.Text += myLine + "\r\n";
   }
   txtMinimum.Focus();
}
```

This code reads the input values and determines the diameter range. It writes some header information and then, for each diameter, computes and prints geometries. Values are right justified.

7. Save the application (saved in **Example 7-5** folder in **LearnVCS\VCS Code\Class 7** folder). Run the application. When I used 30 and 70 for minimum and maximum diameters, respectively, I obtain this neatly formatted table of results:

Configuration Files

Earlier in this chapter, we discussed one possible application for a sequential file - an **initialization** or **configuration file**. These files are used to save user selected options from one execution of an application to the next. With such files, the user avoids the headache of re-establishing desired values each time an application is run.

Every Windows application uses configuration files. For example, a word processor remembers your favorite page settings, what font you like to use, what toolbars you want displayed, and many other options. How does it do this? When you start the program, it opens and reads the configuration file and sets your choices. When you exit the program, the configuration file is written back to disk, making note of any changes you may have made while using the word processor.

You can add the same capability to Visual C# applications. How do you decide what your configuration file will contain and how it will be formatted? That is completely up to you, the application designer. Typical information stored in a **configuration** file includes: current dates and times, check box settings, radio button settings, selected colors, font name, font style, font size, and selected menu options. You decide what is important in your application. You develop variables to save information and read and write these variables from and to the sequential configuration file. There is usually one variable (numeric, string, date, Boolean) for each option being saved. And, I usually place each variable on its own line (using **WriteLine** method) in the configuration file. That way, no 'tokenizing' is required.

Once you've decided on values to save and the format of your file, how do you proceed? A first step is to create an initial file using a text editor. Save your configuration file in your project's application path (**Bin\Debug** folder). Configuration files will always be kept in the application path. And, the usual three letter file extension for a configuration file is **ini** (for initialization). When distributing your application to other users, be sure to include a copy of the configuration file. When creating a **Setup** program for an application using a configuration file, you need to include the file in **Step 4** of the **Setup Wizard** (refer to those steps in Chapter 6).

Once you have developed the configuration file, you need to write code to fit this framework:

When your application begins (Form **Load** event), open (**StreamReader** object) and read (**ReadLine** method) the configuration file and use the variables to establish the respective options. Establishing options involves things like setting Font objects, establishing colors, simulating click events on check boxes and radio buttons, and setting properties.

When your application ends (Form **FormClosing** event), examine all options to be saved, establish respective variables to represent these options, and open (**StreamWriter** method) and write (**WriteLine** method, usually) the configuration file. We write the configuration file in the Form FormClosing event for two reasons. Usually an application will have an Exit button or an Exit option in the menu structure. The code to exit an application is usually:

```
this.Close();
```

This statement will activate the Form **FormClosing** event. Also, most Windows applications have a little box with an **X** in the upper right hand corner of the form that can be used to stop an application. In fact, in most applications we have built in this class, we need to use this box to stop things. When this 'X box' is clicked, any exit routine you have coded is **ignored** and the program immediately transfers to the Form **FormClosing** event.

Example 7-6

Configuration Files

1. We will modify the Note Editor built in Chapter 6 to save four pieces of information in a configuration file: bold status, italic status, underline status and selected font size. Open the **Note Editor** project. Use either **Example 6-4** or **Problem 6-2**, if you did that problem. I use Problem 6-2 (it includes an About form).

2. Add this line at the top of the code window with the other **using** statements:

```
using System.IO;
```

3. Use this code in the **frmEdit Load** event method:

```
private void FrmEdit_Load(object sender, EventArgs e)
{
    int i;
    // Open configuration file and set font values
    StreamReader inputFile = new
StreamReader(Application.StartupPath + "\\note.ini");
    mnuFmtBold.Checked =
Convert.ToBoolean(inputFile.ReadLine());
    mnuFmtItalic.Checked =
Convert.ToBoolean(inputFile.ReadLine());
    mnuFmtUnderline.Checked =
Convert.ToBoolean(inputFile.ReadLine());
    i = Convert.ToInt32(inputFile.ReadLine());
    switch (i)
    {
        case 1:
            mnuFmtSizeSmall.PerformClick();
            break;
        case 2:
            mnuFmtSizeMedium.PerformClick();
            break;
        case 3:
            mnuFmtSizeLarge.PerformClick();
            break;
    }
    inputFile.Close();
    ChangeFont();
}
```

In this code, the configuration file (named **note.ini**) is opened. We read three Boolean values that establish whether checks should be next to bold, italic and underline, respectively, in the menu structure. Then, an integer is read and used to set font size (1-small, 2-medium, 3-large). Note use of the **PerformClick** method to simulate clicking on the corresponding menu option.

4. Use this code in the **frmEdit FormClosing** event method:

```
private void FrmEdit_FormClosing(object sender,
FormClosingEventArgs e)
{
  // Open configuration file and write font values
  StreamWriter outputFile = new
StreamWriter(Application.StartupPath + "\\note.ini");
  outputFile.WriteLine(mnuFmtBold.Checked);
  outputFile.WriteLine(mnuFmtItalic.Checked);
  outputFile.WriteLine(mnuFmtUnderline.Checked);
  if (mnuFmtSizeSmall.Checked)
  {
    outputFile.WriteLine(1);
  }
  else if (mnuFmtSizeMedium.Checked)
  {
    outputFile.WriteLine(2);
  }
  else
  {
    outputFile.WriteLine(3);
  }
  outputFile.Close();
}
```

This code does the 'inverse' of the procedure followed in the frmEdit Load event. The configuration file is opened for output. Three Boolean variables representing current status of the bold, italic, and underline check marks are written to the file. Then, an integer representing the selected font size is written prior to closing and saving the file.

5. Save the application (saved in **Example 7-6** folder in **LearnVCS\VCS Code\Class 7** folder). Run the application. You will see this error message:

and this line of code is highlighted:

```
StreamReader inputFile = new
StreamReader(Application.StartupPath + "\\note.ini");
```

This message is telling us that the configuration file cannot be found. Of course, it can't - we forgot to create it! If you are using configuration files, you must always create an initial version. Open a text editor (**Notepad** will work) and type these four lines:

```
False
False
False
1
```

This says that bold, italic and underline options will be unchecked (False) and the font size will be small (represented by the 1). Save this four line file as **note.ini** in the application directory (the **Bin\Debug** folder within your project folder). Try running it again and things should be fine. Try changing any of the saved options and exit the program. Run it again and you should see the selected options are still there. Any text typed will have disappeared. We'll solve the 'disappearing text' problem next when we look at how to save text in a sequential file.

Writing and Reading Text Using Sequential Files

In many applications, we would like to be able to save text information and retrieve it for later reference. This information could be a **text file** created by an application or the contents of a Visual C# **text box** control. . Writing and reading text using sequential files involves some functions we have already seen and a couple of new ones.

To **write** a sequential text file, we follow the simple procedure: open the file for output, write the file, close the file. If the file is a line-by-line text file, each line of the file is written to disk using a single **Write** or **WriteLine** statement. Use **Write** if a line already has a new line (\r\n) character appended to it. Use **WriteLine** if there is no such character. So, to write **myLine** to **outputFile**, use either:

```
outputFile.Write(myLine);
```

or

```
outputFile.WriteLine(myLine);
```

This assumes you have somehow generated the string **myLine**. How you generate this data depends on your particular application. You may have lines of text or may form the lines using techniques just discussed. The **Write** or **WriteLine** statement should be in a loop that encompasses all lines of the file. You must know the number of lines in your file, beforehand. A typical code segment to accomplish this task is:

```
StreamWriter outputFile = new StreamWriter(myFile);
for (int i = o; i < numberLines; i++)
{
..// need code here to generate string data myLine
..outputFile.WriteLine(myLine);
}
outputFile.Close();
```

This code writes **numberLines** text lines to the sequential file **myFile**.

If we want to write the contents of the **Text** property of a text box named **txtExample** to a file named **c:\MyFolder\MyFile.txt**, we only need three lines of code:

```
StreamWriter outputFile = new
StreamWriter("c:\\MyFolder\\MyFile.txt");
outputFile.Write(txtExample.Text);
outputFile.Close();
```

The text is now saved in the file for later retrieval.

To **read** the contents of a previously-saved text file, we follow similar steps to the writing process: open the file (**StreamReader** object), read the file, close the file. If the file is a text file, we read each individual line with the **ReadLine** method:

```
myLine = inputFile.ReadLine();
```

This line is usually placed in a **do/while** structure that is repeated until all lines of the file are read in. The **Peek** method can be used to detect an end-of-file condition, if you don't know, beforehand, how many lines are in the file. A typical code segment to accomplish this task is:

```
StreamReader inputFile = new StreamReader(myFile);
do
{
  myLine = inputFile.ReadLine();
   // do something with the line of text
}
while (inputFile.Peek() != -1);
```

This code reads text lines from the sequential file **myFile** until the end-of-file is reached. You could put a counter in the loop to count lines if you like.

To place the contents of a sequential file into a text box control, we use a new method, **ReadToEnd.** This method reads a text file until the end is reached. So, to place the contents of a previously saved sequential file (**c:\MyFolder\MyFile.txt**) into the **Text** property of a text box control named **txtExample**, we need these three lines of code:

```
StreamReader inputFile = new
StreamReader("c:\\MyFolder\\MyFile.txt");
txtExample.Text = inputFile.ReadToEnd();
inputFile.Close();
```

SaveFileDialog Control

In Toolbox:

Below Form (Default Properties):

As mentioned earlier, when a sequential file is opened using **StreamWriter**, if the file being opened already exists, it is first erased. This is fine for files like configuration files. We want to overwrite these files. But, for other files, this might not be desirable behavior. Hence, prior to overwriting a sequential file, we want to make sure it is acceptable. Using the **SaveFileDialog** control to obtain filenames will provide this "safety factor." This control insures that any path selected for saving a file exists and that if an existing file is selected, the user has agreed to overwriting that file.

SaveFileDialog **Properties:**

Name	Gets or sets the name of the save file dialog (I usually name this control **dlgSave**).
AddExtension	Indicates whether the dialog box automatically adds an extension to a file name if the user omits the extension.
CheckFileExists	Indicates whether the whether the dialog box displays a warning if the user specifies a file name that does not exist. Useful if you want the user to save to an existing file.
CheckPathExists	Indicates whether the dialog box displays a warning if the user specifies a path that does not exist.
CreatePrompt	Indicates whether the dialog box prompts the user for permission to create a file if the user specifies a file that does not exist.
DefaultExt	Gets or sets the default file extension.
FileName	Gets or sets a string containing the file name selected in the file dialog box.
Filter	Gets or sets the current file name filter string, which determines the choices that appear in "Files of type" box.

SaveFileDialog **Properties** (continued)

FilterIndex	Gets or sets the index of the filter currently selected in the file dialog box.
InitialDirectory	Gets or sets the initial directory displayed by the file dialog box.
OverwritePrompt	Indicates whether the dialog box displays a warning if the user specifies a file name that already exists. Default value is True.
Title	Gets or sets the file dialog box title.

SaveFileDialog **Methods**:

ShowDialog	Displays the dialog box. Returned value indicates which button was clicked by user (**OK** or **Cancel**).

The **SaveFileDialog** control will appear in the tray area of the design window. The **ShowDialog** method is used to display the **SaveFileDialog** control. For a control named **dlgSave**, the appropriate code is:

```
dlgSave.ShowDialog();
```

And the displayed dialog box is:

The user types a name in the File name box (or selects a file using the dialog control). The file type is selected form the **Files of type** box (values here set with the **Filter** property). Once selected, the **Save** button is clicked. **Cancel** can be clicked to cancel the save operation. If the user selects an existing file and clicks **Save**, the following dialog will appear:

This is the aforementioned protection against inadvertently overwriting an existing file.

The ShowDialog method returns the clicked button. It returns **DialogResult.OK** if Save is clicked and returns **DialogResult.Cancel** if Cancel is clicked. The **FileName** property contains the complete path to the selected file.

Typical use of **SaveFileDialog** control:

  ➤ Set the **Name, DefaultExt, Filter,** and **Title** properties.
  ➤ Use **ShowDialog** method to display dialog box.
  ➤ Read **FileName** property to determine selected file

Example 7-7

Note Editor - Reading and Saving Text Files

1. We'll now add the capability to read in and save the contents of the text box in the Note Editor application we modified in Example 7-6. Load that application (saved in the **Example 7-6** folder in **LearnVCS\VCS Code\Class 7** folder). If you started a new project folder for this modification, make sure to copy the configuration file (**note.ini**) to the **Bin\Debug** folder in the project folder (you may have to create the folder first). Add **OpenFileDialog** and **SaveFileDialog** controls to the project.

2. Set these properties:

    openFileDialog1:
Name	dlgOpen
FileName	[blank]
Filter	Text Files (*.txt)|*.txt
Title	Open File

    saveFileDialog1:
Name	dlgSave
DefaultExt	txt
FileName	[Blank]
Filter	Text Files (*.txt)|*.txt
Title	Save File

3. Modify the **File** menu in your application, such that **Open** and **Save** options are included. To do this, click on the **File** option, right-click the separator bar and choose **Insert New**. A blank item will appear above the separator bar. Repeat the insert process to add another item. Type the **Text** properties. The File menu should now read:

File
   New
   Open
   Save
   ———

   Exit

Properties for these new menu items should be:

Text	Name
&Open	mnuFileOpen
&Save	mnuFileSave

4. The two new menu options need code. Use this code in the **mnuFileOpen Click** event:

```
private void MnuFileOpen_Click(object sender, EventArgs e)
{
  if (dlgOpen.ShowDialog() == DialogResult.OK)
  {
    StreamReader inputFile = new
StreamReader(dlgOpen.FileName);
    txtEdit.Text = inputFile.ReadToEnd();
    inputFile.Close();
    txtEdit.SelectionLength = 0;
  }
}
```

5. And for the **MnuFileSave Click** method, use this code:

```
private void mnuFileSave_Click(object sender, EventArgs e)
{
  if (dlgSave.ShowDialog() == DialogResult.OK)
  {
    StreamWriter outputFile = new
StreamWriter(dlgSave.FileName);
    outputFile.Write(txtEdit.Text);
    outputFile.Close();
  }
}
```

6. Save your application (saved in **Example 7-7** folder in the **LearnVCS\VCS Code\Class 7** folder). Run it and test the **Open** and **Save** functions. Note you have to save a file before you can open one.

Note, too, that after opening a file, text is displayed based on current format settings. It would be nice to save formatting information along with the text. You could do this by saving an additional file with the format settings (bold, italic, underline status and font size). Then, when opening the text file, open the accompanying format file and set the saved format. Note this is much like having a configuration file for each saved text file. See if you can make these modifications. In Class 10, we will see another text control (the rich text box) that saves formatting at the same time it saves the text.

Another thing you could try: Modify the message box that appears when you try to **Exit**. Make it ask if you wish to save your file before exiting - provide **Yes**, **No, Cancel** buttons. Program the code corresponding to each possible response. Use calls to existing methods, if possible.

Error Handling

No matter how hard we try, **errors** do creep into our applications. These errors can be grouped into three categories:

1. **Syntax** errors
2. **Run-time** errors
3. **Logic** errors

Syntax errors occur when you mistype a command, leave out an expected phrase or argument, or omit needed punctuation. Visual C# and the Intellisense feature detects these errors as they occur and even provides help in correcting them. You cannot run a Visual C# program until all syntax errors have been corrected. The **Task** window in the Visual C# IDE lists all syntax errors and identifies the line they occur in. To help locate syntax errors, it is advisable to turn on the line number option in the code window. To do this, select the **Tools** menu item in the IDE. Then, choose **Options**. In the left side of the window that appears (make sure **Show all settings** is checked), choose **Text Editor** (and perhaps **C#**). Then, choose the **Line Numbers** option.

Run-time errors are usually beyond your program's control. Examples include: when a variable takes on an unexpected value (divide by zero), invalid text box entries, when a drive door is left open, or when a file is not found. We saw examples of run-time errors in building one of our sequential file examples. In Example 7-6, we encountered a missing file error when trying to read a configuration file. Visual C# lets us trap such errors and make attempts to correct them. Doing so precludes our program from unceremoniously stopping. User's do not like programs that stop unexpectedly!

Logic errors are the most difficult to find. With logic errors, the program will usually run, but will produce incorrect or unexpected results. The Visual C# debugger is an aid in detecting logic errors.

Some ways to minimize errors are:

> ➤ Design your application carefully. More design time means less debugging time.
> ➤ Use comments where applicable to help you remember what you were trying to do.
> ➤ Use consistent and meaningful naming conventions for your variables, controls, objects, and methods.

Run-Time Error Trapping and Handling

Run-time errors (referred to in Visual C# as **exceptions**) are "catchable." That is, Visual C# recognizes an error has occurred and enables you to catch it and take corrective action (handle the error). As mentioned, if an error occurs and is not caught, your program will usually end in a rather unceremonious manner. Most run-time errors occur when your application is working with files, either trying to open, read, write or save a file. Other common run-time errors are divide by zero, overflow (exceeding a data type's range) and improper data types.

Visual C# uses a structured approach to catching and handling exceptions. The structure is referred to as a **try/catch/finally** block. And the annotated syntax for using this block is:

```
try
{
  // here is code you try where some kind of
  // error may occur

}
catch (ExceptionType ex)
{
  // if error described by exception of ExceptionType
  // occurs, process this code

}
catch (Exception ex)
{
  // if any other error occurs, process this code

}
finally
{
  // Execute this code whether error occurred or not
  // this block is optional

}
// Execution continues here
```

The above code works from the top, down. It 'tries' the code between **try** and the first **catch** statement. If no error is encountered, any code in the **finally** block will be executed and the program will continue after the right brace closing the **try/catch/finally** block. If an exception (error) occurs, the program will look to find, if any, the first **catch** statement (you can have multiple catch statements and must have at least one) that matches the exception that occurred. If one is found, the code in that respective block is executed (code to help clear up the error - the exception handling), then the code in the **finally** block, then program execution continues after the closing brace. If an error occurs that doesn't match a particular exception, the code in the 'generic' **catch** block is executed, followed by the code in the **finally** block. And, program execution continues after the closing brace.

This structure can be used to trap and handle any **Type** of exception defined in the Visual C# **Exception** class. There are hundreds of possible exceptions related to data access, input and output functions, graphics functions, data types and numerical computations. Here is a list of example exception types (their names are descriptive of the corresponding error condition):

`ArgumentException`	`ArgumentNullException`
`ArgumentOutOfRangeException`	`ArithmeticException`
`ArrayTypeMismatchException`	`DivideByZeroException`
`DllNotFoundException`	`Exception`
`FormatException`	`IndexOutOfRangeException`
`DirectoryNotFoundException`	`EndOfStreamException`
`FileNotFoundException`	`IOException`
`OutOfMemoryException`	`OverflowException`

Let's take a closer look at the **catch** block. When you define a catch block, you define the exception type you want to catch. For example, if want to catch a divide by zero condition, an **DivideByZeroException**, we use:

```
catch (DivideByZeroException ex)
{
   // Code to execute if divide by zero occurs
}
```

If in the **try** block, a divide by zero occurs, the code following this **catch** statement will be executed. You would probably put a message box here to tell the user what happened and provide him or her with options of how to fix the problem. To help with the messaging capability, the optional variable you define as the exception (**ex**, in this case) has a **Message** property you can use. The message is retrieved using **ex.Message**.

A **try** block may be exited using the **break** statement. Be aware any code in the **finally** block will still be executed even if break is encountered. Once the finally code is executed, program execution continues after the brace closing the try block.

Example of **try** block to catch a "file not found" error:

```
try
{
   // Code to open file
}
catch (FileNotFoundException ex)
{
   // message box describing the error
   MessageBox.Show(ex.Message, "Error",
MessageBoxButtons.OK, MessageBoxIcon.Error);
}
finally
{
   //Code to close file (even if error occurred)
}
```

Example of **try** block to catch a "formatting" error (happens when trying to convert an empty text string to a numeric value):

```
try
{
   // Code to format text string
}
catch (FormatException ex)
{
   // write code that just sets numeric value to 0.0
}
finally
{
   //Code to close file (even if error occurred)
}
```

Example of a **generic** error catching routine:

```
try
{
  // Code to try
}
catch (Exception ex)
{
  // message box describing the error
  MessageBox.Show(ex.Message, "Error",
MessageBoxButtons.OK, MessageBoxIcon.Error);
}
finally
{
  //Code to finish the block
}
```

We've only taken a brief look at the structured run-time error handling capabilities of Visual C#. It is difficult to be more specific without knowing just what an application's purpose is. You need to know what type of errors you are looking for and what corrective actions should be taken if these errors are encountered. As you build and run your own applications, you will encounter run-time errors. These errors may be due to errors in your code. If so, fix them. But, they may also be errors that arise due to some invalid inputs from your user, because a file does not meet certain specifications or because a disk drive is not ready. You need to use error handling to keep such errors from shutting down your application, leaving your user in a frustrated state.

Example 7-8

Note Editor - Error Trapping

1. Many times, users may delete files (including configuration files) not knowing what they're doing. In this example, we modify the Note Editor application (again) so that if the configuration file cannot be found, the program will still run. We use error trapping to catch the 'file not found' exception. If the file can't be found, we'll establish values for the four missing format variables and continue Load Example 7-7 (saved in the **Example 7-7** folder in **LearnVCS\VCS Code\Class 7** folder). Make sure the **note.ini** file is <u>not</u> in your project's **Bin\Debug** folder. We want to see if our program works without it.

2. Modify the **frmEdit Load** event to enable error trapping (new code is shaded):

```
private void FrmEdit_Load(object sender, EventArgs e)
{
  int i;
  try
  {
    // Open configuration file and set font values
    StreamReader inputFile = new StreamReader("note.ini");
    mnuFmtBold.Checked =
Convert.ToBoolean(inputFile.ReadLine());
    mnuFmtItalic.Checked =
Convert.ToBoolean(inputFile.ReadLine());
    mnuFmtUnderline.Checked =
Convert.ToBoolean(inputFile.ReadLine());
    i = Convert.ToInt32(inputFile.ReadLine());
    switch (i)
    {
      case 1:
        mnuFmtSizeSmall.PerformClick();
        break;
      case 2:
        mnuFmtSizeMedium.PerformClick();
        break;
      case 3:
        mnuFmtSizeLarge.PerformClick();
        break;
    }
    inputFile.Close();
  }
  catch (FileNotFoundException)
```

```
    {
      MessageBox.Show("Configuration file not found.",
"Default Reset");
      mnuFmtBold.Checked = false;
      mnuFmtItalic.Checked = false;
      mnuFmtUnderline.Checked = false;
      mnuFmtSizeSmall.PerformClick();
    }
  ChangeFont();
}
```

In this code, if the file is not found, the **catch** block establishes values for the bold, italic and underline status (all False) and a font size (small). This allows the program to run to completion.

3. Save your application (saved in **Example 7-8** folder in the **LearnVCS\VCS Code\Class 7** folder). Run it and you should see this:

If you don't get this message and the program runs, stop the application and delete the **note.ini** file from the project's **Bin\Debug** folder. Then, run again and you should see the above message box generated in the catch block.

Choose some formatting features, stop the application and run it again. The error message box will not be seen - why? The reason you don't see the error message again is that when you exited the program, it wrote the **note.ini** file in the proper folder. The neat thing about such code is that we fixed a problem without the user even knowing there was a problem.

Debugging Visual C# Programs

We now consider the search for, and elimination of, **logic errors**. These are errors that don't prevent an application from running, but cause incorrect or unexpected results. Logic errors are sometimes difficult to find; they may be very subtle. Visual C# provides an excellent set of **debugging** tools to aid in this search.

A typical logic error could involve an **if** structure. Look at this example:

```
if (a > 5 && b < 4)
{
..// do this code
}
else if (a == 6)
{
   // do this code
}
```

In this example, if a is 6 and b is 2, the **else if** statement (which you wanted executed if a is 6) will never be seen. In this case, swap the two **if** clauses to get the desired behavior. Or, another possible source of a logic error:

```
StreamReader inputFile = new
StreamReader(dlgOpen.FileName);
inputFile.ReadLine(myLine);
```

In this little 'snippet,' a file the user selected using an file open dialog control is opened and the first line read. It looks okay, but what if the user selected a file that really wasn't meant to be used by your application. This would be a classic case of GIGO (garbage in - garbage out).

Debugging code is an art, not a science. There are no prescribed processes that you can follow to eliminate all logic errors in your program. The usual approach is to eliminate them as they are discovered.

What we'll do here is present the debugging tools available in the Visual C# environment and describe their use with an example. You, as the program designer, should select the debugging approach and tools you feel most comfortable with. The more you use the debugger, the more you will learn about it. Fortunately, the simpler tools will accomplish the tasks for most debugging applications.

The interface between your application and the debugging tools is via several different windows in the Visual C# IDE: the **Output** window, the **Locals** window, the **Breakpoints** window, the **Watch** window, and the **Auto** window. These windows can be accessed from the **View** menu (the Immediate window can also be accessed by pressing **Ctrl+G**). Or, they can be selected from the dropdown button on the **Debug Toolbar** (accessed using the **Toolbars** option under the **View** menu):

We will examine other buttons on this toolbar as we continue. This toolbar can be customized with more features using the **Options** button. Consult on-line help for the procedure to do this.

All debugging using the debug window is done when your application is in **Debugging** (or **break**) mode. Recall the application mode is always displayed in the title bar of Visual C#. You usually enter break mode by setting **breakpoints** (we'll look at this in a bit), pressing the **Break** button on the toolbar when your program encounters an untrapped run-time error, the program usually goes into debugging mode.

Once in debugging mode, the debug windows and other tools can be used to:

> ➢ Determine values of variables
> ➢ Set breakpoints
> ➢ Set watch variables and expressions
> ➢ Manually control the application
> ➢ Determine which methods have been called
> ➢ Change the values of variables and properties

The best way to learn proper debugging is do an example. We'll build that example now, then learn how to use the Visual C# debugger.

Example 7-9

Debugging Example

1. This example simply has a form with two button controls used to execute some code. You can either build it or just load it from the course notes (saved in **Example 7-9** folder in **LearnVCS\VCS Code\Class 7** folder).

2. If you choose to build, start a new application and put two button controls on the form. **Name** the buttons **btnMethod1** and **btnMethod2**. Set the buttons' **Text** properties to **Method &1** and **Method &2**, respectively. My little form looks like this:

3. The application has two variables with form level scope:

```
int xCount = 0, ySum = 0;
```

xCount keeps track of the number of times each of two counter variables is incremented. **ySum** sums all computed Y values.

4. The first button's **Name** property is **btnMethod1**. The code for its **Click** event is:

```
private void BtnMethod1_Click(object sender, EventArgs e)
{
  int x1 = -1, y1;
  do
  {
    x1++;
    y1 = Fcn(x1);
    xCount++;
    ySum += y1;
  }
  while (x1 < 20);
}
```

This code uses a **do/while** structure to increment the counter variable **x1** from 0 to 20. For each x1, a corresponding **y1** is computed using the general method **Fcn**. In each cycle of the do/while, the form level variables **xCount** and **ySum** are adjusted accordingly.

5. The general method (**Fcn**) used by this method is:

```
public int Fcn(int x)
{
  double value;
  value = 0.1 * x * x;
  return ((int) value);
}
```

This code just computes an 'integer parabola.' No need to know what that means. Just recognize, given an x value, it computes and returns a y.

6. The **Click** event for the second button (**Name btnMethod2**) is:

```
private void BtnMethod2_Click(object sender, EventArgs e)
{
   int x2, y2;
   for (x2 = -10; x2 <= 10; x2++)
   {
     y2 = 5 * Fcn(x2);
     xCount++;
     ySum += y2;
   }
}
```

This code is similar to that for the other button. It uses a **for** structure to increment the counter variable **x2** from -10 to 10. For each x2, a corresponding **y2** is computed using the same general method **Fcn**. In each cycle of the for loop, the form level variables **xCount** and **ySum** are adjusted accordingly.

7. Save and run the application (as mentioned, saved in **Example 7-9** folder in **LearnVCS\VCS Code\Class 7** folder). Notice not much happens if you click either button. Admittedly, this code doesn't do much, especially without any output, but it makes a good example for looking at debugger use. So, get ready to try debugging.

Using the Debugging Tools

There are several **debugging tools** available for use in Visual C#. Access to these tools is provided via both menu options and buttons on the **Debug** toolbar. Some of the tools we will examine are:

> ➤ **Breakpoints** which let us stop our application.
> ➤ **Locals, Watch** and **Autos windows** which let us examine variable values.
> ➤ **Call stack** which let us determine how we got to a certain point in code.
> ➤ **Step into, step over** and **step out** which provide manual execution of our code.

These tools work in conjunction with the various debugger windows.

Writing to the Output Window:

There is even a simpler debugging tool than any of those mentioned above. You can write directly to the **output** window while an application is running. Sometimes, this is all the debugging you may need. A few carefully placed write statements can sometimes clear up all logic errors, especially in small applications. To write to the output window, use the **WriteLine** method of the **Console** object:

    Console.WriteLine(StringData);

This will write the string information **StringData** as a line in the output window. Hence, the output window can be used as a kind of scratch pad for your application. Any information written here is just for your use. Your users will never see it. You also must maintain the output window. Nothing is ever deleted. To manually clear the window, right-click it and select **Clear All**.

Console.WriteLine Example:

1. Modify the **btnMethod1 Click** event in Example 7-9 by including the shaded line:

```
private void BtnMethod1_Click(object sender, EventArgs e)
{
   int x1 = -1, y1;
   do
   {
     x1++;
     y1 = Fcn(x1);
     Console.WriteLine(x1.ToString() + " " +
y1.ToString());
     xCount++;
     ySum += y1;
   }
   while (x1 < 20);
}
```

Run the application. Click the **Method 1** button.

2. Examine the output window. To view the output window, select the **View** menu option. Select **Output** from the next submenu. The window should show:

```
Output                                                    ▾ ☐ ✕
Show output from: Debug                                   ▾  ⌐  "
 The thread 0x1ffc has exited with code 0 (0x0).
 'Example 7-9.vshost.exe' (CLR v2.0.50727: Example 7-9.vshost.e
 0 0
 1 0
 2 0
 3 0
 4 1
 5 2
 6 3
 7 4
 8 6
 9 8
 10 10
 11 12
 12 14
 13 16
 14 19
 15 22|
 16 25
 17 28
 18 32
 19 36
 20 40
 The program '[7152] Example 7-9.vshost.exe' has exited with cc
                                                            ▾
 ◀  ▭▭▭▭▭                                                   ▶
```

Note how, at each iteration of the loop, the program prints the value of x1 and y1. You can use this information to make sure x1 is incrementing correctly, ending at the proper value and that y1 values look acceptable. You can get a lot of information using **Console.WriteLine**. If needed, you can add additional text information in the WriteLine argument to provide specific details on what is printed (variable names, method names, etc.).

3. Before leaving this example, delete the **Console.WriteLine** statement.

Breakpoints:

In the above example, the program ran to completion before we could look at the output window. In many applications, we want to stop the application while it is running, examine variables and then continue running. This can be done with **breakpoints.** A breakpoint marks a line in code where you want to stop (temporarily) program execution, that is force the program into **break** mode. One way to set a breakpoint is to put the cursor in the line of code you want to break at and press **<F9>**. Or, a simpler way is to click next to the desired line of code in the vertical shaded bar at the left of the code window:

```
18        int xCount = 0, ySum = 0;
19
20   ⊟    private void btnMethod1_Click(object sender, EventArgs e)
21        {
22          int x1 = -1, y1;
23          do
24          {
25            x1++;
26            y1 = fcn(x1);
27            xCount++;
28            ySum += y1;
29          }
30          while (x1 < 20);
31        }
32   ⊟    public int fcn(int x)
33        {
34          double value;
35          value = 0.1 * x * x:
```

Click here to set a breakpoint in Line 27

Once set, a large red dot marks the line along with shading:

```
18        int xCount = 0, ySum = 0;
19
20   ⊟    private void btnMethod1_Click(object sender, EventArgs e)
21        {
22          int x1 = -1, y1;
23          do
24          {
25            x1++;
26            y1 = fcn(x1);
27            xCount++;
28            ySum += y1;
29          }
30          while (x1 < 20);
31        }
32   ⊟    public int fcn(int x)
33        {
34          double value;
35          value = 0.1 * x * x;
```

To remove a breakpoint, repeat the above process. Pressing **<F9>** or clicking the line at the left will 'toggle' the breakpoint. If you need to clear all breakpoints in an application, select the **Debug** menu item and the **Delete All Breakpoints** option. Breakpoints can be added/deleted at **design** time or in **break** mode.

When you run your application, Visual C# will stop when it reaches lines with breakpoints and allow you to check variables and expressions. To continue program operation after a breakpoint, press **<F5>**, click the **Continue** button on the toolbar, or choose **Continue** from the **Debug** menu.

Breakpoint Example:

1. Set a breakpoint on the **xCount++** line in the **btnMethod1 Click** event (as demonstrated above). Run the program and click the **Method 1** button. The program will stop at the desired line (it will be highlighted). Hold the cursor over **x1** two lines above this line and you should see:

```
17
18        int xCount = 0, ySum = 0;
19
20        private void btnMethod1_Click(object sender, EventArgs e)
21        {
22            int x1 = -1, y1;
23            do
24            {
25                x1++;
26                y1  ⊘ x1  0   x1);
27                xCount++;
28                ySum += y1;
29            }
30            while (x1 < 20);
31        }
```

Notice a tooltip appears displaying the current value of this variable (**x1 = 0**). You can move the cursor onto any variable in this method to see its value. If you check values on lines prior to the line with the breakpoint, you will be given the current value. If you check values on lines at or after the breakpoint, you will get their last computed value.

2. Continue running the program (click the **Continue** button or press **<F5>**). The program will again stop at this line, but **x1** will now be equal to **1**. Check it. Continue running the program, examining **x1** and **x1** (and **xCount** and **ySum** too).

3. Try other breakpoints in the application if you have time. Once done, make sure you clear all the breakpoints you used.

Viewing Variables in the Locals Window:

In the breakpoint example, we used tooltips to examine variable values. We could see variable values, no matter what their scope. The **locals** window can also be used to view variables, but only those with method level scope. As execution switches from method to method, the contents of the local window change to reflect only the variables applicable to the current method. The locals window can be viewed using the dropdown button on the debug toolbar or select the **Debug** menu option, choose **Windows**, then **Locals**.

Locals Window Example:

1. Set breakpoints on the **xCount++** lines in both the **btnMethod1 Click** event and the **btnMethod2 Click** event. Run the program and click the **Method 1** button. The program will stop at the desired line. View the locals window and you should see:

All the variables local to the this method are seen. Continue running the application (click **Continue** button or press **<F5>**), watching x1 and y1 change with each loop execution.

2. Eventually (once x1 exceeds 20), the application form will reappear. When it does, click the **Method 2** button. The program will stop at the desired line in that method and you will see:

which are initial values for the local variables (x2 and y2) in this method. Continue running, watching the values change. Stop the example whenever you want. Remove the breakpoint in the **btnMethod2 Click** event.

Viewing Variables in the Watch Window:

Watch windows can also be used to examine variables. They can maintain values for both local and form level variables. And, you can even change the values of variables in the watch window (be careful if you do this; strange things can happen). The watch window can only be accessed in **break** mode. At that time, you simply right-click on any variables you want to add to the watch window and select the **Add Watch** option. A watch window can be viewed using the dropdown button on the debug toolbar or select the **Debug** menu option, choose **Windows,** then **Watch,** then one of four available watch windows.

Watch Window Example:

1. Make sure there is still a breakpoint on the **xCount++** line in the **btnMethod1 Click** event. Run the program and click the **Method 1** button. The program will stop at the desired line. Open a watch window. Right-click on the **xCount** variable and select **Add Watch**. Do the same for the **ySum** variable. You should now see:

The current value of **xCount** and **ySum** are seen. They are both zero. Continue running the application (click **Continue** button or press **<F5>**), watching xCount and ySum change with each loop execution.

2. When the form reappears, click **Method 2**. Then, click **Method 1** again. The program will again stop at the marked line. The values of xCount and ySum should have changed significantly with the new values added when the btnMethod2 Click event was executed.

The two watch variables can be deleted by right-clicking the variable name in the watch window and selecting **Delete Watch**. Again, you can only do this in **break** mode.

Viewing Variables in the Autos Window:

The **autos window** combines features of the locals and watch windows. This window displays values of all local and form level variables for the current method. As program control moves from one method to another, the autos window adapts to the new variable set. The autos window can only be accessed in **break** mode. The auto window can be viewed using the dropdown button on the debug toolbar or select the **Debug** menu option, choose **Windows**, then **Autos**.

Autos Window Example:

1. Set breakpoints on the **xCount++** lines in both the **btnMethod1 Click** event and the **btnMethod2 Click** event. Run the program and click the **Method 1** button. The program will stop at the desired line. View the autos window, click on the + next to the keyword **this** and you should see:

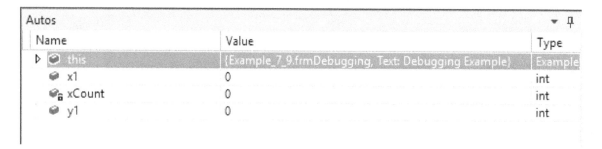

All the variables used in this method (local and form level scope) are seen. Continue running the application (click **Continue** button or press **<F5>**), watching the values change with each loop execution.

2. Eventually, the application form will reappear. When it does, click the
Method 2 button. The program will stop at the desired line in that method
and you will see:

which are current values for the local and form level scope variables in this
method. Continue running, watching the values change. Stop the example
whenever you want. Remove all breakpoints.

Call Stack Window:

General methods can be called from many places in an application. That's the idea of using a general method! If an error occurs in such a method, it is helpful to know which method was calling it. While in break mode, the **Call Stack** window will provide will display all active methods, that is those that have not been exited. The call stack window provides a road map of how you got to the point you are in the code. The call stack window can be viewed using the dropdown button on the debug toolbar or select the **Debug** menu option, choose **Windows**, then **Call Stack**.

Call Stack Window Example:

1. Set a breakpoint on the `value = 0.1 * x * x` line in the general method (**Fcn**). Run the application. Click **Method 1**. The program will break at the marked line. Open the call stack window and you will see:

The information of use to use is the top two lines. These lines tell us we are in **Fcn** method and it was called by the **BtnMethod1_Click** method on a form named **frmDebugging**. This would be very useful information if there were an error occurring in the method.

2. Keep running the application until the form appears again. Click **Method 2** and view the call stack window. You should now be able to see the method has been called by **BtnMethod2_Click**.

Single Stepping (Step Into) An Application:

A powerful feature of the Visual C# debugger is the ability to manually control execution of the code in your application. The **Step Into** option lets you execute your program one line at a time. It lets you watch how variables   choosing the **Step Into** option in the **Debug** menu, or by clicking the **Step Into** button on the toolbar:

You may choose to step through several lines at a time by using **Run To Cursor** option. With this option, click on a line below your current point of execution. Then, right-click the desired line and choose **Run To Cursor** in the dropdown menu. The program will run through every line up to the cursor location, then stop.

Step Into Example:

1. Set a breakpoint at the **for (x2 = -10; x2 <= 10; x2++)** line in the **btnMethod2 Click** event. Run the application. Click **Method 2**. The program will stop and the marked line will be highlighted in the code window:

```
37 ┤       }
38 ┌─     private void btnMethod2_Click(object sender, EventArgs e)
39 │      {
40 │        int x2, y2;
41 │        for (|x2 = -10; x2 <= 10; x2++)
42 │        {
43 │          y2 = 5 * fcn(x2);
44 │          xCount++;
45 │          ySum += y2;
46 │        }
47 ┤     }
```

2. Open the locals window and use the **Step Into** button to single step through the program. It's fun to see the program logic being followed. Notice how the contents of the locals window change as program control moves from the **btnMethod2 Click** event to the general method **Fcn**. When you are in the btnMethod2 Click method, values for **x2** and **y2** are listed. When in the function, values for **x** and **value** are given.

3. At some point, put the cursor on the closing right brace line in the **btnMethod2 Click** event. Try the **Run To Cursor** option. The method will finish its **for** loop without stopping again. Now, press <F5> to continue and the form will reappear.

Method Stepping (Step Over):

Did you notice in the example just studied that, after a while, it became annoying to have to single step through the function evaluation at every step of the for loop? While single stepping your program, if you come to a method call that you know operates properly, you can perform **method stepping**. This simply executes the entire method at once, treating as a single line of code, rather than one step at a time.

To move through a method in this manner, while in break mode, press <F10>, choose **Step Over** from the **Debug** menu, or press the **Step Over** button on the toolbar:

Step Over Example:

1. Run the previous example. Single step through it a couple of times.

2. One time through, when you are at the line calling the **Fcn** method, press the **Step Over** button. Notice how the program did not single step through the function as it did previously.

Method Exit (Step Out):

While stepping through your program, if you wish to complete the execution of a method you are in, without stepping through it line-by-line, choose the **Step Out** option. The method will be completed and you will be returned to the method accessing that function.

To perform this step out, press **Shift+<F11>**, choose **Step Out** from the **Debug** menu, or press the **Step Out** button on the toolbar

Step Out Example:

1. Run the previous example. Single step through it a couple of times. Also, try stepping over the function.

2. At some point, while single stepping through the function, press the **Step Out** button. Notice how control is immediately returned to the calling method (**btnMethod2 Click** event).

3. At some point, while in the **btnMethod2 Click** event, press the **Step Out** button. The method will be completed and the application form will reappear with the two button controls displayed.

Debugging Strategies

We've looked at each debugging tool briefly. Be aware this is a cursory introduction. Use the on-line help to delve into the details of each tool described. In particular, you might like to look at the **immediate** window and the **breakpoints** window. In the immediate window, you can type any legal Visual C# construct. You can print variable values, change values and run little snippets of code. In the breakpoints window, you can see a summary of all breakpoints and even add counters which keep track of how many times a breakpoint has been reached.

Only through lots of use and practice can you become a proficient debugger. You'll get this practice, too. Every time your application encounters a run-time error, the dialog box describing the error will have a **Break** button. Click that button to start using your new found debugging skills.

There are some common sense guidelines to follow when debugging. My first suggestion is: keep it **simple**. Many times, you only have one or two bad lines of code. And you, knowing your code best, can usually quickly narrow down the areas with bad lines. Don't set up some elaborate debugging method if you haven't tried a simple approach to find your error(s) first. Many times, just a few intelligently-placed **Console.WriteLine** statements or a few examinations of the watch and locals windows can solve your problem.

A tried and true approach to debugging can be called **Divide and Conquer**. If you're not sure where your error is, guess somewhere in the middle of your application code. Set a breakpoint there. If the error hasn't shown up by then, you know it's in the second half of your code. If it has shown up, it's in the first half. Repeat this division process until you've narrowed your search.

And, of course, the best debugging strategy is to be careful when you first design and write your application to minimize searching for errors later.

Class Review

After completing this class, you should understand:

- How to read and write sequential files (and the difference between using Write and WriteLine methods)
- How to use the Application.StartupPath parameter
- How to parse and build a text string
- How to use configuration files in an application
- How to use the FileSaveDialog control to save files
- How to implement run-time error trapping and handling in a Visual C# method
- How to use the various capabilities of the Visual C# debugger to find and eliminate logic errors

Practice Problems 7

Problem 7-1. Option Saving Problem. Load **Problem 4-1** (in the **LearnVCS\VCS Code\Class 4** folder), the practice problem used to examine sample message boxes. Modify this program to allow saving of the user inputs when application ends. Use a text file to save the information. When the application begins, it should reflect this set of saved inputs.

Problem 7-2. Text File Problem. Build an application that lets you look through your computer directories for text files (.txt extension) and view those files in a text box. The image viewer (Example 5-4) built in Class 5 is a good starting point.

Problem 7-3. Data File Problem. In the **LearnVCS\VCS Code\Class 7\Problem 7-3** folder is a file entitled **MAR95.DAT**. Open this file using the Windows Notepad. The first several lines of the file are:

```
144
"4/27/95","Detroit        ",2,3,0,"Opening Night  "
"4/28/95","Detroit        ",2,8,2,"               "
"4/29/95","Detroit        ",2,11,1,"               "
"4/30/95","Detroit        ",2,1,10,"               "
"5/1/95","Texas           ",1,4,1,"                "
"5/2/95","Texas           ",1,15,3,"               "
"5/3/95","Texas           ",1,5,1,"                "
"5/5/95","California      ",1,0,10,"               "
"5/6/95","California      ",1,5,7,"                "
"5/7/95","California      ",1,3,2,"                "
```

This file chronicles the strike-shortened 1995 season of the Seattle Mariners baseball team, their most exciting year. (Our apologies to foreign readers who don't understand the game of baseball!) The first line tells how many lines are in the file. Each subsequent line represents a single game. There are six variables on each line:

Variable Number	Variable Type	Description
1	String	Date of Game
2	String	Opponent
3	Integer	(1-Away game, 2-Home game)
4	Integer	Mariners runs
5	Integer	Opponent runs
6	String	Comment

Write an application that reads this file, determines which team won each game and outputs to another file (a comma-separated, or **csv**, file) the game number and current Mariners winning or losing streak (consecutive wins or losses). Use positive integers for wins, negative integers for losses.

As an example, the corresponding output file for the lines displayed above would be:

1,1 (a win)
2,2 (a win)
3,3 (a win)
4,-1 (a loss)
5,1 (a win)
6,2 (a win)
7,3 (a win)
8,-1 (a loss)
9,-2 (a loss)
10,1 (a win)

There will be 144 lines in this output file. Load the resulting file in Excel and obtain a bar chart for the output data.

Problem 7-4. Debugging Problem. Load the **Problem 7-4** project in the **LearnVCS\VCS Code\Class 7\Problem 7-4** folder. It's the temperature conversion example from Class 5 with some errors introduced. Run the application. It shouldn't run. Debug the program and get it running correctly.

Exercise 7-1

Information Tracking

Design and develop an application that allows the user to enter (on a daily basis) some piece of information that is to be saved for future review and reference. Examples could be stock price, weight, or high temperature for the day. The input screen should display the current date and an input box for the desired information. All values should be saved on disk for future retrieval and update. A scroll bar should be available for reviewing all previously-stored values.

Exercise 7-2

'Recent Files' Menu Option

Under the File menu on nearly every application (that opens files) is a list of the four most recently-used files (usually right above the Exit option). Modify your information tracker (Exercise 7-1) to implement such a feature. This is not trivial -- there are lots of things to consider. For example, you'll need a file to store the last four file names. You need to open that file and initialize the corresponding menu entries when you run the application -- you need to rewrite that file when you exit the application. You need logic to re-order file names when a new file is opened or saved. You need logic to establish new menu items as new files are used. You'll need additional error-trapping in the open procedure, in case a file selected from the menu no longer exists. Like I said, a lot to consider here.

8. Graphics Techniques with Visual C#

Review and Preview

In Chapter 5, we looked at using the picture box control to display graphics files. In this chapter, we extend our graphics programming skills to learn how to perform simple animations, build little games, draw lines, rectangles and ellipses and do some basic plotting of lines, bars and pie segments.

Most of the examples in this class will be relatively short. We show you how to do many graphics tasks. You can expand the examples to fit your needs.

Simple Animation

One of the more fun things to do with Visual C# programs is to create animated graphics. We'll look at a few simple **animation** techniques here. In Chapter 9, we look at even more detailed animations.

One of the simplest animation effects is achieved by **toggling** between two **images**. For example, you may have a picture of a stoplight with a red light. By quickly changing this picture to one with a green light, we achieve a dynamic effect - animation. Other two image animations could be open and closed file drawers, open and closed mail or smiling and frowning faces. The **Picture Box** control is used to achieve this animated effect.

The idea here is simple. A picture box control displays some picture (set via the **Image** property). Some event, for example clicking on the picture box or clicking on a button control, occurs. When this event occurs, we want to change or toggle the **Image** property to another picture.

In Chapter 5, we saw that one way to change the Image property of a picture box control at run-time was via the **FromFile** method of the **Image** object. You need to provide this method with a complete path to the graphics file to load into the picture box. Once given this path, the **FromFile** method loads the image from the specified disk file. In a simple animation, accessing a disk file each time the picture is toggled can cause problems. First, for detailed graphics files, the toggling effect may be slowed as the file is loaded. Second, you must insure the graphics file being accessed exists in the specified directory. Finally, if you plan to distribute your application, you need to remember to include any graphics files with the deployment package. Let's simplify this process a bit.

A better approach to simple animation is to include, in your project, an additional picture box control for each picture in the animation sequence (here, just two pictures). Set the **Image** property (at design time) of these controls to the pictures in the sequence. Set the **Visible** property of these controls to **False** so they are not seen at run-time. You will still have the visible picture box displaying the animation. Upon detection of the toggling event, simply set the **Image** property of this displaying picture box to the **Image** property of the appropriate 'hidden' picture box. With this approach, toggling is quick and no disk files are accessed. The graphics in the sequence are 'attached' to the form and do not have to be included as separate files with any deployment package.

The C# code for 'two-state' simple animation is straightforward. Define a form level scope variable (**pictureNumber**) that keeps track of the currently displayed picture (either a 0 or 1).

```
int pictureNumber;
```

Then, in the toggling event method use this code (**picDisplay** is the displaying picture box control, **picChoice0** is a hidden picture box with one graphic, **picChoice0** is another hidden picture box with the 'toggled' graphic):

```
if (pictureNumber == 0)
{
  picDisplay.Image = picChoice0.Image;
  pictureNumber = 1;
}
else
{
  picDisplay.Image = picChoice1.Image;
  pictureNumber = 0;
}
```

One question you may be asking is where do I get the graphics for toggling pictures? Search web sites and find graphics files available for purchase. You've probably seen the CD-ROM sets with 100,000 graphics! Also, look for icons and bitmaps installed on your computer by other applications.

Example 8-1

Simple Animation

1. Start a new application. We'll build a simple two-picture animation example showing mail entering a mailbox. Place three picture box controls on the form. The form should look like this:

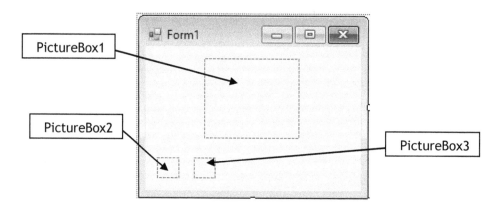

2. Set the following properties:

Form1:
Name	frmSimple
FormBorderStyle	SingleFixed
StartPosition	CenterScreen
Text	Simple Animation

pictureBox1:
Name	picDisplay
Image	image0.gif (found in **Example 8-1** folder of **LearnVCS\VCS Code\Class 8** folder)
SizeMode	AutoSize
Visible	True

pictureBox2:
Name	picChoice0
Image	image0.gif (found in **Example 8-1** folder of **LearnVCS\VCS Code\Class 8** folder)
SizeMode	StretchImage
Visible	False

pictureBox3:

Name	picChoice1
Image	image1.gif (found in **Example 8-1** folder of **LearnVCS\VCS Code\Class 8** folder)
SizeMode	StretchImage
Visible	False

When done, my form looks like this:

picDisplay is our display box, while the other picture box controls (**picChoice0** and **picChoice1**) store the images we toggle.

3. Use this form level scope declaration that declares and initializes **pictureNumber**:

```
int pictureNumber;
```

4. Use the following code in the **picDisplay Click** method:

```
private void PicDisplay_Click(object sender, EventArgs e)
{
  if (pictureNumber == 0)
  {
    picDisplay.Image = picChoice0.Image;
    pictureNumber = 1;
  }
  else
  {
    picDisplay.Image = picChoice1.Image;
    pictureNumber = 0;
  }
}
```

5. Save and run the application (saved in **Example 8-1** folder in **LearnVCS\VCS Code\Class 8** folder). Click the graphic and watch the letter go in the mailbox. Here's the sequence:

 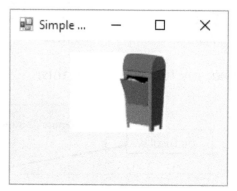

Timer Control

In Toolbox:

 Timer

Below Form (Default Properties):

Timer1

If want to expand simple animation to more than two graphics, the first step is to add additional pictures to the sequence. But, then how do we cycle through the pictures? We could ask a user to keep clicking on a button or picture to see all the pictures. That's one solution, but perhaps not a desirable one. What would be nice is to have the pictures cycle without user interaction. To do this, we need to have the capability to generate events without user interaction.

The Visual C# **Timer** control (looked at very briefly way back in Class 1) provides this capability of generating events. The timer control is very easy to implement and provides useful functionality beyond simple animation tasks. Other control events can be detected while the timer control processes events in the background. This multi-tasking allows more than one thing to be happening in your application.

Timer **Properties**:

Name	Gets or sets the name of the timer control (three letter prefix is **tim**).
Enabled	Used to turn the timer on and off. When True, timer control continues to operate until the Enabled property is set to False.
Interval	Number of milliseconds (there are 1000 milliseconds in one second) between each invocation of the timer control's **Tick** event.

Timer **Events**:

Tick	Event method invoked every **Interval** milliseconds while timer control's **Enabled** property is **True** (**default** event).

To use the **Timer** control, we add it to our application the same as any control. There is no user interface, so it will appear in the tray area below the form in the design window. You write code in the timer control's **Tick** event. This is the code you want to repeat every **Interval** milliseconds. In the animation-sequencing example, this is where you would change the picture box **Image** property.

The timer control's **Enabled** property is **False** at design time. You 'turn on' a timer in code by changing this property to **True**. Usually, you will have some control that toggles the timer control's **Enabled** property. That is, you might have a button that turns a timer on and off. The logical Not (**!**) operator is very useful for this toggling operation. If you have a timer control named **timExample**, this line of code will turn it on (set Enabled to True) if it is off (Enabled is False). It will do the reverse if the timer is already on:

```
timExample.Enabled = !timExample.Enabled;
```

It is best to start and end applications with the timer controls off (**Enabled** set to **False**).

Applications can (and many times do) have multiple timer controls. You need separate timer controls if you have events that occur with different regularity (different **Interval** values). Timer controls are used for two primary purposes. First, you use timer controls to periodically repeat some code segment. This is like our animation example. Second, you can use a timer control to implement some 'wait time' established by the **Interval** property. In this case, you simply start the timer and when the Interval is reached, have the **Tick** event turn its corresponding timer off.

Typical use of **Timer** control:

> ➤ Set the **Name** property and **Interval** property.
> ➤ Write code in **Tick** event.
> ➤ At some point in your application, set **Enabled** to **True** to start timer. Also, have capability to reset **Enabled** to **False**, when desired.

Example 8-2

Timer Control

1. Start a new application. We want an application that makes a button control disappear and reappear every second. Place a single button control on the form. Add a Timer control. Set the following properties:

Form1:

Name	frmTimer
FormBorderStyle	SingleFixed
StartPosition	CenterScreen
Text	Timer Example

Button1:

Name	btnStart
FontSize	14
Text	&Start

Timer1:

Name	timFlash
Interval	1000

When done, my form looks like this:

Other controls in tray:

2. Use this code in the **btnStart Click** event (this code toggles the timer and button text):

```
private void BtnStart_Click(object sender, EventArgs e)
{
  // toggle timer and button text
  timFlash.Enabled = !timFlash.Enabled;
  if (timFlash.Enabled)
  {
    btnStart.Text = "&Stop";
  }
  else
  {
    btnStart.Text = "&Start";
  }
}
```

3. Use the following code in the **timFlash Tick** method to toggle the Visible property of the button making it disappear then reappear:

```
private void TimFlash_Tick(object sender, EventArgs e)
{
  btnStart.Visible = !btnStart.Visible;
}
```

4. Save and run the application (saved in **Example 8-2** folder in **LearnVCS\VCS Code\Class 8** folder). Watch the button come and go. Stop whenever you want – note the button has to be there to click to stop.

Basic Animation

We return to the question of how to do animation with more than two pictures. More detailed animations are obtained by rotating through several pictures - each a slight change in the previous picture. This is the principle motion pictures are based on. In a movie, pictures flash by us at 24 frames per second and our eyes are tricked into believing things are smoothly moving.

Basic animation is done in a Visual C# application by adding hidden picture controls for each picture in the animation sequence. A timer control changes the display - with each **Tick** event, a new picture is seen. Once the end of the sequence is reached, you can 'loop' back to the first picture and repeat or you can simply stop. To achieve this effect in code, we have a form level scope variable that keeps track of the currently displayed picture (**pictureNumber**):

```
int pictureNumber;
```

You need to initialize this at some point, either in this declaration or when you start the timer.

Assume we have **n** pictures to cycle through. We will have n hidden picture box controls with the respective animation pictures. If **picDisplay** is the displaying picture box control and **picChoice0**, **picChoice1**, ... are the hidden picture boxes, the code in the Timer control's **Tick** method is:

```
switch (pictureNumber)
{
  case 0:
    picDisplay.Image = picChoice0.Image;
    break;
  case 1:
    picDisplay.Image = picChoice1.Image;
    break;
  case 2:
    picDisplay.Image = picChoice2.Image;
    break;
    .
    // there will be a case for each image up to n-1
    .
}
pictureNumber++;
```

You need to check when **pictureNumber** reaches **n**. When it does, you can stop the sequence (stop the timer). Or, you can reset **pictureNumber** to **0** to repeat the animation sequence.

More elaborate effects can be achieved by moving an image while, at the same time, changing the displayed picture. Effects such as a little guy walking across the screen are easily achieved. Appearance of control movement is achieved by incrementing or decrementing the **Left** and **Top** properties. For example, to move our picture box (**picDisplay**) 20 pixels to the right at the same time we update the picture, we use:

```
picDisplay.Left += 20;
```

The techniques shown here work fine for animation sequences with fewer than 10 pictures or so. With more pictures, you need to use more sophisticated tools. Consult Visual C# on-line help for information about the **ImageList** control. It is helpful with animations.

Example 8-3

Basic Animation

1. Start a new application. We'll build an animation example that uses the timer control to display a spinning earth! Place seven picture box controls and a button control on the form. Add a timer control. The form should look like this:

Other controls in tray:

2. Set the following properties:

Form1:

Name	frmAnimation
FormBorderStyle	SingleFixed
StartPosition	CenterScreen
Text	Animation Example

pictureBox1:
    Name   picDisplay
    Image   earth0.gif (found in **Example 8-3** folder of
                            LearnVCS\VCS Code\Class 8 folder)
    SizeMode   AutoSize
    Visible   True

pictureBox2:
    Name   picChoice0
    Image   earth0.gif (found in **Example 8-3** folder of
                            LearnVCS\VCS Code\Class 8 folder)
    SizeMode   StretchImage
    Visible   False

pictureBox3:
    Name   picChoice1
    Image   earth1.gif (found in **Example 8-3** folder of
                            LearnVCS\VCS Code\Class 8 folder)
    SizeMode   StretchImage
    Visible   False

pictureBox4:
    Name   picChoice2
    Image   earth2.gif (found in **Example 8-3** folder of
                            LearnVCS\VCS Code\Class 8 folder)
    SizeMode   StretchImage
    Visible   False

pictureBox5:
    Name   picChoice3
    Image   earth3.gif (found in **Example 8-3** folder of
                            LearnVCS\VCS Code\Class 8 folder)
    SizeMode   StretchImage
    Visible   False

pictureBox6:
    Name   picChoice4
    Image   earth4.gif (found in **Example 8-3** folder of
                            LearnVCS\VCS Code\Class 8 folder)
    SizeMode   StretchImage
    Visible   False

pictureBox7:

Name	picChoice5
Image	earth5.gif (found in **Example 8-3** folder of **LearnVCS\VCS Code\Class 8** folder)
SizeMode	StretchImage
Visible	False

button1:

Name	btnTimer
Text	Start/Stop

timer1:

Name	timAnimation
Interval	500

When done, my form looks like this:

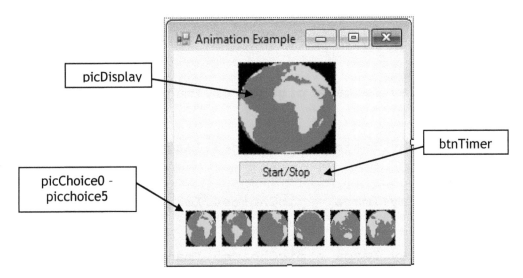

picDisplay is our display box, while the other picture box controls (**picChoice0**, **picChoice1**, **picChoice2**, **picChoice3**, **picChoice4** and **picChoice5**) store the images we cycle through.

3. Use this form level scope declaration that declares and initializes **pictureNumber**:

```
int pictureNumber;
```

4. Use the following code in the **btnTimer Click** method to toggle the timer:

```
private void BtnTimer_Click(object sender, EventArgs e)
{
    timAnimation.Enabled = !timAnimation.Enabled;
}
```

5. Use this code in the **timAnimation Tick** event to cycle through the different pictures (I choose to repeat the sequence when the end is reached):

```
private void TimAnimation_Tick(object sender, EventArgs e)
{
    switch (pictureNumber)
    {
        case 0:
            picDisplay.Image = picChoice0.Image;
            break;
        case 1:
            picDisplay.Image = picChoice1.Image;
            break;
        case 2:
            picDisplay.Image = picChoice2.Image;
            break;
        case 3:
            picDisplay.Image = picChoice3.Image;
            break;
        case 4:
            picDisplay.Image = picChoice4.Image;
            break;
        case 5:
            picDisplay.Image = picChoice5.Image;
            break;
    }
    pictureNumber++;
    if (pictureNumber == 6)
    {
        // restart sequence
        pictureNumber = 0;
    }
}
```

6. Save and run the application (saved in **Example 8-3** folder in **LearnVCS\VCS Code\Class 8** folder). Start and stop the timer control and watch the earth spin! Here's my spinning earth:

Add this line of code after the `pictureNumber++;` line in the timer **Tick** event:

```
picDisplay.Left += 10;
```

This will make the picture move to the right at the same time it is spinning. Make your form fairly wide. Run the application again and watch the earth 'walk off' the right side of the form. Can you think of logic that makes it scroll around to the left side after it disappears? Just study the geometry of the situation (**Left** and **Width** properties).

Random Numbers (Revisited) and Games

A fun thing to do with Visual C# is to create **games**. You can write games that you play against the computer or against another opponent. Graphics and animations play a big part in most games. And, each time we play a game, we want the response to be different. It would be boring playing a game like Solitaire if the same cards were dealt each time you played. Here, we review the random number object introduced back in Chapter 2.

To introduce chaos and randomness into games, we use **random numbers**. Random numbers are used to have the computer roll a die, spin a roulette wheel, deal a deck of cards, and draw bingo numbers. Visual C# develops random numbers using a built-in **random number generator.**

The random number generator we use in Visual C# must be declared and created. The statement to do this (assuming the object is named **myRandom**):

```
Random myRandom = new Random();
```

This statement is placed with the variable declaration statements.

Once created, when you need a random integer value, use the **Next** method of this Random object:

```
myRandom.Next(Limit)
```

This statement generates a random integer value that is greater than or equal to 0 and less than **Limit**. Note it is less than limit, not equal to. For example, the method:

```
myRandom.Next(5)
```

will generate random numbers from 0 to 4. The possible values will be 0, 1, 2, 3 and 4.

Random Object **Examples**:

To roll a six-sided die, the number of spots would be computed using:

```
numberSpots = myRandom.Next (6) + 1;
```

To randomly choose a card from a deck of 52 cards (indexed from 0 to 51), use:

```
cardValue = myRandom.Next(52);
```

To pick a number from 50 to 150, use:

```
number = myRandom.Next(101) + 50;
```

Let's use our new animation skills and random numbers to build a little game.

Example 8-4

One-Buttoned Bandit

1. Start a new application. In this example, we will build a computer version of a slot machine. We'll use random numbers and timers to display three random pictures. Certain combinations of pictures win you points. You'll need seven picture box controls (three for display, four for hiding pictures), a panel control, two label controls, two button controls and two timer controls. The form should look like this:

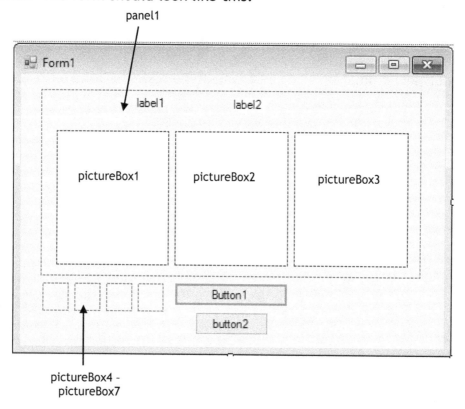

Other controls in tray:

     ⏱ Timer1   ⏱ Timer2

2. Set the following properties (doing the buttons first so their properties are available):

button1:

Name	btnSpin
Text	&Spin It

button2:

Name	btnExit
Text	E&xit

Form1:

Name	frmBandit
AcceptButton	btnSpin
FormBorderStyle	FixedSingle
StartPosition	CenterScreen
Text	One-Buttoned Bandit

panel1:

Name	pnlBandit
BackColor	Blue

label1:

BackColor	Blue
Font	Bold, Italic, Size 14
ForeColor	Yellow
Text	Bankroll

label2:

Name	lblBank
AutoSize	False
BackColor	White
BorderStyle	Fixed3D
Font	Bold, Size 14
Text	100
TextAlign	MiddleCenter

pictureBox1:

Name	picBandit0
BackColor	White
BorderStyle	Fixed3D
SizeMode	StretchImage

pictureBox2:
    Name   picBandit1
    BackColor   White
    BorderStyle   Fixed3D
    SizeMode   StretchImage

pictureBox3:
    Name   picBandit2
    BackColor   White
    BorderStyle   Fixed3D
    SizeMode   StretchImage

pictureBox4:
    Name   picChoice0
    Image   arrow.gif (in **Example 8-4** folder in **LearnVCS\VCS Code\Class 8** folder)
    SizeMode   StretchImage
    Visible   False

pictureBox5:
    Name   picChoice1
    Image   ball.gif (in **Example 8-4** folder in **LearnVCS\VCS Code\Class 8** folder)
    SizeMode   StretchImage
    Visible   False

pictureBox6:
    Name   picChoice2
    Image   bullseye.gif (in **Example 8-4** folder in **LearnVCS\VCS Code\Class 8** folder)
    SizeMode   StretchImage
    Visible   False

pictureBox7:
    Name   picChoice3
    Image   jackpot.gif (in **Example 8-4** folder in **LearnVCS\VCS Code\Class 8** folder)
    SizeMode   StretchImage
    Visible   False

timer1:

Name	timSpin
Enabled	False
Interval	100

timer2:

Name	timDone
Enabled	False
Interval	2000

When done, the form should look something like this:

A few words on what we're doing. We will randomly fill the three large picture boxes by choosing from the four choices in the non-visible picture boxes. One timer (**timSpin**) will be used to flash pictures (every 0.1 seconds) in the boxes. One timer (**timDone**) will be used to time the entire process (lasts 2.0 seconds).

3. Use this code for form level scope declarations (**Bankroll** is your winnings):

```
int bankRoll;
Random myRandom = new Random();
```

4. Use this code in the **frmBandit Load** method.

```
private void FrmBandit_Load(object sender, EventArgs e)
{
    bankRoll = Convert.ToInt32(lblBank.Text);
}
```

Here, we initialize your bankroll.

5. Attach this code to the **btnSpin_Click** event.

```
private void BtnSpin_Click(object sender, EventArgs e)
{
    if (bankRoll == 0)
    {
        MessageBox.Show("Out of Cash!", "Game Over",
MessageBoxButtons.OK);
        this.Close();
    }
    bankRoll--;
    lblBank.Text = bankRoll.ToString();
    btnSpin.Enabled = false;
    timSpin.Enabled = true;
    timDone.Enabled = true;
}
```

Here, we first check to see if you're out of cash. If so, the game ends. If not, you are charged 1 point and the timers are turned on.

6. This is the code for the **timSpin Tick** event.

```
private void TimSpin_Tick(object sender, EventArgs e)
{
  picBandit0.Image = ShowImage(myRandom.Next(4));
  picBandit1.Image = ShowImage(myRandom.Next(4));
  picBandit2.Image = ShowImage(myRandom.Next(4));
}
```

which uses this **ShowImage** general method:

```
private Image ShowImage(int i)
{
  switch (i)
  {
    case 0:
      return (picChoice0.Image);
    case 1:
      return (picChoice1.Image);
    case 2:
      return (picChoice2.Image);
    case 3:
      return (picChoice3.Image);
    default:
      return (null);
  }
}
```

Every 0.1 seconds (100 milliseconds), the three visible picture boxes are filled with a random image. This gives the effect of the spinning slot machine.

7. And, the code for the **timDone Tick** event. This event is triggered after the bandit spins for 2 seconds (2000 milliseconds).

```
private void TimDone_Tick(object sender, EventArgs e)
{
  int p0, p1, p2;
  int winnings = 0;
  const int jackpot = 3;
  btnSpin.Enabled = true;
  timSpin.Enabled = false;
  timDone.Enabled = false;
  // pick final pictures and see if it's a winner
  p0 = myRandom.Next(4);
  p1 = myRandom.Next(4);
  p2 = myRandom.Next(4);
  picBandit0.Image = ShowImage(p0);
```

```
  picBandit1.Image = ShowImage(p1);
  picBandit2.Image = ShowImage(p2);
  if (p0 == jackpot)
  {
    winnings = 1;
    if (p1 == jackpot)
    {
      winnings = 3;
      if (p2 == jackpot)
      {
        winnings = 10;
      }
    }
  }
  else if (p0 == p1)
  {
    winnings = 2;
    if (p1== p2)
    {
      winnings = 4;
    }
  }
  bankRoll += winnings;
  lblBank.Text = bankRoll.ToString();
}
```

First, the timers are turned off. Final pictures are displayed in each position. Then, the pictures are checked to see if you won anything.

8. Use this code in the **btnExit Click** event.

```
private void BtnExit_Click(object sender, EventArgs e)
{
  MessageBox.Show("You ended up with " +
bankRoll.ToString() + " points.", "Game Over",
MessageBoxButtons.OK);
  this.Close();
}
```

When you exit, your final earnings are displayed in a message box.

9. Save and run the application (saved in **Example 8-4** folder in **LearnVCS\VCS Code\Class 8** folder). See if you can become wealthy. Here's what I got after a few spins:

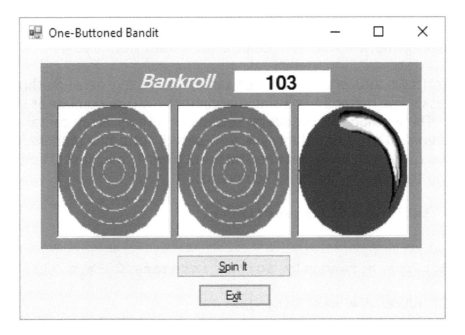

I'm quitting while I'm ahead! If you have time, try these things.

A. Rather than display the three final pictures almost simultaneously, see if you can stop each picture from spinning at a different time. You'll need a few more **Timer** controls.

B. Do something flashy when you win something!!

C. See if you can figure out the logic I used to specify winning. See if you can show the one-buttoned bandit returns 95.3 percent of all the 'money' put in the machine. (Hint: there are 64 possible combinations of pictures, each one equally likely.) This is higher than what Vegas machines return. But, with truly random operation, Vegas is guaranteed their return. They can't lose!

Randomly Sorting Integers

In many games, we have the need to randomly sort a sequence of integers. For example, to shuffle a deck of cards, we sort the integers from 0 to 51 (giving us 52 integers to represent the cards). To randomly sort the state names in a states/capitals game, we would randomize the values from 0 to 49.

Randomly sorting n integers is a common task. Here is a general method that does that task. The method has a single argument - **n** (the number of integers to be sorted). The method (**SortIntegers**) returns an integer array containing the random integers. The returned array is zero-based, returning random integers from 0 to n - 1, not 1 to n. If you need integers from 1 to n, just simply add 1 to each value in the returned array! The code is:

```
public int[] SortIntegers(int n)
{
  /*
  *   Returns n randomly sorted integers 0 -> n - 1
  */
  int[] nArray = new int[n];
  int temp, s;
  Random sortRandom = new Random();
  //   initialize array from 0 to n - 1
  for (int i = 0; i < n; i++)
  {
    nArray[i] = i;
  }
  //   i is number of items remaining in list
  for (int i = n; i >= 1; i--)
  {
    s = sortRandom.Next(i);
    temp = nArray[s];
    nArray[s] = nArray[i - 1];
    nArray[i - 1] = temp;
  }
  return(nArray);
}
```

Look at the code, one number is pulled from the original sorted array and put at the bottom of the array. Then a number is pulled from the remaining unsorted values and put at the 'new' bottom. This selection continues until all the numbers have been sorted. This routine has been called a 'one card shuffle' because it's like shuffling a deck of cards by pulling one card out of the deck at a time and laying it aside in a pile.

This method has a wide range of applications. We'll use it in Exercise 8-1 to play Blackjack. I've used it to randomize the letters of the alphabet, scramble words in spelling games, randomize answers in multiple choice tests, and even playback compact disc songs in random order (yes, you can build a CD player with Visual C#).

Example 8-5

Random Integers

1. Start a new application. We want an application that randomly sorts a selected number of integers. Add a list box control, a numeric updown control and a button control to the form. The form should look like this:

2. Set the following properties:

Form1:

Name	frmRandom
FormBorderStyle	SingleFixed
StartPosition	CenterScreen
Text	Random Sort

listBox1:

Name	lstValues

numericUpDown1:

Name	nudValue
Maximum	100
Minimum	2
TextAlign	Right
Value	2

button1:

Name	btnSort
Text	&Sort Integers

When done, my form looks like this:

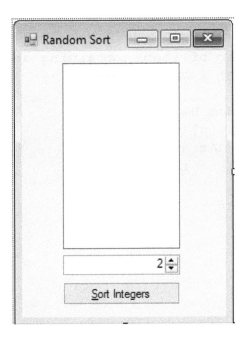

3. Include the **SortIntegers** method:

```csharp
public int[] SortIntegers(int n)
{
  /*
   *  Returns n randomly sorted integers 0 -> n - 1
   */
  int[] nArray = new int[n];
  int temp, s;
  Random sortRandom = new Random();
  //  initialize array from 0 to n - 1
  for (int i = 0; i < n; i++)
  {
    nArray[i] = i;
  }
  //  i is number of items remaining in list
  for (int i = n; i >= 1; i--)
  {
    s = sortRandom.Next(i);
    temp = nArray[s];
    nArray[s] = nArray[i - 1];
    nArray[i - 1] = temp;
  }
  return(nArray);
}
```

4. Use this code in the **btnSort Click** event method:

```
private void BtnSort_Click(object sender, EventArgs e)
{
  int arraySize = Convert.ToInt32(nudValue.Value);
  int[] integerArray = new int[arraySize];
  // Clear list box
  lstValues.Items.Clear();
  // sort  integers
  integerArray = SortIntegers(arraySize);
  // display sorted integers
  for (int i = 0; i < arraySize; i++)
  {
    lstValues.Items.Add(integerArray[i].ToString());
  }
}
```

This code reads the value of the updown control establishes the array dimension and calls **SortIntegers**. The sorted values are displayed in the list box control.

5. Save and run the application (saved in **Example 8-5** folder in **LearnVCS\VCS Code\Class 8** folder). Try sorting different numbers of integers. Here's a couple of runs I did sorting 10 integers:

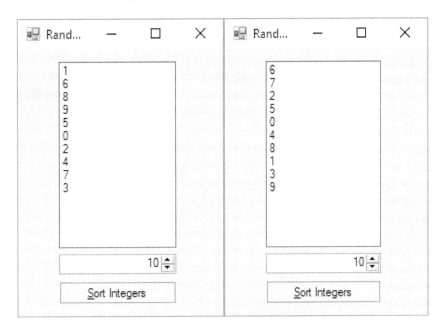

Notice you get different results every time you do a sort.

Graphics Methods

We now know how to display graphics files (pictures) in Visual C# applications and how to do basic animations. Visual C# also offers a wealth of **graphics methods** that let us draw lines, rectangles, ellipses, pie shapes and polygons. With these methods, you can draw anything! These methods are provided by the **GDI+** (graphical device interface), an improved version of previous interfaces.

The graphics methods examined in this chapter are part of the Visual C# **Drawing** namespace. The methods are applied to **Graphics** objects. Using graphics objects is a little detailed, but worth the time to learn. There is a new vocabulary with many new objects to study. We'll cover every step. The basic approach to drawing with graphics objects will always be:

> ➢ Create a **Graphics** object
> ➢ Create **Pen** objects and **Brush** objects
> ➢ Draw to Graphics object using drawing methods
> ➢ Dispose of Pen and Brush objects when done with them
> ➢ Dispose of Graphics object when done with it

The process is like drawing on paper. You get your paper (graphics object) and your pens and brushes. You do all your drawing and coloring and then put your supplies away!

All the drawing methods we study are **overloaded** functions. Recall this means there are many ways to invoke a function, using different numbers and types of arguments. For each drawing method, we will look at one or two implementations of that particular method. You are encouraged to examine other implementations using the Visual C# on-line help facilities.

In this chapter, we will learn about **Graphics** objects, **Pen** objects, **Brush** objects and the use of **colors**. We'll learn how to draw **lines**, draw and fill **rectangles**, draw and fill **ellipses** and draw **pie** segments. We'll use these skills to build basic plotting packages and, in Chapter 9, a simple paintbrush program. Let's get started.

Graphics Object

As mentioned, graphics methods (drawing functions) are applied to graphics objects. **Graphics objects** provide the "surface" for drawing methods and can be created using many of the Visual C# controls. The usual controls for graphics methods are the **form**, the **picture box** control, and the **panel** control. In this course, we will primarily use the panel control for　It provides a nicely "contained" drawing area.

There are two steps involved in creating a **graphics object**. We first declare the object (in the **Drawing** namespace) using the standard statement:

```
Graphics myGraphics;
```

Placement of this statement depends on scope. Place it in a method for method level scope. Place it with other form level declarations for form level scope. Once declared, the object is created using the **CreateGraphics** method:

```
myGraphics = hostControlName.CreateGraphics();
```

where **HostControlName** is the name of the control hosting the graphics object [the form (**this**), any other control (**Name** property)].

Once a graphics object is created, all graphics methods are applied to this object. Hence, to apply a drawing method named **DrawingMethod** to the **myGraphics** object, use:

myGraphics.**DrawingMethod** (**Arguments**);

where **Arguments** are any needed arguments.

There are two important drawing methods we introduce now. First, after all of your hard work drawing in a graphics object, there are times you will want to erase or clear the object. This is done with the **Clear** method:

```
myGraphics.Clear(Color);
```

This statement will clear a graphics object and fill it with the specified **Color**. We will look at colors next. The usual color argument for clearing a graphics object is the background color of the host control, or:

```
myGraphics.Clear(hostControlName.BackColor);
```

Once you are done drawing to an object and need it no longer, it should be properly disposed to clear up system resources. The syntax for disposing of our example graphics object uses the **Dispose** method:

```
myGraphics.Dispose();
```

All graphics methods use the **client coordinates** of the hosting control:

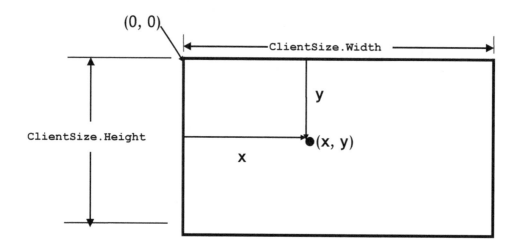

The client dimensions, **ClientSize.Width** and **ClientSize.Height** represent the "graphics" region of the control hosting the graphics object. Due to border space, they are <u>not</u> the same as the **Width** and **Height** properties. ClientSize.Width is less than Width and ClientSize.Height is less than Height. For example, you won't be able to draw in the title bar region of a form object.

Points in client coordinates will be referred to by a Cartesian pair, **(x, y)**. In the diagram, note the **x** (horizontal) coordinate runs from left to right, starting at **0** and extending to **ClientSize.Width - 1**. The **y** (vertical) coordinate goes from top to bottom, starting at **0** and ending at **ClientSize.Height - 1**. All measurements are integers and in units of **pixels**. Later, we will see how we can use any coordinate system we want.

Colors

Colors play a big part in Visual C# applications. We have seen colors in designing some of our previous applications. At design time, we have selected background colors (**BackColor** property) and foreground colors (**ForeColor** property) for different controls. Such choices are made by selecting the desired property in the properties window. Once selected, a palette of customizable colors appears for you to choose from.

Most of the graphics methods we study will use **pen** and **brush** objects (we'll look at these objects soon). Both pen objects and brush objects have **Color** arguments that specify just what color they draw or paint in. Unlike control color properties, these colors cannot be selected at design time. They must be defined in code. How do we do this? There are two approaches we will take: (1) use built-in colors and (2) create a color.

The colors built into Visual C# are specified by the **Color** structure (from the **Drawing** namespace). A color is specified using:

```
Color.ColorName
```

where **ColorName** is a reserved color name. There are many, many color names (I counted 141). To see a list, consult on-line help for the **Color** structure and click **Members**. There are colors like **BlanchedAlmond**, **Linen**, **NavajoWhite**, **PeachPuff** and **SpringGreen**. You don't have to remember these names. Whenever you type the word **Color**, followed by a dot (.), in the code window, the Intellisense feature of the IDE will pop up with a list of color selections. Just choose from the list to complete the color specification. You will have to remember the difference between BlanchedAlmond and Linen though! Personally, as my lovely wife will attest, I can only distinguish a few colors (I'm a blue, red, yellow kind of guy).

If for some reason, the selection provided by the **Color** structure does not fit your needs, there is a method that allows you to create over 16 million different colors. The method (**FromArgb**) works with the **Color** structure. The syntax to specify a color is:

```
Color.FromArgb(red, green, blue)
```

where **red, green**, and **blue** are integer measures of intensity of the corresponding primary colors. These measures can range from 0 (least intensity) to 255 (greatest intensity). For example, `Color.FromArgb(255, 255, 0)` will produce yellow. Sorry, but I can't tell you what values to use to create **PeachPuff**.

It is easy to specify colors for graphics methods using the **Color** structure. Any time you need a color, just use one of the built-in colors or the **FromArgb** method. These techniques to represent color are not limited to just providing colors for graphics methods. They can be used anywhere Visual C# requires a color; for example, **Backcolor** and **Forecolor** properties can also be set (at run-time) using these techniques. For example, to change your form background color to **PeachPuff**, use:

```
this.BackColor = Color.PeachPuff;
```

If you want to allow your users the capability of changing colors at run-time, the **ColorDialog** control, examined next, is a very useful tool.

ColorDialog Control

In Toolbox:

Below Form (Default Properties):

The **ColorDialog** control is a pre-configured dialog box that allows the user to select a color from a palette and to add custom colors to that palette. It is the same dialog box that you see in other Windows applications. The selected color can be used to set control properties or select colors needed by graphics objects and methods.

ColorDialog **Properties:**

Name	Gets or sets the name of the color dialog (I usually name this control **dlgColor**).
AllowFullOpen	Gets or sets a value indicating whether the user can use the dialog box to define custom colors.
AnyColor	Gets or sets a value indicating whether the dialog box displays all available colors in the set of basic colors.
Color	Indicates selected color.
CustomColors	Gets or sets the set of custom colors shown in the dialog box.
FullOpen	Gets or sets a value indicating whether the controls used to create custom colors are visible when the dialog box is opened.
SolidColorOnly	Gets or sets a value indicating whether the dialog box will restrict users to selecting solid colors only.

ColorDialog **Methods:**

ShowDialog	Displays the dialog box. Returned value indicates which button was clicked by user (**OK** or **Cancel**).

To use the **ColorDialog** control, we add it to our application the same as any control. It will appear in the tray below the form. Once added, we set a few properties. Then, we write code to make the dialog box appear when desired. The user then makes selections and closes the dialog box. At this point, we use the selected **Color** property for our tasks.

The **ShowDialog** method is used to display the **ColorDialog** control. For a control named **dlgColor**, the appropriate code is:

```
dlgColor.ShowDialog();
```

And the displayed dialog box is:

The user selects a color by making relevant choices. Once complete, the **OK** button is clicked. At this point, the **Color** property is available for use. **Cancel** can be clicked to cancel the color change. The ShowDialog method returns the clicked button. It returns **DialogResult.OK** if OK is clicked and returns **DialogResult.Cancel** if Cancel is clicked.

Typical use of **ColorDialog** control:

> ➤ Set the **Name** property (perhaps change defaults concerning what color options are displayed).
> ➤ Use **ShowDialog** method to display dialog box.
> ➤ Use **Color** property in appropriate place in code.

Pen Object

As mentioned, many of the graphics methods we study require a **Pen** object. This virtual pen is just like the pen you use to write and draw. You can choose color, width and style of the pen. You can use pens built-in to Visual C# or create your own pen.

In many cases, the pen objects built into Visual C# are sufficient. The **Pens** class will draw a line **1** pixel wide in a color you choose (Intellisense will present the list to choose from). If the selected color is **ColorName** (one of the 141 built-in color names), the syntax to refer to such a pen is:

```
Pens.ColorName
```

To create your own **Pen** object (in **Drawing** namespace), you first declare the pen using:

```
Pen myPen;
```

The pen is then created using the **Pen** constructor:

```
myPen = new Pen(color, width);
```

where **color** is the color your new pen will draw in and **width** is the integer width of the line (in pixels) drawn. This pen will draw a solid line. The **color** argument can be one of the built-in colors or one generated with the **FromArgb** function. Using some of the overloaded versions of the pen constructor allow you to create pens that can draw dashed and other line styles. Consult on-line help for details.

Once created, you can change the color and width at any time using the **Color** and **Width** properties of the pen object. The syntax is:

```
myPen.Color = newColor;
myPen.Width = newWidth;
```

Here, **newColor** is a newly specified color and **newWidth** is a new integer pen width.

When done drawing with a pen object, it should be disposed using the **Dispose** method:

```
myPen.Dispose();
```

DrawLine Method

The first graphics (drawing) method we learn is **DrawLine**. This method is used to connect two Cartesian points with a straight-line segment. It operates on a previously created graphics object. If that object is **myGraphics** and we wish to connect the point (**x1, y1**) with (**x2, y2**) using a pen object **myPen**, the syntax is:

```
myGraphics.DrawLine(myPen, x1, y1, x2, y2);
```

Each coordinate value is an integer type. As mentioned, all graphics methods (including **DrawLine**) are overloaded functions. There are other implementations of DrawLine in Visual C#. This is just one of them.

Using a black pen with a line width of 1 (**Pens.Black**), the **DrawLine** method with these points is:

```
myGraphics.DrawLine(Pens.Black, x1, y1, x2, y2);
```

This produces on a form (**myGraphics** object):

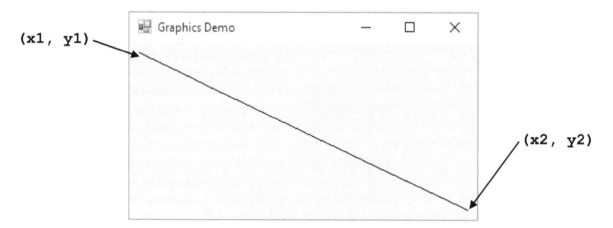

For every line segment you need to draw, you will need a separate **DrawLine** statement. Of course, you can choose to change pen color or pen width at any time you wish.

Graphics Methods (Revisited)

Before continuing, let's build and look at a little example to demonstrate a couple of (perhaps unexpected) features of graphics methods in Visual C#. Start a new project. Place a single button control (**Text** property of **Draw Line**) in the middle of the form. We won't be concerned with proper naming conventions here. We're just playing around. When we click the button, we want to draw a blue line on the form from the upper left corner to the lower right corner. When we click the button again, we want the line to disappear.

This code (the **button1 Click** event method) does the trick:

```
private void Button1_Click(object sender, EventArgs e)
{
  Graphics myGraphics;
  // toggle button text property
  if (button1.Text == "Draw Line")
  {
    button1.Text = "Clear Line";
    lineThere = true;
  }
  else
  {
    button1.Text = "Draw Line";
    lineThere = false;
  }
  myGraphics = this.CreateGraphics();
  if (lineThere)
  {
    myGraphics.DrawLine(Pens.Blue, 0, 0,
this.ClientSize.Width - 1, this.ClientSize.Height - 1);
  }
  else
  {
    myGraphics.Clear(this.BackColor);
  }
  myGraphics.Dispose();
}
```

Add this code to the little example.

You need to define and initialize one variable (**lineThere**) as having form level scope:

```
bool lineThere = false;
```

This variable is true when a line has been drawn and false when there is no line. It is initially false, since there will be no line when the application begins.

Since this is the first graphics code we've seen, let's look at it closely. It first 'toggles' the button's **Text** property and establishes a value for **lineThere**. It then creates the **Graphics** object **myGraphics** using the form (**this**) as the host control. If checks the status of **lineThere** to determine if we're drawing a line or clearing the line. If drawing (**lineThere** = **true**), a blue pen draws a line. If clearing, the graphics object is cleared to the form's background color. Before leaving the method, the object is disposed.

Run this little application and click the button one time. You should see something like this (your results will vary assuming your form is a different size):

The first feature to see here is that the line appears <u>behind</u> the button control. Graphics objects are created and maintained (as a **bitmap** graphic) in their own "layer" of the hosting control. In a form, this layer lies behind the "layer" with all the controls. When you clear the graphics object, it clears this back layer. It won't clear any objects placed on the form. Click the button a few times to see how this works.

To see the second feature of graphics methods, make sure a line appears on the form and reduce the form to an icon by clicking the **Minimize** button (the one with an underscore character) in the upper right-hand corner of the form. Then, restore the form to the screen by clicking the form entry on your task bar. Here's what you should see:

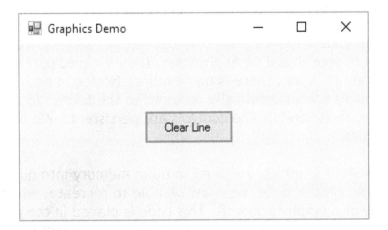

The button control is still there, but the line we carefully drew has disappeared! What happened? We'll answer that question next.

Persistent Graphics

Why did the line disappear in our little example when the form went away for a bit? Visual C# graphics objects have <u>no</u> memory. They only display what has been last drawn on them. If you reduce your form to an icon and restore it, the graphics object cannot remember what was displayed previously – it will be cleared. Similarly, if you switch from an active Visual C# application to some other application, your Visual C# form may become partially or fully obscured. When you return to your Visual C# application, the obscured part of any graphics object will be erased. Again, there is no memory. Notice in both these cases, however, all controls are automatically restored to the form. Your application remembers these, fortunately! The controls are persistent. We also want **persistent graphics**.

To maintain persistent graphics, we need to build memory into our graphics objects using code. In this code, we must be able to recreate, when needed, the current state of a graphics object. This code is placed in the host control's **Paint** event. This event is called whenever an obscured object becomes unobscured. The **Paint** event will be automatically called for each object when a form is first activated and when a form is restored from an icon or whenever an obscured object is viewable again.

Maintaining persistent graphics does require a bit of work on your part. You need to always know what is in your graphics objects and how to recreate the objects, when needed. This usually involves developing some program variables that describe how to recreate the graphics object. And, you usually need to develop some ad hoc rules for re-creation. As you build your first few **Paint** events, you will begin to develop your own ways for maintaining persistent graphics. At certain times, you'll need to force a "repaint" of your form or control. To do this, for an object named **objectName** use:

```
objectName_Paint(null, null);
```

That is, you simply call the **Paint** event for the object you want to repaint. Use the keyword **null** for both arguments. These arguments are not used in any Paint events we create, hence are disregarded. One hint: always check for the actual name assigned to a **Paint** event by Visual C#. You want to make sure you call the correct event.

Let's see how to maintain persistent graphics in our little example. First, cut and paste all the graphics statements out of the **button1 Click** event method into the **Form1 Paint** event. The lines to move are shaded:

```
private void Button1_Click(object sender, EventArgs e)
{
  Graphics myGraphics;
  // toggle button text property
  if (button1.Text == "Draw Line")
  {
    button1.Text = "Clear Line";
    lineThere = true;
  }
  else
  {
    button1.Text = "Draw Line";
    lineThere = false;
  }
  myGraphics = this.CreateGraphics();
  if (lineThere)
  {
    myGraphics.DrawLine(Pens.Blue, 0, 0,
this.ClientSize.Width - 1, this.ClientSize.Height - 1);
  }
  else
  {
    myGraphics.Clear(this.BackColor);
  }
  myGraphics.Dispose();
}
```

Hence, the **Form1 Paint** event will be:

```
private void Form1_Paint(object sender, PaintEventArgs e)
{
  Graphics myGraphics;
  myGraphics = this.CreateGraphics();
  if (lineThere)
  {
    myGraphics.DrawLine(Pens.Blue, 0, 0,
this.ClientSize.Width - 1, this.ClientSize.Height - 1);
  }
  else
  {
    myGraphics.Clear(this.BackColor);
  }
  myGraphics.Dispose();
}
```

With this code, the line will be drawn when **lineThere** is **true,** else the graphics object will be cleared. And the modified **button1 Click** event will now be:

```
private void Button1_Click(object sender, EventArgs e)
{
  // toggle button text property
  if (button1.Text == "Draw Line")
  {
    button1.Text = "Clear Line";
    lineThere = true;
  }
  else
  {
    button1.Text = "Draw Line";
    lineThere = false;
  }
}
```

Run the application with these changes in place. Try drawing and clearing the line. The graphics should be persistent, meaning the line will be there when it's supposed to and not there when it's not supposed to be there. The last incarnation of this little graphics example is saved in the **GraphicsDemo** folder in the **LearnVCS\VCS Code\Class 8** folder.

So, to use persistent graphics, you need to do a little work. Once you've done that work, make sure you truly have persistent graphics. Perform checks similar to those we did for our little example here. The Visual C# environment makes doing these checks very easy. It's simple to make changes and immediately see the effects of those changes. A particular place to check is to make sure the initial loading of graphics objects display correctly. Sometimes, Paint events cause incorrect results the first time they are invoked.

And, though, including **Paint** events in a Visual C# application require extra coding, it also has the advantage of centralizing all graphics operations in one method. This usually helps to simplify the tasks of code modification and maintenance. I've found that the persistent graphics problem makes me look more deeply at my code. In the end, I write better code. I believe you'll find the same is true with your applications.

Example 8-6

Drawing Lines

1. Start a new application. In this application, we will draw random line segments in a panel control using **DrawLine**. Add a panel control and two button controls to the form. The form should look like this:

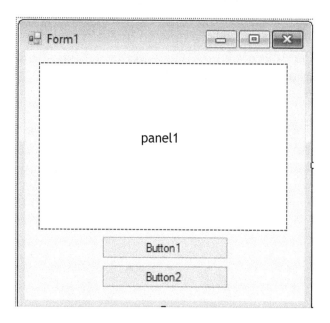

2. Set the following properties:

Form1:

Name	frmLine
FormBorderStyle	SingleFixed
StartPosition	CenterScreen
Text	Drawing Lines

panel1:

Name	pnlDraw
BackColor	White
BorderStyle	Fixed3D

button1:

Name	btnDraw
Text	&Draw Lines

button2:
>Name   btnClear
>
>Text   &Clear Lines

When done, my form looks like this:

3. We define an **EndPoint** class (**EndPoint.cs**) to keep track of each line segment drawn:

```
class Endpoint
{
  public int X;
  public int Y;
}
```
4. Return to the form code window. Form level scope declarations:

```
int numberPoints = 0;
const int maxPoints = 50;
Random myRandom = new Random();
Endpoint[] LineEnds = new Endpoint[maxPoints];
```

5. Use this code in the **btnDraw Click** event method:

```
private void BtnDraw_Click(object sender, EventArgs e)
{
  // add new random point to line array and redraw
  // create two points first time through
  do
  {
    LineEnds[numberPoints] = new Endpoint();
    LineEnds[numberPoints].X =
myRandom.Next(pnlDraw.ClientSize.Width);
    LineEnds[numberPoints].Y =
myRandom.Next(pnlDraw.ClientSize.Height);
    numberPoints += 1;
  }
  while (numberPoints < 2);
  pnlDraw_Paint(null, null);
  // no more clicks if maxpoints exceeded
  if (numberPoints == maxPoints)
  {
    btnDraw.Enabled = false;
  }
}
```

With each click of the button, a new point is added to the array to draw.

6. Use this code in **btnClear Click** event – this clears the graphics object and allows new line segments to be drawn:

```
private void BtnClear_Click(object sender, EventArgs e)
{
  // clear region
  numberPoints = 0;
  btnDraw.Enabled = true;
  pnlDraw_Paint(null, null);
}
```

7. Use this code in the **pnlDraw Paint** event. This code draws the line segments defined by the X and Y arrays:

```
private void PnlDraw_Paint(object sender, PaintEventArgs e)
{
  // create graphics object and connect points in x, y arrays
  Graphics myGraphics;
  Pen myPen;
  myGraphics = pnlDraw.CreateGraphics();
  myPen = new Pen(Color.Blue, 3);
  if (numberPoints != 0)
  {
    for (int i = 1; i < numberPoints; i++)
    {
      myGraphics.DrawLine(myPen, LineEnds[i - 1].X,
LineEnds[i - 1].Y, LineEnds[i].X, LineEnds[i].Y);
    }
  }
  else
  {
    myGraphics.Clear(pnlDraw.BackColor);
  }
  myPen.Dispose();
  myGraphics.Dispose();
}
```

8. Save and run the application (saved in **Example 8-6** folder in **LearnVCS\VCS Code\Class 8** folder). Try drawing (click **Draw Lines** several times) and clearing random line segments. Note that the graphics are persistent. Try obscuring the form to prove this. Here's some segments I drew:

Rectangle Structure

We now begin looking at two-dimensional graphics methods. These include methods for drawing rectangles, ellipses and pie segments. Each of these methods uses a bounding rectangle within a graphics object to specify the drawing area. This rectangle is specified by a **Rectangle** structure (from the **Drawing** namespace). A structure is similar to an object; it has properties and methods. One difference between a structure and an object is you don't have to dispose of any structure you create.

Rectangle Structure **Properties**:

Bottom	Gets the y-coordinate of the lower-right corner of the rectangle
Height	Gets or sets the width of the rectangle
Left	Gets the x-coordinate of the upper-left corner of the rectangle
Right	Gets the x-coordinate of the lower-right corner of the rectangle
Top	Gets the y-coordinate of the upper-left corner of the rectangular
Width	Gets or sets the height of the rectangle
X	Gets or sets the x-coordinate of the upper-left corner of the rectangle
Y	Gets or sets the y-coordinate of the upper-left corner of the rectangle

All of the relative measurements (**Bottom**, **Left**, **Right**, **Top**, X, Y) are relative to the graphics object. A diagram shows everything:

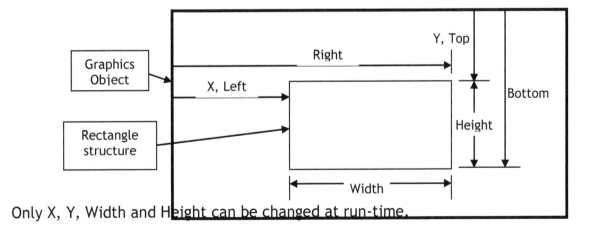

Only X, Y, Width and Height can be changed at run-time.

There are two steps involved in creating a **rectangle structure**. We first declare the structure (in the **Drawing** namespace) using the standard statement:

```
Rectangle myRectangle;
```

Placement of this statement depends on scope. Place it in a method for method level scope. Place it with other form level declarations for form level scope. Once declared, the structure is created using the **Rectangle** constructor:

```
myRectangle = new Rectangle(left, top, width, height);
```

where **left**, **top**, **width** and **height** are the desired integer measurements (in pixels).

You can move and resize the rectangle in code, by changing any of four properties:

```
myRectangle.X = newX;
myRectangle.Y = newY;
myRectangle.Width = newWidth;
myRectangle.Height = newHeight;
```

where **newX**, **newY**, **newWidth**, and **newHeight** represent new values for the respective properties.

DrawRectangle Method

The **DrawRectangle** method will draw a rectangle in a **rectangle structure** within a **graphic object**. To draw a rectangle, you first create the graphics object. Then you create the rectangle structure using the just-defined constructor. Assuming you have created a graphics object named **myGraphics** and a rectangle structure named **myRectangle**, the syntax to draw a rectangle with pen object **myPen** is:

```
myGraphics.DrawRectangle(myPen, myRectangle);
```

Using a black pen with a line width of 1 (**Pens.Black**), the code to draw a rectangle that takes up 80 percent of the width and height of the client area of a form-hosted graphics object is:

```
Graphics myGraphics;
Rectangle myRectangle;
myGraphics = this.CreateGraphics();
int left = (int) (0.1 * this.ClientSize.Width);
int top = (int) (0.1 * this.ClientSize.Height);
int width = (int) (0.8 * this.ClientSize.Width);
int height = (int) (0.8 * this.ClientSize.Height);
myRectangle = new Rectangle(left, top, width, height);
myGraphics.DrawRectangle(Pens.Black, myRectangle);
myGraphics.Dispose();
```

This code produces this rectangle:

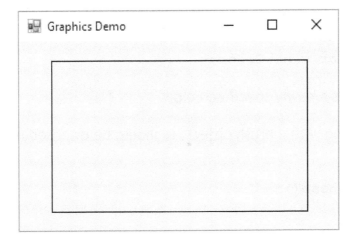

Brush Object

The rectangle we just drew is pretty boring. It would be nice to have the capability to fill it with a color and/or pattern. Filling of regions in Visual C# is done with a **Brush** object. Like the Pen object, a brush is just like a brush you use to paint – just pick a color. You can use brushes built-in to Visual C# or create your own brush. In this chapter, we only look at solid color brushes. Advanced brush effects are studied in Chapter 9.

In most cases, the brush objects built into Visual C# are sufficient. The **Brushes** class provides brush objects that paint using one of the 141 built-in color names we've seen before. The syntax to refer to such a brush is:

```
Brushes.ColorName
```

To create your own **Brush** object (from the **Drawing** namespace), you first declare the brush using:

```
Brush myBrush;
```

The solid color brush is then created using the **SolidBrush** constructor:

```
myBrush = new SolidBrush(color);
```

where **color** is the color your new brush will paint with. This color argument can be one of the built-in colors or one generated with the **FromArgb** function.

Once created, you can change the color of a brush any time using the **Color** property of the brush object. The syntax is:

```
myBrush.Color = newColor;
```

where **newColor** is a newly specified color.

When done painting with a brush object, it should be disposed using the **Dispose** method:

```
myBrush.Dispose();
```

FillRectangle Method

The **FillRectangle** method will draw a filled rectangle in a **rectangle structure** within a **graphic object**. To fill a rectangle, you first create the graphics object. Then you create the rectangle structure using the rectangle constructor. Assuming you have created a graphics object named **myGraphics** and a rectangle structure named **myRectangle**, the syntax to fill a rectangle with brush object **myBrush** is:

```
myGraphics.FillRectangle(myBrush, myRectangle);
```

Using a red solid brush (**Brushes.Red**), the code to fill a rectangle that takes up 80 percent of the width and height of the client area of a form-hosted graphics object is:

```
Graphics myGraphics;
Rectangle myRectangle;
myGraphics = this.CreateGraphics();
int left = (int) (0.1 * this.ClientSize.Width);
int top = (int) (0.1 * this.ClientSize.Height);
int width = (int) (0.8 * this.ClientSize.Width);
int height = (int) (0.8 * this.ClientSize.Height);
myRectangle = new Rectangle(left, top, width, height);
myGraphics.FillRectangle(Brushes.Red, myRectangle);
myGraphics.Dispose();
```

This code produces this rectangle:

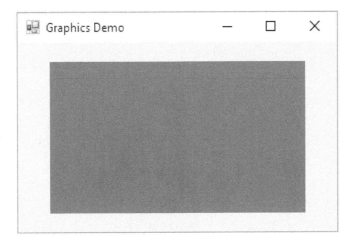

Notice the FillRectangle method fills the entire region with the selected color. If you had previously used DrawRectangle to form a border region, the fill will blot out that border. If you want a bordered, filled region, do the **fill** operation **first**, **then** the **draw** operation.

DrawEllipse Method

Ellipses can be drawn in Visual C# using methods nearly identical to the rectangle methods. The **DrawEllipse** method will draw an ellipse in a **rectangle structure** within a **graphic object**. To draw an ellipse, you first create the graphics object. Then you create the rectangle structure using the constructor. Assuming you have created a graphics object named **myGraphics** and a rectangle structure named **myRectangle**, the syntax to draw an ellipse with pen object **myPen** is:

```
myGraphics.DrawEllipse(myPen, myRectangle);
```

Using a black pen with a line width of 1 (**Pens.Black**), the code to draw an ellipse that takes up 80 percent of the width and height of the client area of a form-hosted graphics object is:

```
Graphics myGraphics;
Rectangle myRectangle;
myGraphics = this.CreateGraphics();
int left = (int) (0.1 * this.ClientSize.Width);
int top = (int) (0.1 * this.ClientSize.Height);
int width = (int) (0.8 * this.ClientSize.Width);
int height = (int) (0.8 * this.ClientSize.Height);
myRectangle = new Rectangle(left, top, width, height);
myGraphics.DrawEllipse(Pens.Black, myRectangle);
myGraphics.Dispose();
```

This code produces this ellipse:

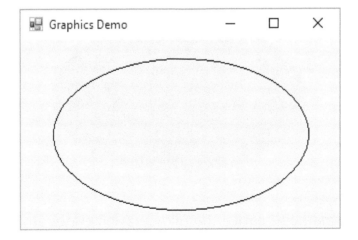

FillEllipse Method

The **FillEllipse** method will draw a filled ellipse in a **rectangle structure** within a **graphic object**. To fill an ellipse, you first create the graphics object. Then you create the rectangle structure. Assuming you have created a graphics object named **myGraphics** and a rectangle structure named **myRectangle**, the syntax to fill an ellipse with brush object **myBrush** is:

```
myGraphics.FillEllipse(myBrush, myRectangle);
```

Using a green solid brush (**Brushes.Green**), the code to fill an ellipse that takes up 80 percent of the width and height of the client area of a form-hosted graphics object is:

```
Graphics myGraphics;
Rectangle myRectangle;
myGraphics = this.CreateGraphics();
int left = (int) (0.1 * this.ClientSize.Width);
int top = (int) (0.1 * this.ClientSize.Height);
int width = (int) (0.8 * this.ClientSize.Width);
int height = (int) (0.8 * this.ClientSize.Height);
myRectangle = new Rectangle(left, top, width, height);
myGraphics.FillEllipse(Brushes.Green, myRectangle);
myGraphics.Dispose();
```

This code produces this ellipse:

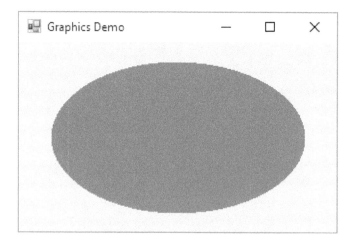

Like the rectangle methods, notice the fill operation erases any border that may have been there after a draw operation. For a bordered, filled ellipse, do the fill, then the draw.

Example 8-7

Drawing Rectangles and Ellipses

1. Start a new application. In this application, we will draw and fill random rectangles or ellipses in a panel control. The rectangles or ellipses will be filled with random colors. Add a panel control, two radio buttons and three button controls to the form. The form should look like this:

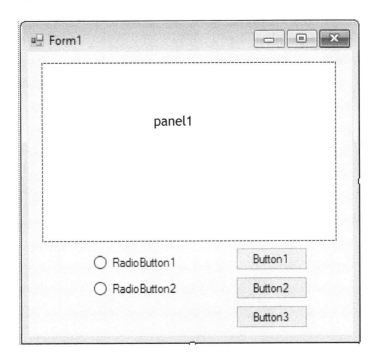

2. Set the following properties:

Form1:

Name	frmRectangle
FormBorderStyle	SingleFixed
StartPosition	CenterScreen
Text	Drawing Rectangles

panel1:

Name	pnlDraw
BackColor	White
BorderStyle	Fixed3D

radioButton1:

Name	rdoRectangle
Checked	True
Text	&Rectangle

radioButton2:

Name	rdoEllipse
Text	&Ellipse

button1:

Name	btnDraw
Text	&Draw

button2:

Name	btnFill
Enabled	False
Text	&Fill

button3:

Name	btnClear
Enabled	False
Text	&Clear

When done, my form looks like this:

3. Form level scope declarations:

```
Rectangle myRectangle;
bool isDrawn = false;
bool isFilled = false;
int fillRed, fillBlue, fillGreen;
Random myRandom = new Random();
```

4. Use this code in the **btnDraw Click** event method:

```
private void BtnDraw_Click(object sender, EventArgs e)
{
  // generate new random rectangle structure
  // rectangle is centered, taking up 20 to 90 percent of
each dimension
  int w = (int) (pnlDraw.ClientSize.Width *
(myRandom.Next(71) + 20) / 100);
  int h = (int) (pnlDraw.ClientSize.Height *
(myRandom.Next(71) + 20) / 100);
  int l = (int) (0.5 * (pnlDraw.ClientSize.Width - w));
  int t = (int) (0.5 * (pnlDraw.ClientSize.Height - h));
  myRectangle = new Rectangle(l, t, w, h);
  isDrawn = true;
  isFilled = false;
  btnDraw.Enabled = false;
  btnFill.Enabled = true;
  btnClear.Enabled = true;
  pnlDraw_Paint(null, null);
}
```

This code establishes a new rectangle structure and draws a rectangle or ellipse.

5. Use this code in the **btnFill Click** event method:

```
private void BtnFill_Click(object sender, EventArgs e)
{
  // fill rectangle or ellipse with brush
  isFilled = true;
  btnDraw.Enabled = false;
  // pick colors at random
  fillRed = myRandom.Next(256);
  fillGreen = myRandom.Next(256);
  fillBlue = myRandom.Next(256);
  pnlDraw_Paint(null, null);
}
```

Here, random colors are picked and the existing rectangle or ellipse is filled.

6. Use this code in **btnClear Click** event – this clears the graphics object and allows another rectangle or ellipse to be drawn:

```
private void BtnClear_Click(object sender, EventArgs e)
{
  // clear region
  isDrawn = false;
  isFilled = false;
  btnDraw.Enabled = true;
  btnFill.Enabled = false;
  btnClear.Enabled = false;
  pnlDraw_Paint(null, null);
}
```

7. Use this code in the **pnlDraw Paint** event. This code draws/fills the rectangle or ellipse if it is in the panel control:

```csharp
private void PnlDraw_Paint(object sender, PaintEventArgs e)
{
  Graphics myGraphics;
  Pen myPen;
  Brush myBrush;
  myGraphics = pnlDraw.CreateGraphics();
  myGraphics.Clear(pnlDraw.BackColor);
  // fill before draw to keep border
  if (isFilled)
  {
    // paint with brush of random color
    myBrush = new SolidBrush(Color.FromArgb(fillRed, fillGreen, fillBlue));
    if (rdoRectangle.Checked)
    {
      myGraphics.FillRectangle(myBrush, myRectangle);
    }
    else
    {
      myGraphics.FillEllipse(myBrush, myRectangle);
    }
    myBrush.Dispose();
  }
  if (isDrawn)
  {
    // draw with pen 3 pixels wide
    myPen = new Pen(Color.Black, 3);
    if (rdoRectangle.Checked)
    {
      myGraphics.DrawRectangle(myPen, myRectangle);
    }
    else
    {
      myGraphics.DrawEllipse(myPen, myRectangle);
    }
    myPen.Dispose();
  }
  myGraphics.Dispose();
}
```

8. Lastly, if either radio button is clicked, we clear the drawing region so a new shape can be drawn. The corresponding **rdoShape_CheckedChanged** event procedure (handles both radio buttons) is:

```
private void RdoShape_CheckedChanged(object sender,
EventArgs e)
{
  // shape changes - clear drawing area
  btnClear_Click(null,null);
}
```

9. Save and run the application (saved in **Example 8-7** folder in **LearnVCS\VCS Code\Class 8** folder). Try drawing and filling rectangles and ellipses. Notice how the random colors work. Notice how the button controls are enabled and disabled at different points. Note that the graphics are persistent. Here's a rectangle I drew:

and now it's filled:

Here's an elliptical border:

and its filled counterpart:

DrawPie Method

The **DrawPie** method will draw a segment of an ellipse (a slice of pie) in a **rectangle structure** within a **graphic object**. To draw a pie segment, you first create the graphics object. Then you create the rectangle structure. Assuming you have created a graphics object named **myGraphics** and a rectangle structure named **myRectangle**, the syntax to draw a pie segment with pen object **myPen** is:

```
myGraphics.DrawPie(myPen, myRectangle, startAngle,
sweepAngle);
```

where **startAngle** and **sweepAngle** are angles (both **float** data types, measured in **degrees**) bounding the pie segment.

A diagram indicates these bounding angles:

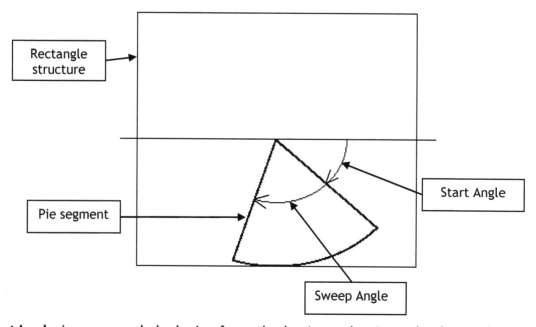

startAngle is measured clockwise from the horizontal axis to the first side of the pie segment. **sweepAngle** is the clockwise angle starting at startAngle and ending at the second side of the pie segment. Notice if startAngle = 0 and sweepAngle = 360, the DrawPie method draws the same figure as DrawEllipse (you get the whole pie!).

Using a black pen with a line width of 1 (**Pens.Black**), the code to draw a pie segment (**startAngle = 120**, **sweepAngle = 80**) within a rectangle structure that takes up 80 percent of the width and height of the client area of a form-hosted graphics object is:

```
Graphics myGraphics;
Rectangle myRectangle;
myGraphics = this.CreateGraphics();
int left = (int) (0.1 * this.ClientSize.Width);
int top = (int) (0.1 * this.ClientSize.Height);
int width = (int) (0.8 * this.ClientSize.Width);
int height = (int) (0.8 * this.ClientSize.Height);
myRectangle = new Rectangle(left, top, width, height);
myGraphics.DrawPie(Pens.Black, myRectangle, 120, 80);
myGraphics.Dispose();
```

This code produces this pie segment:

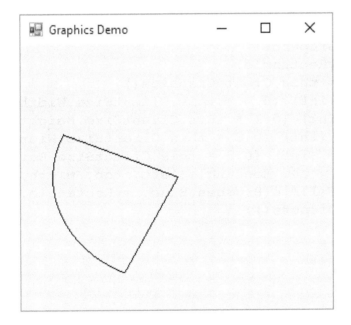

FillPie Method

The **FillPie** method will fill a segment of an ellipse (a slice of pie) in a **rectangle structure** within a **graphic object**. To fill a pie segment, you first create the graphics object. Then you create the rectangle structure. Assuming you have created a graphics object named **myGraphics** and a rectangle structure named **myRectangle**, the syntax to fill a pie segment with brush object **myBrush** is:

```
myGraphics.FillPie(myBrush, myRectangle, startAngle,
    sweepAngle)
```

where **startAngle** and **sweepAngle** are the segment bounding angles (both **float** data types, measured in **degrees,** in a clockwise direction).

Using a blue solid brush (**Brushes. Blue**), the code to fill a pie segment (**startAngle = 120, sweepAngle = 80**) within a rectangle structure that takes up 80 percent of the width and height of the client area of a form-hosted graphics object is:

```
Graphics myGraphics;
Rectangle myRectangle;
myGraphics = this.CreateGraphics();
int left = (int) (0.1 * this.ClientSize.Width);
int top = (int) (0.1 * this.ClientSize.Height);
int width = (int) (0.8 * this.ClientSize.Width);
int height = (int) (0.8 * this.ClientSize.Height);
myRectangle = new Rectangle(left, top, width, height);
myGraphics.FillPie(Brushes.Blue, myRectangle, 120, 80);
myGraphics.Dispose();
```

This code produces this pie segment:

Like the rectangle and ellipse methods, notice the fill operation erases any border that may have been there after a draw operation. For a bordered, filled pie segment, do the fill, then the draw.

Example 8-8

Drawing Pie Segments

1. Start a new application. In this application, we will draw an ellipse (in panel control) and fill it with a random number (2 to 6) of pie segments. Each segment will be a different color. Add a panel control and two button controls to the form. The form should look like this:

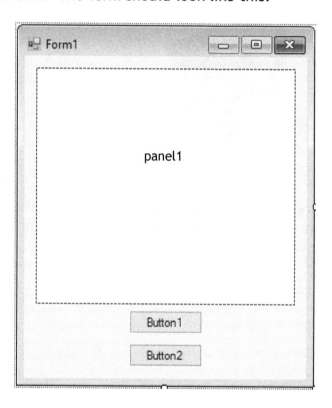

2. Set the following properties:

Form1:

Name	frmPie
FormBorderStyle	SingleFixed
StartPosition	CenterScreen
Text	Drawing Pie Segments

panel1:

Name	pnlDraw
BackColor	White
BorderStyle	Fixed3D

button1:

Name	btnDraw
Text	&Draw/Fill Pie

button2:

Name	btnClear
Enabled	False
Text	&Clear Pie

When done, my form looks like this:

3. Add the **PieSlice** class (**PieSlice.cs**) to store information about each slice. Also, allows construction of a slice knowing the sweep angle and color:

```csharp
class PieSlice
{
  public float SweepAngle;
  public System.Drawing.Color SliceColor;
  public PieSlice(float a, System.Drawing.Color c)
  {
    this.SweepAngle = a;
    this.SliceColor = c;
  }
}
```

4. Return to the form code window. Form level scope declarations:

```csharp
Rectangle myRectangle;
int numberSlices;
PieSlice[] slices = new PieSlice[6];
Color[] myColors = new Color[6];
bool isDrawn = false;
Random myRandom = new Random();
```

5. Use this code in **frmPie Load** to define the rectangle structure and set colors for the pie segments:

```csharp
private void FrmPie_Load(object sender, EventArgs e)
{
  // set up rectangle and colors
  myRectangle = new Rectangle(20, 20,
pnlDraw.ClientSize.Width - 40, pnlDraw.ClientSize.Height -
40);
  myColors[0] = Color.Red;
  myColors[1] = Color.Green;
  myColors[2] = Color.Yellow;
  myColors[3] = Color.Blue;
  myColors[4] = Color.Magenta;
  myColors[5] = Color.Cyan;
}
```

6. Use this code in **btnClear Click** event – this clears the graphics object and allows another pie to be drawn:

```
private void BtnClear_Click(object sender, EventArgs e)
{
  // clear region
  isDrawn = false;
  btnDraw.Enabled = true;
  btnClear.Enabled = false;
  pnlDraw_Paint(null, null);
}
```

7. Use this code in the **btnDraw Click** event method:

```
private void BtnDraw_Click(object sender, EventArgs e)
{
  // new pie - get number of slices (2-6), sweep angles
and draw it
  float degreesRemaining;
  // draw bounding ellipse
  // choose 2 to 6 slices at random
  numberSlices = myRandom.Next(5) + 2;
  degreesRemaining = 360;
  // for each slice choose a sweep angle
  for (int n = 0; n < numberSlices; n++)
  {
    if (n < numberSlices - 1)
    {
      slices[n] = new PieSlice(myRandom.Next((int)(0.5 *
degreesRemaining)) + 1, myColors[n]);
    }
    else
    {
      slices[n] = new PieSlice(degreesRemaining,
myColors[n]);
    }
    degreesRemaining -= slices[n].SweepAngle;
  }
  isDrawn = true;
  btnDraw.Enabled = false;
  btnClear.Enabled = true;
  pnlDraw_Paint(null, null);
}
```

This code establishes the pie segments and draws them.

8. Use this code in the **pnlDraw Paint** event. This code draws/fills an ellipse with pie segments if it is in the panel control:

```csharp
private void PnlDraw_Paint(object sender, PaintEventArgs e)
{
  Graphics myGraphics;
  Brush myBrush;
  float startAngle;
  myGraphics = pnlDraw.CreateGraphics();
  if (isDrawn)
  {
    // draw pie
    startAngle = 0;
    // for each slice fill and draw
    for (int n = 0; n < numberSlices; n++)
    {
      myBrush = new SolidBrush(slices[n].SliceColor);
      myGraphics.FillPie(myBrush, myRectangle, startAngle, slices[n].SweepAngle);
      myGraphics.DrawPie(Pens.Black, myRectangle, startAngle, slices[n].SweepAngle);
      startAngle += slices[n].SweepAngle;
      myBrush.Dispose();
    }
    // draw bounding ellipse
    myGraphics.DrawEllipse(Pens.Black, myRectangle);
  }
  else
  {
    // clear pie
    myGraphics.Clear(pnlDraw.BackColor);
  }
  myGraphics.Dispose();
}
```

9. Save and run the application (saved in **Example 8-8** folder in **LearnVCS\VCS Code\Class 8** folder). Click **Draw/Fill Pie** to draw a segmented pie. Try several – each will be different. Note that the graphics are persistent. Here's a run I made:

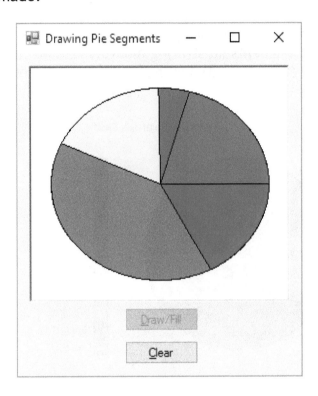

Pie Charts

The example just discussed suggests an immediate application for such capabilities – drawing **pie charts**. Pie charts are used to compare values of like information or to show what makes up a particular quantity. For example, a pie chart could illustrate what categories your monthly expenses fit into. Or, here is a pie chart with 12 segments illustrating monthly rainfall (in inches) for my hometown of Seattle (the segments for the winter months are very big!):

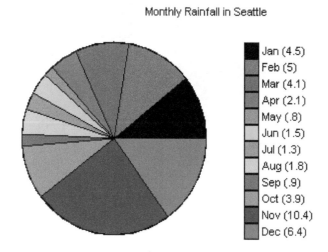

Monthly Rainfall in Seattle

Jan (4.5)
Feb (5)
Mar (4.1)
Apr (2.1)
May (.8)
Jun (1.5)
Jul (1.3)
Aug (1.8)
Sep (.9)
Oct (3.9)
Nov (10.4)
Dec (6.4)

This chart was created with Visual C#, by the way.

The steps for drawing a pie chart are straightforward. Assume you have **n** pieces of data (monthly rainfall, categorized expenditures, seasonal air traffic, various income sources). Follow these steps to create a pie chart using the Visual C# graphics methods:

> ➢ Generate **n** pieces of data to be plotted. Store this data in an array **y[n]** (a 0-based array).
> ➢ Sum the n elements of the y array to obtain a total value.
> ➢ Divide each y element by the computed total to obtain the proportional contributions of each.
> ➢ Multiply each proportion by 360 degrees – the resulting values will be the **sweepAngle** arguments in the **DrawPie** and **FillPie** functions.
> ➢ Draw each pie segment (pick a unique, identifying color) using **FillPie** and **DrawPie** (fill then draw to maintain border). Initialize the **startAngle** at zero. After drawing each segment, the next **startAngle** will be the previous value incremented by the current **sweepAngle**.

This code is a general class (**PieChart**) to draw a pie chart in a panel control. It uses another class (**PieSlice**, from Example 8-8) which is used to define each slice. You should be able to identify each of the steps listed above. The constructor has as arguments: **n**, the number of pie segments, **y**, the array of data (**double** data type) and **c**, an array of pie segment colors. Once constructed, the **Draw** method is used to draw the pie chart in **p**, the panel hosting the chart.

```
class PieChart
{
  PieSlice[] slice;
  public PieChart(int n, double[] y,
System.Drawing.Color[] c)
  {
    // builds slices for pie chart
    // n - number of pie segments to draw
    // y - array of points (double type) to chart (lower
index is 0, upper index is n-1)
    // c - color of pie segments
    // find sum of values
    slice = new PieSlice[n];
    double sum = 0;
    for (int i = 0; i < n; i++)
    {
      sum += y[i];
    }
    // for each slice assign sweep angle and color
    for (int i = 0; i < n; i++)
    {
```

```csharp
      slice[i] = new PieSlice((float)(360.0 * y[i] / sum),
c[i]);
    }
  }
  public void Draw(System.Windows.Forms.Panel p)
  {
    // draws a pie chart on panel p
    System.Drawing.Graphics pieChart;
    System.Drawing.Brush myBrush;
    System.Drawing.Rectangle myRectangle;
    float startAngle;
    // start drawing - use circle centered in narrowest
dimension of plot area
    if (p.ClientSize.Height < p.ClientSize.Width)
    {
      myRectangle = new System.Drawing.Rectangle((int)(0.5
* p.ClientSize.Width - 0.45 * p.ClientSize.Height),
(int)(0.05 * p.ClientSize.Height), (int)(0.9 *
p.ClientSize.Height), (int)(0.9 * p.ClientSize.Height));
    }
    else
    {
      myRectangle = new System.Drawing.Rectangle((int)(0.5
* p.ClientSize.Width - 0.45 * p.ClientSize.Width),
(int)(0.5 * p.ClientSize.Height - 0.45 *
p.ClientSize.Width), (int)(0.9 * p.ClientSize.Width),
(int)(0.9 * p.ClientSize.Width));
    }
    pieChart = p.CreateGraphics();
    pieChart.Clear(p.BackColor);
    startAngle = 0;
    // for each slice compute sweep angle, fill and draw
    for (int i = 0; i < slice.Length; i++)
    {
      myBrush = new
System.Drawing.SolidBrush(slice[i].SliceColor);
      pieChart.FillPie(myBrush, myRectangle, startAngle,
slice[i].SweepAngle);
      pieChart.DrawPie(System.Drawing.Pens.Black,
myRectangle, startAngle, slice[i].SweepAngle);
      startAngle += slice[i].SweepAngle;
      myBrush.Dispose();
    }
    pieChart.DrawEllipse(System.Drawing.Pens.Black,
myRectangle);
    pieChart.Dispose();
  }
```

```
}
class PieSlice
{
  public float SweepAngle;
  public System.Drawing.Color SliceColor;
  public PieSlice(float a, System.Drawing.Color c)
  {
    this.SweepAngle = a;
    this.SliceColor = c;
  }
}
```

Each of the drawing object/methods is prefaced with **System.Drawing**. This can be avoided by placing this line:

```
using System.Drawing;
```

at the top of the class definition file with the other **using** statements.

To use the **PieChart** class in your application, first add the class to your project. Then determine the number of slices (**n**), the array of values (**y**) and an array of colors (**c**). Of course, you can name these variables anything you'd like. The pie chart is then constructed using:

```
PieChart myPieChart;
myPieChart = new PieChart(n, y, c);
```

To draw this chart on a panel control (**myPanel**), use the **Draw** method:

```
myPieChart.Draw(myPanel);
```

Line Charts and Bar Charts

In addition to pie charts, two other useful data display tools are **line charts** and **bar charts**. Line charts are used to plot Cartesian pairs of data (x, y) generated using some function. They are useful for seeing trends in data. As an example, you could plot your weight while following a diet and exercise regime. And, here is a line chart (created with Visual C#) of yearly attendance at the Seattle Mariners baseball games from 1991 to 2000:

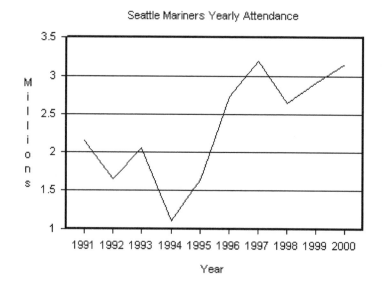

You can see there was increased interest in the team after the 1995 year (that's the exciting year we've alluded to in some of our problems – for example, see Problem 8-4 at the end of this chapter).

The Visual C# **DrawLine** function can be used to create line charts. The steps for generating such a chart are simple:

➢ Generate **n** Cartesian pairs of data to be plotted. Store the horizontal values in an array **x[n]**, the corresponding vertical values in an array **x[n]** (both 0-based arrays).
➢ Loop through all n points, connecting consecutive points using the **DrawLine** function.

Bar charts plot values as horizontal or vertical bars (referenced to some base value, many times zero). They can also be used to see trends and to compare values, like pie charts. Here's a vertical bar chart (drawn with Visual C# methods) of the same attendance data in the line chart above (the base value is 1 million):

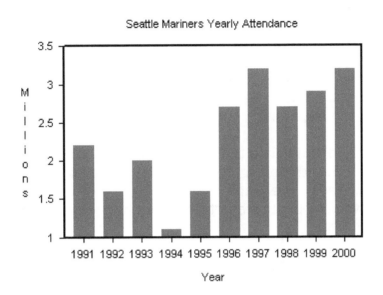

The increase in attendance after 1995 is very pronounced. And, here's a bar chart (base value of zero) of Seattle's monthly rainfall (again, note how big the 'winter' bars are):

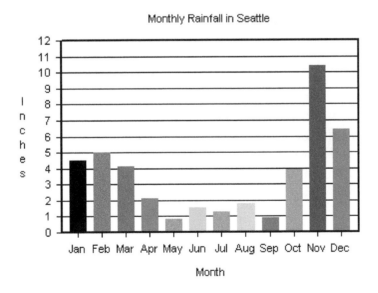

Yes, this, too, was created with Visual C#.

The **FillRectangle** graphics method can be used for bar charts. The steps for generating a vertical bar chart:

> ➢ Generate **n** pieces of data to be plotted. Store this data in an array **y[n]** (a 0-based array).
> ➢ Determine the width of each bar, using width of the graphics object as a guide. I usually allow some space between each bar.
> ➢ Select a base value (the value at the bottom of the bar). This is often zero.
> ➢ For each bar, determine horizontal position based on bar width and current bar being drawn. Draw each bar (pick a unique, identifying color, if desired) using **FillRectangle**. The bar height begins at the base value and ends at the respective **y** value.

At this point, we could write code to implement general methods for drawing line and bar charts. But, there's a problem. And, that problem relates to the **client coordinates** used by the graphics objects. Let me illustrate. Say we wanted to draw a very simple line chart described by the four Cartesian points given by:

x = 0, y = 2
x = 2, y = 7
x = 5, y = 11
x = 6, y = 13

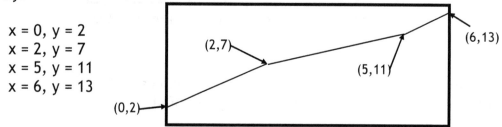

In this plot, the horizontal axis value (x) begins at 0 and reaches a maximum of 6. The vertical axis value (y) has a minimum value of 2, a maximum of 13. And, y increases in an upward direction.

Recall, the client coordinates of the graphics object has an origin of **(0, 0)** at the upper left corner. The maximum x value is **ClientSize.Width - 1**, the maximum y value is **ClientSize.Height -1** and y increases in a downward direction. Hence, to plot our data, we need to first compute where each (x, y) pair in our 'user-coordinates' fits within the dimensions of the graphics object specified by the **ClientSize.Width** and **ClientSize.Height** properties. This is a straightforward coordinate conversion computation.

Coordinate Conversions

Drawing in the graphics object is done in **client coordinates** (measured in pixels, an integer type). Data for plotting line and bar charts is usually in some physically meaningful units (inches, degrees, dollars) we'll call **user coordinates.** In order to draw a line or bar chart, we need to be able to convert from user coordinates to client coordinates. We will do each axis (horizontal and vertical) separately.

The horizontal (**xClient** axis) in **client coordinates** is **ClientSize.Width** pixels wide. The far left pixel is at **xClient = 0** and the far right is at **xClient = ClientSize.Width - 1**. xClient increases from left to right:

0   **xClient**   **ClientSize.Width - 1**

Assume the horizontal data (**xUser** axis) in our user coordinates runs from a minimum, **xMin,** at the left to a maximum, **xMax,** at the right. Thus, the first pixel on the horizontal axis of our user coordinates will be xMin and the last will be xMax:

xMin   **xUser**   **xMax**

With these two depictions, we can compute the **xClient** value corresponding to a given **xUser** value using simple **proportions,** dividing the distance from some point on the axis to the minimum value by the total distance. The process is also called **linear interpolation.** These proportions show:

$$\frac{\textbf{xUser - xMin}}{\textbf{xMax - xMin}} = \frac{\textbf{xClient - 0}}{\textbf{ClientSize.Width} - 1 - 0}$$

Solving this for **xClient** yields the desired conversion from a user value on the horizontal axis (**xUser**) to a client value for plotting:

xClient = (xUser - xMin)(ClientSize.Width - 1)/(xMax - xMin)

You can see this is correct at each extreme value. When **xUser = xMin, xClient = 0.** When **xUser = xMax, xClient = ClientSize.Width - 1.**

Now, we find the corresponding conversion for the vertical axis. We'll place the two axes side-by-side for easy comparison:

Client Axis: **User Axis:**

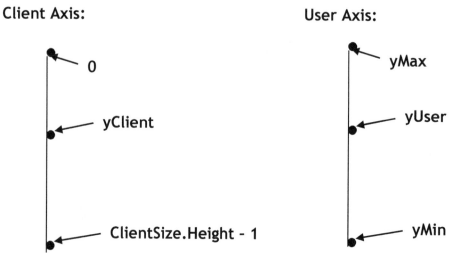

The vertical (**yClient** axis) in **client coordinates** is **ClientSize.Height** pixels high. The topmost pixel is at **yClient = 0** and the bottom is at **yClient = ClientSize.Height – 1. yClient** increases from top to bottom. The vertical data (**yUser** axis) in our user coordinates, runs from a minimum, **yMin**, at the bottom, to a maximum, **yMax**, at the top. Thus, the top pixel on the vertical axis of our user coordinates will be **yMax** and the bottom will be **yMin** (note our user axis increases up, rather than down).

With these two depictions, we can compute the **yClient** value corresponding to a given **yUser** value using linear interpolation. The computations show:

$$\frac{yUser - yMin}{yMax - yMin} = \frac{yClient - (ClientSize.Height - 1)}{0 - (ClientSize.Height - 1)}$$

Solving this for **yClient** yields the desired conversion from a user value on the vertical axis (**yUser**) to a client value for plotting (this requires a bit algebra, but it's straightforward):

   yClient = (yMax - yUser)(ClientSize.Height - 1)/(yMax - yMin)

Again, check the extremes. When **yUser = yMin, yClient = ClientSize.Height - 1.** When **yUser = yMax, yClient = 0.** It looks good.

Whenever we need to plot real, physical data in a graphics object, we will need coordinate conversions. In these notes, we use two general methods to do the conversions. First, for the horizontal axis, we use **xUserToxClient**. This function has four input arguments: **p** the panel control hosting the graphics object, the **xUser** value, the minimum user value, **xMin**, and the maximum value, **xMax**. All values are of **double** data type. The function returns the client coordinate (an **int** type):

```
public int xUserToxClient(Panel p, double xUser, double
xMin, double xMax)
{
   return((int) ((p.ClientSize.Width - 1) * (xUser - xMin)
/ (xMax - xMin)));
}
```

For the vertical axis, we use **yUserToyClient**. This function has four input arguments: **p** the panel control hosting the graphics object, the **yUser** value, the minimum user value, **yMin**, and the maximum value, **yMax**. All values are of **double** data type. The function returns the client coordinate (an **int** type):

```
public int yUserToyClient(Panel p, double yUser, double
yMin, double yMax)
{
   return((int) ((p.ClientSize.Height - 1) * (yMax - yUser)
/ (yMax - yMin)));
}
```

With the ability to transform coordinates, we can now develop general-purpose line and bar chart methods, similar to that developed for the pie chart. The modified steps to create a line chart are:

➤ Generate **n** Cartesian pairs of data to be plotted. Store the horizontal values in an array **x[n]**, the corresponding vertical values in an array **y[n]** (both 0-based arrays).
➤ Loop through all n points to determine the minimum and maximum x and y values.
➤ Again, loop through all n points. For each point, convert the x and y values to client coordinates, then connect the current point with the previous point using the **DrawLine** function.

This code is a general class (**LineChart**) to draw a line chart in a panel control. It incorporates the two coordinate conversion functions. You should be able to identify each of the steps listed above (most involve finding the minimum and maximum values). The constructor has as arguments: **p**, the panel control hosting the chart, **n**, the number of points to plot, **x**, the array of horizontal values, and **y** the array of vertical values. The **x** and **y** arrays are of type **double**. Once constructed, the **Draw** method is used to draw the line chart in **p** using the line color **c**.

```csharp
class LineChart
{
  private int[] xClient;
  private int[] yClient;
  public LineChart(System.Windows.Forms.Panel p, int n,
  double[] x, double[] y)
  {
    // Constructs a line chart - pairs of (x, y)
coordinates
    // p - panel control to draw plot
    // n - number of points to plot
    // x - array of x points (lower index is 0, upper
index is n-1)
    // y - array of y points (lower index is 0, upper
index is n-1)
    // need at least two points to plot
    if (n < 2)
    {
      return;
    }
    // find minimums and maximums
    double xMin, xMax;
    double yMin, yMax;
    xMin = x[0]; xMax = x[0];
    yMin = y[0]; yMax = y[0];
    for (int i = 1; i < n; i++)
    {
      if (x[i] < xMin)
        xMin = x[i];
      if (x[i] > xMax)
        xMax = x[i];
      if (y[i] < yMin)
        yMin = y[i];
      if (y[i] > yMax)
        yMax = y[i];
    }
    // Extend Y values a bit so bars are not right on
borders
```

```
    yMin = (double)((1 - 0.05 * Math.Sign(yMin)) * yMin);
    yMax = (double)((1 + 0.05 * Math.Sign(yMax)) * yMax);
    // get client coordinates
    xClient = new int[n];
    yClient = new int[n];
    for (int i = 0; i < n ; i++)
    {
      xClient[i] = xUserToxClient(p, x[i], xMin, xMax);
      yClient[i] = yUserToyClient(p, y[i], yMin, yMax);
    }
  }
  public void Draw(System.Windows.Forms.Panel p,
System.Drawing.Color c)
  {
    // Draws a line in p
    // p - panel control to draw plot
    // n - number of points to plot
    // xclient - array of x points (lower index is 0,
upper index is n-1)
    // yclient - array of y points (lower index is 0,
upper index is n-1)
    // c - color of line
    System.Drawing.Graphics lineChart;
    System.Drawing.Pen myPen;
    lineChart = p.CreateGraphics();
    myPen = new System.Drawing.Pen(c);
    lineChart.Clear(p.BackColor);
    for (int i = 0; i < xClient.Length - 1; i++)
    {
      // plot in client coordinates
      lineChart.DrawLine(myPen, xClient[i], yClient[i],
xClient[i + 1], yClient[i + 1]);
    }
    lineChart.Dispose();
    myPen.Dispose();
  }
  public int xUserToxClient(System.Windows.Forms.Panel p,
double xUser, double xMin, double xMax)
  {
    return ((int)((p.ClientSize.Width - 1) * (xUser -
xMin) / (xMax - xMin)));
  }
  public int yUserToyClient(System.Windows.Forms.Panel p,
double yUser, double yMin, double yMax)
  {
    return ((int)((p.ClientSize.Height - 1) * (yMax -
yUser) / (yMax - yMin)));
```

```
    }
}
```

Each of the drawing object/methods is prefaced with **System.Drawing**. This can be avoided by placing this line:

```
using System.Drawing;
```

at the top of the class definition file with the other **using** statements.

To use the **LineChart** class in your application, first add the class to your project. Then determine the number of points (**n**), the arrays of points (**x** and **y**) and a line color (**c**). Of course, you can name these variables anything you'd like. The line chart is then constructed for use in a panel control named **myPanel** using:

```
LineChart myLineChart;
myLineChart = new LineChart(myPanel, n, x, y);
```

To draw this chart on the panel control using color **c**, use the **Draw** method:

```
myLineChart.Draw(myPanel, c);
```

The modified steps to create a bar chart are:

> ➢ Generate **n** pieces of data to be plotted. Store this data in an array **y[n]** (a 0-based array).
> ➢ Determine the width of each bar, using width of the graphics object as a guide. I usually allow some space (one-half a bar width) between each bar.
> ➢ Loop through all n points to determine the minimum and maximum y value.
> ➢ Select a base value (the value at the bottom of the bar). This is often zero. Convert the base value to client coordinates.
> ➢ For each bar, determine horizontal position based on bar width and current bar being drawn. Draw each bar (pick a unique, identifying color, if desired) using **FillRectangle**. The bar height begins at the base value and ends at the respective **y** value (converted to client coordinates).

This code is a general class (**BarChart**) to draw a bar chart in a panel control. It incorporates the vertical coordinate conversion function. You should be able to identify each of the steps listed above (most involve finding minimums and maximums). The constructor arguments are **p**, the panel control hosting the chart, **n**, the number of points to plot, **y** the array of values (type **double**),and **b** the base value (type **double**). Once constructed, the **Draw** method is used to draw the bar chart in **p** with **c** the bar color array. This routine uses a version of **FillRectangle** that does not use the rectangle structure. It simply defines the rectangle using the usual Left, Top, Width and Height properties. Also, note different coding is needed depending whether the bar value is higher or lower than the base value (i.e., whether the bar goes up or down).

```
class BarChart
{
  int[] yClient;
  int bClient;
  public BarChart(System.Windows.Forms.Panel p, int n,
double[] y, double b)
    {
      // Constructs a vertical bar chart
      // p - panel control to draw plot
      // n - number of points to plot
      // c - color of bars
      // b - base value (lower limit of bar drawn)
      // need at least one point to draw bar chart
      if (n < 1)
      {
        return;
      }
      // find minimums and maximums
```

```
      double yMin, yMax;
      yMin = y[0]; yMax = y[0];
      if (n > 1)
      {
        for (int i = 1; i < n; i++)
        {
          if (y[i] < yMin)
            yMin = y[i];
          if (y[i] > yMax)
            yMax = y[i];
        }
      }
      // Extend Y values a bit so bars are not right on
borders
      yMin = (double)((1 - 0.05 * Math.Sign(yMin)) * yMin);
      yMax = (double)((1 + 0.05 * Math.Sign(yMax)) * yMax);
      // determine client values
      bClient = yUserToyClient(p, b, yMin, yMax);
      yClient = new int[n];
      for (int i = 0; i < n; i++)
      {
        yClient[i] = yUserToyClient(p, y[i], yMin, yMax);
      }
    }
  public void Draw(System.Windows.Forms.Panel p,
System.Drawing.Color[] c)
    {
      // Draws a vertical bar chart on p
      // p - panel control to draw plot
      // n - number of points to plot
      // yclient - array of points to chart (lower index is
0, upper index is n-1)
      // c - color of bars
      // bclient - base value (lower limit of bar drawn)
      System.Drawing.Graphics barChart;
      System.Drawing.Brush myBrush;
      int barWidth;
      barChart = p.CreateGraphics();
      barChart.Clear(p.BackColor);
      // Find bar width in client coordinates
      // use half bar-width as margins between bars
      barWidth = (int)(2 * (p.ClientSize.Width - 1) / (3 *
yClient.Length + 1));
      for (int i = 0; i < yClient.Length; i++)
      {
        myBrush = new System.Drawing.SolidBrush(c[i]);
        // draw bars
```

```
        if (bClient > yClient[i])
        {
          barChart.FillRectangle(myBrush, (int)((1.5 * i +
0.5) * barWidth), yClient[i], barWidth, bClient -
yClient[i]);
        }
        else
        {
          barChart.FillRectangle(myBrush, (int)((1.5 * i +
0.5) * barWidth), bClient, barWidth, yClient[i] -
bClient);
        }
        myBrush.Dispose();
      }
      // line at base
      barChart.DrawLine(System.Drawing.Pens.Black, 0,
bClient, p.ClientSize.Width - 1, bClient);
      barChart.Dispose();
    }
    public int yUserToyClient(System.Windows.Forms.Panel p,
double yUser, double yMin, double yMax)
    {
      return ((int)((p.ClientSize.Height - 1) * (yMax -
yUser) / (yMax - yMin)));
    }
  }
```

Each of the drawing object/methods is prefaced with **System.Drawing**. This can be avoided by placing this line:

```
using System.Drawing;
```

at the top of the class definition file with the other **using** statements.

To use the **BarChart** class in your application, first add the class to your project. Then determine the number of points (**n**), the array of points (**y**), a base value (**b**) and a bar color array (**c**). Of course, you can name these variables anything you'd like. The bar chart is then constructed for use in a panel control named **myPanel** using:

```
BarChart myBarChart;
myBarChart = new BarChart(myPanel, n, y, b);
```

To draw this chart on the panel control using color array **c**, use the **Draw** method:

```
myBarChart.Draw(myPanel, c);
```

Example 8-9

Line, Bar and Pie Charts

1. Start a new application. Here, we'll use the classes we developed to plot line, bar and pie charts. The data for the plots will be random.

2. Put a panel control and menu strip control (**Name mnuMainPlot**) on a form. Set up this simple menu structure:

<u>P</u>lot
    <u>L</u>ine Chart
    <u>B</u>ar Chart
    <u>S</u>piral Chart
    <u>P</u>ie Chart
    ——————

    E<u>x</u>it

Properties for these menu items should be:

Text	Name	Shortcut
&Plot	mnuPlot	[None]
&Line Chart	mnuPlotLine	CtrlL
&Bar Chart	mnuPlotBar	CtrlB
&Spiral Chart	mnuPlotSpiral	CtrlS
&Pie Chart	mnuPlotPie	CtrlP
-	mnuPlotSep	[None]
E&xit	mnuPlotExit	[None]

Other properties should be:

Form1:

Name	frmPlot
FormBorderStyle	Fixed Single
MainMenuStrip	mnuMainPlot
StartPosition	CenterScreen
Text	Plotting Examples

panel1:

Name	pnlPlot
BackColor	White

The form should resemble this (menu is opened):

Other controls in tray:

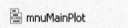

3. Form level scope declarations:

```
int whichPlot = 0;
// data arrays
double[] x = new double[200];
double[] y = new double[200];
double[] yd = new double[200];
// color array
Color[] plotColor = new Color[10];
// information to construct line charts (whichplot = 1, 2)
double alpha, beta;
Color lineColor;
// information to construct bar chart (whichplot = 3)
int numberBars;
// information for pie chart (whichplot = 4)
int numberSlices;
Random myRandom = new Random();
```

4. Use this code in the **frmPlot Load** method. This sets colors to use:

```
private void FrmPlot_Load(object sender, EventArgs e)
{
    // colors to use
    plotColor[0] = Color.Black;
    plotColor[1] = Color.DarkBlue;
    plotColor[2] = Color.DarkGreen;
    plotColor[3] = Color.DarkCyan;
    plotColor[4] = Color.DarkRed;
    plotColor[5] = Color.DarkMagenta;
    plotColor[6] = Color.Brown;
    plotColor[7] = Color.Blue;
    plotColor[8] = Color.Gray;
    plotColor[9] = Color.Red;
}
```

5. Add this code to the **mnuPlotLine Click** method (handles both **mnuPlotLine** and **mnuPlotSpiral Click** events). This code generates random data to plot using the **LineChart** class:

```
private void MnuPlotLine_Click(object sender, EventArgs e)
{
  ToolStripMenuItem itemClicked = (ToolStripMenuItem)
sender;
  // clear checks
  mnuPlotLine.Checked = false;
  mnuPlotSpiral.Checked = false;
  mnuPlotBar.Checked = false;
  mnuPlotPie.Checked = false;
  // check item selected
  itemClicked.Checked = true;
  // Create a sinusoid with 200 points
  alpha = (100.0 - myRandom.Next(200)) / 1000.0;
  beta = myRandom.Next(1000) / 100.0 + 5.0;
  for (int i = 0; i < 200; i++)
  {
    x[i] = i;
    y[i] = (double) (Math.Exp(-alpha * i) *
Math.Sin(Math.PI * i / beta));
    yd[i] = (double) (Math.Exp(-alpha * i) * (Math.PI *
Math.Cos(Math.PI * i / beta) / beta - alpha *
Math.Sin(Math.PI * i / beta)));
  }
  // choose random color
  lineColor = plotColor[myRandom.Next(10)];
  // Draw plots
  if (mnuPlotLine.Checked)
  {
    whichPlot = 1;
  }
  else
  {
    whichPlot = 2;
  }
  pnlPlot_Paint(null, null);
}
```

6. Add this code to the **mnuPlotBar Click**. This code generates random data to plot using the **BarChart** method:

```csharp
private void MnuPlotBar_Click(object sender, EventArgs e)
{
  // generate 5-10 bars with values from -10 to 10 and
draw bar chart
  // check item selected
  mnuPlotLine.Checked = false;
  mnuPlotSpiral.Checked = false;
  mnuPlotBar.Checked = true;
  mnuPlotPie.Checked = false;
  numberBars = myRandom.Next(6) + 5;
  for (int i = 0; i < numberBars; i++)
  {
    y[i] = (double) (myRandom.Next(2000) / 100.0 - 10.0);
  }
  whichPlot = 3;
  pnlPlot_Paint(null, null);
}
```

7. Add this code to the **mnuPlotPie Click**. This code generates random data to plot using the **PieChart** method:

```csharp
private void MnuPlotPie_Click(object sender, EventArgs e)
{
  // Generate 3 to 10 slices at random with values from 1
to 5
  // check item selected
  mnuPlotLine.Checked = false;
  mnuPlotSpiral.Checked = false;
  mnuPlotBar.Checked = false;
  mnuPlotPie.Checked = true;
  numberSlices = myRandom.Next(8) + 3;
  for (int i = 0; i < numberSlices; i++)
  {
    y[i] = (double) (myRandom.Next(5000) / 100.0 + 1.0);
  }
  whichPlot = 4;
  pnlPlot_Paint(null, null);
}
```

8. Use this code in the **pnlPlot Paint** event. This code draws the plot based on user selection:

```
private void PnlPlot_Paint(object sender, PaintEventArgs e)
{
  switch (whichPlot)
  {
    case 0:
      return;
    case 1:
      // line chart (x/y)
      LineChart myLineChart;
      myLineChart = new LineChart(pnlPlot, 200, x, y);
      myLineChart.Draw(pnlPlot, lineColor);
      break;
    case 2:
      // spiral chart
      LineChart mySpiralChart;
      mySpiralChart = new LineChart(pnlPlot, 200, y, yd);
      mySpiralChart.Draw(pnlPlot, lineColor);
      break;
    case 3:
      // bar chart
      BarChart myBarChart;
      myBarChart = new BarChart(pnlPlot, numberBars, y, 0);
      myBarChart.Draw(pnlPlot, plotColor);
      break;
    case 4:
      // pie chart
      PieChart myPieChart;
      myPieChart = new PieChart(numberSlices, y, plotColor);
      myPieChart.Draw(pnlPlot);
      break;
  }
}
```

9. Add this code to the **mnuPlotExit Click** event method:

```
private void MnuPlotExit_Click(object sender, EventArgs e)
{
   this.Close();
}
```

10. Make sure to create the **LineChart (LineChart.cs)**, **BarChart (BarChart.cs)**, and **PieChart (PieChart.cs)** classes and add them to your project.

11. Finally, save and run the application (saved in **Example 8-9** folder in **LearnVCS\VCS Code\Class 8** folder). Run it and try all the plotting options. Each time you draw any plot it will be different because of the randomness programmed in. Here's an example of each plot type:

Line Chart:

Bar Chart:

Spiral Chart:

Pie Chart:

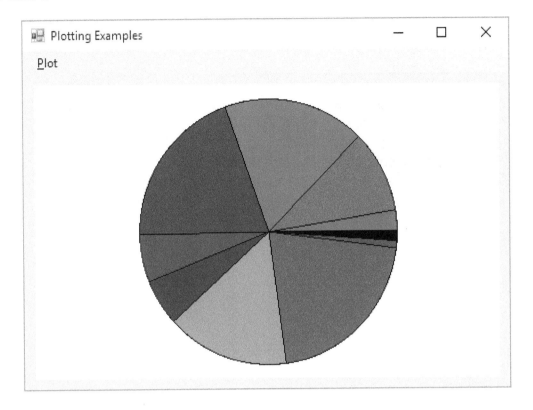

You're ready to tackle any plotting job now.

These routines just call out for enhancements. Some things you might try:

A. Draw grid lines on the plots. Use dotted or dashed lines at regular intervals.

B. Modify the line and chart classes to allow plotting more than one function. Use colors or different line styles to differentiate the lines and bars. Add a legend defining each plot.

C. Label the plot axes. Put titling information on the axes and the plot. Consult the **DrawString** method described in Chapter 9.

Class Review

After completing this class, you should understand:

- ➤ How to do simple animation with the picture box control
- ➤ How the timer control works – its properties and the Tick event
- ➤ The basics of simple games using the random number generator
- ➤ The graphics methods and objects that allow drawing directly to the graphics object
- ➤ Ways to specify colors with the graphics methods, for setting properties and use of the ColorDialog control
- ➤ The concept of persistent graphics and use of the Paint event
- ➤ The difference between client coordinates and user coordinates and conversion from one to the other
- ➤ How to draw simple line charts, bar charts and pie charts.

Practice Problems 8

Problem 8-1. Bounce Problem. Bouncing balls are fun. An equation that computes the **Top** property for a bouncing **control** (usually a picture box) on a **Form** (given the control's **Left** property) is:

```
control.Top = (int) ((this.ClientSize.Height -
control.Height) * (1 - Math.Abs(Math.Cos(Math.PI * nBounces
* control.Left / this.ClientSize.Width))));
```

where **nBounces** is the number of bounces you want across the form. This equation was derived with just a bit of trigonometry. Use this equation to make a ball bounce across the form by varying the control **Left** property. When it hits an end, make it switch direction.

Problem 8-2. Dice Rolling Problem. Build an application that rolls two dice and displays the results (graphics of the six die faces are included in the **LearnVCS\VCS Code\Class 8\Problem 8-2** folder). Have each die 'stop rolling' at different times.

Problem 8-3. RGB Colors Problem. Build an application with three scroll bars and a label control. Use the scroll bars to adjust the red, green and blue contributions to the **FromArgb** function of the Color structure. Let the background color of the label control be set by those contributions.

Problem 8-4. Plotting Problem. Build an application that opens the output file created in Practice Problem 7-3 (the Mariners win streak file - saved as **MAR95.CSV** in the **LearnVCS\VCS Code\Class 7\Problem 7-3\Bin\Debug** folder) and plots the information as a bar chart in a panel control. You'll want to first copy the **CSV** file into the **Bin\Debug** folder of this new application.

Problem 8-5. Pie Chart Problem. Build an application where the user can enter a list of numbers and build a pie chart from that list.

Exercise 8-1

Blackjack

Develop an application that simulates the playing of the card game Blackjack. The idea of Blackjack is to score higher than a Dealer's hand without exceeding twenty-one. Cards count their value, except face cards (jacks, queens, kings) count for ten, and aces count for either one or eleven (your pick). If you beat the Dealer, you get 10 points. If you get Blackjack (21 with just two cards) and beat the Dealer, you get 15 points. This is not a trivial application to build.

The game starts by giving two cards (from a standard 52 card deck) to the Dealer (one face down) and two cards to the player. The player decides whether to Hit (get another card) or Stay. The player can choose as many extra cards as desired. If the player exceeds 21 before staying, it is a loss (-10 points). If the player does not exceed 21, it becomes the dealer's turn. The Dealer adds cards until 16 is exceeded. When this occurs, if the dealer also exceeds 21 or if his total is less than the player's, he loses. If the dealer total is greater than the player total (and under 21), the dealer wins. If the dealer and player have the same total, it is a Push (no points added or subtracted). There are lots of other things you can do in Blackjack, but these simple rules should suffice here. The cards should be reshuffled whenever there are fewer than fifteen (or so) cards remaining in the deck.

Exercise 8-2

Information Tracking Plotting

Add plotting capabilities to the information tracker you developed in Exercise 7-1 and Exercise 7-2. Plot whatever information you stored versus the date. Use a line or bar chart.

9. More Graphics Methods and Multimedia Effects

Review and Preview

In the last class, we learned a lot about graphics methods in Visual C#. Yet, everything we drew was static; there was no user interaction. In this chapter, we extend our graphics methods knowledge by learning how to detect mouse events. An example paintbrush program is built.

We look at new brush objects and how to 'draw' text. We then are introduced to concepts needed for multimedia (game) programming – animation, collision detection and sounds. Like Chapter 8, we will build lots of relatively short examples to demonstrate concepts. You'll learn to modify the examples for your needs.

Mouse Events

In Chapter 8, we learned about the graphics object, the rectangle structure and many drawing methods. We learned how to draw lines, rectangles, ellipses and pie segments. We learned how to incorporate these drawing elements into methods for line charts, bar charts and pie charts. Everything drawn with these elements was static; there was no user interaction. We set the parameters in code and drew our shapes or plots. We (the users) just sat there and watched pretty things appear.

In this chapter, the user becomes involved. To provide user interaction with an application, we can use the mouse as an interface for drawing graphics with Visual C#. To do this, we need to understand **mouse events**. Mouse events are similar to control events. Certain event methods are invoked when certain mouse actions are detected. Here, we see how to use mouse events for drawing on forms and panel controls.

We've used the mouse to click on controls in past applications. For example, we've written code for many button control **Click** events. To use the mouse for drawing purposes, however, a simple click event is not sufficient. We need to know not only that a control was clicked, but also need to know where it was clicked to provide a point to draw to. The mouse event that provides this information is the **MouseDown** event. The **MouseDown** event method is triggered whenever a mouse button is pressed while the mouse cursor is over a control. The form of this method is:

```
private void ControlName_MouseDown(object sender,
MouseEventArgs e)
{

}
```

The arguments are:

sender	Control clicked to invoke method
e	Event handler revealing which button was clicked and the coordinate of mouse cursor when button was pressed.

We are interested in three properties of the event handler **e**:

e.Button	Mouse button pressed. Possible values are: **MouseButtons.Left**, **MouseButtons.Center**, **MouseButtons.Right**
e.X	X coordinate of mouse cursor when mouse was clicked
e.Y	Y coordinate of mouse cursor when mouse was clicked

In drawing applications, the **MouseDown** event is used to initialize a drawing process. The point clicked is used to start drawing a line and the button clicked is often used to select line color.

Another common task for drawing with the mouse is moving the mouse while holding down a mouse button. The mouse event that provides this information is the **MouseMove** event. The **MouseMove** event is continuously triggered whenever the mouse is being moved over a control. The form of this method is:

```
private void ControlName_MouseMove(object sender,
MouseEventArgs e)
{

}
```

Its arguments are identical to those of the **MouseDown** event:

sender	Control clicked to invoke method
e	Event handler revealing which button is pressed and the current coordinate of mouse.

Properties for the event handler **e** are the same:

e.Button	Mouse button pressed (if any). Possible values are: **MouseButtons.Left**, **MouseButtons.Center**, **MouseButtons.Right**, **MouseButtons.None**
e.X	X coordinate of mouse cursor
e.Y	Y coordinate of mouse cursor

In drawing processes, the **MouseMove** event is used to detect the continuation of a previously started line. If drawing is continuing, the current point is connected to the previous point using the current pen.

Lastly, we would like to be able to detect the release of a mouse button. The **MouseUp** event is the opposite of the **MouseDown** event. It is triggered whenever a previously pressed mouse button is released. The method outline is:

```
private void ControlName_MouseUp(object sender,
MouseEventArgs e)
{

}
```

The arguments are:

sender	Control invoking method
e	Event handler revealing which button was released and the coordinate of mouse cursor when button was released.

We are interested in three properties of the event handler **e**:

e.Button	Mouse button released. Possible values are: **MouseButtons.Left**, **MouseButtons.Center**, **MouseButtons.Right**
e.X	X coordinate of mouse cursor when button was released
e.Y	Y coordinate of mouse cursor when button was released

In a drawing program, the **MouseUp** event signifies the halting of the current drawing process. We'll find the **MouseDown**, **MouseMove** and **MouseUp** events are integral parts of any Visual C# drawing program. We use them now (in conjunction with the **DrawLine** method) to build a paintbrush program called the **Blackboard**.

Example 9-1

Blackboard

1. Start a new application. Here, we will build a blackboard we can scribble on with the mouse (using colored 'chalk'). The left and right mouse buttons will draw with different (selectable) colors. Place a large panel control and two label controls on a form. Place a group box with 8 small label controls in it. The form should resemble this:

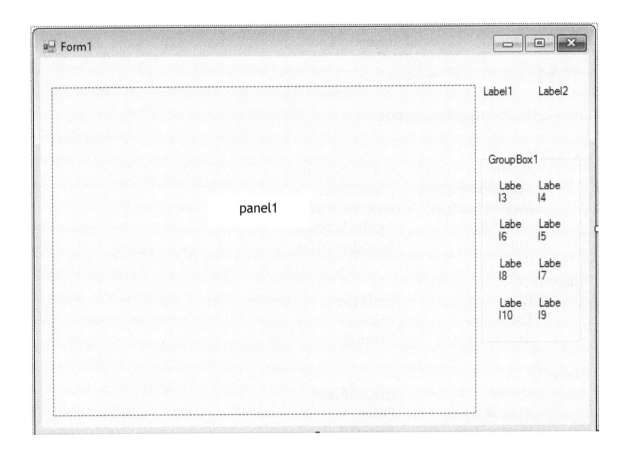

2. Add a menu strip control (**Name mnuBlackboard**). Set up a simple menu
    structure for your application. The menu should be:

    F̲ile
        N̲ew
        _____
        E̲xit

Properties for these menu items should be:

Text	Name
&File	mnuFile
&New	mnuFileNew
-	mnuFileSep
E&xit	mnuFileExit

3. Now, set the following properties:

Form1:

Name	frmBlackboard
FormBorderStyle	FixedSingle
MainMenuStrip	mnuBlackboard
StartPosition	CenterScreen
Text	Blackboard

panel1:

Name	pnlDraw
BackColor	Black
BorderStyle	Fixed3D

label1:

Name	lblLeftColor
AutoSize	False
BorderStyle	Fixed3D
Text	[Blank]

label2:

Name	lblRightColor
AutoSize	False
BorderStyle	Fixed3D
Text	[Blank]

groupBox1:

Name	grpColors
Font Size	10
Text	Colors

label3:

Name	lblGray
AutoSize	False
BorderStyle	Fixed3D
Text	[Blank]

label4:

Name	lblBlue
AutoSize	False
BorderStyle	Fixed3D
Text	[Blank]

label5:

Name	lblCyan
AutoSize	False
BorderStyle	Fixed3D
Text	[Blank]

label6:

Name	lblGreen
AutoSize	False
BorderStyle	Fixed3D
Text	[Blank]

label7:

Name	lblMagenta
AutoSize	False
BorderStyle	Fixed3D
Text	[Blank]

label8:

Name	lblRed
AutoSize	False
BorderStyle	Fixed3D
Text	[Blank]

label9:

Name	lblWhite
AutoSize	False
BorderStyle	Fixed3D
Text	[Blank]

label10:

Name	lblYellow
AutoSize	False
BorderStyle	Fixed3D
Text	[Blank]

The finished form (menu opened) should look something like:

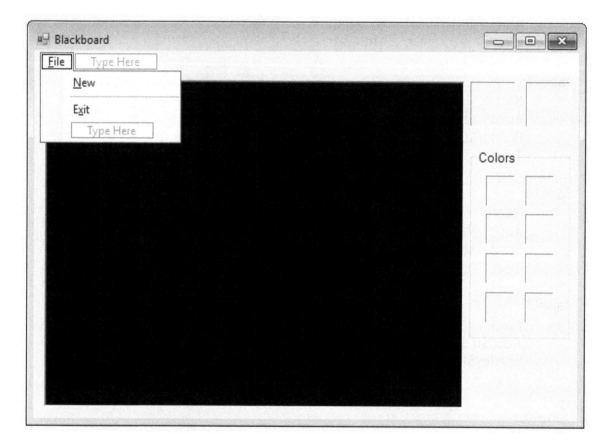

Other controls in tray:

     mnuBlackboard

4. Form level scope declarations code:

```
Graphics blackboard;
Pen myPen;
bool drawingOn;
int xPrevious, yPrevious;
Color leftColor, rightColor;
```

These are used to do drawing. **drawingOn** indicates if drawing process is active.

5. Use this code in each indicated method.

Use this code in the **frmBlackboard Load** method to set up selection and drawing colors and form drawing objects:

```
private void FrmBlackboard_Load(object sender, EventArgs e)
{
  // establish color choices
  lblGray.BackColor = Color.Gray;
  lblBlue.BackColor = Color.Blue;
  lblGreen.BackColor = Color.LightGreen;
  lblCyan.BackColor = Color.Cyan;
  lblRed.BackColor = Color.Red;
  lblMagenta.BackColor = Color.Magenta;
  lblYellow.BackColor = Color.Yellow;
  lblWhite.BackColor = Color.White;
  // set up graphics object and drawing pen
  leftColor = Color.Gray;
  lblLeftColor.BackColor = leftColor;
  rightColor = Color.White;
  lblRightColor.BackColor = rightColor;
  // create objects
  blackboard = pnlDraw.CreateGraphics();
  myPen = new Pen(leftColor);
}
```

Code for **mnuFileNew Click** event where we check to see if the drawing should be erased.

```
private void MnuFileNew_Click(object sender, EventArgs e)
{
  // Make sure user wants to start over
  if (MessageBox.Show("Are you sure you want to start a
new drawing?", "New Drawing", MessageBoxButtons.YesNo,
MessageBoxIcon.Question) == DialogResult.Yes)
  {
    blackboard.Clear(Color.Black);
  }
}
```

In **mnuFileExit Click**, make sure the user really wants to stop the application.

```
private void MnuFileExit_Click(object sender, EventArgs e)
{
  // Make sure user wants to quit
  if (MessageBox.Show("Are you sure you want to exit the
Blackboard?", "Exit Blackboard", MessageBoxButtons.YesNo,
MessageBoxIcon.Error, MessageBoxDefaultButton.Button2) ==
DialogResult.Yes)
  {
    this.Close();
  }
  else
  {
    return;
  }
}
```

In the **frmBlackboard FormClosing** event, dispose of the graphics objects.

```
private void FrmBlackboard_FormClosing(object sender,
FormClosingEventArgs e)
{
  // dispose graphics objects
  blackboard.Dispose();
  myPen.Dispose();
}
```

Code for **lblColor MouseDown** event to select color (handles clicking on any of eight color choice label controls).

```
private void LblColor_MouseDown(object sender,
MouseEventArgs e)
{
  Label colorClicked = (Label) sender;
  // set drawing color
  if (e.Button == MouseButtons.Left)
  {
    leftColor = colorClicked.BackColor;
    lblLeftColor.BackColor = leftColor;
  }
  else if (e.Button == MouseButtons.Right)
  {
    rightColor = colorClicked.BackColor;
    lblRightColor.BackColor = rightColor;
  }
}
```

When a mouse button is clicked (left or right button), drawing is initialized at the mouse cursor location with the respective color in the **pnlDraw MouseDown** event.

```
private void PnlDraw_MouseDown(object sender,
MouseEventArgs e)
{
  // if left button or right button clicked, set color and
  start drawing process
  if (e.Button == MouseButtons.Left || e.Button ==
  MouseButtons.Right)
  {
    drawingOn = true;
    xPrevious = e.X;
    yPrevious = e.Y;
    if (e.Button == MouseButtons.Left)
    {
      myPen.Color = leftColor;
    }
    else
    {
      myPen.Color = rightColor;
    }
  }
}
```

While mouse is being moved and **DrawingOn** is **True**, draw lines in current color in **pnlDraw MouseMove** event.

```csharp
private void PnlDraw_MouseMove(object sender,
MouseEventArgs e)
{
  // if drawing, connect previous point with new point
  if (drawingOn)
  {
    blackboard.DrawLine(myPen, xPrevious, yPrevious, e.X,
e.Y);
    xPrevious = e.X;
    yPrevious = e.Y;
  }
}
```

When a mouse button is released, stop drawing current line in the **pnlDraw MouseUp** event.

```csharp
private void PnlDraw_MouseUp(object sender, MouseEventArgs
e)
{
  // if left or button released,connect last point and
turn drawing off
  if (drawingOn && (e.Button == MouseButtons.Left ||
e.Button == MouseButtons.Right))
  {
    blackboard.DrawLine(myPen, xPrevious, yPrevious, e.X,
e.Y);
    drawingOn = false;
  }
}
```

6. Run the application. Try drawing. The left mouse button draws with one color and the right button draws with another. The current drawing colors are displayed at the top right corner of the form. To change a color, left or right click on the desired color in the **Colors** group box. Fun, huh? Here's one of my sketches:

Save the application (saved in **Example 9-1** folder in **LearnVCS\VCS Code\Class 9** folder). This is a neat application, but there's a problem. Draw a little something and then reduce the application to an icon. When the form is restored, your masterpiece is gone! The graphics here are not persistent. In Chapter 8, we used the panel control's **Paint** event to insure persistence. In this application, it would be difficult to always know what is displayed in the panel control. We would have to somehow store every point and every color used in the picture. Then, in the **Paint** event, every drawing step taken by the user would need to be reproduced. This is a difficult problem. We need another solution. We'll look at a potential solution next.

Persistent Graphics, Revisited (Image and Bitmap Objects)

In most of the graphics examples we studied in Chapter 8, we were able to recreate the contents of a graphics object in the **Paint** event. This allowed easy restoration of whatever was in the graphics object when the form was reactivated. In the **Blackboard** example, the user can draw anything they want in any color they want. This makes it difficult to recreate their drawing.

If we expect our graphics object to have complex graphics that are difficult to recreate in a **Paint** event, we take a different approach. The approach involves creating another type of graphics object, one that will always have a current copy of what is drawn. This copy will be maintained in a **bitmap object** using the **BackgroundImage** property of the host control (form, picture box or panel control, for example). The **BackgroundImage** property is just what it says – it sets or gets the image stored in the background of a control, a perfect choice for our Blackboard and other graphics examples. This **bitmap object** gives our graphics object some **memory**.

The idea here is based on the fact that the **BackgroundImage** property of an object is persistent. For example, if you set the **BackgroundImage** property of a control at design time, that image is persistent. You don't have to redraw it in a **Paint** event. There are three basic steps involved in creating a **graphics object** with **memory**. First, as always, declare the graphics object:

```
Graphics myGraphics;
```

Second, create a blank **bitmap** object for the **BackgroundImage** property of the host control for **myGraphics**. If that control is named **myObject** (usually a panel control), the **Bitmap** constructor is:

```
myObject.BackgroundImage = new
Bitmap(myObject.ClientSize.Width,
myObject.ClientSize.Height, PixelFormat);
```

Let's look at this constructor.

The first two arguments define the bitmap as having the same dimensions (**Width** and **Height** properties of the client rectangle) as the host control.

The final argument specifies what format is used to maintain the graphics object. There are many possible values for **PixelFormat**, each of the form `System.Drawing.Imaging.PixelFormat.FormatValue` where:

FormatValue	Description
Format16bppArgb1555	The pixel format is 16 bits per pixel. The color information specifies 32,768 shades of color, of which 5 bits are red, 5 bits are green, 5 bits are blue, and 1 bit is alpha.
Format16bppGrayScale	The pixel format is 16 bits per pixel. The color information specifies 65536 shades of gray.
Format16bppRgb555	The pixel format is 16 bits per pixel. The color information specifies 32768 shades of color of which 5 bits are red, 5 bits are green and 5 bits are blue.
Format16bppRgb565	The pixel format is 16 bits per pixel. The color information specifies 32,768 shades of color, of which 5 bits are red, 6 bits are green, and 5 bits are blue.
Format24bppRgb	The pixel format is 24 bits per pixel. The color information specifies 16,777,216 shades of color, of which 8 bits are red, 8 bits are green, and 8 bits are blue.
Format32bppArgb	The pixel format is 32 bits per pixel. The color information specifies 16,777,216 shades of color, of which 8 bits are red, 8 bits are green, and 8 bits are blue. The 8 additional bits are alpha bits.
Format32bppPArgb	The pixel format is 32 bits per pixel. The color information specifies 16,777,216 shades of color, of which 8 bits are red, 8 bits are green, and 8 bits are blue. The 8 additional bits are premultiplied alpha bits.

For our work, we will select a 'medium resolution' value of **Format24bppRgb**. You can try other formats if you like.

Finally, we create the graphics object using the new bitmap object:

```
myGraphics = Graphics.FromImage(myObject.BackgroundImage);
```

Anything drawn to this graphics object will be remembered and easily restored (without a **Paint** event) when needed. To provide this memory, after every drawing operation to the object, the host object needs to be refreshed (copies last drawn information to the **BackgroundImage**). The syntax for this is:

```
myObject.Refresh();
```

A side benefit of using such a graphics object is the ability to save and then, at some time, reload images. To **save** the image (a bitmap), use:

```
myObject.BackgroundImage.Save(FileName,
System.Drawing.Imaging.ImageFormat.Bmp);
```

where **FileName** is a complete path to the saved file (use a save file dialog control to obtain the name).

Then, to load (or **open**) a previously saved file into the host control (**myObject**) of the graphics object, use:

```
myObject.BackgroundImage = Image.FromFile(FileName);
```

where **FileName** is the saved file path. An open file dialog control can be used to obtain the file name. Once the **BackgroundImage** is loaded from file, the graphics object must be reconstructed using:

```
myGraphics = Graphics.FromImage(myObject.BackgroundImage);
```

A good question to ask at this point is why don't we always provide memory (persistent graphics) for our graphics objects? With these new techniques, we don't need to write code in a **Paint** event, where we always have to remember what is displayed in our graphics objects. The reasons we don't do this are **speed** and **resources**. Maintaining a bitmap object in memory consumes resources and slows the drawing process significantly. The more complex the object, the slower things become. You will notice the loss of speed when we modify the **Blackboard** example. You, the programmer, need to decide when to provide persistence to your graphics objects.

Example 9-2

Blackboard (Revisited)

1. Here, we will modify the **Blackboard** example so the graphics are persistent. That way, you'll never lose your masterpiece! The modifications are simple. Load **Example 9-1**.

2. We need to change how the panel graphics object is constructed. This is done in the **frmBlackboard Load** event (the new and/or modified code is shaded):

```csharp
private void FrmBlackboard_Load(object sender, EventArgs e)
{
  // establish color choices
  lblGray.BackColor = Color.Gray;
  lblBlue.BackColor = Color.Blue;
  lblGreen.BackColor = Color.LightGreen;
  lblCyan.BackColor = Color.Cyan;
  lblRed.BackColor = Color.Red;
  lblMagenta.BackColor = Color.Magenta;
  lblYellow.BackColor = Color.Yellow;
  lblWhite.BackColor = Color.White;
  // set up graphics object and drawing pen
  leftColor = Color.Gray;
  lblLeftColor.BackColor = leftColor;
  rightColor = Color.White;
  lblRightColor.BackColor = rightColor;
  // create objects
  pnlDraw.BackgroundImage = new
Bitmap(pnlDraw.ClientSize.Width,
pnlDraw.ClientSize.Height,
System.Drawing.Imaging.PixelFormat.Format24bppRgb);
  blackboard =
Graphics.FromImage(pnlDraw.BackgroundImage);
  myPen = new Pen(leftColor);
}
```

3. A new bitmap and graphics object must be generated when starting a new drawing in the **mnuFileNew Click** event (added code is shaded):

```
private void MnuFileNew_Click(object sender, EventArgs e)
{
   // Make sure user wants to start over
   if (MessageBox.Show("Are you sure you want to start a
new drawing?", "New Drawing", MessageBoxButtons.YesNo,
MessageBoxIcon.Question) == DialogResult.Yes)
   {
      pnlDraw.BackgroundImage = new
Bitmap(pnlDraw.ClientSize.Width,
pnlDraw.ClientSize.Height,
System.Drawing.Imaging.PixelFormat.Format24bppRgb);
      blackboard =
Graphics.FromImage(pnlDraw.BackgroundImage);
   }
}
```

4. We need to **Refresh** the object after each drawing method. A **Refresh** is needed in the **pnlDraw MouseMove** and **pnlDraw MouseUp** events (added code is shaded):

```
private void PnlDraw_MouseMove(object sender,
MouseEventArgs e)
{
   // if drawing, connect previous point with new point
   if (drawingOn)
   {
      blackboard.DrawLine(myPen, xPrevious, yPrevious, e.X,
e.Y);
      pnlDraw.Refresh();
      xPrevious = e.X;
      yPrevious = e.Y;
   }
}
```

```
private void PnlDraw_MouseUp(object sender, MouseEventArgs
e)
{
  // if left or button released,connect last point and
turn drawing off
  if (drawingOn && (e.Button == MouseButtons.Left ||
e.Button == MouseButtons.Right))
  {
    blackboard.DrawLine(myPen, xPrevious, yPrevious, e.X,
e.Y);
    pnlDraw.Refresh();
    drawingOn = false;
  }
}
```

That's all there is to change. Save (saved in **Example 9-2** folder in **LearnVCS\VCS Code\Class 9** folder) and run the application. Try drawing. Once you have a few lines (with different colors) on the blackboard, reduce the program to an icon. Restore the application. Your picture is still there! The graphics are persistent. But, you should also note the drawing process is slower and the lines appear more jagged. This performance degradation is due to the resources needed to maintain the bitmap object.

A challenge for those who like challenges - add **Open** and **Save** options that allow you to load and save pictures you draw (you'll get a chance to do this in Problem 9-1).

More Graphics Methods

In Chapter 8, we learned about the graphics object, the rectangle structure and many drawing methods. We learned how to draw lines, rectangles, ellipses and pie segments. We learned how to incorporate these drawing elements into methods for line charts, bar charts and pie charts. The GDI+ in Visual C# is vast and offers many graphics methods.

Here, we look a few more graphics methods to use in our applications. We learn how to draw connected line segments, polygons and filled polygons. We study connected curves, closed curves and filled closed curves. And, we learn about non-solid brush objects and how to add text to a graphics object.

The steps for drawing here are exactly the same as those followed in Chapter 8:

> ➢ Create a **Graphics** object
> ➢ Create **Pen** objects and **Brush** objects
> ➢ Draw to Graphics object using drawing methods
> ➢ Dispose of Pen and Brush objects when done with them
> ➢ Dispose of Graphics object when done with it

Before studying the new methods, we look at another graphics structure, the **Point** structure.

Point Structure

We will look at graphics methods that draw line and curve segments by connecting points. These methods use a concept known as a **point structure** to define each connected point. This structure (in the is similar to the rectangle structure studied in Chapter 8. The point structure has just two properties: X, the horizontal coordinate, and Y, the vertical coordinate.

There are two steps involved in creating a **point** structure. We first declare the structure using the standard statement:

```
Point myPoint;
```

Placement of this statement depends on scope. Place it in a method for method level scope. Place it with other form level declarations for form level scope. Once declared, the structure is created using the **Point** constructor:

```
myPoint = new Point(x, y);
```

where **x** and **y** are the desired coordinates (in pixels).

You can change the structure's properties at any time in code:

```
myPoint.X = newX;
myPoint.Y = newY;
```

where **newX** and **newY** represent new values for the respective properties.

More often than not, we work with arrays of point structures. This lets us define many points for drawing purposes. To declare an array of 30 such points, we use:

```
Point[] myPoints = new Point[30];
```

To change the coordinates of element 15 of this array, we use:

```
myPoints[15].X = newX;
myPoints[15].Y = newY;
```

DrawLines Method

I know you're already asking "didn't we look at the **DrawLines** method in Chapter 8?" No, we looked at **DrawLine**, not **DrawLines**. The DrawLine method connects two points with a line segment. The **DrawLines** method connects an array of points with a series of line segments. The connected points are specified using the **Point** structure. The method operates on a previously created graphics object (use **CreateGraphics** method with the desired control or use the **FromImage** method discussed with persistent graphics). If that object is **myGraphics** and we are using a pen object **myPen**, the syntax to connect an array of points **myPoints** is:

```
myGraphics.DrawLines(myPen, myPoints);
```

Let's see how to develop the array **myPoints**.

We first need to know how many points will be in the array. The graphics methods that use point structures assume the arrays are zero-based. So, if there are **numberPoints** in the array, it is dimensioned using:

```
Point[] myPoints = new Point[numberPoints];
```

Then, in code, specify the **x** and **y** coordinate of each point (**int** values) in the array. Once all points are specified, the **DrawLines** method begins at the **0** element in the array and consecutively connects points, ending at the **numberPoints - 1** element.

As an example, say we have 5 points to connect with line segments. First, dimension the array to **5**:

```
Point[] myPoints = new Point[5];
```

Then assign values to each set of coordinates (no specific values are applied here):

```
myPoints[0].X = x0; myPoints[0].Y = y0;
myPoints[1].X = x1; myPoints[1].Y = y1;
myPoints[2].X = x2; myPoints[2].Y = y2;
myPoints[3].X = x3; myPoints[3].Y = y3;
myPoints[4].X = x4; myPoints[4].Y = y4;
```

With many points, this assignment is usually in some form of loop.

Using a black pen with line width of 1 (**Pens.Black**), the **DrawLines** method with this array (**myPoints**) is:

```
myGraphics.DrawLines(Pens.Black, myPoints);
```

This produces on a form (**myGraphics** object):

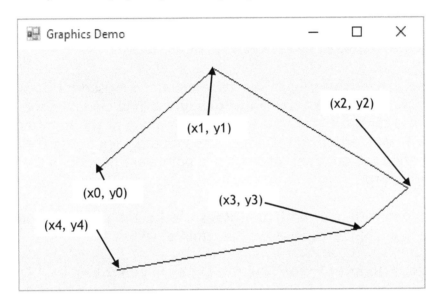

DrawLines connects every point in the given array of points.

DrawPolygon Method

The **DrawPolygon** method is similar to DrawLines. It connects a series of points (**Point** structure) with line segments, but also connects the final point with the first point, forming a closed polygon. The method assumes a graphic object has been created. For a graphics object **myGraphics**, a pen **myPen** and a series of points **myPoints**, the syntax is:

```
myGraphics.DrawPolygon(myPen, myPoints)
```

The **myPoints** array is specified in the same manner we used for DrawLines. Once all points are specified, the **DrawPolygon** method begins at the **0** element in the array and consecutively connects points, ending at the **numberPoints - 1** element. As a last step, this final point is connected back to the **0** element point, completing the polygon. At least two points are needed in the point array or an error will occur.

Using a black pen with line width of 1 (**Pens.Black**), the **DrawPolygon** method with the example point array used earlier (**myPoints**) is:

```
myGraphics.DrawPolygon(Pens.Black, myPoints);
```

This produces on a form (**myGraphics** object):

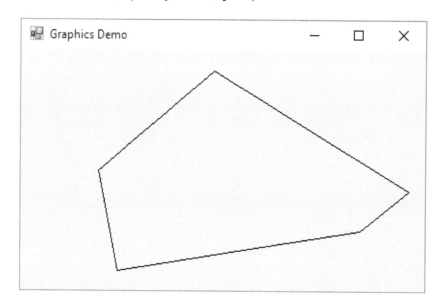

FillPolygon Method

The **FillPolygon** method will draw and fill a polygon. It connects a series of points (**Point** structure) with line segments and, like DrawPolygon, connects the final point with the first point, forming a closed polygon. That polygon is then filled using a specified **Brush** object. For a graphics object **myGraphics**, a brush **myBrush** and a series of points **myPoints**, the syntax is:

```
myGraphics.FillPolygon(myBrush, myPoints);
```

The **myPoints** array is specified in the same manner as DrawLines and DrawPolygon. Once all points are specified, the **FillPolygon** method draws and fills the polygon bounded by the points. At least two points are needed in the point array or an error will occur.

Using a red solid brush (**Brushes.Red**), the **FillPolygon** method with the example point array used earlier (**myPoints**) is:

```
myGraphics.FillPolygon(Brushes.Red, myPoints);
```

This produces on a form (**myGraphics** object):

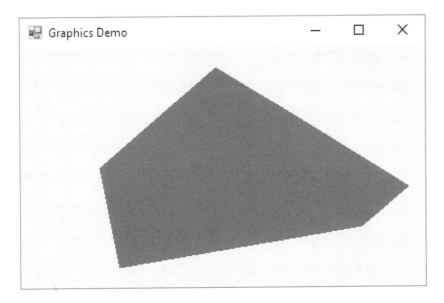

Notice the FillPolygon method fills the entire region with the selected color. If you had previously used DrawPolygon to form a border region, the fill will blot out that border. If you want a bordered, filled region, do the **fill** operation **first**, **then** the **draw** operation.

DrawCurve Method

We now look at three methods very similar to DrawLines, DrawPolygon and FillPolygon. The first is **DrawCurve.** Like DrawLines, DrawCurve connects an array of points. However, rather than connect the points with straight lines, they are connected with something called a **cardinal spline.** That's just fancy mathematics talk for a smooth curve. The connected points are specified using the **Point** structure. The method operates on a previously created graphics object (use **CreateGraphics** method with desired control, or use a bitmap object as discussed in persistence graphics). If that object is **myGraphics** and we are using a pen object **myPens**, the syntax to connect an array of points **myPoints** is:

```
myGraphics.DrawCurve(myPen, myPoints);
```

The **myPoints** array is specified in the same manner we used for DrawLines and other methods. Once all points are specified, the **DrawCurve** method begins at the **0** element in the array and consecutively connects points, ending at the **numberPoints - 1** element.

Using a black pen with line width of 1 (**Pens.Black**), the **DrawCurve** method with a point array **myPoints** is:

```
myGraphics.DrawCurve(Pens.Black, myPoints);
```

Assuming **myPoints** contains five points distributed on a form (**myGraphics** object), we would see:

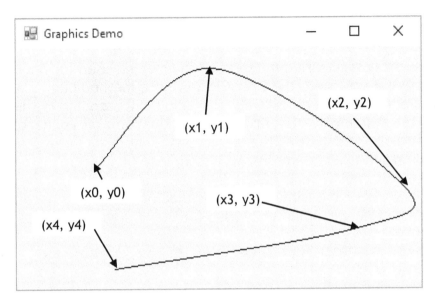

Notice the nice smooth curve that is drawn.

DrawClosedCurve Method

The **DrawClosedCurve** method is similar to DrawCurve. It connects a series of points (**Point** structure) with splines, but also connects the final point with the first point, forming a closed curve. The method assumes a graphic object has been created. For a graphics object **myGraphics**, a pen **myPen** and a series of points **myPoints**, the syntax is:

```
myGraphics.DrawClosedCurve(myPen, myPoints);
```

The **myPoints** array is specified in the same manner we used for DrawCurve. Once all points are specified, the **DrawClosedCurve** method begins at the **0** element in the array and consecutively connects points, ending at the **numberPoints - 1** element. As a last step, this final point is connected back to the 0 element point, completing the closed curve. At least three points are needed in the point array or an error will occur.

Using a black pen with line width of 1 (**Pens.Black**), the **DrawClosedCurve** method with the example point array used for DrawCurve (**myPoints**) is:

```
myGraphics.DrawClosedCurve(Pens.Black, myPoints);
```

This produces on a form (**myGraphics** object):

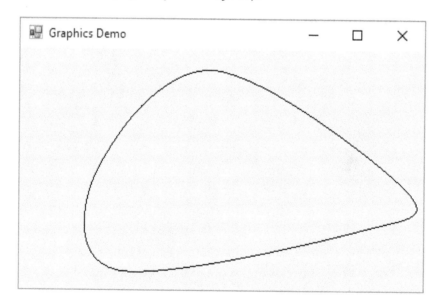

FillClosedCurve Method

The **FillClosedCurve** method will draw and fill a closed curve. It connects a series of points (**Point** structure) with splines and, like DrawClosedCurve, connects the final point with the first point, forming a closed curve. That curve is then filled using a specified **Brush** object. For a graphics object **myGraphics**, a brush **myBrush** and a series of points **myPoints**, the syntax is:

```
myGraphics.FillClosedCurve(myBrush, myPoints);
```

The **myPoints** array is specified in the same manner as DrawCurve and DrawClosedCurve. Once all points are specified, the **FillClosedCurve** method draws and fills the closed curve bounded by the points. At least three points are needed in the point array or an error will occur.

Using a green solid brush (**Brushes.Green**), the **FillClosedCurve** method with the example point array used earlier (**myPoints**) is:

```
myGraphics.FillClosedCurve(Brushes.Green, myPoints);
```

This produces on a form (**myGraphics** object):

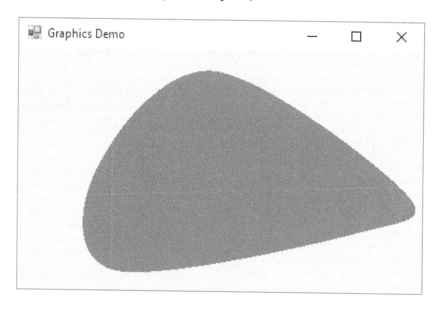

Notice the FillClosedCurve method fills the entire region with the selected color. If you had previously used DrawClosedCurve to form a border region, the fill will blot out that border. If you want a bordered, filled region, do the **fill** operation **first, then** the **draw** operation.

Now, let's use the **DrawLines, DrawPolygon, FillPolygon, DrawCurve, DrawClosedCurve** and **FillClosedCurve** methods, in conjunction with the **MouseDown** event, to build an example that lets a user do some interactive drawing.

Example 9-3

Drawing Lines, Polygons, Curves, Closed Curves

1. Start a new application. In this application, the user will click on a form specifying a set of points. These points will be used to draw line segments, a polygon, a filled (random color) polygon, a curve, a closed curve or a filled closed curve. Add three button controls and two radio buttons to the form. The form should look like this:

2. Set the following properties:

> **Form1:**
>
> | | |
> |---|---|
> | Name | frmDrawing |
> | FormBorderStyle | SingleFixed |
> | StartPosition | CenterScreen |
> | Text | Lines and Curves Example |
>
> **button1:**
>
> | | |
> |---|---|
> | Name | btnDraw |
> | Enabled | False |
> | Text | &Draw |
>
> **button2:**
>
> | | |
> |---|---|
> | Name | btnClose |
> | Enabled | False |
> | Text | &Close |
>
> **button3:**
>
> | | |
> |---|---|
> | Name | btnFill |
> | Enabled | False |
> | Text | &Fill |
>
> **radioButton1:**
>
> | | |
> |---|---|
> | Name | rdoLines |
> | Checked | True |
> | Text | Lines |
>
> **radioButton2:**
>
> | | |
> |---|---|
> | Name | rdoCurves |
> | Text | Curves |

When done, my form looks like this:

3. Form level scope declarations:

```
Point[] clickedPoint = new Point[30];
Point[] drawingPoint;
int maximumPoint;
bool isDrawn;
Graphics myDrawing;
Random myRandom = new Random();
```

4. Use this code in **frmDrawing Load** method:

```
private void FrmDrawing_Load(object sender, EventArgs e)
{
  isDrawn = true; // set to true to initialize properly
  myDrawing = this.CreateGraphics();
}
```

5. Use this code in the form's **MouseDown** method. It saves the clicked points and marks them with a red dot:

```csharp
private void FrmDrawing_MouseDown(object sender,
MouseEventArgs e)
{
  if (isDrawn)
  {
    // starting over with new drawing
    btnDraw.Enabled = true;
    btnClose.Enabled = false;
    btnFill.Enabled = false;
    rdoLines.Enabled = true;
    rdoCurves.Enabled = true;
    isDrawn = false;
    maximumPoint = 0;
    myDrawing.Clear(this.BackColor);
  }
  else if (maximumPoint > 29)
  {
    MessageBox.Show("Maximum points exceeded.", "Error",
MessageBoxButtons.OK, MessageBoxIcon.Information);
    return;
  }
  // Save clicked point and mark with red dot
  clickedPoint[maximumPoint].X = e.X;
  clickedPoint[maximumPoint].Y = e.Y;
  myDrawing.FillEllipse(Brushes.Red,
clickedPoint[maximumPoint].X - 1,
clickedPoint[maximumPoint].Y - 1, 3, 3);
  maximumPoint++;
}
```

6. Use this code in the **btnDraw Click** event method:

```csharp
private void BtnDraw_Click(object sender, EventArgs e)
{
  drawingPoint = new Point[maximumPoint];
  //copy saved points into line/polygon points
  for (int n = 0; n < maximumPoint; n++)
  {
    drawingPoint[n] = new Point(clickedPoint[n].X,
clickedPoint[n].Y);
  }
  // draw lines unless there's less than three points
  if (maximumPoint < 3)
  {
    return;
  }
  else
  {
    rdoLines.Enabled = false;
    rdoCurves.Enabled = false;
    btnDraw.Enabled = false;
    btnClose.Enabled = true; // allow closing
    if (rdoLines.Checked)
    {
      myDrawing.DrawLines(Pens.Black, drawingPoint);
    }
    else
    {
      myDrawing.DrawCurve(Pens.Black, drawingPoint);
    }
    isDrawn = true;
  }
}
```

This code copies the clicked points to the point structure for drawing and connects those points.

7. Code for the **BtnClose** Click method:

```
private void btnClose_Click(object sender, EventArgs e)
{
  // close polygon/curve
  btnClose.Enabled = false;
  btnFill.Enabled = true; // allow filling
  if (rdoLines.Checked)
  {
    // polygon
    myDrawing.DrawPolygon(Pens.Black, drawingPoint);
  }
  else
  {
    // curve
    myDrawing.DrawClosedCurve(Pens.Black, drawingPoint);
  }
}
```

This code closes the line segments or curve drawn.

8. Use this code in the **BtnFill Click** event method:

```
private void btnFill_Click(object sender, EventArgs e)
{
  Brush myBrush;
  // fill
  myBrush = new
SolidBrush(Color.FromArgb(myRandom.Next(256),
myRandom.Next(256), myRandom.Next(256)));
  if (rdoLines.Checked)
  {
    myDrawing.FillPolygon(myBrush, drawingPoint);
    myDrawing.DrawPolygon(Pens.Black, drawingPoint);
  }
  else
  {
    myDrawing.FillClosedCurve(myBrush, drawingPoint);
    myDrawing.DrawClosedCurve(Pens.Black, drawingPoint);
  }
  myBrush.Dispose();
}
```

The closed polygon or curve is filled with a random color.

9. Use this code in the **frmDrawing FormClosing** event:

```
private void FrmDrawing_FormClosing(object sender,
FormClosingEventArgs e)
{
  myDrawing.Dispose();
}
```

10. Save and run the application (saved in **Example 9-3** folder in **LearnVCS\VCS Code\Class 9** folder). Try drawing points (just click the form with any button of the mouse), lines, polygons, curves and closed curves. Fill the polygons and curves. Notice how the random colors work. Notice how the button controls are enabled and disabled at different points. To start a new drawing once complete, just click the form with a new starting point. Try overlapping points to see some nice effects. Here's a polygon I drew:

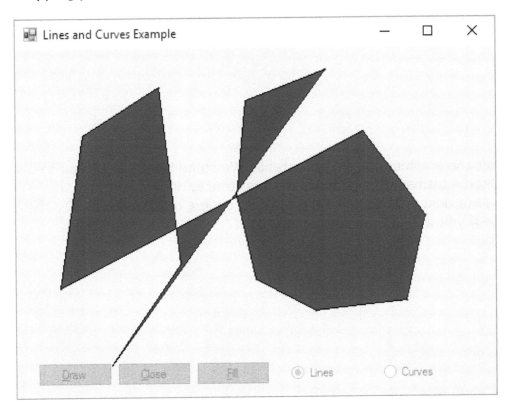

and here's a filled closed curve:

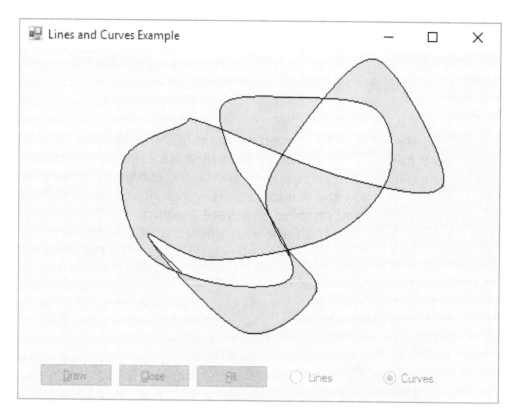

Note that the graphics are <u>not</u> persistent. We could have used a **Paint** event or maintained a **bitmap object** to insure persistence. In this example, however, we have not done that to make the drawing code a little clearer. Try the next example if you want to see something cool!!

Example 9-4

Drawing Animated Lines and Curves

1. In this example, we will modify the program just built to draw curves. In this modification, when the user fills the shape, the shape will change itself over time! Load **Example 9-3**.

2. Add a timer control to do the animation. Set these properties:

   timer1:

Name	timCurve
Interval	100

3. Make **myBrush** a form level object. Remove its declaration from the **btnFill Click** event and place it in the general declarations area (this allows us to fill the curve from another method):

```
Brush myBrush;
```

Also, remove line disposing of **myBrush** object.

4. We want to start the timer when the user clicks **Fill Curve**. This is done in the **btnFill Click** event (new code is shaded):

```
private void BtnFill_Click(object sender, EventArgs e)
{
  // myBrush declaration used to be here
  // fill
  myBrush = new
SolidBrush(Color.FromArgb(myRandom.Next(256),
myRandom.Next(256), myRandom.Next(256)));
  if (rdoLines.Checked)
  {
    myDrawing.FillPolygon(myBrush, drawingPoint);
    myDrawing.DrawPolygon(Pens.Black, drawingPoint);
  }
  else
  {
    myDrawing.FillClosedCurve(myBrush, drawingPoint);
    myDrawing.DrawClosedCurve(Pens.Black, drawingPoint);
  }
  // myBrush disposal used to be here
  timCurve.Enabled = true;
}
```

We turn off the timer when a new curve is started in the **frmDrawing MouseDown** event (new code is shaded):

```csharp
private void FrmDrawing_MouseDown(object sender,
MouseEventArgs e)
{
  if (isDrawn)
  {
    // starting over with new drawing
    timCurve.Enabled = false;
    btnDraw.Enabled = true;
    btnClose.Enabled = false;
    btnFill.Enabled = false;
    rdoLines.Enabled = true;
    rdoCurves.Enabled = true;
    isDrawn = false;
    maximumPoint = 0;
    myDrawing.Clear(this.BackColor);
  }
  else if (maximumPoint > 29)
  {
    MessageBox.Show("Maximum points exceeded.", "Error",
MessageBoxButtons.OK, MessageBoxIcon.Information);
    return;
  }
  // Save clicked point and mark with red dot
  clickedPoint[maximumPoint].X = e.X;
  clickedPoint[maximumPoint].Y = e.Y;
  myDrawing.FillEllipse(Brushes.Red,
clickedPoint[maximumPoint].X - 1,
clickedPoint[maximumPoint].Y - 1, 3, 3);
  maximumPoint++;
}
```

5. Use this code for the **timCurves Tick** event (a new method):

```
private void TimCurve_Tick(object sender, EventArgs e)
{
  // Tweak all points a bit
  for (int i = 0; i < maximumPoint; i++)
  {
    drawingPoint[i].X += myRandom.Next(21) - 10;
    drawingPoint[i].Y += myRandom.Next(21) - 10;
  }
  // clear frame and redraw
  myDrawing.Clear(this.BackColor);
  if (rdoLines.Checked)
  {
    myDrawing.FillPolygon(myBrush, drawingPoint);
    myDrawing.DrawPolygon(Pens.Black, drawingPoint);
  }
  else
  {
    myDrawing.FillClosedCurve(myBrush, drawingPoint);
    myDrawing.DrawClosedCurve(Pens.Black, drawingPoint);
  }
}
```

In this procedure, we go through the points defining the polygon/curve and randomly change them a bit. This will 'perturb' the displayed polygon/curve giving the effect of animation.

6. Save and run the application (saved in **Example 9-4** folder in **LearnVCS\VCS Code\Class 9** folder). Create and fill a polygon or curve. Once filled, be amazed at its animated performance. You might like to also change colors as the animation is going on.

HatchBrush Object

The filled polygons and filled curves are pretty, but it would be nice to have them filled with something other than a solid color. Visual C# provides other brush objects that provide interesting fill effects. These brushes are part of the **Drawing2D** namespace. To use such objects, you need to add the following **using** line at the top of your code window with other such statements:

```
using System.Drawing.Drawing2D;
```

Here, we look at the **HatchBrush** object. Hatch brushes fill a region with a specific style of line. You can specify the color of the line and the background color of the fill.

To create your own **HatchBrush** object, you first declare the brush using:

```
HatchBrush myBrush;
```

The brush is then created using the **HatchBrush** constructor:

```
myBrush = new HatchBrush(HatchStyle, foregroundColor,
backgroundColor);
```

where **HatchStyle** defines the line 'hatch' style, **foregroundColor** is the line color and **backgroundColor** the fill color. The color arguments can be one of the built-in colors or one generated with the **FromArgb** function.

There are numerous **HatchStyle** values (**Drawing2D** namespace) to choose from. Here are some of the values; consult on-line help for a complete list (each value describes the hatch appearance):

```
BackwardDiagonal          Plaid
Cross                     Shingle
DiagonalBrick             SolidDiamond
DiagonalCross             Sphere
Divot                     Trellis
ForwardDiagonal           Vertical
Horizontal                Wave
HorizontalBrick           Weave
LargeCheckerBoard         ZigZag
LargeConfetti
LargeGrid
```

Hence, to create a hatch brush with a **HorizontalBrick** pattern, **blue** foreground, and **white** background, use this constructor:

```
myBrush = new HatchBrush(HatchStyle.HorizontalBrick,
Color.Blue, Color.White);
```

Once created, you can change the hatch style or either color of a hatch brush in code using the respective properties of the hatch brush object. The syntax is:

```
myBrush.HatchStyle = newStyle;
myBrush.ForegroundColor = newForegroundColor;
myBrush.BackgroundColor = newBackgroundColor;
```

where **newStyle**, **newForegroundColor** and **newBackgroundColor** are newly specified values.

When done painting with a hatch brush object, it should be disposed using the Dispose method:

```
myBrush.Dispose();
```

Example 9-5

Hatch Brush

In the **LearnVCS\VCS Code\Class 9** folder is a project named **Example 9-5**. We will not build this project (or any other brush example; not much would be gained in the way of learning), but will use it to demonstrate the different effects provided by a hatch brush. If desired, you can look through the code to see how things are done.

Open and run that project. You should see:

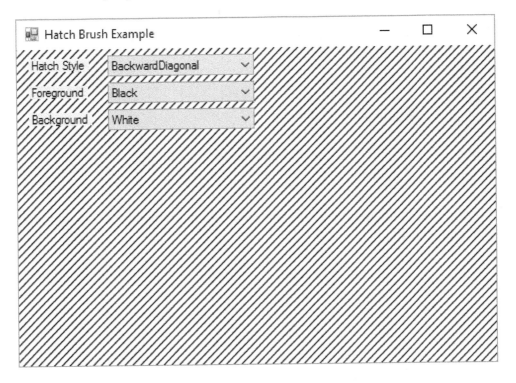

Select different hatch styles, foreground colors and background colors. Here's a diagonal brick pattern:

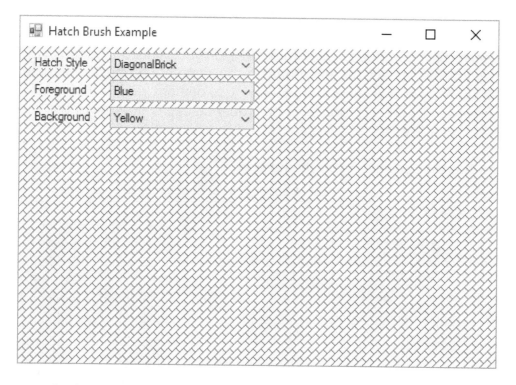

Once a combo box is active, you can use the cursor arrows on the keyboard to 'scroll' through the list.

LinearGradientBrush Object

Another brush in the **Drawing2D** namespace is the **LinearGradientBrush**. This brush fills a graphics object with a blending of two colors. It starts with one color and gradually 'becomes' the other color in a specified direction. You specify the colors and direction of the 'gradient.' Recall you will need this **using** statement.

```
using System.Drawing.Drawing2D;
```

To create your own **LinearGradientBrush** object, you first declare the brush using:

```
LinearGradientBrush myBrush;
```

The brush is then created using the **LinearGradientBrush** constructor:

```
myBrush = new LinearGradientBrush(rectangle, startColor,
endColor, LinearGradientMode);
```

where **rectangle** defines the rectangular region where the gradient starts and ends, **startColor** is the gradient start color, **endColor** the gradient end color, and **LinearGradientMode**, the gradient direction. The color arguments can be one of the built-in colors or one generated with the **FromArgb** function.

You can achieve interesting effects by changing the size of the rectangular region (**rectangle** argument) assigned to the brush. Small regions give 'tight' gradients, while large rectangles yield gradients spread over long distances.

There are four **LinearGradientMode** values (**Drawing2D** namespace) to choose from:

```
BackwardDiagonal        ForwardDiagonal
Horizontal              Vertical
```

Hence, to create a linear gradient brush with a Rectangle structure **myRectangle**, a **green** starting color, a **yellow** ending color and a **Horizontal** direction, use this constructor:

```
myBrush = new LinearGradientBrush(myRectangle,
Color.Green, Color.Yellow, LinearGradientMode.Horizontal);
```

Once created, you can the brush in code using the respective properties. The syntax is:

```
myBrush.LinearColors(0) = newStartColor;
myBrush.LinearColors(1) = newEndColor;
myBrush.LinearGradientMode = newLinearGradientMode;
```

where **newStartColor, newEndColor** and **newLinearGradientMode** are newly specified values.

When done painting with a linear gradient brush object, it should be disposed using the Dispose method:

```
myBrush.Dispose()
```

Example 9-6

Linear Gradient Brush

We have built an application to view different linear gradient brush directions, colors and sizes. Open **Example 9-6** in the **LearnVCS\VCS Code\Class 9** folder. Run the application and you should see:

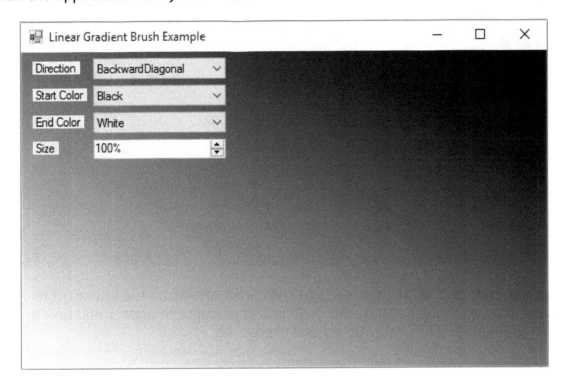

Select different gradient directions and colors. Notice how the size selection can provide interesting effects. Here's a pretty effect:

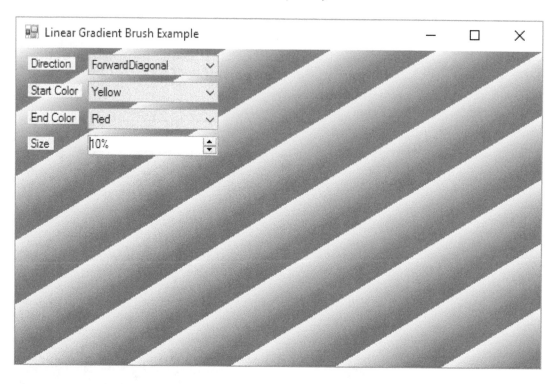

Once any control is active, you can use the cursor arrows on the keyboard to 'scroll' through the list. Study the code in this example to understand how a linear gradient brush is constructed and used.

TextureBrush Object

The last brush we study is the **TextureBrush**. This brush (in the **Drawing** namespace) fills a graphics object with an image – fun effects are possible.

To create your own **TextureBrush** object, you first declare the brush and the **Image** object it will use:

```
TextureBrush myBrush;
Image myImage;
```

The brush is then created using the **TextureBrush** constructor:

```
myBrush = new TextureBrush(myImage);
```

The **Image** object can be a bitmap, an icon or a metafile. The object needs to be defined using the appropriate constructor. To create an **Image** object using the **Bitmap** constructor (seen earlier in this chapter), use:

```
myImage = new Bitmap(FileName);
```

where **FileName** is a complete path to the desired bitmap graphic file. Icons and metafile objects are created with their respective constructors (**Icon**, **Metafile**).

When done painting with a texture brush object, it should be disposed using the Dispose method:

```
myBrush.Dispose();
```

We've only introduced the **Texture** brush. There are many other properties that can be used to obtain interesting effects. Study the on-line help for further details.

Example 9-7

Texture Brush

We have built an application to view different texture brushes (using bitmap images). Open **Example 9-7** in the **LearnVCS\VCS Code\Class 9** folder. Run the application and you should see:

Click **Change Background** to change the background graphic. Select different bitmaps (a few are in the project folder) for painting the form. Here's a denim background:

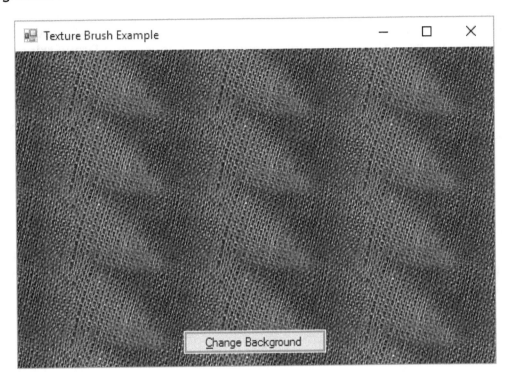

Notice you can resize the form and it's still painted correctly. Study the code in this example to understand how a texture brush is constructed and used.

DrawString Method

The last drawing method we study 'draws' text information on a graphics object using a brush object. Text adds useful information to graphics objects, especially for plots. The line, bar and pie chart examples built in Chapter 8 are rather boring without the usual titles, labels and legends. The **DrawString** method will let us add text to any graphic object.

The **DrawString** method is easy to use. You need to know what text you want to draw, what font you want to use, what brush object to use and where you want to locate the text. The method operates on a previously created graphics object (use **CreateGraphics** method with a control). The syntax is:

```
myGraphics.DrawString(myString, myFont, myBrush, x, y);
```

where **myGraphics** is the graphics object, **myString** is the text to display (a **string** type), **myFont** is the font to use (**Font** object), **myBrush** is the selected brush (**Brush** object) and (**x, y**) is the Cartesian coordinate (**int** type) specifying location of the upper left corner of the text string

Let's look at an example. Can you see what this snippet of code will produce?

```
// left-justified text at 0, 0
Graphics myGraphics;
myGraphics = this.CreateGraphics();
myGraphics.DrawString("Hello World!", new Font("Arial",
24), Brushes.Red, 0, 0);
```

First, a graphics object (**myGraphics**) is created using the form. Then, the string "**Hello World!**" is 'drawn' using an **Arial**, Size **24**, font and a **red solid brush** in the upper left hand corner (**x = 0, y = 0**) of the graphics object. This code produces:

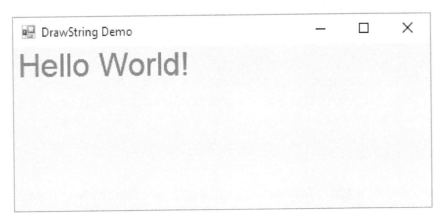

A key decision in using **DrawString** is placement. That is, what **x** and **y** values should you use? To help in this decision, it is helpful to know what size a particular text string is. If we know how wide and how tall (in pixels) a string is, we can perform precise placements, including left, center and right justifications.

If you are only interested in obtaining the height of a string for correct vertical placement, you can use the Visual C# **GetHeight** method. This method operates on the font object. If you have a font object named **myFont**, the height is given by:

   myHeight = myFont.GetHeight();

The returned **myHeight** value (**float** data type) is in pixels.

If you need both width and height, the Visual C# method **MeasureString** gives us this information. The size (**mySize**) of a string **myString** written to a graphics object **myGraphics** using **myFont** is computed using:

```
mySize = myGraphics.MeasureString(myString, myFont);
```

The returned value **mySize** is a **SizeF** structure with two properties, **Width** and **Height**. This is the information we want. **SizeF** is another Visual C# structure similar to the **Rectangle** and **Point** structures. To determine string size, we need such a structure.

There are two steps involved in creating a **SizeF** structure. We first declare the structure using the standard statement:

```
SizeF mySize;
```

Placement of this statement depends on scope. Place it in a method for method level scope. Place it with other form level declarations for form level scope. Once declared, the structure is created using the **SizeF** constructor:

```
mySize = new SizeF();
```

No arguments are needed. You can assign width and height arguments, but we don't need to. We are just using **mySize** to determine such properties.

Let's use a **SizeF** structure with our previous example. The code needed to measure the string **"Hello World!"** 'drawn' using an **Arial**, Size **24**, font is:

```
// string size
SizeF mySize;
mySize = new SizeF();
mySize = myGraphics.MeasureString("Hello World!", new
Font("Arial", 24));
Console.WriteLine(mySize.Width);
Console.WriteLine(mySize.Height);
```

From this we can determine (looking in the debugger output window):

```
mySize.Width = 190.151
mySize.Height = 39.75
```

These measurements are floating point representations (type **float**) of pixels. The 'F' in **SizeF** implies a floating point, rather than integer, number. There is also a **Size** structure in Visual C# that provides integer information. This structure, though, can't be used with **MeasureString**.

The height of a string lets us know how much to increment the desired vertical position after printing each line in multiple lines of text. Or, it can be used to 'vertically justify' a string within the client rectangle of a graphics object. For example, assume we have found the height of a string (**mySize.Height**). To vertically justify this string in the host control (**myObject**) for a graphics object, the **y** coordinate (converted to an **int** type needed by **DrawString**) would be:

```
y = (int) (0.5 * (myObject.ClientSize.Height -
mySize.Height));
```

This assumes the string is 'shorter' than the graphics object client rectangle.

Similarly, the width of a string lets us define margins and left, right or center justify a string within the client rectangle of a graphics object. For left justification, establish a left margin and set the x coordinate to this value in the **DrawString** method. If we know the width of a string (**mySize.Width**), it is centered justified in the client area of a graphics object's host control **myObject** using an **x** value of (again converted to **int** type):

```
x = (int) (0.5 * (myObject.ClientSize.Width -
mySize.Width));
```

To right justify the same string, use:

```
x = (int) (myObject.ClientSize.Width - mySize.Width);
```

Both of the above equations, of course, assume the string is 'narrower' than the graphics object.

Let's go back and apply these relations to our **"Hello World!"** example. Code to **center** the text both **vertically** <u>and</u> **horizontally** on the form is:

```
// vertically centered, horizontally centered text
Graphics myGraphics = this.CreateGraphics();
SizeF mySize = new SizeF();
string myString = "Hello World!";
Font myFont = new Font("Arial", 24);
mySize = myGraphics.MeasureString(myString, myFont);
myGraphics.DrawString(myString, myFont, Brushes.Red, (int)
(0.5 * (this.ClientSize.Width - mySize.Width)), (int) (0.5
* (this.ClientSize.Height - mySize.Height)));
```

Notice we have combined the declaration and construction of the graphics object and SizeF object into single lines. This is perfectly acceptable, though I prefer separate lines. This code results in:

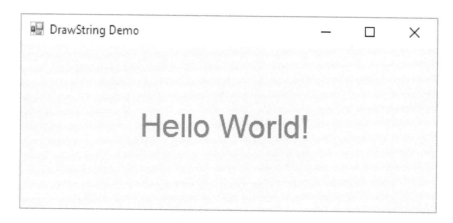

Code to **vertically center** and **right justify** the text on the form is:

```
// vertically centered, right-justified text
Graphics myGraphics = this.CreateGraphics();
SizeF mySize = new SizeF();
string myString = "Hello World!";
Font myFont = new Font("Arial", 24);
mySize = myGraphics.MeasureString(myString, myFont);
myGraphics.DrawString(myString, myFont, Brushes.Red, (int)
(this.ClientSize.Width - mySize.Width), (int) (0.5 *
(this.ClientSize.Height - mySize.Height)));
```

which results in:

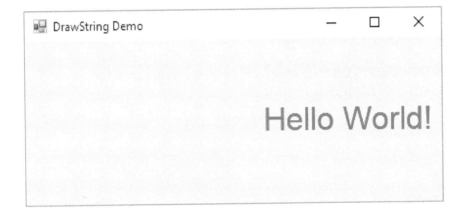

Even more interesting effects can be obtained using other brushes. Try drawing strings with hatch, linear gradient and texture brushes. Here's the code for the "Hello World!" example to use a larger font and a 'denim' textured brush:

```
// vertically centered, horizontally centered text
// using denim brush
Graphics myGraphics = this.CreateGraphics();
SizeF mySize = new SizeF();
string myString = "Hello World!";
Font myFont = new Font("Arial Black", 36);
TextureBrush myBrush = new TextureBrush(new
Bitmap(Application.StartupPath + "\\denim.bmp"));
mySize = myGraphics.MeasureString(myString, myFont);
myGraphics.DrawString(myString, myFont, myBrush, (int)
(0.5 * (this.ClientSize.Width - mySize.Width)), (int) (0.5
* (this.ClientSize.Height - mySize.Height)));
```

The result is (the denim bitmap must be in the **Bin\Debug** folder and was taken from the Example 9-7 folder):

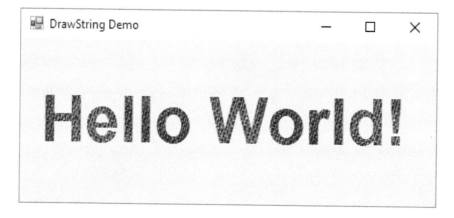

We won't do much more with the **DrawString** method here. You will, however, see the **DrawString** method again in Chapter 10. This method is integral in obtaining printed information from a Visual C# application. And, you will see its use is identical. You need to determine what to print, in what font, with what brush and where on the page it needs to be. For reference, each of the examples studied here is saved in the **DrawString Demo** folder in the **LearnVCS\VCS Code\Class 9** folder (code not being used is 'commented out').

Multimedia Effects

Everywhere you look in the world of computers today, you see **multimedia effects**. Computer games, web sites and meeting presentations are filled with animated graphics and fun sounds. It is relatively easy to add such effects to our Visual C# applications.

In Chapter 8, we achieved simple animation effects by changing the image in a picture box control and, if desired, moving the control by modifying **Left** and **Top** properties. Sophisticated animation relies on the ability to move several changing objects over a changing background. The simple techniques we learned cannot be used here. To achieve more sophisticated animation, we will use the Visual C# **DrawImage** method.

Animation requires the moving of rectangular regions. We need ways to move these rectangular regions. The mouse (using mouse events) is one option. Another option considered is movement using **keyboard events**. And, many times we want to know if these rectangular regions overlap to detect things like files reaching trash cans, balls hitting paddles or little creatures eating power pellets. We will learn how to detect if two **rectangles intersect**.

And, multimedia presentations also use **sounds**. Visual C# uses the **SoundPlayer** class to play sound files.

Animation with DrawImage Method

To achieve animation in a Visual C# application, whether it is background scrolling, sprite animation, or other special effects, we use the **DrawImage** graphics method. In its simplest form, this method draws an **Image** object at a particular position in a graphics object. Changing and/or moving the image within the graphics object achieves animation. And, multiple images can be moved/changed within the graphics object. There are many overloaded versions of **DrawImage**. We will look a few of them in this chapter. We encourage you to study the other forms, as you need them.

Before using **DrawImage**, you need two things: a **graphics** object to draw to and an **image** object to draw. The graphics and image objects are declared in the usual manner:

```
Graphics myGraphics;
Image myImage;
```

We create the graphics object (assume **myObject** is the host object):

```
myGraphics = myObject.CreateGraphics();
```

The **Image** object is usually created from a graphics file:

```
myImage = Image.FromFile(FileName);
```

where **FileName** is a complete path to the graphics file describing the image to draw. At this point, we can draw **myImage** in **myGraphics**.

In its simplest form, the **DrawImage** method is:

```
myGraphics.DrawImage(myImage, myRectangle);
```

where **myRectangle** is a rectangle structure that positions **myImage** within **myGraphics**. **myRectangle** is specified by **x** the horizontal position, **y** the vertical position, the width **w** and height **h**:

```
myRectangle = new Rectangle(x, y, w, h);
```

The width and height can be the original image size or scaled up or down. It's your choice.

A picture illustrates what's going on with **DrawImage**:

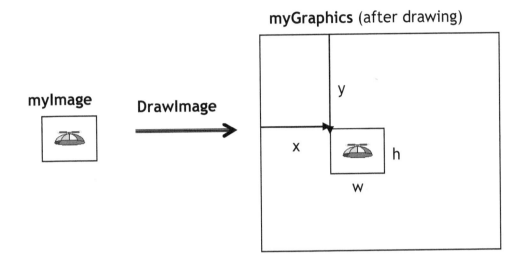

Note how the transfer of the rectangular region occurs. Successive bitmap transfers give the impression of motion, or animation. Recall **w** and **h** in the graphics object do not have to necessarily match the width and height of the **Image** object. Scaling (up or down) is possible.

Example 9-8

Bouncing Ball

1. We'll build an application with a ball bouncing from the top to the bottom (and back) as an illustration of the use of **DrawImage**. Start a new application. Add a panel control (will display the animation), a timer control, and a button. Set these properties:

Form1:

Name	frmBall
FormBorderStyle	FixedSingle
StartPosition	CenterScreen
Text	Bouncing Balls

timer1:

Name	timBall
Interval	100

panel1:

Name	pnlDisplay
BackColor	Light Blue
BorderStyle	Fixed3D

button1:

Name	btnStart
Text	&Start

When done, my form looks like this:

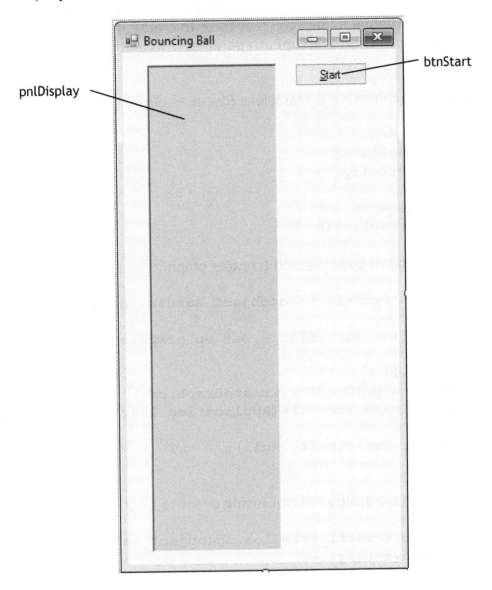

Other controls in tray:

⏱ timBall

2. In the **LearnVCS\VCS Code\Class 9\Example 9-8** folder is a graphics file named **ball.gif**. This will be our bouncing ball. Copy this file into the application **Bin\Debug** folder (you may have to create the folder first). We will use the **Application.StartupPath** parameter to load the file into the **Image** object.

3. Form level scope variable declarations (declares objects and movement variables):

```
int ballY, ballDir;
Graphics myDisplay;
Image myBall;
int ballSize = 50;
Rectangle myRectangle;
```

4. Add code to **frmBall Load** method (creates graphics and image objects):

```
private void FrmBall_Load(object sender, EventArgs e)
{
  // initialize variables - set up graphics objects
  ballY = 0;
  ballDir = 1;
  myDisplay = pnlDisplay.CreateGraphics();
  myBall = Image.FromFile(Application.StartupPath +
"\\ball.gif");
  pnlDisplay_Paint(null, null);
}
```

5. Use this code in the **frmBall FormClosing** event to dispose of objects:

```
private void FrmBall_FormClosing(object sender,
FormClosingEventArgs e)
{
  // dispose of objects
  myDisplay.Dispose();
  myBall.Dispose();
}
```

6. Write a **btnStart Click** event method to toggle the timer:

```
private void BtnStart_Click(object sender, EventArgs e)
{
  // toggle timer
  if (timBall.Enabled)
  {
    timBall.Enabled = false;
    btnStart.Text = "&Start";
  }
  else
  {
    timBall.Enabled = true;
    btnStart.Text = "&Stop";
  }
}
```

7. The **timBall Tick** event controls the bouncing ball position:

```
private void TimBall_Tick(object sender, EventArgs e)
{
  // determine ball position and draw it
  ballY += (int) (ballDir * pnlDisplay.ClientSize.Height /
50);
  // check for bounce
  if (ballY < 0)
  {
    ballY = 0;
    ballDir = 1;
  }
  else if (ballY + ballSize >
pnlDisplay.ClientSize.Height)
  {
    ballY = pnlDisplay.ClientSize.Height - ballSize;
    ballDir = -1;
  }
  pnlDisplay_Paint(null, null);
}
```

8. And, the **pnlDisplay Paint** event does the actual image drawing:

```
private void PnlDisplay_Paint(object sender,
PaintEventArgs e)
{
   // horizontally center ball in display rectangle
   myRectangle = new Rectangle((int) (0.5 *
(pnlDisplay.ClientSize.Width - ballSize)), ballY,
ballSize, ballSize);
   myDisplay.Clear(pnlDisplay.BackColor);
   myDisplay.DrawImage(myBall, myRectangle);
}
```

9. Once everything is together, save it (saved in **Example 9-8** folder in the **LearnVCS\VCS Code\Class 9** folder), run it and follow the bouncing ball!

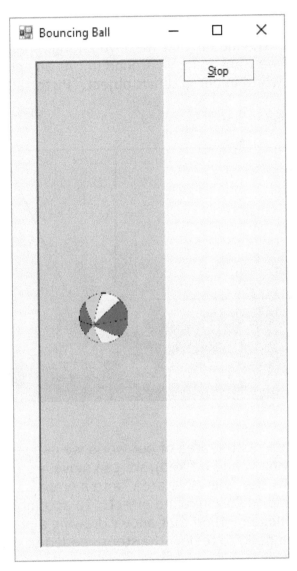

Note we have added a **Paint** event to make the graphics (ball position) persistent.

Scrolling Backgrounds

Most action arcade games employ scrolling or moving backgrounds. What looks like a very sophisticated effect is really just a simple application of the **DrawImage** method. The idea is that we have a large image representing the background "world" we want to move around in. At any point, we can view a small region of that world in our graphics object. Pictorially, we have:

Background image   Viewable area

The boxed area represents the area of our world we can see at any one time. By varying **x** and **y** (leaving **w** and **h** fixed), we can move around in this world. As x and y vary, if we draw the "viewable area" into a graphics object of the same size, we obtain the moving background effect. To accomplish this task, we need a form of the **DrawImage** method that allows drawing a portion of a source image. But, first, we need to review the steps needed to use **DrawImage**.

Before using **DrawImage**, we need: a **Graphics** object to draw to and an **Image** object to draw from. The graphics and image objects are declared in the usual manner:

```
Graphics myGraphics;
Image myImage;
```

Create the graphics object (assume **myObject** is the host object) and **Image** object:

```
myGraphics = myObject.CreateGraphics();
myImage = Image.FromFile(FileName);
```

where **FileName** is a complete path to the graphics file describing the background image to draw.

To draw a portion of the source image (**myImage**) in the graphics object (**myGraphics**), we use an overloaded version of the **DrawImage** method:

```
myGraphics.DrawImage(myImage, rectangleDest, rectangleSrc,
GraphicsUnit.Pixel);
```

where:

rectangleDest	A rectangle structure within the graphics object (the destination location) where the image will be drawn.
rectangleSrc	A rectangle structure within the image object (the source location) defining the portion of the image to draw in the graphics object.

The last argument is the physical unit used in measuring the graphics. We use **pixels.**

For scrolling backgrounds, the 'destination' rectangle (**rectangleDest**) encompasses the entire control (**myObject**) hosting the graphics object used as the viewing area:

```
rectangleDest = new Rectangle(0, 0,
MyObject.ClientSize.Width, MyObject.ClientSize.Height);
```

The 'source' rectangle (**rectangleSrc**) contains the portion of the image we want to copy into the graphics object. This rectangle has the same dimensions (width and height) as the destination rectangle, with the upper left corner described by a desired position (x, y) within the source image:

```
rectangleSrc = new Rectangle(x, y,
myObject.ClientSize.Width, myObject.ClientSize.Height);
```

An example using our beach photo should clear things up (hopefully). Applying the **DrawImage** using **myImage** will result in the following display in **myGraphics:**

myImage

In this picture, **w** is the width of the client rectangle (**ClientSize.Width**) of the graphics object host control and **h** is the height of that rectangle (**ClientSize.Height**).

Hence, the process for moving (or scrolling) backgrounds is simple (once the image is available):

> ➢ Decide on the desired viewing area (set width **w** and height **h**).
> ➢ Choose a mechanism for varying **x** and **y**. Scroll bars and cursor control keys are often used, or they can be varied using Timer controls.
> ➢ As x and y vary, use **DrawImage** to draw the current "viewable area" of the source image into the viewer (graphics object).

Example 9-9

Horizontally Scrolling Background

1. Start a new application. In this project, we'll view a horizontally scrolling seascape. Add a horizontal scroll bar, a panel control, and a timer control. Set these properties:

Form1:

Name	frmScroll
FormBorderStyle	FixedSingle
StartPosition	CenterScreen
Text	Scrolling Background

hScrollBar1:

Name	hsbScroll
LargeChange	2
Maximum	20
Minimum	0
SmallChange	1
Value	0

panel1:

Name	pnlViewer
BorderStyle	FixedSingle

timer1:

Name	timScroll
Interval	50
Enabled	True

When done, my form looks like this:

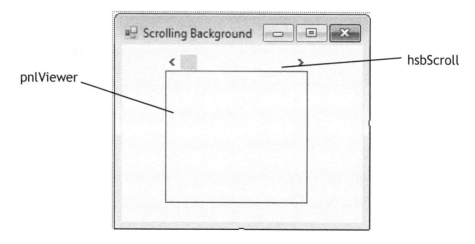

pnlViewer

hsbScroll

Other controls in tray:

⏱ timScroll

2. In the **LearnVCS\VCS Code\Class 9\Example 9-9** folder is a graphics file
    named **undrsea1.bmp**. This will be our background. Copy this file into the
    application **Bin\Debug** folder (you may have to create the folder first). Here
    is the graphic:

As x increases, the background appears to scroll to the left. Note as x reaches
the end of this source image, we need to copy a little of both ends to the
destination graphics object. We will use our **Application.StartupPath** parameter
to load this file into the **Image** object.

3. Form level scope variable declarations (declares objects and movement variables):

```
Graphics viewer;
Image background;
int scrollX = 0;
```

4. Add code to **frmScroll Load** method (creates graphics and image objects):

```
private void FrmScroll_Load(object sender, EventArgs e)
{
  background = Image.FromFile(Application.StartupPath +
"\\undrseal.bmp");
  // make sure viewer is same height as background image
  pnlViewer.Height = background.Height;
  viewer = pnlViewer.CreateGraphics();
}
```

5. Use this code in the **frmScroll FormClosing** event to dispose of objects:

```
private void FrmScroll_FormClosing(object sender,
FormClosingEventArgs e)
{
  // dispose of objects
  viewer.Dispose();
  background.Dispose();
}
```

6. The **timScroll Tick** event controls scrolling. At each program cycle, we update the position on the background image and draw the result.

```csharp
private void TimScroll_Tick(object sender, EventArgs e)
{
  int addedWidth;
  Rectangle rectangleDest, rectangleSrc;
  // Find next location on background
  scrollX += hsbScroll.Value;
  if (scrollX > background.Width)
  {
    scrollX = 0;
  }
  // When x is near right edge, we need to copy
  // two segments of the background into viewer
  if (scrollX > (background.Width -
pnlViewer.ClientSize.Width))
    {
      addedWidth = background.Width - scrollX;
      rectangleDest = new Rectangle(0, 0, addedWidth,
pnlViewer.ClientSize.Height);
      rectangleSrc = new Rectangle(scrollX, 0, addedWidth,
background.Height);
      viewer.DrawImage(background, rectangleDest,
rectangleSrc, GraphicsUnit.Pixel);
      rectangleDest = new Rectangle(addedWidth, 0,
pnlViewer.ClientSize.Width - addedWidth,
pnlViewer.ClientSize.Height);
      rectangleSrc = new Rectangle(0, 0,
pnlViewer.ClientSize.Width - addedWidth,
background.Height);
      viewer.DrawImage(background, rectangleDest,
rectangleSrc, GraphicsUnit.Pixel);
    }
    else
    {
      rectangleDest = new Rectangle(0, 0,
pnlViewer.ClientSize.Width, pnlViewer.ClientSize.Height);
      rectangleSrc = new Rectangle(scrollX, 0,
pnlViewer.ClientSize.Width, background.Height);
      viewer.DrawImage(background, rectangleDest,
rectangleSrc, GraphicsUnit.Pixel);
    }
}
```

7. Save the application (saved in **Example 9-9** folder in the **LearnVCS\VCS Code\Class 9** folder) and run it. Watch the sea go by. The scroll bar is used to control the speed of the scrolling (the amount X increases each time a tick event occurs). Here's my sea scrolling:

Notice the graphics are persistent, even though there is no **Paint** event. The reason this occurs is because the timer control **Tick** event is automatically updating the displayed picture 20 times each second.

Sprite Animation

Using the **DrawImage** method to draw a scrolling background leads us to an obvious question. Can we make an object move across the background – the kind of effect you see in video games? Yes we can – it just takes a little more effort. The moving picture is called a **sprite**. Working with the previous example, say we want a fish to bob up and down through the moving waters. The first thing we need is a bitmap picture of a fish – draw one with a painting program or borrow one from somewhere and convert it to bitmap format (**bmp** extension). Here's one (**fish.bmp**) I came up with:

If you copy this picture onto the background using the **DrawImage** method, the fish will be there, but the background will be gray. We could paint the background the same color as the water and things would look OK, but what if the fish jumps out of the water or swims near the rocks? The background is obliterated. We want whatever background the fish is swimming in to "come through." We accomplish this via **sprite animation.**

Sprite animation is done by invoking a different version of the DrawImage method using an **ImageAttributes** object. Such an object will allow us to declare one color within the bitmap to be transparent. Then, when the bitmap is drawn over a background, that background will show through. Let's go through the necessary steps for sprite animation.

The **ImageAttributes** object is part of the **Imaging** namespace. To use such and object, you need to add the following **using** line at the top of your code window with other such statements:

```
using System.Drawing.Imaging;
```

The ImageAttributes object (**myImageAttributes**) is constructed using:

```
ImageAttributes myImageAttributes = new ImageAttributes();
```

The desired transparent color (**clearColor**) is established using the **SetColorKey** method:

```
myImageAttributes.SetColorKey(clearColor, clearColor);
```

You may wonder why the color argument is repeated. The **SetColorKey** method actually allows specification of a range of colors that can be considered transparent. The two arguments specify a **low** color and a **high** color. In our example, we only want a single color; hence both arguments are the same.

Finally, to draw the entire source image (**myImage**) using the ImageAttributes object in a graphics object (**myGraphics**), we use this version of the **DrawImage** method:

```
myGraphics.DrawImage(myImage, rectangleDest, 0, 0,
myImage.Width, myImage.Height, GraphicsUnit.Pixel,
myImageAttributes);
```

where **rectangleDest** is the rectangle structure within the graphics object (the destination location) where the image will be drawn. Arguments 3 (**0**), 4 (**0**), 5 (**myImage.Width**), and 6 (**myImage.Height**) specify the source rectangle. These are respectively, the desired **x** within the source image, **y** within the source image, **width** from the source image, and **height** from source image. The values used will copy the entire source image. If you only want to copy a portion of the source, you would adjust these arguments. With this method (now including the ImageAttributes object), **myImage** will be drawn in **myGraphics** with the desired transparent color.

One question is lingering – how do you determine the desired transparent color? In our fish example, it is a gray, but that's not a real definite specification. The **clearColor** argument must be a Visual C# **Color** object, usually using the **FromArgb** method with values for the red, green and blue contributions. How do you come up with such values? I'll give you one approach using the little fish bitmap as an example.

Here's a snippet of code to identify the background color in the fish bitmap:

```
Image fish = Image.FromFile(Application.StartupPath +
"\\fish.bmp");
Bitmap fishBitmap = new Bitmap(fish);
Console.WriteLine(fishBitmap.GetPixel(0, 0));
```

First, the fish image is loaded from its file. Next, the **Image** object is converted to a **Bitmap** object. We can determine the color of individual pixels in such objects. That is what is done in the final line of code – we read the color, using **GetPixel**, of the pixel in the upper left corner of **fishBitmap** (part of the background) and print it to the output window. Doing this results in:

```
Output
Show output from:  Debug
The thread 0x26d0 has exited with code 0 (0x0).
The thread 0x4b4 has exited with code 0 (0x0).
'WindowsApplication9.vshost.exe' (CLR v4.0.30319
'WindowsApplication9.vshost.exe' (CLR v4.0.30319
Color [A=255, R=192, G=192, B=192]
The thread 0x33cc has exited with code 0 (0x0).
The thread 0x3aec has exited with code 0 (0x0).
The program '[5348] WindowsApplication9.vshost.e
```

This tells us the red contribution is 192 (R=192), the green contribution is 192 (G=192) and the blue contribution is 192 (B=192). Hence, the background color can be represented by:

```
Color.FromArgb(192, 192, 192)
```

This is the color argument we would use in the **ImageAttributes** object to make the background of the fish transparent.

We'll place the fish in our scrolling background soon, but first let's look at ways to move the fish once it's in the picture.

Keyboard Events

In multimedia applications, particularly games, you often need to move objects around. This movement can be automatic (using the **Timer** control) for animation effects. But then there are times you want the user to have the ability to move objects. One possibility (studied earlier in this chapter) is using the mouse and the corresponding mouse events. Here, we consider an alternate movement technique: **keyboard events**. We learn how to detect both the pressing of keys and the releasing of keys. These events can be used to trigger desired effects (such as object movement) in your application.

In applications using text box controls, we've already seen one keyboard event, the **KeyPress** event. In that event, we were able to examine user keystrokes and determine if they were acceptable in the context of the current control. The **KeyPress** event is useful for detecting keys with ASCII representations. It cannot detect keys without such representations. Examples of keys without ASCII values are the Alt, Ctrl, Shift, cursor control and other control keys. To detect pressing such keys (and ASCII keys) and combinations of such keys, we use the **KeyDown** event method. The form of this method is:

```
private void ControlName_KeyDown(object sender,
KeyEventArgs e)
{
    .
}
```

The arguments are:

sender	Control active when key pressed to invoke method
e	Event handler revealing which key was pressed and status of certain control keys when key was pressed

We are interested in several properties of the event handler **e**:

e.Alt	Boolean property that indicates if Alt key is pressed
e.Control	Boolean property that indicates if Ctrl key is pressed
e.KeyCode	Gives the key code for the key pressed
e.Shift	Boolean property that indicates if either Shift key is pressed

The **KeyCode** property is a member of the **Keys** class. There are values for every key that can be pressed (see on-line help). The Intellisense feature of the Visual C# IDE will provide **KeyCode** values when needed (just type **Keys** followed by a dot and a list of choices will appear). The **KeyDown** event usually has a **switch** structure with a **case** clause for each possible key (or key combination) expected.

You may also want to detect the release of a previously pressed key. This can be done by the **KeyUp** event. The method outline is:

```
private void ControlName_KeyUp(object sender, KeyEventArgs e)
{
    .
}
```

The arguments are:

sender	Control active when key released to invoke method
e	Event handler revealing which key was released and status of certain control keys when key was released

We are interested in several properties of the event handler **e**:

e.Alt	Boolean property that indicates if Alt key is pressed
e.Control	Boolean property that indicates if Ctrl key is pressed
e.KeyCode	Gives the key code for the key released
e.Shift	Boolean property that indicates if either Shift key is pressed

The **KeyCode** property is used as it is in the **KeyDown** event.

When using either the KeyDown or KeyUp methods to move objects, it is recommended that the form's **KeyPreview** property be set to **True**. In this case, the form will receive all KeyPress, KeyDown, and KeyUp events. After the form's event handlers have completed processing the keystroke, the keystroke is then assigned to the control with focus. To handle keyboard events only at the form level and not allow controls to receive keyboard events, set the **e.Handled** parameter in your form's **KeyPress** or **KeyDown** event to **true**.

Example 9-10

Sprite Animation

1. In this application, we will add a swimming fish to the scrolling background implemented in Example 9-9. And, we use cursor control keys to move the fish up and down. We just need to make a couple of changes to the code. Open **Example 9-9**.

2. In the **LearnVCS\VCS Code\Class 9\Example 9-10** folder is a graphics file named **fish.bmp**. This is the fish graphics. Copy this file into the application **Bin\Debug** folder (you may have to create the folder first).

3. Set the **frmScroll KeyPreview** property to **True**.

4. Add this line at the top of the code window with the other **using** statements:

    ```
    using System.Drawing.Imaging;
    ```

5. Add these 'fish' variables to the form level declarations:

    ```
    Image fish;
    ImageAttributes fishAttributes = new ImageAttributes();
    int fishX, fishY;
    ```

6. Add the shaded code to the **frmScroll Load** method to initialize the 'fish' variables:

```
private void FrmScroll_Load(object sender, EventArgs e)
{
  background = Image.FromFile(Application.StartupPath +
"\\undrsea1.bmp");
  // make sure viewer is same height as background image
  pnlViewer.Height = background.Height;
  viewer = pnlViewer.CreateGraphics();
  fishAttributes.SetColorKey(Color.FromArgb(192, 192,
192), Color.FromArgb(192, 192, 192));
  fish = Image.FromFile(Application.StartupPath +
"\\fish.bmp");
  // draw fish in middle of viewer
  fishX = (int) (0.5 * (pnlViewer.ClientSize.Width -
fish.Width));
  fishY = (int) (0.5 * (pnlViewer.ClientSize.Height -
fish.Height));
}
```

7. Add the shaded code to the **timScroll Tick** method to draw the fish on the background:

```
private void TimScroll_Tick(object sender, EventArgs e)
{
  int addedWidth;
  Rectangle rectangleDest, rectangleSrc;
  // Find next location on background
  scrollX += hsbScroll.Value;
  if (scrollX > background.Width)
  {
    scrollX = 0;
  }
  // When x is near right edge, we need to copy
  // two segments of the background into viewer
  if (scrollX > (background.Width -
pnlViewer.ClientSize.Width))
    {
      addedWidth = background.Width - scrollX;
      rectangleDest = new Rectangle(0, 0, addedWidth,
pnlViewer.ClientSize.Height);
      rectangleSrc = new Rectangle(scrollX, 0, addedWidth,
background.Height);
      viewer.DrawImage(background, rectangleDest,
rectangleSrc, GraphicsUnit.Pixel);
```

```
    rectangleDest = new Rectangle(addedWidth, 0,
pnlViewer.ClientSize.Width - addedWidth,
pnlViewer.ClientSize.Height);
    rectangleSrc = new Rectangle(0, 0,
pnlViewer.ClientSize.Width - addedWidth,
background.Height);
    viewer.DrawImage(background, rectangleDest,
rectangleSrc, GraphicsUnit.Pixel);
  }
  else
  {
    rectangleDest = new Rectangle(0, 0,
pnlViewer.ClientSize.Width, pnlViewer.ClientSize.Height);
    rectangleSrc = new Rectangle(scrollX, 0,
pnlViewer.ClientSize.Width, background.Height);
    viewer.DrawImage(background, rectangleDest,
rectangleSrc, GraphicsUnit.Pixel);
  }
  // draw fish
  Rectangle fishDest = new Rectangle(fishX, fishY,
fish.Width, fish.Height);
  viewer.DrawImage(fish, fishDest, 0, 0, fish.Width,
fish.Height, GraphicsUnit.Pixel, fishAttributes);
}
```

8. Use this code in the **frmScroll KeyDown** method (new code):

```
private void FrmScroll_KeyDown(object sender, KeyEventArgs
e)
{
  if (e.KeyCode == Keys.Up)
  {
    fishY -= 5;
  }
  else if (e.KeyCode == Keys.Down)
  {
    fishY += 5;
  }
  e.Handled = true;
}
```

This moves the fish up (up cursor key) and down (down cursor key).

9. Run the application and save it (saved in **Example 9-10** folder in **LearnVCS\VCS Code\Class 9** folder). Use the up cursor key to move the fish up and the down cursor key to move the fish down. Notice that, no matter where the fish is, the background shows through. Here's the fish in the middle of the water:

Here's the fish down by the rocks:

And, here's a fabulous flying fish:

You now know the secrets of doing animations in video games – scrolling backgrounds and the use of sprites.

Collision Detection

As objects move in a multimedia presentation or video game, we need some way to see if two items collide or overlap. For example, in a basketball game, you need to see if the ball goes in the hoop. In a solitaire card game, you need to see if a card is placed on another card properly. In a file disposal application, you want to know when the file reaches the trashcan. Rectangular regions describe all the moving objects in a multimedia application. Hence, we want to know if two rectangles intersect. In Visual C#, this test can be accomplished using the **IntersectsWith** method of the **Rectangle** structure we've seen before.

To use the IntersectsWith method, we need two **Rectangle** structures. If **rectangle1** and **rectangle2** describe the rectangles being checked for intersection, this expression:

```
rectangle1.IntersectsWith(rectangle2)
```

will return one of two Boolean values. It returns **true** if rectangle1 and rectangle2 intersect. It returns **false** if there is no intersection between rectangle1 and rectangle2.

Just because two rectangles intersect, you may not want to declare a collision. There are other methods (look at the **Intersect** method) that actually determine not only if there is an intersection, but also determine the size of the overlap between the two rectangles. With these alternates, you can detect an intersection and, once detected, see how large the intersection area is. If this intersection area is small compared to the size of the compared rectangles, you might not allow the collision. Or, you might want different response depending on location of the intersection region. For example, if a ball hits (collides with) a paddle on one side, the ball will go in one direction. If the ball hits the paddle on the other side, a different rebound direction is assumed.

Example 9-11

Collision Detection

1. In this application, we will add a paddle (a **Rectangle** object) at the bottom of the bouncing ball application built in Example 9-8. If the ball collides with the paddle, we allow it to bounce back up. If it misses the paddle, we let it drop off the bottom of the form. The paddle will be moved to the **left** using the **F** key and to the **right** using the **J** key. These keys were selected because they are in a natural typing position. Open **Example 9-8**.

2. First, widen the panel control to give the paddle room to move. My modified form looks like this:

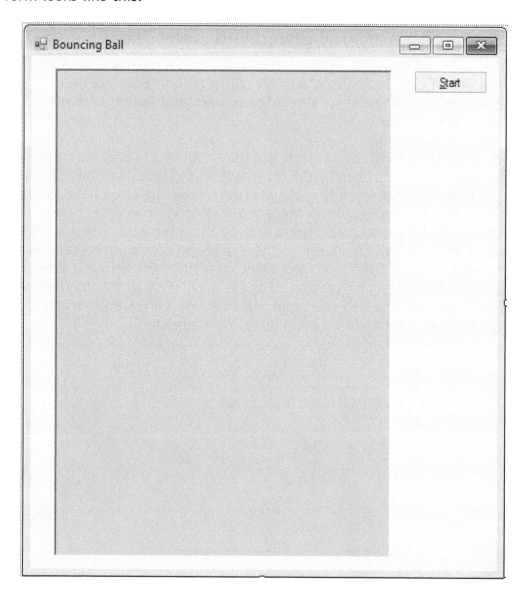

3. Set the **frmBall KeyPreview** property to **True**.

4. Add these variables to the form level declarations:

```
Rectangle myPaddle;
int paddleX = 100;
```

5. Add the shaded code to the **frmBall Load** method. This creates the paddle rectangle structure:

```
private void FrmBall_Load(object sender, EventArgs e)
{
  // initialize variables - set up graphics objects
  ballY = 0;
  ballDir = 1;
  myDisplay = pnlDisplay.CreateGraphics();
  myBall = Image.FromFile(Application.StartupPath +
"\\ball.gif");
  myPaddle = new Rectangle(paddleX, pnlDisplay.Height -
20, ballSize, 10);
  pnlDisplay_Paint(null, null);
}
```

6. Modify the **timBall Tick** method to add checking for a collision between the paddle and the ball (changes are shaded):

```
private void TimBall_Tick(object sender, EventArgs e)
{
  // determine ball position and draw it
  ballY += (int) (ballDir * pnlDisplay.ClientSize.Height /
50);
  // check for bounce
  if (ballY < 0)
  {
    ballY = 0;
    ballDir = 1;
  }
  else
  {
    // check for collision with paddle
    if (myRectangle.IntersectsWith(myPaddle))
    {
      ballY = myPaddle.Y - ballSize;
      ballDir = -1;
    }
  }
  // check to see if ball went off bottom - if so,
reposition at top
  if (ballY > pnlDisplay.ClientSize.Height)
  {
    ballY = - ballSize;
  }
  pnlDisplay_Paint(null, null);
}
```

7. Add the shaded code to the **pnlDisplay Paint** method. This draws the paddle:

```
private void PnlDisplay_Paint(object sender,
PaintEventArgs e)
{
  // horizontally center ball in display rectangle
  myRectangle = new Rectangle((int) (0.5 *
(pnlDisplay.ClientSize.Width - ballSize)), ballY,
ballSize, ballSize);
  myDisplay.Clear(pnlDisplay.BackColor);
  myDisplay.DrawImage(myBall, myRectangle);
  // draw paddle
  myDisplay.FillRectangle(Brushes.Red, myPaddle);
}
```

8. Add a **frmBall KeyDown** method to move the paddle (new code):

```
private void FrmBall_KeyDown(object sender, KeyEventArgs
e)
{
  if (e.KeyCode == Keys.F)
  {
    paddleX -= 5;
  }
  else if (e.KeyCode == Keys.J)
  {
    paddleX += 5;
  }
  myPaddle.X = paddleX;
}
```

9. Save and run the application (saved in **Example 9-11** in the **LearnVCS\VCS Code\Class 9** folder). Use the keyboard **F** key to move the paddle to the left and the **J** key to move it to the right. Make sure it can bounce off the paddle. Make sure it goes off the screen if it misses the paddle (note the code to make it reappear if this happens). Here's a run I made:

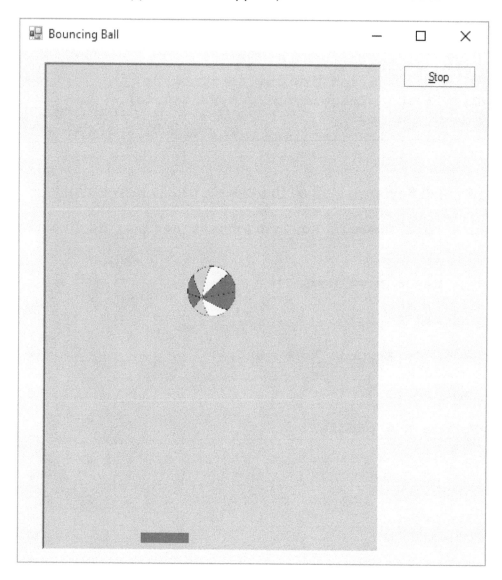

Playing Sounds

Most games feature sounds that take advantage of stereo sound cards. By using the Visual C# **SoundPlayer** class, we can add such sounds to our projects. This class uses the Visual C# **Media** namespace, so for any application using sounds, you will need to add this line:

```
using System.Media;
```

at the top of the code window with the other directives.

The **SoundPlayer** class is used to play one particular type of sound, those represented by **wav** files (files with wav extensions). Most sounds you hear played in Windows applications are saved as **wav** files. These are the files formed when you record using one of the many sound recorder programs available

Prior to playing a sound, a **SoundPlayer** object (**mySound**) must be declared using the usual statement.

```
SoundPlayer mySound;
```

The object is then constructed using:

```
mySound = new SoundPlayer(SoundFile);
```

where **SoundFile** is a complete path to the **wav** file to be played.

A sound is loaded into memory using the **Load** method of the **SoundPlayer** class:

```
mySound.Load();
```

This is an <u>optional</u> step that should be done for sounds that will be played often - it allows them to be played quickly.

There are two methods available to play a sound, the **Play** method and the **PlaySync** method:

```
mySound.Play();
mySound.PlaySync();
```

With the **Play** method, a sound is played **asynchronously**. This means that execution of code continues as the sound is played. With **PlaySync**, the sound is played **synchronously**. In this case, the sound is played to completion, and then code execution continues. With either method, if the sound is not loaded into memory, it will be loaded first. This will slow down your program depending on how big the file is. This is why we preload sounds (using the **Load** method) that are played often.

It is normal practice to include any sound files an application uses in the same directory as the application executable file (the **Bin\Debug folder**). This makes them easily accessible (use the **Application.StartupPath** parameter). As such, when building a deployment package for an application, you must remember to include the sound files in the package. And, you must insure these files are installed in the proper directory.

Example 9-12

Bouncing Ball with Sound!

1. Open **Example 9-11**, the bouncing ball example. We will play one sound when the ball bounces and another sound when the ball leaves the bottom of the panel. In the **LearnVCS\VCS Code\Class 9\Example 9-12** is a bouncing sound (**bong.wav**) and a miss sound (**missed.wav**). Copy these files to the application's **Bin\Debug** folder (you may have to create the folder first). Also copy the **ball.gif** file (the bouncing ball) to the same folder.

2. Add this line at the top of the code window with the other **using** statements:

```
using System.Media;
```

3. Add these variables to the form level declarations:

```
SoundPlayer missSound;
SoundPlayer bounceSound;
```

4. Modify the **frmBall Load** procedure to create the sound variables (new code is shaded):

```
private void FrmBall_Load(object sender, EventArgs e)
{
  // initialize variables - set up graphics objects
  ballY = 0;
  ballDir = 1;
  myDisplay = pnlDisplay.CreateGraphics();
  myBall = Image.FromFile(Application.StartupPath +
"\\ball.gif");
  myPaddle = new Rectangle(paddleX, pnlDisplay.Height -
20, ballSize, 10);
  pnlDisplay_Paint(null, null);
  bounceSound = new SoundPlayer(Application.StartupPath +
"\\bong.wav");
  missSound = new SoundPlayer(Application.StartupPath +
"\\missed.wav");
}
```

5. Add code to the **timBall Tick** procedure to play the 'bounce' and 'missed' sounds when needed (added code is shaded):

```csharp
private void TimBall_Tick(object sender, EventArgs e)
{
    // determine ball position and draw it
    ballY += (int)(ballDir * pnlDisplay.ClientSize.Height /
50);
    // check for bounce
    if (ballY < 0)
    {
        ballY = 0;
        ballDir = 1;
        bounceSound.Play();
    }
    else
    {
        // check for collision with paddle
        if (myRectangle.IntersectsWith(myPaddle))
        {
            ballY = myPaddle.Y - ballSize;
            ballDir = -1;
            bounceSound.Play();
        }
    }
    // check to see if ball went off bottom - if so,
reposition at top
    if (ballY > pnlDisplay.ClientSize.Height)
    {
        ballY = -ballSize;
        missSound.PlaySync();
    }
    pnlDisplay_Paint(null, null);
}
```

The bounce sound is played asynchronously, while the miss sound is played synchronously.

6. Save the application and run it (saved in **Example 9-12** in the **LearnVCS\VCS Code\Class 9** folder). Each time the ball bounces, you should hear a bonk! When it misses the paddle and falls off the bottom, you hear another sound.

Class Review

After completing this class, you should understand:

- How to detect and use mouse events
- How to add persistence to graphics objects without a Paint event
- How to draw lines, polygons and filled polygons
- How to draw curves, closed curves and filled closed curves
- How to use hatch, gradient and texture brushes
- How to add text to a graphics object
- How to do animation using DrawImage
- How to work with scrolling backgrounds
- The basics of sprite animation
- How to use keyboard events and detect collision of two rectangular regions
- How to play sound files

Practice Problems 9

Problem 9-1. Blackboard Problem. Modify the **Blackboard** application (Example 9-2) to allow adjustable line width while drawing. Also, allow saving and opening of drawing files.

Problem 9-2. Rubber Band Problem. Build an application where the user draws a 'rubber band' rectangle on the form. Let a left-click start drawing (defining upper left corner). Then move the mouse until the rectangle is as desired and release the mouse button. When the 'rubber band' is complete, draw an ellipse in the defined region.

Problem 9-3. Shape Guessing Game. Build a game where the user is presented with three different shapes. Give the user one shape name and have them identify the matching shape.

Problem 9-4. Plot Labels Problem. In Problem 8-4, we built an application that plotted the win streak for the Seattle Mariners 1995 season. Use the DrawString method to add any labeling information desired.

Problem 9-5. Bouncing Balls Problem. Build an application with two bouncing balls. When they collide make them disappear with some kind of sound. Add any other effects you might like.

Problem 9-6. Moon Problem. In the **LearnVCS\VCS Code\Class 9\Problem 9-6** folder is a bitmap file named **THEMOON.BMP**. It is a large (450 pixels high, 640 pixels wide) lunar landscape. Build an application that lets you traverse this landscape in a small viewing window. Use cursor control keys to move horizontally and vertically.

Problem 9-7. Sound Files Problem. Build an application that lets you look through your computer directories for sound files (.wav extension). When you select a file, play it using the **SoundPlayer** object. The image viewer (Example 5-4) built in Class 5 is a good starting point.

Exercise 9

The Original Video Game - Pong!

In the early 1970's, Nolan Bushnell began the video game revolution with Atari's Pong game -- a very simple Ping-Pong kind of game. Try to replicate this game using Visual C#. In the game, a ball bounces from one end of a court to another, bouncing off sidewalls. Players try to deflect the ball at each end using a controllable paddle. Use sounds where appropriate.

10. Other Windows Application Topics

Review and Preview

In this class, we conclude our discussion of general Visual C# Windows applications. We look at some other controls, how to add and use controls at run-time, how to print from an application, how to use the Windows API (Application Programming Interface) and how to add help systems to our applications. In the final chapter (Chapter 11), we look at how to use Visual C# for database management and an exciting new feature of Visual C# – the Web form. This form lets us build applications that work on the Internet.

Other Controls

In the past several chapters, we've looked at many of the controls in the Visual C# toolbox. But, there are still others. We will look at several of these **other controls** in this chapter. For each control, we will build a short example to demonstrate its use. With your programming skills, you should be able to expand these examples to fit your particular needs.

What if you can't find the exact control you need for a particular task? Another skill you can develop, using the knowledge gained in this course, is the ability to build and deploy your own Visual C# controls. You can modify an existing control (seen in Chapter 3), build a control made up of several existing controls or create an entirely new control. Building your own controls is beyond the scope of this course. There are several excellent texts and websites that address this topic.

LinkLabel Control

In Toolbox:

On Form (Default Properties):

linkLabel1

A **LinkLabel** control is like the **Label** control we've used many times before, with one important additional feature. The LinkLabel control allows you to put web style URL (Universal Resource Locator; a web page address) links in a Visual C# application. This lets your user visit relevant web sites from within an application.

LinkLabel **Properties:**

Name	Gets or sets the name of the link label (three letter prefix for label name is **lkl**).
ActiveLinkColor	Gets or sets the color used to display an active link.
AutoSize	Gets or sets a value indicating whether the link label is automatically resized to display its entire contents.
BackColor	Get or sets the link label background color.
BorderStyle	Gets or sets the border style for the link label.
DisabledLinkColor	Gets or sets the color used when displaying a disabled link.
Font	Gets or sets font name, style, size.
ForeColor	Gets or sets color of text or graphics.
LinkArea	Gets or sets the range in the text to treat as a link.
LinkBehavior	Gets or sets a value that represents the behavior of a link.
LinkColor	Gets or sets the color used when displaying a normal link.
LinkVisited	Gets or sets a value indicating whether a link should be displayed as though it were visited.
Text	Gets or sets string displayed on link label.
TextAlign	Gets or sets the alignment of text in the link label.
VisitedLinkColor	Gets or sets the color used when displaying a link that that has been previously visited.

LinkLabel **Methods:**

Refresh   Forces an update of the link label control contents.

LinkLabel **Events:**

LinkClicked   Occurs when a link is clicked within the control
                               (**default** event).

Once a link is clicked in the link label control, we need to know how to display
the specified web page. Knowing a URL (the **Text** property of the link label
control), the web page is displayed using the **Process.Start** method in the Visual
C# **System.Diagnostics** namespace. In code, this line would be for a control
named **lklExample:**

```
System.Diagnostics.Process.Start(lklExample.Text);
```

Typical use of **LinkLabel** control:

> ➢ Set the **Name** and **Text** property (the URL for the web page).
> ➢ You may also want to change the **Font** and various **link colors.**
> ➢ Write code in the link label's **LinkClicked** event. This code should access
>   the web page (using **Process.Start**) and set the **LinkVisited** property to
>   **True.**

Example 10-1

Link Label Control

1. Start a new project. In this project, you'll use the link label control to visit some web site (we've selected ours; you can use any one you want). This is a popular feature of many commercial applications. Place a link label control on the form.

2. Set the properties of the form and each object.

    Form1:
Name	frmLinkLabel
FormBorderStyle	FixedSingle
StartPosition	CenterScreen
Text	Link Label Example

    linkLabel1:
Name	lklURL
Text	Visit Our Web Site!
Font Size	14

Your finished form should look like this:

4. Use the following code in the **lklURL LinkClicked** event.

```
private void LklURL_LinkClicked(object sender,
LinkLabelLinkClickedEventArgs e)
{
  // Call the Process.Start method to open the default
browser
  // with a URL:
  lklURL.LinkVisited = true;

System.Diagnostics.Process.Start("http://www.kidwaresoftwa
re.com");
}
```

5. Save your project (saved in **Example 10-1** folder in the **LearnVCS\VCS Code\Class 10** folder). Run the application. Click the link. What happens next depends on the state of your computer. Here's the running project after I clicked the link:

So what happens after clicking the link? If you're already logged on to the Internet and your browser is running, program control will switch to the browser and you'll see our web site's home page. If you're logged in, but your browser is not running, the browser will start and then you'll see the web page. If not logged in, your browser will start and your default login procedure will begin. If you successfully log in, our web site will appear. All of this performance comes with no extra code!

MonthCalendar Control

In Toolbox:

 MonthCalendar

On Form (Default Properties):

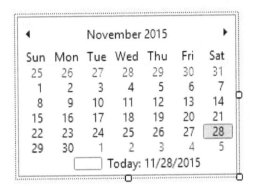

The **MonthCalendar** control allows a user to select a date. It is a very easy to use int
erface – just point and click. This control is useful for ordering information, making reservations or choosing the current date. It can be used to select a single date or a range of dates.

MonthCalendar **Properties:**

Name	Gets or sets the name of the month calendar (three letter prefix for label name is **cal**).
BackColor	Get or sets the month calendar background color.
CalendarDimensions	Gets or sets the number of columns and rows of months displayed.
FirstDayOfWeek	Gets or sets the first day of the week as displayed in the month calendar.
Font	Gets or sets font name, style, size.
ForeColor	Gets or sets color of text or graphics.
MaxDate	Gets or sets the maximum allowable date.
MaxSelectionCount	The maximum number of days that can be selected in a month calendar control.
MinDate	Gets or sets the minimum allowable date.
SelectionEnd	Gets or sets the end date of the selected range of dates.

MonthCalendar **Properties** (continued):

SelectionRange	Retrieves the selected range of dates for a month calendar control.
SelectionStart	Gets or sets the start date of the selected range of dates.
ShowToday	Gets or sets a value indicating whether the date represent by the TodayDate property is shown at the bottom of the control.
ShowTodayCircle	Gets or sets a value indicating whether today's date is circled.
TodayDate	Gets or sets the value that is used by MonthCalendar as today's date.

MonthCalendar **Methods:**

SetDate	Sets date as the current selected date.

MonthCalendar **Events:**

DateChanged	Occurs when the date in the MonthCalendar changes (**default** event).
DateSelected	Occurs when a date is selected.

Typical use of **MonthCalendar** control:

➢ Set the **Name** property. Set **MaxSelection** Count (set to 1 if just picking a single date).
➢ Monitor **DateChanged** and/or **DateSelected** events to determine date value(s). Values are between **SelectionStart** and **SelectionEnd** properties.

DateTimePicker Control

In Toolbox:

 DateTimePicker

On Form (Default Properties):

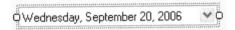 Wednesday, September 20, 2006

The **DateTimePicker** control works like the MonthCalendar control with a different interface and formatting options. It allows the user to select a single date. The selected date appears in a combo box. The calendar portion is available as a 'drop down.' This control can also be used to select a time; we won't look at that option.

DateTimePicker **Properties:**

Name	Gets or sets the name of the date/time picker control (three letter prefix for label name is **dtp**).
BackColor	Get or sets the control background color.
Font	Gets or sets font name, style, size.
ForeColor	Gets or sets color of text or graphics.
Format	Gets or sets the format of the date displayed in the control.
MaxDate	Gets or sets the maximum allowable date.
MinDate	Gets or sets the minimum allowable date.
Value	Gets or sets the date value assigned to the control.

DateTimePicker **Events:**

ValueChanged	Occurs when the **Value** property changes (**default** event).

Typical use of **DateTimePicker** control:

➢ Set the **Name** and Format properties.
➢ When needed, read **Value** property for selected date.

Example 10-2

Date Selections

1. Start a new project. In this project, we'll look at single date selection using the **MonthCalendar** and **DateTimePicker** controls. Add one of each of these controls to the form.

2. Set the properties of the form and each object.

Form1:

Name	frmMonth
FormBorderStyle	FixedSingle
StartPosition	CenterScreen
Text	Calendar Examples

monthCalendar1:

Name	calExample
MaxSelectionCount	1

dateTimePicker1:

Name	dtpExample
Format	Long

Your form should look like this:

3. Use this code in the **calExample DateSelected** event:

```
private void CalExample_DateSelected(object sender,
DateRangeEventArgs e)
{
  MessageBox.Show("You selected " +
calExample.SelectionStart.ToLongDateString(), "Date
Selected in Month Calendar Control");
}
```

4. Save your project (saved in **Example 10-2** folder in the **LearnVCS\VCS Code\Class 10** folder). Run the application. Notice how easy it is to select dates for your applications. Here's my birthday (yes, I'm getting old) in the top calendar and today's in the lower control:

When I click the date in the MonthCalendar control, I see:

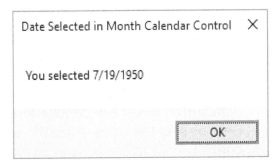

Play with the date time picker control too – can you write code to display its selection in a message box.

RichTextbox Control

In Toolbox:

On Form (Default Properties):

The **RichTextBox** control allows the user to enter and edit text, providing more advanced formatting features than the conventional textbox control. You can use different fonts and font styles for different text sections (see the '**Selection**' properties). You can even control indents, hanging indents, and bulleted paragraphs. Possible uses for this control include: reading and viewing large text files or implementing a full-featured text editor into any applications.

RichTextBox **Properties:**

Name	Gets or sets the name of the rich text box (three letter prefix for text box name is **rtb**).
AutoSize	Gets or sets a value indicating whether the height of the text box automatically adjusts when the font assigned to the control is changed.
BackColor	Get or sets the text box background color.
BorderStyle	Gets or sets the border style for the text box.
Font	Gets or sets font name, style, size.
ForeColor	Gets or sets color of text or graphics.
HideSelection	Gets or sets a value indicating whether the selected text in the text box control remains highlighted when the control loses focus.
Lines	Gets or sets the lines of text in a text box control.

RichTextBox **Properties** (continued):

MaxLength	Gets or sets the maximum number of characters the user can type into the text box control.
MultiLine	Gets or sets a value indicating whether this is a multiline text box control.
ReadOnly	Gets or sets a value indicating whether text in the text box is read-only.
ScrollBars	Gets or sets which scroll bars should appear in a multiline TextBox control.
SelectedText	Gets or sets a value indicating the currently selected text in the control.
SelectionColor	Gets or sets the text color of the current text selection or insertion point.
SelectionFont	Gets or sets the font of the current text selection or insertion point.
SelectionLength	Gets or sets the number of characters selected in the text box.
SelectionStart	Gets or sets the starting point of text selected in the text box.
Tag	Stores a string expression.
Text	Gets or sets the current text in the text box.
TextAlign	Gets or sets the alignment of text in the text box.
TextLength	Gets length of text in text box.

RichTextBox **Methods:**

AppendText	Appends text to the current text of text box.
Clear	Clears all text in text box.
Copy	Copies selected text to clipboard.
Cut	Moves selected text to clipboard.
Focus	Places the cursor in a specified text box.
LoadFile	Loads the contents of a file into the RichTextBox control.
Paste	Replaces the current selection in the text box with the contents of the Clipboard.
SaveFile	Saves the contents (including all formatting) of the RichTextBox to a file.
Undo	Undoes the last edit operation in the text box.

RichTextBox **Events:**

Click	Occurs when the user clicks the text box.
Focused	Occurs when the control receives focus.
KeyDown	Occurs when a key is pressed down while the control has focus.
KeyPress	Occurs when a key is pressed while the control has focus – used for key trapping.
Leave	Triggered when the user leaves the text box. This is a good place to examine the contents of a text box after editing.
TextChanged	Occurs when the Text property value has changed (**default** event).

Note particularly the **LoadFile** and **SaveFile** methods. **SaveFile** will save the contents of the rich text box control as an **rtf** (rich text format) file. Almost all word processing programs can open such a document. The format for a rich text box control named **rtbExample** is:

```
rtbExample.SaveFile(FileName);
```

where **FileName** is a complete path to the file. To open a previously saved file, the format is:

```
rtbExample.LoadFile(FileName);
```

Typical use of **RichTextBox** control as display control:

> ➤ Set the **Name** property. Initialize **Text** property to desired string.
> ➤ If displaying more than one line, set **MultiLine** property to **True**.
> ➤ Assign **Text** property in code where needed.
> ➤ If desired, write code to selectively format displayed text.

Typical use of **RichTextBox** control as input device:

> ➤ Set the **Name** property. Initialize **Text** property to desired string.
> ➤ If it is possible to input multiple lines, set **MultiLine** property to **True**.
> ➤ In code, give **Focus** to control when needed. Provide key trapping code in **KeyPress** event. Read **Text** property when **LostFocus** event occurs.
> ➤ If desired, write code to selectively format displayed text.

Example 10-3

Rich Text Box Example

1. Start a new project. In this project, we'll change the font of selected text using the rich text box control. Add a rich text box control, a button control and a font dialog control to the project.

2. Set the properties of the form and each object.

Form1:

Name	frmRichTextBox
FormBorderStyle	FixedSingle
StartPosition	CenterScreen
Text	Rich Text Box Example

richTextBox1:

Name	rtbExample
MultiLine	True
ScrollBars	Vertical
Text	[Blank]

button1:

Name	btnFont
Text	&Change Font

fontDialog1:

Name	dlgFont

Your form should look like this:

Other controls in tray:

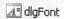

3. Use this code in the **btnFont Click** event:

```
private void BtnFont_Click(object sender, EventArgs e)
{
  if (dlgFont.ShowDialog() == DialogResult.OK)
  {
    rtbExample.SelectionFont = dlgFont.Font;
  }
}
```

4. Save your project (saved in **Example 10-3** folder in the **LearnVCS\VCS Code\Class 10** folder). Run the application. Type some text in the text box. Select a section of text and click **Change Font** to change the font. Notice you can format as many text selections as your desire. Here's some text with various formats:

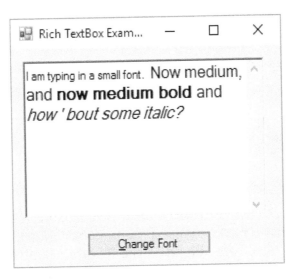

ToolStrip (Toolbar) Control

In Toolbox:

On Form (Default Properties):

Below Form (Default Properties):

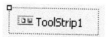

Almost all Windows applications these days use toolbars. A toolbar provides quick access to the most frequently used menu commands in an application. The **ToolStrip** control (also referred to as the **Toolbar** control) is a mini-application in itself. It provides everything you need to design and implement a toolbar into your application. Possible uses for this control include: provide a consistent interface between applications with matching toolbars, place commonly used functions in an easily-accessed space and provide an intuitive, graphical interface for your application.

ToolStrip **Properties:**

Name	Gets or sets the name of the toolstrip (toolbar) control (three letter prefix for label name is **tlb**).
BackColor	Background color of toolstrip.
Items	Gets the collection of controls assigned to the toolstrip control.
LayoutStyle	Establishes whether toolbar is vertical or horizontal.
Dock	Establishes location of toolbar on form.

The primary property of concern is the **Items** collection. This establishes each item in the toolbar. Choosing the **Items** property in the Properties window and clicking the ellipsis that appears will display the **Items Collection Editor**. With this editor, you can add, delete, insert and move items. We will look at adding just two types of items: **ToolStripButton** and **ToolStripSeparator** (used to separate tool bar buttons). To add a button, make sure **ToolStripButton** appears in the drop-down box and click the **Add** button. A name will be assigned to a button. After adding one button, the editor will look like this:

Add as many buttons as you like. You can change any property you desire in the **Properties** area.

ToolStripButton **Properties:**

Name	Gets or sets the name of the button (three letter prefix for control name is **tlb**).
DisplayStyle	Sets whether image, text or both are displayed on button.
Image	Image to display on button.
Text	Caption information on the button, often blank.
TextImageRelation	Where text appears relative to image.
ToolTipText	Text to display in button tool tip.

To add a separator, make sure **ToolStripSeparator** appears in drop-down box and click **Add**. When done editing buttons, click **OK** to leave the Items Collection Editor.

Setting the **Image** property requires a few steps (a process similar to that used for the picture box control). First, click the ellipsis next to the **Image** property in the property window. This **Select Resource** window will appear:

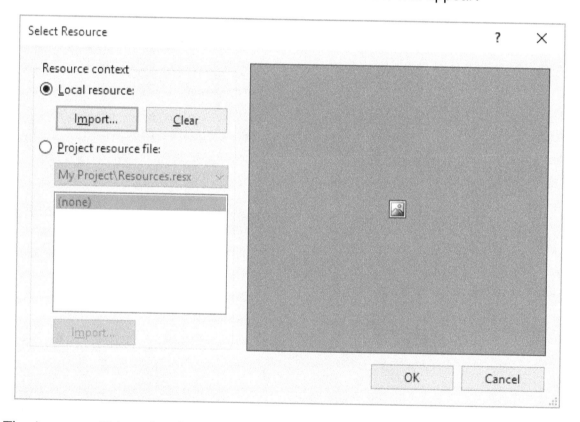

The images will be a local resource, so select the **Local resource** radio button and click the **Import** button.

An **Open** window will display graphics files (if you want to see an **ico** file, you must change **Files of type** to **All Files**). In the **LearnVCS\VCS Code\Class 10** folder is a folder named **Toolbar Graphics.** In this folder, there are many bitmap files for toolbar use:

Select the desired file and click **Open.** Once an image is selected, click **OK** in the **Select Resource** window. It will be assigned to the **Image** property

After setting up the toolbar, you need to write code for the **Click** event for each toolbar button. This event is the same **Click** event we encounter for button controls.

Typical use of **ToolStrip** control:

> Set the **Name** property and desired location.
> Decide on image, text, and tooltip text for each button.
> Establish each button/separator using the **Items Collection Editor.**
> Write code for the each toolbar button's **Click** event.

Example 10-4

Note Editor Toolbar

1. Back in Chapters 6 and 7, we built and modified a **Note Editor** application. In the application, we could type and format text in a text box control. In this example, we'll add a toolbar to that application. Load **Example 7-8** (the last incarnation of the Note Editor). You will probably have to resize the form and move the text box to make room for the toolbar. Name the toolbar **tlbNoteEditor**. The form should look like this:

tlbNoteEditor

Added control in tray:

tlbNoteEditor

2. The toolbar will have six buttons: one to create a **new** file, one to **open** a file, one to **save** a file, one to **bold** text, one to **italicize** text and one to **underline** text. Click on the **Items** property of the toolbar control. The **Items Collection Editor** will appear. We use this editor to sequentially add seven buttons to the toolbar: the six mentioned above plus one button as a space holder between file functions (New, Open, Save) and edit functions (Bold, Italicize, Underline). So, **Add** seven buttons with these properties:

toolBarButton1:

Name	tlbNew
Image	new.bmp
Text	[Blank]
ToolTipText	New File

toolBarButton2:

Name	tlbOpen
Image	open.bmp
Text	[Blank]
ToolTipText	Open File

toolBarButton3:

Name	tlbSave
Image	save.bmp
Text	[Blank]
ToolTipText	Save File

toolBarButton4:

Name	tlbSpace
Style	Separator

toolBarButton5:

Name	tlbBold
Image	bld.bmp
Text	[Blank]
ToolTipText	Bold Text

toolBarButton6:

Name	tlbItalic
Image	itl.bmp
Text	[Blank]
ToolTipText	Italicize Text

toolBarButton7:

Name	tlbUnderline
Image	undrln.bmp
Text	[Blank]
ToolTipText	Underline Text

Note six images are needed with the buttons. Recall these are added using the **Select Resource** window (click the **Image** property for one of the buttons). All the graphics files are included in the **LearnVCS\VCS Code\Class 10\Toolbar Graphics** folder.

Also, note (as desired) **tlbSpace** is a placeholder button (choose **Separator** as the type before adding) that puts some space between the file and formatting buttons.

The finished **Items Collection Editor** window appears as:

Click **OK** to close this box.

The top of my form now looks like this:

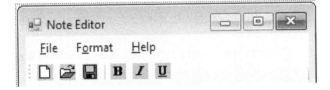

Notice the separator 'button.'

3. Lastly, add this code to the **tlbNoteEditor Click** event (handles the **Click** event for each toolbar button). Each toolbar button replicates an existing menu item, so the code is simply a 'click' on the corresponding menu option (using the **PerformClick** method):

```
private void TlbNoteEditor_Click(object sender, EventArgs
e)
{
  ToolStripButton toolButton = (ToolStripButton) sender;
  if (toolButton.Name.Equals("tlbNew"))
  {
    mnuFileNew.PerformClick();
  }
  else if (toolButton.Name.Equals("tlbOpen"))
  {
    mnuFileOpen.PerformClick();
  }
  else if (toolButton.Name.Equals("tlbSave"))
  {
    mnuFileSave.PerformClick();
  }
  else if (toolButton.Name.Equals("tlbBold"))
  {
    mnuFmtBold.PerformClick();
  }
  else if (toolButton.Name.Equals("tlbItalic"))
  {
    mnuFmtItalic.PerformClick();
  }
  else if (toolButton.Name.Equals("tlbUnderline"))
  {
    mnuFmtUnderline.PerformClick();
  }
}
```

4. Save (saved in **Example 10-4** folder in the **LearnVCS\VCS Code\Class 10** folder) and run the application. Make sure all the toolbar buttons work properly. Check out how the tool tips work. Here's the Note Editor with toolbar added:

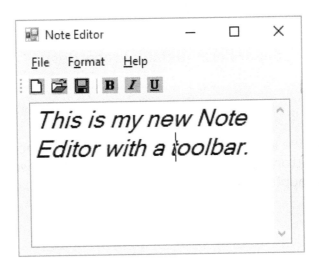

ToolTip Control

In Toolbox:

Below Form (Default Properties):

In the last example, we saw that tool tips are useful for indicating what a particular toolbar button does. Using the **ToolTip** control, we can add tool tips to any control in an application. This can be used to help explain a control's use and purpose.

ToolTip **Properties:**

Name	Gets or sets the name of the tooltip control (three letter prefix for label name is **tlt**).
AutomaticDelay	Sets the length of time that the ToolTip string is shown, how long the user must point at the control for the ToolTip to appear, and how long it takes for subsequent ToolTip windows to appear. Usually, the default values are quite adequate.

Once added to an application, all controls in the application will have an additional property: **ToolTip**. Just set a value of this property for each control you want to have a tool tip. It's that easy! Try using tool tips in applications you build.

Adding Controls at Run-Time

In building Visual C# applications, the process of adding controls and setting properties at design time is straightforward and simple. There are times, however, when it might be advantageous to add controls at run-time. For example, what if the number of radio button controls displayed for a certain choice depended on some user input. Or, perhaps the task of adding many similar controls is a lot of tedious work. With just a bit of code, we can automate the task of **adding controls** to a form at **run-time**. We can also remove controls if desired. This is a review of some material seen back in Chapter 3, where we introduced object-oriented programming.

To add a control at run-time, we need to follow five steps: (1) declare the control, (2) create the control, (3) set control properties, (4) add control to form and (5) connect event handlers. We look at each step separately for a generic control named **myControl** of type **ControlType**.

The first step is to declare a control using the usual statement:

```
ControlType myControl;
```

Quite often we declare an array of controls. The control is created using the respective constructor:

```
myControl = new ControlType();
```

At this point, **myControl** is established with a default set of properties. You can overwrite any properties you choose. In particular, you must set values for the **Left** and **Top** properties. If you don't, all your new controls will be stacked in the upper left corner of the form (Left = 0, Top = 0). You probably also want to change the **Width** and **Height** properties. Once the properties are set, the control is added to the form using the **Add** method of the **Controls** object:

```
this.Controls.Add(myControl);
```

If you are adding the control to a group box or panel control, you would replace **this** (referring to the form) in the above statement with the container control's name.

So, now the control is created and on the form, but recognizes no events. Decide what events you want your control to respond to. If you want event **MyEvent** to be handled by a method **MyMethod**, an event handler is created using:

```
myControl.MyEvent += new
System.EventHandler(this.MyMethod);
```

Before using this statement, the method **MyMethod** should exist in the code window. It could be a method corresponding to an existing control or a new method you create. If you create it, the format is:

```
private void MyMethod(object sender, EventArgs e)
{
    .
    .
}
```

You would write code in this method, assuming event handlers are added at run-time.

As an aside, you can add event methods in code for existing controls also. This sometimes saves a little typing at design time. For example, say you have a method that handles clicking on 20 button controls. Rather than assign the event method 20 times in the properties window, you could add it in code.

You can also remove controls from your application. To remove a control (named **myControl**) from the form, use:

```
this.Controls.Remove(myControl);
```

If you are removing a control from a group box or panel control, replace the keyword **this** with the container control's name. When the control is removed, all event handlers for this control are modified to no longer include the removed control. This also happens when a control is deleted at design time.

Example 10-5

Rolodex - Adding Controls at Run-Time

1. Start a new project. In this project, we'll build a computer rolodex index. We will neatly format 26 button controls in two rows across a form. Each button will have a letter of the alphabet. Such a 'control array' could be used for searching a database for information, looking for a last name, or finding a word in a dictionary. Set these properties (all we have is a form):

   Form1:
Name	frmControls
FormBorderStyle	FixedSingle
StartPosition	CenterScreen
Text	Adding Controls

Make your form fairly wide (it needs to hold 2 rows of 13 buttons):

The trickiest part is determining the width of each button. It's essentially the form width divided by 13, since there are 13 buttons in each row. In the code, we add a little space for margins. For each button, we need to establish **Left**, **Top**, **Width** and **Height** properties. We also set the **ForeColor**, **BackColor** and **Text** properties. See the code for our solution.

2. All the buttons are created in the **frmControls Load** event (you should be able to follow the commented code):

```csharp
private void FrmControls_Load(object sender, EventArgs e)
{
    int w, l, lStart, t;
    int buttonHeight = 35;
    Button[] rolodex = new Button[26];
    // determine button width (do not round up)
    w = (int)(this.ClientRectangle.Width / 14);
    // center the resulting buttons
    lStart = (int)(0.5 * (this.ClientSize.Width - 13 * w));
    l = lStart;
    t = (int)(0.5 * (this.ClientSize.Height - 2 *
buttonHeight));
    // create and position 26 buttons
    for (int i = 0; i < 26; i++)
    {
        // create and position new button
        rolodex[i] = new Button();
        rolodex[i].TabStop = false;
        rolodex[i].Text = ((char)(65 + i)).ToString();
        rolodex[i].Width = w;
        rolodex[i].Height = buttonHeight;
        rolodex[i].Left = l;
        rolodex[i].Top = t;
        // give cool colors
        rolodex[i].BackColor = Color.Red;
        rolodex[i].ForeColor = Color.Yellow;
        // add button to form
        this.Controls.Add(rolodex[i]);
        // add event handler
        rolodex[i].Click += new
System.EventHandler(this.Rolodex_Click);
        // next left
        l += w;
        if (i == 12)
        {
            // move to next row
            l = lStart;
            t += buttonHeight;
        }
    }
}
```

3. Use this code for the **Rolodex Click** event (handles clicks on all buttons – handlers added in code):

```
private void Rolodex_Click(object sender, EventArgs e)
{
  Button buttonClicked = (Button) sender;
  MessageBox.Show("You clicked the " + buttonClicked.Text
+ " button.", "", MessageBoxButtons.OK);
}
```

4. Save your project (saved in **Example 10-5** folder in the **LearnVCS\VCS Code\Class 10** folder). Run the application. Notice the nicely spaced buttons.

Click on a button and a message box appears telling you what you clicked. Here's the resulting message:

Stop the application and resize the form. See how the new buttons adapt to the new size. This is another nice feature of adding controls at run-time – it adapts to any changes in form size you might make.

Printing with Visual C#

Any serious Visual C# application will use a **printer** to provide the user with a hard copy of any results (text or graphics) they might need. Printing is one of the more tedious programming tasks within Visual C#. But, fortunately, it is straightforward and there are several dialog controls that help with the tasks. We will introduce lots of new topics here. All steps will be reviewed. Objects used in printing are found in the **Drawing.Printing** namespace. For any application with printing, add this using declaration at the top of the code window:

```
using System.Drawing.Printing;
```

To perform printing in Visual C#, we use the **PrintDocument** object. This object controls the printing process and has four important properties:

Property	Description
DefaultPageSettings	Indicates default page settings for the document.
DocumentName	Indicates the name displayed while the document is printing.
PrintController	Indicates the print controller that guides the printing process.
PrinterSettings	Indicates the printer that prints the document.

The steps to print a document (which may include text and graphics) using the **PrintDocument** object are:

➤ Declare a **PrintDocument** object
➤ Create a **PrintDocument** object
➤ Set any properties desired.
➤ Print the document using the **Print** method of the **PrintDocument** object.

The first three steps are straightforward. To declare and create a **PrintDocument** object named **myDocument**, use:

```
PrintDocument myDocument;
     .
     .
     .
myDocument = new PrintDocument();
```

Any properties needed usually come from print dialog boxes we'll examine in a bit.

The last step poses the question: how does the **PrintDocument** object print with the **Print** method? Printing is done in a general Visual C# method associated with the **PrintDocument.PrintPage** event. This is a method you must create and write. The method tells the **PrintDocument** object what goes on each page of your document. Once the method is written, you need to add the event handler in code (we just learned how to do that) so the **PrintDocument** object knows where to go when it's ready to print a page. It may sound confusing now, but once you've done a little printing, it's very straightforward.

The general Visual C# method for printing your pages (**PrintPage** in this case) must be of the form:

```
private void PrintPage(object sender, PrintPageEventArgs e)
{
    .
    .
}
```

In this method, you 'construct' each page that the **PrintDocument** object is to print. And, you'll see the code in this method is familiar.

In the **PrintPage** method, the argument **e** (of type **PrintPageEventArgs**) has many properties with information about the printing process. The most important property is the **graphics object**:

```
e.Graphics
```

Something familiar! **PrintDocument** provides us with a graphics object to 'draw' each page we want to print. This is the same graphics object we used in Chapters 8 and 9 to draw lines, curves, rectangles, ellipses, text and images. And, all the methods we learned there apply here! We'll look at how to do this in detail next. But, first, let's review how to establish and use the **PrintDocument** object.

A diagram summarizes the printing process:

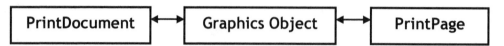

The **PrintDocument** object provides a **Graphics Object** to 'draw' each page. Each page is created in the **PrintPage** event handler (called by the PrintDocument **Print** method).

Here is an annotated code segment that establishes a **PrintDocument** object (**myDocument**) and connects it to a method named **PrintPage** that provides the pages to print via the graphics object:

```
// Declare the document
PrintDocument myDocument;
    .
    .
    .
// Create the document and name it
myDocument = new PrintDocument();
myDocument.DocumentName = "My Document";
    .
    .
    .
// You could set other properties here
    .
    .
// Add code handler
myDocument.PrintPage += new
PrintPageEventHandler(this.PrintPage);

// Print document
myDocument.Print();
// Dispose of document when done printing
myDocument.Dispose();
```

This code assumes the method **PrintPage** is available. Let's see how to build such a method.

Printing Pages of a Document

The **PrintDocument** object provides (in its **PrintPage** event) a graphics object (**e.Graphics**) for 'drawing' our pages. And, that's just what we do using familiar graphics methods. For each page in our printed document, we draw the desired text information (**DrawString** method), any lines (**DrawLine** method), rectangles (**DrawRectangle** method) or images (**DrawImage** method).

Once a page is completely drawn to the graphics object, we 'tell' the **PrintDocument** object to print it. We repeat this process for each page we want to print. This does require a little bit of work on your part. You must know how many pages your document has and what goes on each page. I usually define a page number variable to help keep track of the current page being drawn.

Once a page is complete, there are two possibilities: there are more pages to print or there are no more pages to print. The **e.HasMorePages** property (Boolean) is used specify which possibility exists. If a page is complete and there are still more pages to print, use:

```
e.HasMorePages = true;
```

In this case, the **PrintDocument** object will return to the **PrintPages** event for the next page. If the page is complete and printing is complete (no more pages), use:

```
e.HasMorePages = false;
```

This tells the **PrintDocument** object its job is done. At this point, you should dispose of the **PrintDocument** object.

Let's look at the graphics object for a single page. The boundaries of the
printed page are defined by the **e.MarginBounds** properties (these are
established by the **PrinterSettings** property):

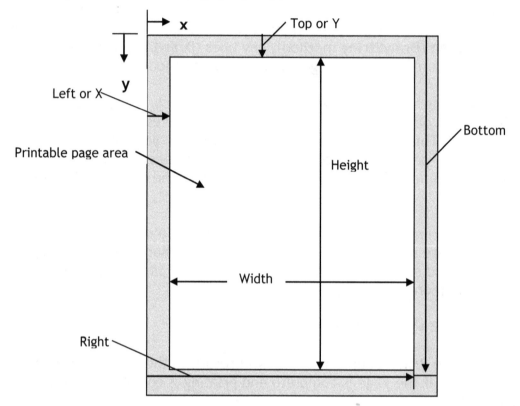

This becomes our palette for positioning items on a page. All values are in units
of 1/100th of an inch. Horizontal position is governed by **x** (increases from 0 to
the right) and vertical position is governed by **y** (increases from 0 to the
bottom).

The process for each page is to decide "what goes where" and then position the
desired information using the appropriate graphics method. Any of the graphics
methods we have learned can be used to put information on the graphic object.
Here, we limit the discussion to printing text, lines, rectangles and images.

To place text on the graphics object (**e.Graphics**), use the **DrawString** method introduced in Chapter 9. To place the string **myString** at position (**x, y**), using the font object **myFont** and brush object **myBrush**, the syntax is:

```
e.Graphics.DrawString(myString, myFont, myBrush, x, y);
```

With this statement, you can place any text, anywhere you like, with any font, any color and any brush style. You just need to make the desired specifications. Each line of text on a printed page will require a **DrawString** statement.

Also in Chapter 9, we discussed methods for determining the size of strings. This is helpful for both vertical and horizontal placement of text on a page. To determine the height (in pixels) of a particular font, use:

```
myFont.GetHeight();
```

If you need width and height of a string use:

```
e.Graphics.MeasureString(myString, myFont);
```

This method returns a **SizeF** structure with two properties: **Width** and **Height** (both in 1/100th of an inch). These two properties are useful for justifying (left, right, center, vertical) text strings.

Many times, you use lines in a document to delineate various sections. To draw a line on the graphics object, use the **DrawLine** method (from Chapter 8):

```
e.Graphics.DrawLine(myPen, x1, y1, x2, y2);
```

This statement will draw a line from (**x1, y1**) to (**x2, y2**) using the pen object **myPen**.

To draw a rectangle (used with tables or graphics regions), use the **DrawRectangle** method (from Chapter 8):

```
e.Graphics.DrawRectangle(myPen, x1, y1, x2, y2);
```

This statement will draw a rectangle with upper left corner at (**x1, y1**) and lower right corner at (**x2, y2**) using the pen object **myPen**.

Finally, the **DrawImage** method (from Chapter 9) is used to position an image (**myImage**) object on a page. The syntax is:

```
e.Graphics.DrawImage(myImage, x, y, width, height);
```

The upper left corner of **myImage** will be at (**x, y**) with the specified **width** and **height**. Any image will be scaled to fit the specified region.

If **DrawImage** is to be used to print the contents of a panel control hosting a graphics object, you must insure the graphics are persistent as discussed in Chapter 9. We review those steps. For a panel named **pnlExample**, establish the **BackgroundImage** as an empty bitmap:

```
pnlExample.BackgroundImage = new
Bitmap(pnlExample.ClientSize.Width,
pnlExample.ClientSize.Height,
Imaging.PixelFormat.Format24bppRgb);
```

Then, establish the drawing object **myObject** using:

```
myObject = Graphics.FromImage(pnlExample.BackgroundImage);
```

Now, any graphics methods applied to this object will be persistent. To maintain this persistence, after each drawing operation to this object, use:

```
pnlExample.Refresh();
```

The image in this object can then be printed with the **DrawImage** method:

```
e.Graphics.DrawImage(pnlExample.BackgroundImage, x, y,
width, height);
```

The upper left corner of the image will be at (**x, y**) with the specified **width** and **height**. The image will be scaled to fit the specified region.

We've seen all of these graphics methods before, so their use should be familiar. You should note that each item on a printed page requires at least one line of code. That results in lots of coding for printing. So, if you're writing lots of code in your print routines, you're probably doing it right. Look at this little code snippet (this assumes we have a picture box control named **picMap** with a persistent **Image** property):

```
// Draw map
e.Graphics.DrawImage(picMap.Image, e.MarginBounds.Left +
20, e.MarginBounds.Top + 20, e.MarginBounds.Width - 40,
(int) (0.5 * e.MarginBounds.Height - 40));

// Draw rectangle around map
e.Graphics.DrawRectangle(Pens.Black, e.MarginBounds.Left +
20, e.MarginBounds.Top + 20, e.MarginBounds.Width - 40,
(int) (0.5 * e.MarginBounds.Height - 40));

// Draw line near middle of page
e.Graphics.DrawLine(Pens.Black, e.MarginBounds.Left,
e.MarginBounds.Top + (int) (0.5 * e.MarginBounds.Height),
e.MarginBounds.Right, e.MarginBounds.Top + (int) (0.5 *
e.MarginBounds.Height));

// Draw string under line
e.Graphics.DrawString("This is my map!!", new
Font("Arial", 48, FontStyle.Bold), Brushes.Black,
e.MarginBounds.Left, e.MarginBounds.Top + (int) (0.5 *
e.MarginBounds.Height + 50));
```

Can you see this code will produce this printed page?

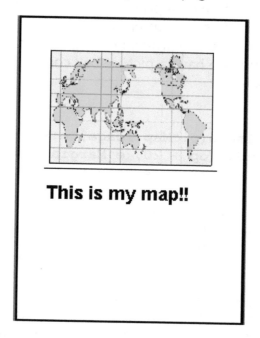

The image (**picMap**) is drawn with a rectangle surrounding it. Then, a line near mid page, then the string "This is my map!!" Of course, this assumes that the PrintDocument object is created and connected to the PrintPage event.

The best way to learn how to print in Visual C# is to do lots of it. You'll develop your own approaches and techniques as you gain familiarity. You might want to see how some of the other graphics methods (**DrawEllipse**, **DrawLines**, **DrawCurves**) might work with printing. Or, look at different brush and pen objects.

Many print jobs just involve the user clicking a button marked '**Print**' and the results appear on printed page with no further interaction. If more interaction is desired, there are three dialog controls that help specify desired printing job properties: **PageSetupDialog**, **PrintDialog**, and **PrintPreviewDialog**. Using these controls adds more code to your application. You must take any user inputs and implement these values in your program. We'll show what each control can do and let you decide if you want to use them in your work. The **PrintPreviewDialog** control is especially cool!!

PageSetupDialog Control

In Toolbox:

Below Form (Default Properties):

The **PageSetupDialog** control allows the user to set various parameters regarding a printing task. This is the same dialog box that appears in most Windows applications. Users can set border and margin adjustments, headers and footers, and portrait vs. landscape orientation.

PageSetupDialog **Properties:**

Name	Gets or sets the name of the page setup dialog (I usually name this control **dlgSetup**).
AllowMargins	Gets or sets a value indicating whether the margins section of the dialog box is enabled.
AllowOrientation	Gets or sets a value indicating whether the orientation section of the dialog box (landscape vs. portrait) is enabled.
AllowPaper	Gets or sets a value indicating whether the paper section of the dialog box (paper size and paper source) is enabled.
AllowPrinter	Gets or sets a value indicating whether the Printer button is enabled.
Document	Gets or sets a value indicating the PrintDocument to get page settings from.
MinMargins	Gets or sets a value indicating the minimum margins the user is allowed to select, in hundredths of an inch.
PageSettings	Gets or sets a value indicating the page settings to modify.
PrinterSettings	Gets or sets the printer settings the dialog box is to modify when the user clicks the Printer button

FontDialog **Methods:**

ShowDialog	Displays the dialog box. Returned value indicates which button was clicked by user (**OK** or **Cancel**).

To use the **PageSetupDialog** control, we add it to our application the same as any control. It will appear in the tray below the form. Once added, we set a few properties. Then, we write code to make the dialog box appear when desired. The user then makes selections and closes the dialog box. At this point, we use the provided information for our tasks.

The **ShowDialog** method is used to display the **PageSetupDialog** control. For a control named **dlgSetup**, the appropriate code is:

```
dlgSetup.ShowDialog();
```

And the displayed dialog box is:

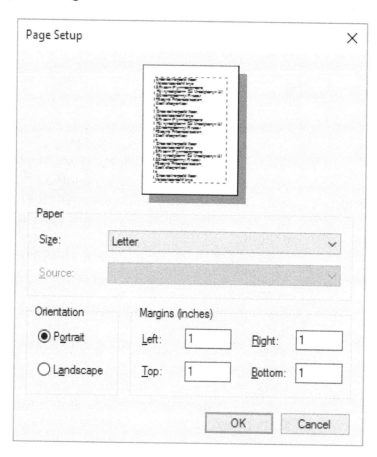

The user makes any desired choices. Once complete, the **OK** button is clicked. At this point, various properties are available for use (namely **PageSettings** and **PrinterSettings**). **Cancel** can be clicked to cancel the changes. The ShowDialog method returns the clicked button. It returns **DialogResult.OK** if OK is clicked and returns **DialogResult.Cancel** if Cancel is clicked.

Typical use of **PageSetupDialog** control:

> ➢ Set the **Name** property. Decide what options should be available.
> ➢ Use **ShowDialog** method to display dialog box, prior to printing.
> ➢ Use **PageSettings** and **PrinterSetting** properties to change printed output.

PrintDialog Control

In Toolbox:

Below Form (Default Properties):

The **PrintDialog** control allows the user to select which printer to use, choose page orientation, printed page range and number of copies. This is the same dialog box that appears in many Windows applications.

PrintDialog **Properties:**

Name	Gets or sets the name of the print dialog (I usually name this control **dlgPrint**).
AllowPrintToFile	Gets or sets a value indicating whether the Print to file check box is enabled.
AllowSelection	Gets or sets a value indicating whether the From... To... Page option button is enabled.
AllowSomePages	Gets or sets a value indicating whether the Pages option button is enabled.
Document	Gets or sets a value indicating the PrintDocument used to obtain PrinterSettings.
PrinterSettings	Gets or sets the PrinterSettings the dialog box is to modify.
PrintToFile	Gets or sets a value indicating whether the Print to file check box is checked

PrintDialog **Methods:**

ShowDialog	Displays the dialog box. Returned value indicates which button was clicked by user (**OK** or **Cancel**).

To use the **PrintDialog** control, we add it to our application the same as any control. It will appear in the tray below the form. Once added, we set a few properties. Then, we write code to make the dialog box appear when desired. The user then makes selections and closes the dialog box. At this point, we use the provided information for our tasks.

The **ShowDialog** method is used to display the **PrintDialog** control. For a control named **dlgPrint**, the appropriate code is:

```
dlgPrint.ShowDialog();
```

And the displayed dialog box is:

The user makes any desired choices. Once complete, the **OK** button is clicked. At this point, various properties are available for use (namely **PrinterSettings**). **Cancel** can be clicked to cancel the changes. The ShowDialog method returns the clicked button. It returns **DialogResult.OK** if OK is clicked and returns **DialogResult.Cancel** if Cancel is clicked.

Typical use of **PrintDialog** control:

> ➤ Set the **Name** property. Decide what options should be available.
> ➤ Use **ShowDialog** method to display dialog box, prior to printing with the PrintDocument object.
> ➤ Use **PrinterSettings** properties to change printed output.

PrintPreviewDialog Control

In Toolbox:

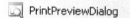

Below Form (Default Properties):

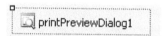

The **PrintPreviewDialog** control is a great addition to Visual C#. It lets the user see printed output in preview mode. They can view all pages, format page views and zoom in on or out of any. The previewed document can also be printed from this control. This is also a useful "temporary" control for a programmer to use while developing printing routines. By viewing printed pages in a preview mode, rather than on a printed page, many trees are saved as you fine tune your printing code.

PrintPreviewDialog **Properties**:

Name	Gets or sets the name of the print preview dialog (I usually name this control **dlgPreview**)
AcceptButton	Gets or sets the button on the form that is clicked when the user presses the <Enter> key.
Document	Gets or sets the document to preview.
Text	Gets or sets the text associated with this control.

PrintPreviewDialog **Methods**:

ShowDialog	Displays the dialog box. Returned value indicates which button was clicked by user (**OK** or **Cancel**).

To use the **PrintDialog** control, we add it to our application the same as any control. It will appear in the tray below the form. Once added, we set a few properties, primarily **Document**. Make sure the **PrintPage** event Is properly coded for the selected **Document**. Add code to make the dialog box appear when desired. The document pages will be generated and the user can see it in the preview window.

The **ShowDialog** method is used to display the **PrintPreviewDialog** control. For a control named **dlgPreview**, the appropriate code is:

```
dlgPreview.ShowDialog();
```

And the displayed dialog box (with no document) is:

The user can use the various layout, zoom and print options in previewing the displayed document. When done, the user closes the dialog control.

Typical use of **PrintPreviewDialog** control:

> ➢ Set the **Name** property. Set the **Document** property.
> ➢ Use **ShowDialog** method to display dialog box and see the previewed document.

Example 10-6

Printing

1. Start a new project. In this project, you'll print out a list of countries and capitals, along with a map of the world. Add two button controls to the form. Also add a print preview dialog control and a print dialog control. Set the properties of the form and each object.

   Form1:

Name	frmPrinting
FormBorderStyle	FixedSingle
StartPosition	CenterScreen
Text	Printing Example

   button1:

Name	btnPreview
Text	Preview

   button2:

Name	btnPrint
Text	Print

   printPreviewDialog1:

Name	dlgPreview

   printDialog1:

Name	dlgPrint
AllowPrintToFile	False

Your form should now look like this:

Other controls in tray:

2. In the **LearnVCS\VCS Code\Class 10\Example 10-6** folder is a map graphic named **world.wmf**. Copy this graphic into your application's **Bin\Debug** folder (you may have to create the folder first). The code below assumes the map graphic is in the application folder. We use the **Application.StartupPath** parameter to identify this folder

3. Add this **using** statement at the top of the code window:

```
using System.Drawing.Printing;
```

4. Form Level Scope Declarations:

```
int pageNumber;
PrintDocument myDocument;
Image myImage;
const int numberCountries = 62;
const int countriesPerPage = 25;
string[] country = new string[numberCountries];
string[] capital = new string[numberCountries];
bool lastPage;
```

5. Use the following code in the **frmPrinting Load** event (loads country/capital arrays and map image):

```
private void FrmPrinting_Load(object sender, EventArgs e)
{
    // Load country/capital arrays
    country[0] = "Afghanistan" ; capital[0] = "Kabul";
    country[1] = "Albania" ; capital[1] = "Tirane";
    country[2] = "Australia" ; capital[2] = "Canberra";
    country[3] = "Austria" ; capital[3] = "Vienna";
    country[4] = "Bangladesh" ; capital[4] = "Dacca";
```

```
country[5] = "Barbados" ; capital[5] = "Bridgetown";
country[6] = "Belgium" ; capital[6] = "Brussels";
country[7] = "Bulgaria" ; capital[7] = "Sofia";
country[8] = "Burma" ; capital[8] = "Rangoon";
country[9] = "Cambodia" ; capital[9] = "Phnom Penh";
country[10] = "China" ; capital[10] = "Peking";
country[11] = "Czechoslovakia" ; capital[11] = "Prague";
country[12] = "Denmark" ; capital[12] = "Copenhagen";
country[13] = "Egypt" ; capital[13] = "Cairo";
country[14] = "Finland" ; capital[14] = "Helsinki";
country[15] = "France" ; capital[15] = "Paris";
country[16] = "Germany" ; capital[16] = " Berlin";
country[17] = "Greece" ; capital[17] = "Athens";
country[18] = "Hungary" ; capital[18] = "Budapest";
country[19] = "Iceland" ; capital[19] = "Reykjavik";
country[20] = "India" ; capital[20] = "New Delhi";
country[21] = "Indonesia" ; capital[21] = "Jakarta";
country[22] = "Iran" ; capital[22] = "Tehran";
country[23] = "Iraq" ; capital[23] = "Baghdad";
country[24] = "Ireland" ; capital[24] = "Dublin";
country[25] = "Israel" ; capital[25] = "Jerusalem";
country[26] = "Italy" ; capital[26] = "Rome";
country[27] = "Japan" ; capital[27] = "Tokyo";
country[28] = "Jordan" ; capital[28] = "Amman";
country[29] = "Kuwait" ; capital[29] = "Kuwait";
country[30] = "Laos" ; capital[30] = "Vientiane";
country[31] = "Lebanon" ; capital[31] = "Beirut";
country[32] = "Luxembourg" ; capital[32] = "Luxembourg";
country[33] = "Malaysia" ; capital[33] = "Kuala Lumpur";
country[34] = "Mongolia" ; capital[34] = "Ulaanbaatar";
country[35] = "Nepal" ; capital[35] = "Katmandu";
country[36] = "Netherlands" ; capital[36] = "Amsterdam";
country[37] = "New Zealand" ; capital[37] =
"Wellington";
country[38] = "North Korea" ; capital[38] = "Pyongyang";
country[39] = "Norway" ; capital[39] = "Oslo";
country[40] = "Oman" ; capital[40] = "Muscat";
country[41] = "Pakistan" ; capital[41] = "Islamabad";
country[42] = "Philippines" ; capital[42] = "Manila";
country[43] = "Poland" ; capital[43] = "Warsaw";
country[44] = "Portugal" ; capital[44] = "Lisbon";
country[45] = "Romania" ; capital[45] = "Bucharest";
country[46] = "Russia" ; capital[46] = "Moscow";
country[47] = "Saudi Arabia" ; capital[47] = "Riyadh";
country[48] = "Singapore" ; capital[48] = "Singapore";
country[49] = "South Korea" ; capital[49] = "Seoul";
country[50] = "Spain" ; capital[50] = "Madrid";
```

```
country[51] = "Sri Lanka" ; capital[51] = "Colombo";
country[52] = "Sweden" ; capital[52] = "Stockholm";
country[53] = "Switzerland" ; capital[53] = "Bern";
country[54] = "Syria" ; capital[54] = "Damascus";
country[55] = "Taiwan" ; capital[55] = "Taipei";
country[56] = "Thailand" ; capital[56] = "Bangkok";
country[57] = "Turkey" ; capital[57] = "Ankara";
country[58] = "United Kingdom" ; capital[58] = "London";
country[59] = "Vietnam" ; capital[59] = "Hanoi";
country[60] = "Yemen" ; capital[60] = "Sana";
country[61] = "Yugoslavia" ; capital[61] = "Belgrade";
myImage = Image.FromFile(Application.StartupPath +
"\\world.wmf");
}
```

6. Add this code to the **btnPreview Click** event (sets up document for preview):

```
private void BtnPreview_Click(object sender, EventArgs e)
{
  // preview printing
  pageNumber = 1; lastPage = false;
  // create document
  myDocument = new PrintDocument();
  myDocument.DocumentName = "World Capitals";
  myDocument.PrintPage += new
PrintPageEventHandler(this.PrintPage);
  // preview dialog
  dlgPreview.Document = myDocument;
  dlgPreview.Text = "Countries and Capitals";
  dlgPreview.ShowDialog();
  myDocument.Dispose();
}
```

7. Add this code to the **btnPrint Click** event (sets up document for printing):

```
private void BtnPrint_Click(object sender, EventArgs e)
{
  // do printing
  pageNumber = 1; lastPage = false;
  // create document
  myDocument = new PrintDocument();
  myDocument.DocumentName = "World Capitals";
  myDocument.PrintPage += new
PrintPageEventHandler(this.PrintPage);
  // print dialog
  dlgPrint.Document = myDocument;
  if (dlgPrint.ShowDialog() == DialogResult.OK)
  {
    myDocument.Print();
  }
  myDocument.Dispose();
}
```

8. Create this **PrintPage** general method. This code establishes what is printed on each page:

```
private void PrintPage(object sender, PrintPageEventArgs
e)
{
  Font printFont;
  SizeF sSize;
  int y, i, iEnd;
  float ratio;
  // here you decide what goes on each page and draw it
there
  // print countries/capitals and map on different pages
  if (!lastPage)
  {
    // on firstpages, put titles and countries/capitals
    printFont = new Font("Arial", 20, FontStyle.Bold);
    sSize = e.Graphics.MeasureString("Countries and
Capitals - Page " + pageNumber.ToString(), printFont);
    e.Graphics.DrawString("Countries and Capitals - Page "
+ pageNumber.ToString(), printFont, Brushes.Black,
e.MarginBounds.Left + (int) (0.5 * (e.MarginBounds.Width -
sSize.Width)), e.MarginBounds.Top);
    // starting y position
    printFont = new Font("Arial", 14,
FontStyle.Underline);
```

```
      y = (int) (e.MarginBounds.Top + 4 *
printFont.GetHeight());
      e.Graphics.DrawString("Country", printFont,
Brushes.Black, e.MarginBounds.X, y);
      e.Graphics.DrawString("Capital", printFont,
Brushes.Black, (int) (e.MarginBounds.X + 0.5 *
e.MarginBounds.Width), y);
      y += (int) (2 * printFont.GetHeight());
      printFont = new Font("Arial", 14, FontStyle.Regular);
      iEnd = countriesPerPage * pageNumber;
      if (iEnd > numberCountries)
      {
        iEnd = numberCountries;
        lastPage = true;
      }
      for (i = countriesPerPage * (pageNumber - 1); i <
iEnd; i++)
      {
        e.Graphics.DrawString(country[i], printFont,
Brushes.Black, e.MarginBounds.X, y);
        e.Graphics.DrawString(capital[i], printFont,
Brushes.Black, (int) (e.MarginBounds.X + 0.5 *
e.MarginBounds.Width), y);
        y += (int) (printFont.GetHeight());
      }
      pageNumber++;
      e.HasMorePages = true;
    }
    else
    {
      // on last page draw map and  a rectangle around map
region
      // maintain original width/height ratio
      ratio = ((float) myImage.Width / myImage.Height);
      e.Graphics.DrawImage(myImage, e.MarginBounds.Left,
e.MarginBounds.Top, e.MarginBounds.Width, (int)
(e.MarginBounds.Height / ratio));
      e.Graphics.DrawRectangle(Pens.Black,
e.MarginBounds.Left, e.MarginBounds.Top,
e.MarginBounds.Width, (int) (e.MarginBounds.Height /
ratio));
      e.HasMorePages = false;
      pageNumber = 1;
      lastPage = false;
    }
  }
```

9. Save your project (saved in **Example 10-6** folder in the **LearnVCS\VCS Code\Class 10** folder). Run the application. Try the preview function (click **Preview**) and see how nicely it displays the printed document. Here's the first page:

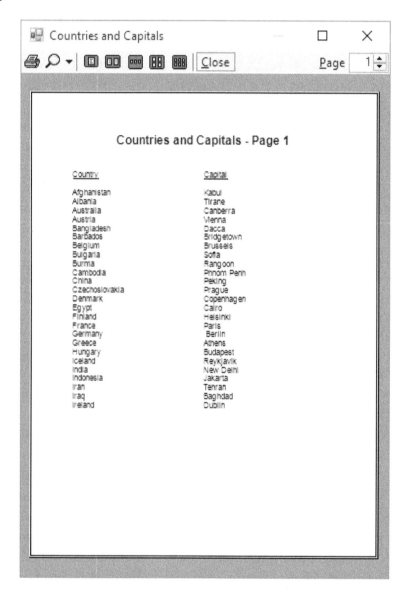

And the map is on the last page:

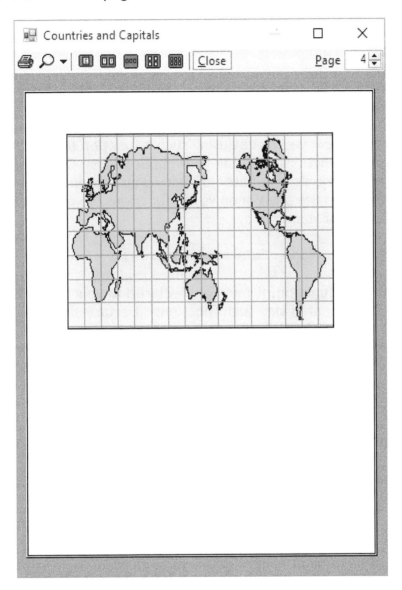

If you want, print out the document on your printer by clicking **Print.**

Using the Windows API

The Windows **Application Programming Interface** (**API**) consists of hundreds of functions (usually written in languages like C and C++). These functions are used by virtually every Windows application to perform functions like displaying windows, file manipulation, printer control, menus and dialog boxes, multimedia, string manipulation, graphics, and managing memory. We can use these functions in a Visual C# application to accomplish tasks not possible using any other methods. Here we look at using such a function for timing. You may choose to find other functions useful in your applications. Consult one of the many API references (either text based or web based) for information on available functions. To use any Windows API functions, you need this **using** statement at the top of your code:

```
using System.Runtime.InteropServices;
```

Before you use an API function, it must be **declared** in your Visual C# code – this lets Visual C# know you are using such functions. Declare statements are placed with form level variables in the code window. The declaration statement informs your program which DLL to use, the name of the API function, and the number, order and type of arguments it takes. This is analogous to function prototyping in the C/C++ languages. For an API function (**APIFcn**), the syntax is:

```
[DllImport(DLLname)] public static extern type
APIFcn([argument list]);
```

where **DLLname** is a string specifying the name of the DLL (dynamic link library) file that contains the method and **type** is the returned value type.

Once declared, using an API function is not much different from using a general method in Visual C#. Just make sure you pass it the correct number and correct type of arguments in the correct order. For our example (**APIFcn**), proper syntax is:

```
returnValue = APIFcn(arguments);
```

The argument list has the usual syntax:

```
type argument1, type argument2, ...
```

It is very important, when using API functions, that argument lists be correct, both regarding number, type and order. If the list is not correct, very bad things can happen. We need to show this same care using built-in and general methods in Visual C#; the consequences of an error are usually not as severe, however.

And, it is critical that the **declaration** statement be correct. Proper formats can be found in any of the multitude of books written on the Windows API and several Internet sites offer help. We will only use one API function. We will provide the correct declaration statement. Declaration statements for other API functions you might want to use are provided with the documentation for the particular API function.

There is a price to pay for using the Windows API. Once you leave the protective surroundings of the Visual C# environment, as you must to use the API, you get to taunt and tease the dreaded general protection fault (**GPF**) monster, which can bring your entire computer system to a screeching halt! So, be careful. And, if you don't have to use API functions, don't.

Lastly, **always, always, always save** your Visual C# application before testing any API calls. More good code has gone down the tubes with GPF's - they are very difficult to recover from. Sometimes, the trusty on-off switch is the only recovery mechanism.

Timing with the Windows API

Often you need some method of **timing** within an application. You may want to know how long a certain routine takes to execute for performance evaluation. You may need to time a student as they take an on-line quiz. You might want to perform "real-time" simulation where the computer produces real-life results. Sports simulations and racing games are examples of such simulations. Or, you might want to build an on-screen clock. Each of these examples requires the ability to compute an elapsed time. Depending on the accuracy you need, there are different methods to compute elapsed time in a Visual C# application.

Visual C# provides some methods for computing times. We looked at one method in the very first chapter - the **Now** method. The **Now** method returns the current date and time as a **DateTime** data type. The time is given in hours, minutes and seconds. Hence, elapsed times can be computed with **one second resolution**. Such resolution is adequate for an on-screen clock, but not very useful for timing a swimmer doing a 50 meter freestyle.

Many computations require **millisecond** (1/1000th of a second) **resolution**. To obtain this level of resolution, we turn to the Windows API and the **GetTickCount** function. This function returns an **int** data type that represents the number of milliseconds that have elapsed since you turned your computer on. The **declaration** statement for **GetTickCount** is:

```
[DllImport("kernel32.dll")]
public static extern int GetTickCount();
```

Note there are no arguments.

GetTickCount (as well as the Visual C# **Now** function) is almost always used to compute an elapsed time (or difference between two times). The actual value returned by **GetTickCount** is not interesting by itself. The only time you might use it is if you had some need to know how long your computer has been on. The usage syntax to compute an elapsed time (in milliseconds) is:

```
int startTime;
int elapsedTime;
     .
startTime = GetTickCount();
     .
  [Do some stuff here]
     .
elapsedTime = GetTickCount() - startTime;
```

<u>**Example 10-7**</u>

Stopwatch Application (Revisited)

1. Remember way back in Class 1 where we built our first Visual C# application, a stopwatch. That stopwatch provided timing with one second of resolution. We'll modify that example here, using **GetTickCount** to do our timing. This will give us resolution to within $1/1000^{th}$ of a second. Load **Example 1-3** from long, long ago (saved in **Example 1-3** folder of **LearnVCS\VCS Code\Class 1** folder).

2. Add this declaration at the top of the code window:

   ```
   using System.Runtime.InteropServices;
   ```

3. Copy the **GetTickCount** declaration statement from these notes and paste it into the code window. Recall this declaration goes in the same area as the form level variables. Also change all times to **double** data types (times will printed as decimal numbers). This code is (new and/or modified code is shaded):

   ```
   double startTime;
   double endTime;
   double elapsedTime;
   [DllImport("kernel32.dll")]
   public static extern int GetTickCount();
   ```

4. Modify the **btnStart Click** procedure where shaded:

   ```
   private void BtnStart_Click(object sender, EventArgs e)
   {
     // Establish and print starting time
     startTime = GetTickCount() / 1000.0;
     txtStart.Text = String.Format("{0:f3}", startTime);
     txtEnd.Text = "";
     txtElapsed.Text = "";
   }
   ```

5. Modify the **btnEnd Click** procedure as shaded:

```
private void BtnEnd_Click(object sender, EventArgs e)
{
    // Find the ending time, compute the elapsed time
    // Put both values in text boxes
    endTime = GetTickCount() / 1000.0;
    elapsedTime = endTime - startTime;
    txtEnd.Text = String.Format("{0:f3}", endTime);
    txtElapsed.Text = String.Format("{0:f3}", elapsedTime);
}
```

6. Run the application and save it (saved in **Example 10-7** folder in the **LearnVCS\VCS Code\Class 10** folder). Note we now have timing with millisecond (as opposed to one second) accuracy. Here's a run I made:

Also note the values in the start and end time label controls are not of much use. There's even a chance they'll be negative numbers! How's that, you ask? The value returned by GetTickCount is an **int** data type. The maximum value that can be represented by this data type is 2,147,483,647. Once that number of milliseconds has elapsed (a little less than 25 days), the value can't increase anymore or an overflow error will result. At this point, the returned value switches to -2,147,483,648, the smallest value possible and starts increasing again. So, if your computer has been on for over 25 days, you may see negative values for **GetTickCount**. The returned value always increases, though. Hence, elapsed times will always be positive. But, think about what happens if you're trying to compute an elapsed time when this switch from a very large positive number to a very large negative number occurs.

Adding a Help System to Your Application

When someone is using a Windows application and gets stumped about what to do next, instinct tells the user to press the **<F1>** function key. Long ago, someone in the old DOS world decided this would be the magic "Help Me!" key. Users expect help when pressing <F1> (I'm sure you rely on it a lot when using Visual C#). If nothing appears after pressing <F1>, user frustration sets in – not a good thing.

All Visual C# applications written for other than your personal use should include some form of an **on-line help system**. It doesn't have to be elegant, but it should be there. Adding a **help file** to your Visual C# application will give it real polish, as well as making it easier to use. In this section, we will show you how to build a very basic on-line help system for your applications. This system will simply have a list of help topics the user can choose from.

We create what is known as an **HTML help** system. HTML stands for **hypertext markup language** and is the 'programming' language of choice for generating web pages. This language will be used to generate and display the topics displayed in the help system. Fortunately, we won't need to learn much (if any) HTML. Building an HTML help system involves several files and several steps. In diagram form, we have:

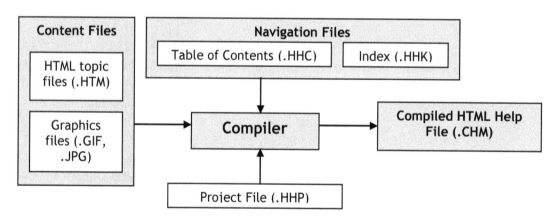

We need to create topic files (.**HTM** files) for each topic in our help system. (We could also add graphics.) These topics are organized by a Table of Contents file (.**HHC**) and Index file (.**HHK**). The Project File (.**HHP**) specifies the components of a help project. All of these files are 'compiled' to create the finished help file (.**CHM**). This file is the file that can be opened for viewing the finished help system.

The developed help system is similar to help systems used by all Windows applications. As an example, here is a help system (.CHM file) that explains how to add or remove programs from your computer:

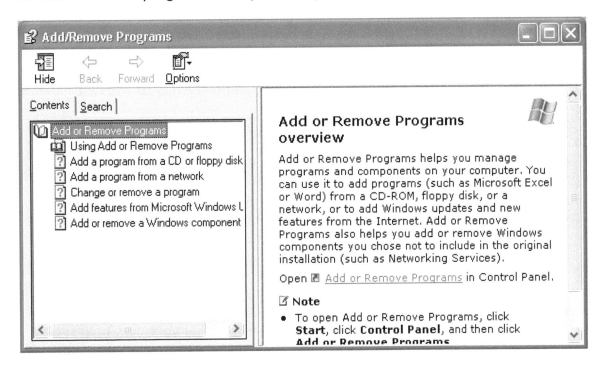

The left frame is a hierarchical structure (**Contents**) of clickable topics. The right frame displays the currently selected topic information. Other tabs in the left frame allow a user to browse an **Index** (none shown here) and **Search** the help file. The file also features several navigation features and print options. The key point here is that this help system is familiar to your user. No new instruction is needed in how to use on-line help.

We will build an HTML help system similar to the one displayed above, but with minimal features. Learning how to build a full-featured help system would be a course in itself. In this chapter, we will learn how to create text-only topics, add a contents file, create a project file and see how to compile the entire package into a useful (if simple) help system.

Creating a Help File

We could create a help system using only text editors if we knew the required structure for the various files. We won't take that approach. The on-line help system will be built using the **Microsoft HTML Help Workshop**. This is a free product from Microsoft that greatly simplifies the building of a help system. The workshop lets you build and organize all the files needed for building the help system. Once built, simple clicks allow compiling and viewing of the help system.

So, obviously, you need to have the workshop installed on your computer. The **HTML Help Workshop** can be downloaded from various Microsoft web sites. To find a download link, go to Microsoft's web site (http://www.microsoft.com). Search on "**HTML Help**" – the search results should display a topic **HTML Downloads**. Select that link and you will be led to a place where you can do the download. Once downloaded, install the workshop as directed.

Creating a complete help file is a major task and sometimes takes as much time as creating the application itself! Because of this, we will only skim over the steps involved, generate a simple example, and provide guidance for further reference. There are five major steps involved in building your own help file:

1. Create your application and develop a hierarchical list of help system topics. This list would consist of headings and topics under specific headings.
2. Create the **topic files** (**HTM** extensions). Please make sure you spell and grammar check your topic files. If there are mistakes in your help system, your user base may not have much confidence in the care you showed in developing your application.
3. Create a **Table of Contents** (**HHC** extension).
4. Create the **Help Project File** (**HHP** extension).
5. Compile the help file to create your finished help system (**CHM** extension).

Step 1 is application-dependent. Here, we'll look at how to use the HTML Help Workshop to complete the last four steps.

Starting the HTML Help Workshop

We will demonstrate the use of the **HTML Help Workshop** to build a very basic help system. The help file will have two headings. Each heading will have three sub-topics:

Heading 1
    Topic 1
    Topic 2
    Topic 3
Heading 2
    Topic 1
    Topic 2
    Topic 3

Though simple, the steps followed here can be used to build an adequate help system. All of the files created while building this help system can be found in the **LearnVCS\VCS Code\Class 10\Sample Help** folder.

If properly installed, there will be an entry for the help workshop on your computer's **Programs** menu. Click **Start**, then **All apps**. Select **HTML Help Workshop**, then **HTML Help Workshop** again. This dialog box should appear:

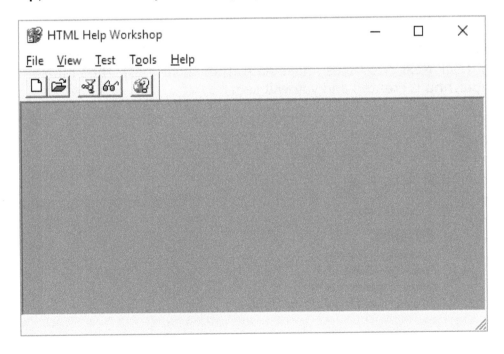

We want to start a new project. Select **New** under the **File** menu. In the selection box that appears, choose **Project** and click **OK**. A cute little **New Project Wizard** appears:

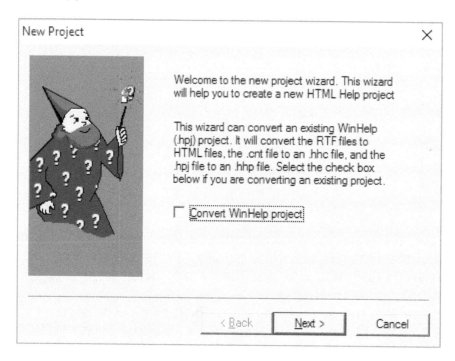

All we need to tell the wizard at this point is the name of our project file. Click **Next**. On the next screen, find (or create) the folder to hold your files (again, I used **LearnVCS\VCS Code\Class 10\Sample Help**) and use the project name **Sample**. Click **Next** two times (make no further selections), then **Finish**. The file **Sample.hhp** is created and you will see:

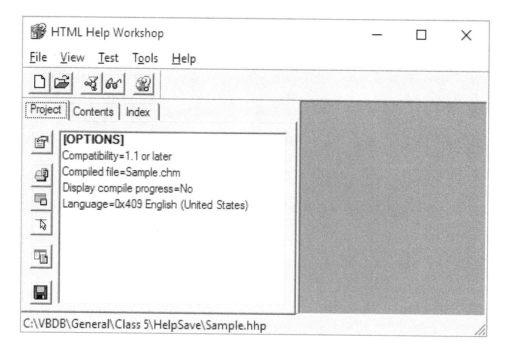

Creating Topic Files

At this point, we are ready to create our topic files. These are the files your user can view for help on topics listed in the contents region of the help system. We will have eight such files in our example (one for each of the two headings and one for each of the two sets of three topics).

Each file is individually created and saved as an HTM file. To create the first file (for Heading 1), choose **New** under the **File** menu. Select **HTML File** and click **OK**. Enter a name for the file (**Heading 1**) and click **OK**. A topic file HTML framework will appear:

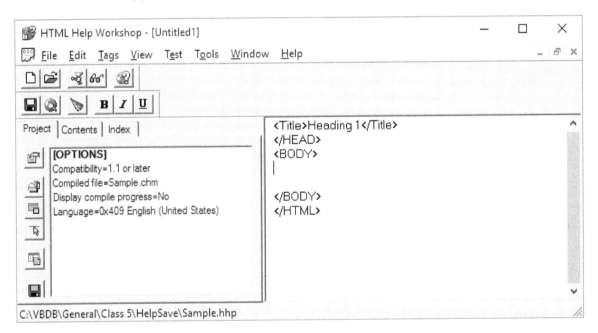

The window on the right is where you type your topic information. The file has some HTML code there already. If you've never seen HTML before, don't panic. We will make it easy. We are only concerned with what goes between the **<BODY>** and **</BODY>** 'tags'. These tags mark the beginning and end of the text displayed when a user selects this particular heading topic.

Most HTML tags work in pairs. The first tag says start something, then the second tag with the slash preface **</>** says stop something. Hence, **<BODY>** says the body of the text starts here. The **</BODY>** tag says the body stops here. It's really pretty easy to understand HTML.

It would help to know just a little more HTML to make your text have a nice appearance. To change the font, use the **FONT** tag:

    <FONT FACE="FontName" SIZE="FontSize">

where **FontName** is the name of the desired font and **FontSize** the desired size. Notice this is very similar to the **Font** constructor in Visual C#. When you are done with one font and want to specify a new one, you must use a **</FONT>** tag before specifying the new font. To bold text, use the **<STRONG>** and **</STRONG>** tags. To delineate a paragraph in HTML, use the **<P>** and **</P>** tags. To cause a line break, use **
**. There is no corresponding </BR> tag.

So, using our minimal HTML knowledge (if you know more, use it), we can create our first topic file. The HTML I used to create the first topic (**Heading1**) is:

```
<BODY>
<STRONG>
This is Heading 1
</STRONG>
<P>
This is where I explain what the subtopics available under this heading are.
</P>
</BODY>
```

This HTML will create this finished topic:

This is Heading 1

This is where I explain what the subtopics available under this heading are.

When done typing this first topic, choose **Close File** under the **File** menu. Select a file name (I used **Heading1.HTM**) to use and save the topic file. Of course, at any time, you can reopen, modify and resave any topic file.

You repeat the above process for every topic in your help system. That is, create a new file, type your topic and save it. You will have an HTM file for every topic in your help system. For our example, create seven more HTM files using whatever text and formatting you desire. The files I created are saved as: **Heading1.HTM, Topic11.HTM, Topic12.HTM, Topic13.HTM, Heading2.HTM, Topic21.HTM, Topic22.HTM, Topic23.HTM.**

Creating HTML topic files using the Help Workshop is a bit tedious. You need to use HTML tags and don't really know what your topic file will look like until you've completed the help system. Using a **WYSIWYG** (what you see is what you get) editor is a better choice. Such editors allow you to create HTML files without knowing any HTML. You just type the file in a normal word processing-type environment, then save it in HTML format. There are several WYSIWYG HTML editors available. Check Internet download sites for options. Also, most word processors offer an option to save a document as an HTML file. I always use a WYSIWYG editor for topic files. I simply save each topic file in the same folder as my help system files, just as if I was using the built-in editor.

Next, we create a **Table of Contents** file. But, before leaving your topic files, make sure they are as complete and accurate as possible. And, again, please check for misspellings - nothing scares a user more than a poorly prepared help file. They quickly draw the conclusion that if the help system is not built with care, the application must also be sloppily built.

Creating Table of Contents File

The **Table of Contents** file specifies the hierarchy of topics to display when the help system's **Contents** tab is selected. In the **HTML Help Workshop**, choose the **New** option under the **File** menu. Choose **Table of Contents**, then click **OK**. The following window appears:

We want to add two headings with three topics under each. To insert a heading, in the right frame, click the toolbar button with a folder (**Insert a heading**). This window appears:

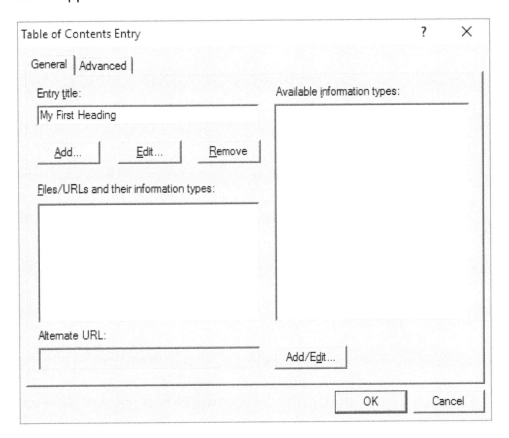

Type a title for the entry in **Entry title** (this is what will appear in the **Contents** – I used **My First Heading**).

You also need to link this topic to its topic file (HTM file). To do this, click **Add** and this appears:

Click the Browse button and 'point' to the corresponding topic file (**Heading1.HTM** in this case). Click **OK** to close this window.

Click **OK** to close the Table of Contents entry window and you'll now see:

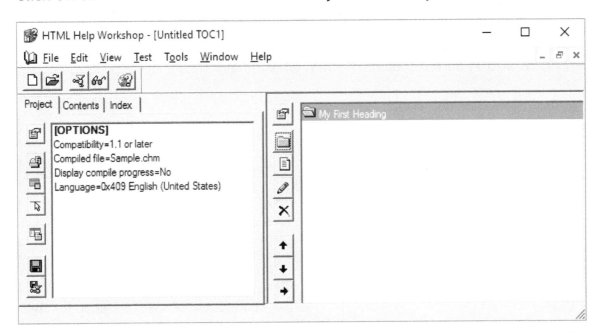

You've created your first entry in the Table of Contents. Notice the icon next to the heading is an 'open folder.' To change this to the more familiar 'open book,' click the top toolbar button (**Contents properties**). In the window that appears, remove the check mark next to '**Use Folders Instead of Books**,' and click **OK**.

Now, we need to enter our first topic under this first heading. Click the toolbar button (**Insert a page**) under the heading button. This dialog will appear:

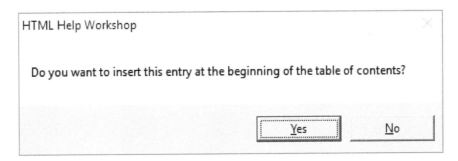

Answer **No** – we want the entry after the heading topic. At this point, you follow the same steps followed for the heading: enter a title and add a link to the topic file.

Add Table of Contents entries for all topic files in our little example. Use whatever titling information you choose. When you enter the second heading, it will be listed under the third topic in the first heading. To move it to the left (making it a major heading), right-click the heading and choose **Move Left**, the left arrow button on the toolbar). When done, I have this:

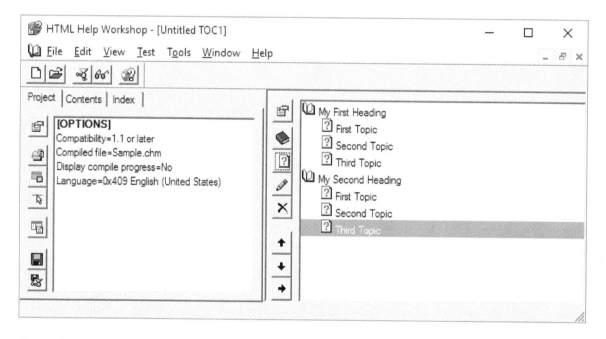

Save the contents file. Choose **Close File** under the **File** menu and assign a name of **Sample.HHC** to this contents file.

Compiling the Help File

We're almost ready to compile and create our help system. Before doing this, we need to add entries to the **Project** file. The project file at this point appears as:

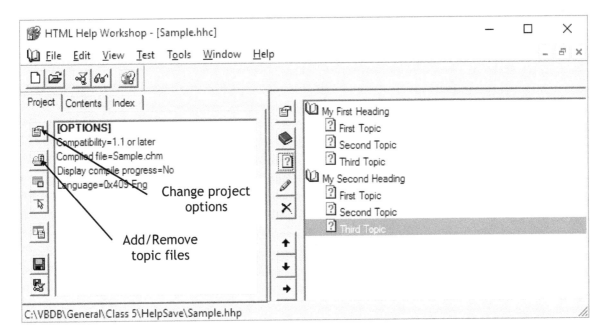

We first need to add our topic files. To do this, choose the **Add/remove topic files** toolbar button. In the window that appears, click **Add**, then select all topics files. You should see:

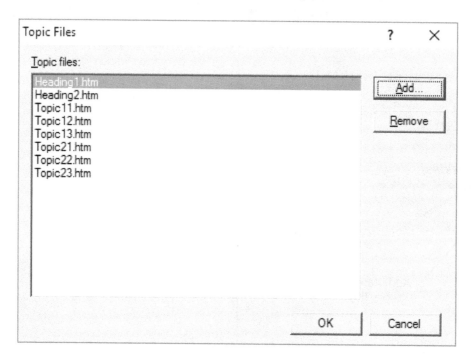

Click **OK.**

Now, the project file has the topic files added:

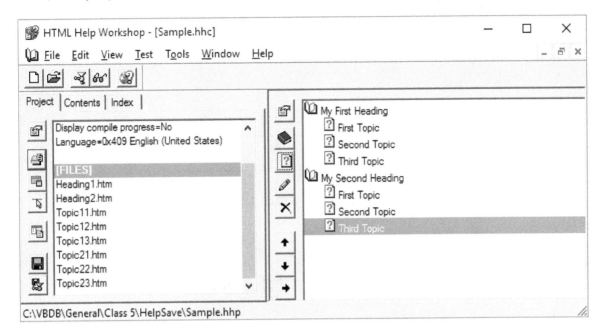

Now, we specify the **Table of Contents** file and set a few other properties. Click the **Change project options** toolbar button. Click the **General** tab and type a title for your help system (I used **My Sample Help File**) and specify the default file (**Heading1.htm**):

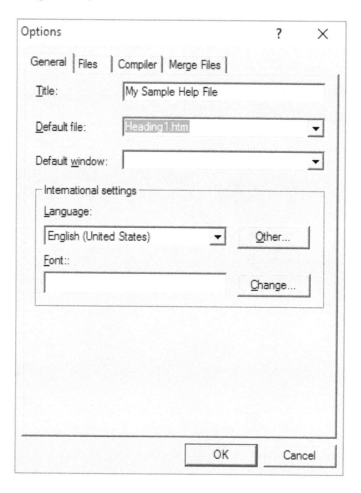

Click on the **Files** tab and select **Sample.hhc** as your contents file. Click **OK** to complete specification of your project file. At this point, save all files by choosing **Save Project** under the **File** menu.

We can now compile our project into the finished product – a complete HTML help system. To do this, click the **Compile HTML file** button (resembles a meat grinder) on the workshop toolbar. **Browse** so your project file (**Sample.hhp**) is selected. Choose **Compile** in the resulting window and things start 'grinding.' If no errors are reported, you should now have a **CHM** file in your directory. If errors did occur, you need to fix any reported problems.

At long last, we can view our finished product. Click on the **View compiled file** button (a pair of sunglasses) on the workshop toolbar. **Browse** so your help file (**Sample.chm**) is selected. Choose **View**, and this will appear (I've expanded the headings to show the topics):

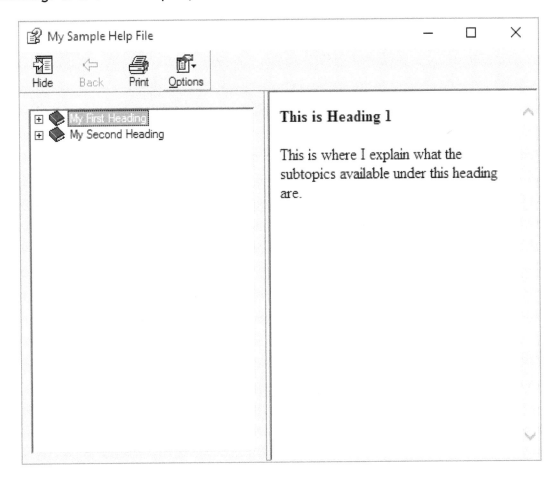

Click to see the various topics and headings displayed.

After all this work, you still only have a simple help file, nothing that rivals those seen in most applications. But, it is a very adequate help system. To improve your help system, you need to add more features. Investigate the HTML Help Workshop for information on tasks such as adding an index file, using context-sensitive help, adding search capabilities and adding graphics to the help system.

HelpProvider Control

In Toolbox:

Below Form (Default Properties):

Once we have a completed HTML help system, we need to connect our Visual C# application to the help file. You need to decide how you want your application to interact with the help system. We will demonstrate a simple approach. We will have the help system appear when the user presses **<F1>** or clicks some control related to obtaining help (menu item, button control). The Visual C# **HelpProvider** control provides this connection.

HelpProvider **Properties:**

Name	Gets or sets the name of the help provider control (three letter prefix for label name is **hlp**).
HelpNamespace	Complete path to compiled help file (**CHM** file)

The **HelpNamespace** property is usually established at run-time. The help file is often installed in the application directory (**Bin\Debug** folder). If this is the case, we can use the **Application.StartupPath** parameter to establish **HelpNamespace**. You also must include the help file in any deployment package you build for your application.

To have the help file appear when a user presses **<F1>,** we set the **HelpNavigator** property of the application form to **TableofContents**. With this setting, the help file will appear displaying the **Table of Contents**, set to the default form.

To have the help file appear in a **Click** event, we use the **ShowHelp** method of the **Help** object. The Visual C# **Help** object allows us to display HTML help files. To replicate the **<F1>** functionality above, we use the syntax:

```
Help.ShowHelp(this, HelpProvider.HelpNamespace);
```

This line of code will display the specified help file.

Typical use of **HelpProvider** control:

> ➢ Set the **Name** property.
> ➢ Set **HelpNameSpace** property in code (file is usually in **Bin\Debug** folder of application).
> ➢ Set **HelpNavigator** property for form to **TableofContents**.
> ➢ Write code for events meant to display the help file (use **Help.ShowHelp**).

The steps above provide minimal, but sufficient, access to an HTML help system. If you need more functionality (context-sensitive help, help on individual controls, pop-up help, adding help to dialog boxes), consult the Visual C# documentation on the **Help Provider** control.

Example 10-8

Help System Display

1. Start a new application. In this simple project, we will show how to display our example help system using <F1> and programmatic control. Add a button control and help provider control to the form. Set these properties:

Form1:
Name	frmHelp
Text	Help Example
HelpNavigator	TableOfContents

button1:
Name	btnHelp
Text	&Help

helpProvider1:
Name	hlpExample

My form now looks like this:

Other controls in tray:

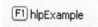

2. Copy the example help file (**Sample.chm** in **LearnVCS\VCS Code\Class 10\Sample Help** folder into the **Bin\Debug** folder of this application (you may have to create the folder first). We will use the **Application.StartupPath** parameter to load the file.

3. Use this code in the **frmHelp Load** event to establish help file path:

```
private void FrmHelp_Load(object sender, EventArgs e)
{
   hlpExample.HelpNamespace = Application.StartupPath +
"\\sample.chm";
}
```

4. Use this code in the **btnHelp Click** event to programmatically display the help file:

```
private void BtnHelp_Click(object sender, EventArgs e)
{
   Help.ShowHelp(this, hlpExample.HelpNamespace);
}
```

5. Save (saved in **Example 10-8** folder in the **LearnVCS\VCS Code\Class 10** folder) and run the application. Click the button and the help system will appear. Press **<F1>** and the help system will appear (I expanded the first heading):

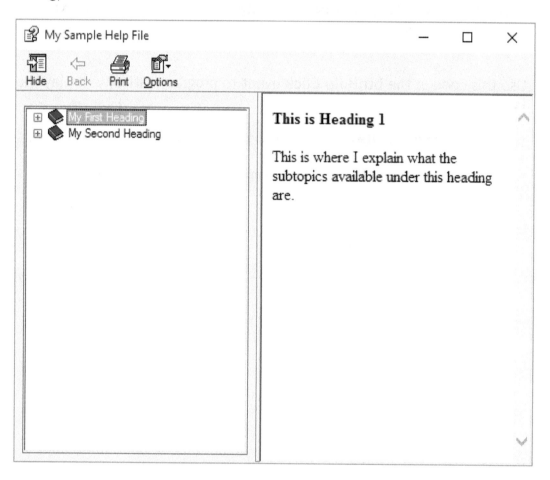

We did it!

Class Review

After completing this class, you should understand:

> ➤ How to use several new controls: link label, date selection controls, rich textbox control
> ➤ How to add a toolbar control and tooltips to a Visual C# application
> ➤ How to add controls at run-time
> ➤ The concepts of printing from a Visual C# application, including use of dialog controls
> ➤ How to use the Windows API for timing
> ➤ How to use the HTML Help Workshop to develop a simple on-line help system
> ➤ How to attach a help file to a Visual C# application, both via function keys and via code

Practice Problems 10

Problem 10-1. Biorhythm Problem. Some people think our lives are guided by biorhythm cycles that begin on the day we are born. There are three cycles: **physical**, **emotional** and **intellectual**. Each cycle can range in value from a low of -100 to a high of +100. If **numberDays** is the number of days since birth, the three cycles are described by these Visual C# equations:

```
physical = 100 * Math.Sin(2 * Math.PI * numberDays / 23);
emotional = 100 * Math.Sin(2 * Math.PI * numberDays / 28);
intellectual = 100 * Math.Sin(2 * Math.PI * numberDays /
33);
```

(For the mathematically inclined, each cycle is a sine wave with different periods.) Build an application that computes these values knowing someone's birth date.

Problem 10-2. Rich Textbox Note Editor Problem. Load the Note Editor example we have been building throughout this course. The last incarnation is in this class where we added a toolbar control (saved as **Example 10-4** in the **LearnVCS\VCS Code\Class 10** folder). Replace the text box control with a rich textbox control. Modify the code to allow selective formatting of text (bold, italics, underline, font size). You will also need to modify the code that opens and saves files (use the **LoadFile** and **SaveFile** methods) to insure saving of the formatting.

Problem 10-3. Loan Printing Problem. . The two lines of Visual C# code that compute the monthly payment on an installment loan are:

```
multiplier = (double) (Math.Pow((1 + interest / 1200),
months));
payment = loan * interest * multiplier / (1200 * (multiplier
- 1));
```

where (all **double** types):

interest	Yearly interest percentage
months	Number of months of payments
loan	Loan amount
multiplier	Interest multiplier
payment	Computed monthly payment

(The 1200 value in these equations converts yearly interest to a monthly rate.) Use this code to build a general method that computes **payment**, given the other three variables.

Now, use this method in an application that computes the payment after the user inputs loan amount, yearly interest and number of months. Allow the user to print out a repayment schedule for the loan. The printed report should include the inputs, computed payments, total of payments and total interest paid. Then, a month-by-month accounting of the declining balance, as the loan is paid, should be printed. In this accounting, include how much of each payment goes toward principal and how much toward interest.

Problem 10-4. Plot Printing Problem. In Problem 9-4, we built an application that displayed a labeled plot of the win streaks for the Seattle Mariners 1995 season. Build an application that prints this plot and its labeling information.

Problem 10-5. Sound Timing Problem. Modify Problem 9-7 (where we played sound files) to include a feature to compute and display the time elapsed (using the Windows API) while the sound plays.

Problem 10-6. Note Editor Help Problem. Develop a help file for the **Note Editor** application (use Problem 10-2 above as a starting point). Explain whatever topics you feel are important. Allow access to this help file via a menu item, a toolbar button and by pressing <F1>.

Exercise 10

Phone Directory

Develop an application that tracks people and phone numbers (include home, work and cell phones). Allow sorting, editing, adding, deleting and saving of entries. Add search capabilities. Allow printing of listings. Develop an on-line help system. In summary, build a full-featured Visual C# phone directory application.

11. Visual C# Database and Web Applications

Review and Preview

Many Visual C# Windows applications are built and deployed as 'front-ends' for databases. That is, they provide the interface between a user and a database. A database is a well-organized system of information.

Visual C# offers a suite of tools that allows viewing, editing, adding, deleting and printing data from a database. We take a brief look at these tools in this last class.

Prior to Visual C#, building and deploying applications that run on the Internet was a major headache. Visual C# introduces the web form that makes the process of building a web application nearly as simple as the process for building a Windows application. We conclude **Learn Visual C#** by introducing the steps involved in building a web application.

Database Applications

In this course, we've presented an in-depth study in the development and deployment of Visual C# Windows applications. A very powerful, and popular, use for such applications is to work as an interface to an existing **database**. Databases are everywhere in today's world: e-commerce sites use databases to track sales and inventories; airlines use databases to schedule flights; doctors use databases to schedule patients; and even sports announcers use databases to provide useless trivial statistics about players.

Products such as Microsoft Access, Microsoft SQL Server, Oracle or Sybase can be used to create databases. Visual C# offers a variety of tools and objects for connecting to, retrieving, viewing and updating data in such databases.

In this class, we look at a few of the tools used for database access. And, we will limit our study to viewing databases created using Microsoft Access. In this class, we will study:

> ➢ Database structure and terminology
> ➢ How to connect to a Microsoft Access database
> ➢ Ways to view data in the database
> ➢ How to navigate within a database

Database Structure and Terminology

Database management has a language all its own. Here, we introduce some of that terminology. In simplest terms, a **database** is a collection of information. This collection is stored in well-defined **tables**, or matrices.

The **rows** in a database table are used to describe similar items. The rows are referred to as database **records**. In general, no two rows in a database table will be alike.

The **columns** in a database table provide characteristics of the records. These characteristics are called database **fields**. Each field contains one specific piece of information. In defining a database field, you specify the data type, assign a length, and describe other attributes.

Here is a simple database example:

Field

ID No	Name	Date of Birth	Height	Weight
1	Bob Jones	01/04/58	72	170
2	Mary Rodgers	11/22/61	65	125
3	Sue Williams	06/11/57	68	130

} **Record**

Table

In this database **table**, each **record** represents a single individual. The **fields** (descriptors of the individuals) include an identification number (ID No), Name, Date of Birth, Height, and Weight.

Most databases use **indexes** to allow faster access to the information in the database. Indexes are sorted lists that point to a particular row in a table. In the example just seen, the **ID No** field could be used as an index.

A database using a single table is called a **flat database**. Most databases are made up of many tables. When using multiple tables within a database, these tables must have some common fields to allow cross-referencing of the tables. The referral of one table to another via a common field is called a **relation**. Such groupings of database tables are called **relational databases**.

In our examples, we will use a sample multi-table database containing information on books about computers. This Microsoft Access database (**books.accdb**) is found in the **LearnVCS\VCS Code\Class 11** folder. Let's look at its relational structure. The **books.accdb** database is made up of four tables:

Authors Table (6246 Records, 3 Fields)

Au_ID	Author	Year Born

Publishers Table (727 Records, 10 Fields)

PubID	Name	Company		Fax	Comments

Title Author Table (16056 Records, 2 Fields)

ISBN	Au_ID

Titles Table (8569 Records, 8 Fields)

Title	Year Pub	ISBN	PubID		Comments

The **Authors** table consists of author identification numbers, the author's name, and the year born. The **Publishers** table has information regarding book publishers. Some of the fields include an identification number, the publisher name, and pertinent phone numbers. The **Title Author** table correlates a book's ISBN (a universal number assigned to books) with an author's identification number. And, the **Titles** table has several fields describing each individual book, including title, ISBN, and publisher identification.

Note each table has two types of information: **source** data and **relational** data. Source data is actual information, such as titles and author names. Relational data are references to data in other tables, such as Au_ID and PubID. In the Authors, Publishers and Title Author tables, the first column is used as the table **index**. In the Titles table, the ISBN value is the **index**.

Using the relational data in the four tables, we should be able to obtain a complete description of any book title in the database. Let's look at one example:

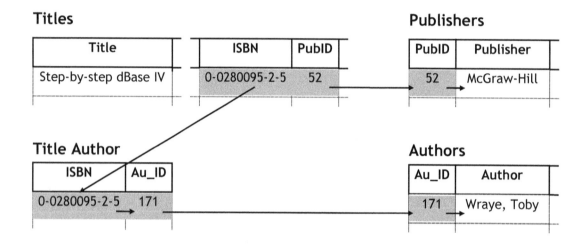

Here, the book in the **Titles** table, entitled "Step-by-step dBase IV," has an ISBN of 0-0280095-2-5 and a PubID of 52. Taking the PubID into the **Publishers** table, determines the book is published by McGraw-Hill and also allows us to access all other information concerning the publisher. Using the ISBN in the **Title Author** table provides us with the author identification (Au_ID) of 171, which, when used in the **Authors** table, tells us the book's author is Toby Wraye.

We can form alternate tables from a database's inherent tables. Such **virtual tables**, or **logical views**, are made using queries of the database. A **query** is simply a request for information from the database tables. As an example with the **books.accdb** database, using pre-defined query languages, we could 'ask' the database to form a table of all authors and books published after 1992, or provide all author names starting with B. We'll look briefly at queries.

Keeping track of all the information in a database is handled by a **database management system** (DBMS). Visual C# provides several tools to help in these management tasks, using what is known as **ADO .NET**. ADO (**ActiveX Data Object**) .NET is the latest incarnation in a series of Visual C# data access technologies.   In this class, we will see how to use Visual C# (and ADO .NET) to perform two tasks: accessing data and displaying data.

DataSet Objects

The **DataSet** object is the heart of ADO .NET. With this object, we can connect to a database and then generate a table (or tables) of data (the **DataSet**) to view. Making **queries** of the database generates tables. The language used to make a query is **SQL** (pronounced 'ess-cue-ell' meaning structured query language). SQL is an English-like language that has evolved into the most widely used database query language. You use SQL to formulate a question to ask of the database. The database 'answers' that question with a new table of records and fields that match your criteria. Sometimes, like in our first example, you don't need any SQL at all – a wizard handles the work for you!

To get data into a **DataSet**, you first establish a connection to the database. The **Connection** object lets you specify the database you will be working with. Communication between the database and **DataSet** is accomplished via the **DataAdapter** object. Connection to the database is done using the **Data Source Configuration Wizard**. The best way to learn to use this wizard and others is by example and that's what we'll do. We will use the wizards to connect to our example database (**books.accdb** in the **LearnVCS\VCS Code\Class 11** folder) and form a table with two fields (**Title**, **ISBN**) from the **Titles** table. Let's go.

But, first, the Access database used here only works with 32-bit operating systems. If you are using a 64-bit version of Visual Studio, you need to make one change to each project you build.

Follow these steps:

> ➤ Once your project is built, choose the **Project** menu item, and select your project's **Properties** entry.
> ➤ In the window that appears, choose the **Compile** tab.
> ➤ Under **Target CPU**, make sure the selection is **x86**, not **AnyCPU**. The changed window should look like this:

> ➤ Close the window to finalize the change.

How will you know if you have an operating system problem? The first symptom is that your application will have no data displayed, indicating the database did not open correctly. Secondly, the **Immediate Window** will have this error message:

An unhandled exception of type 'System.InvalidOperationException' occurred in System.Data.dll

Or, when opening the database, you may see a window similar to this:

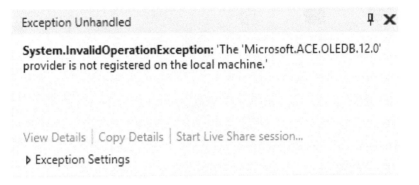

If you see such symptoms, make the above noted correction to your project's properties.

Start a new application in Visual C#. Select the **Project** menu option and choose **Add New Data Source**. This window will appear:

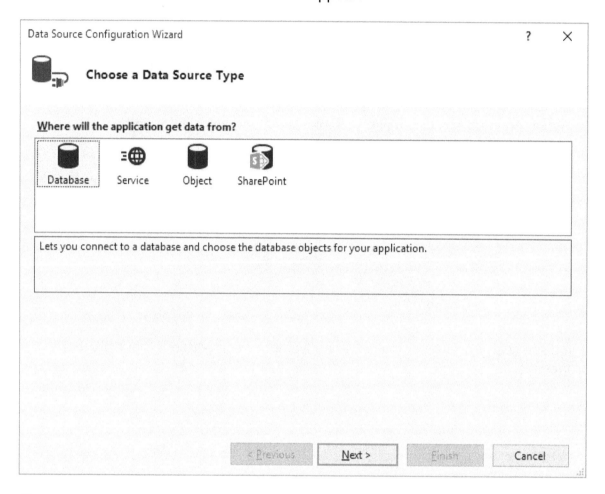

Choose the **Database** application and click **Next**.

You will see a screen asking what **database model** you want to use. Choose **Dataset** and click **Next**.

You next specify where the database is located:

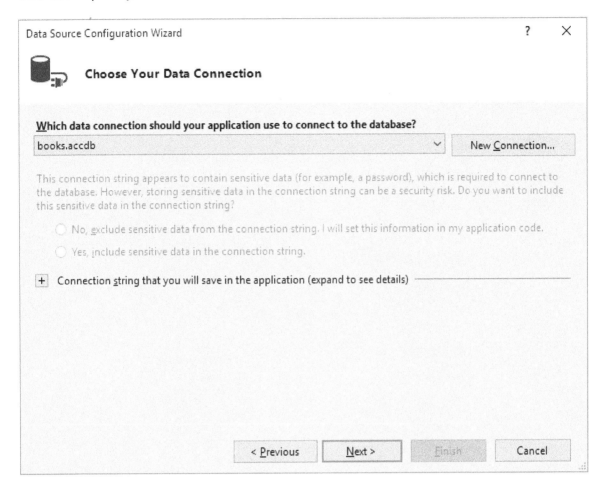

There may or may not be a connection listed in the drop down box. Here is where we will form a needed **Connection string** to connect to the database. Click **New Connection.**

In the next screen, you will see:

```
┌─────────────────────────────────────────────────────────┐
│ Add Connection                              ?      ✕     │
├─────────────────────────────────────────────────────────┤
│  Enter information to connect to the selected data       │
│  source or click "Change" to choose a different data     │
│  source and/or provider.                                 │
│                                                          │
│  Data source:                                            │
│  ┌──────────────────────────────────┐  ┌─────────────┐  │
│  │ Microsoft Access Database File   │  │  Change...  │  │
│  │ (OLE DB)                         │  └─────────────┘  │
│  └──────────────────────────────────┘                   │
│  Database file name:                                     │
│  ┌──────────────────────────────────┐  ┌─────────────┐  │
│  │ |                                │  │  Browse...  │  │
│  └──────────────────────────────────┘  └─────────────┘  │
│  ┌ Log on to the database ───────────────────────────┐  │
│  │                                                    │  │
│  │  User name:  ┌──────────────────────────────────┐ │  │
│  │              │ Admin                            │ │  │
│  │              └──────────────────────────────────┘ │  │
│  │  Password:   ┌──────────────────────────────────┐ │  │
│  │              │                                  │ │  │
│  │              └──────────────────────────────────┘ │  │
│  │              ☐ Save my password                   │  │
│  └────────────────────────────────────────────────────┘  │
│                                       ┌─────────────┐    │
│                                       │ Advanced... │    │
│                                       └─────────────┘    │
│  ───────────────────────────────────────────────────    │
│  ┌──────────────────┐      ┌────────┐  ┌───────────┐    │
│  │ Test Connection  │      │   OK   │  │  Cancel   │    │
│  └──────────────────┘      └────────┘  └───────────┘    │
└─────────────────────────────────────────────────────────┘
```

Make sure the **Data source** shows **Microsoft Access Database File**. If not, click **Change** to see:

As shown, choose **Microsoft Access Database File**. This is the proper choice for a Microsoft Access database. Click **Next**.

You will return to the **Add Connection** window:

Click the **Browse** button and point to the **books.accdb** database (in **LearnVCS\VCS Code\Class 11** folder). Once selected, click **Test Connection** to insure a proper connection.

When testing the connection, you may see:

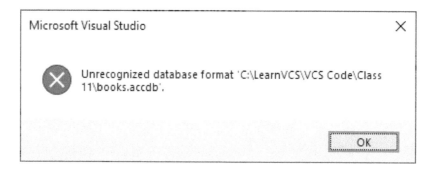

This indicates you are missing the proper driver for the Access Database. To fix this problem, download and install the driver from here:

https://www.microsoft.com/en-us/download/confirmation.aspx?id=13255

Once installed, restart Visual Studio and retry connecting to the database.
When you get to this screen

Click the **Advanced** button.

Select the **Provider** property as shown:

Click **OK** and retest the connection.

Once the connection is verified, click **OK** and you will be returned to the **Data Source Configuration Wizard** main screen. Click **Next** and you will be asked if you want to copy the database to your project:

For our example, answer **No**. When you build applications that actually distribute the database, you would want a copy in your project.

The next screen shows:

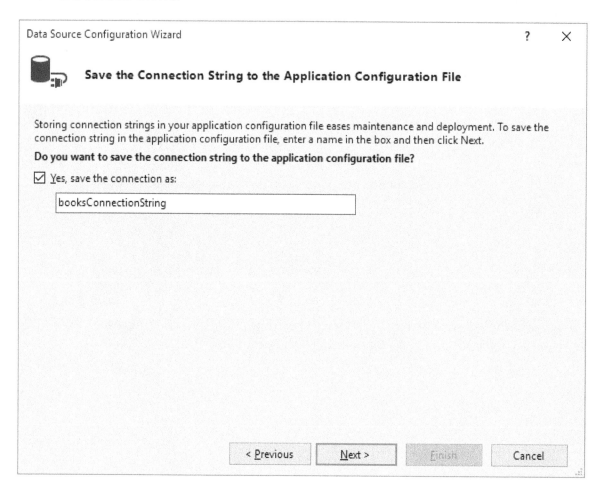

The **connection string** specifies what database fields are used to form the dataset. Choose the default connection string and click **Next**.

The connection is complete; we now need to specify the **DataSet** or table of data we want to generate. We want to choose the **Title** and **ISBN** fields in the **Titles** table. Expand the **Tables** object, then choose the **Titles** table and place checks next to the **Title** and **ISBN** fields:

Once these selections are done, click **Finish** to complete specification of the **DataSet**.

Choose the **Data** menu option and click **Show Data Sources**. Look in the **Data Sources** window in your project and you should see the newly created **DataSet** object (**booksDataSet**):

To form this **DataSet**, Visual C# 'queried' the database (generating its own SQL statement) to pull the **Title** and **ISBN** fields out of the database.

Once generated, there are many properties and methods that allow us to view, edit and modify the dataset. One very useful property is the **Rows** collection. This collection contains all rows in the data set. The **DataRow** object allows us to examine (or establish) fields in each row of the data set. To see all values of a field (**myField**) in a table (**myTable**) existing in a DataSet (**myDataSet**), you could use this code snippet:

```
DataRow myRow;
.

.
for (int i = 0; i < myDataSet.Tables[myTable].Rows.Count;
i++)
{
  myRow = myDataSet.Tables[myTable].Rows[i];
  // Field is available in variable myRow[myField]
.

.
}
```

In this snippet, **myField** is a string data type. Such code could be used to make bulk changes to a database. For example, you could use it to add area codes to all your phone numbers or change the case of particular fields.

In summary, the relationship between the **ConnectionString** property (set using the wizard), the **SQL** query (formed automatically in this example) and the **DataSet** is:

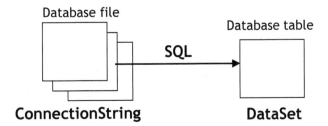

We now need a mechanism to view the information in the database table. This is done using a process known as **data binding.**

Simple Data Binding

Data binding allows us to take data from a data set object and bind it to a particular Visual C# control. This means some property is automatically established by the database.

Most of the Visual C# tools we've studied can be used as **bound** controls. The process of 'connecting' a particular property to a particular database field is known as **simple binding**. Simple binding is best illustrated by example. Add a label control to the form of the example we've been working on – set **AutoSize** to **False** and make it fairly large:

In the properties window for the label control, find the **DataBindings** entry (usually near the top). Expand the entry by clicking the enclosed plus (+) sign. Choose the **Text** property and click the drop-down arrow that appears. Expand the selections until you see this:

Choose **Title**.

We have now 'bound' the **Text** property of the label control to the **Title** field of our dataset. You should also note that three objects have been added to the project (in the tray area under the form):

We recognize the **booksDataSet** object. The **titlesTableAdapter** object is a **DataAdapter** that controls communication between the books database and the dataset. The **titlesBindingSource** controls navigation through the dataset. Important: For proper navigation, all subsequent data bindings for this dataset should connect to this **BindingSource** object, not the original dataset.

One other change has been made to your project. Open the code window. You should see two lines of code have been added to the **Form Load** procedure:

```
// TODO: This line of code loads data into the
'booksDataSet.Titles' table. You can move, or remove it,
as needed.
this.titlesTableAdapter.Fill(this.booksDataSet.Titles);
```

As mentioned in the comment, this is needed to load the data into the dataset.

Guess what? We're finally about to see data! **Run** the sample project. If the database is successfully connected, the data set correctly generated and the label is correctly bound, you will see this on your form:

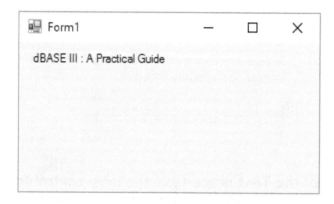

The label control is displaying the **Title** of the first book in the **books.accdb** database! The **Text** property of the control is bound to that field. This is nice, but kind of boring. How can we see the other titles in the database? We need some way to navigate among the rows (records) of the data set table.

Database Navigation

To navigate the rows of a database table, we use the **BindingSource** object associated with the dataset. Recall this object is added to the project once the first data binding is assigned. With just a few properties and methods, we can do quite a few navigation tasks.

For a **BindingSource** named **myBindingSource**, the number of records in the corresponding dataset (table) is given by:

```
myBindingSource.Count
```

The 'record number' for the same binding source is given by:

```
myBindingSource.Position
```

This **Position** property is modified using one of four **BindingSource** methods: **MoveFirst** (move to the first record), **MoveNext** (increment Position by one), **MovePrevious** (decrement Position by one), **MoveLast** (move to the last record). When changed, all controls bound to the dataset will be updated with the current values. The relationship between a data bound control and the Position property is:

The records are a 'zero-based' array, ranging from a low **Position** value of **0** to a high value of **Count - 1**

To help clarify everything, we summarize all the steps for connecting to a database, establishing a dataset, binding controls and database navigation in Example 11-1.

Example 11-1

Accessing the Books Database

1. Start a new application. We'll develop a form where we can skim through the books database, examining Titles and ISBN values. Place four label controls and four buttons on the form. It should look something like this:

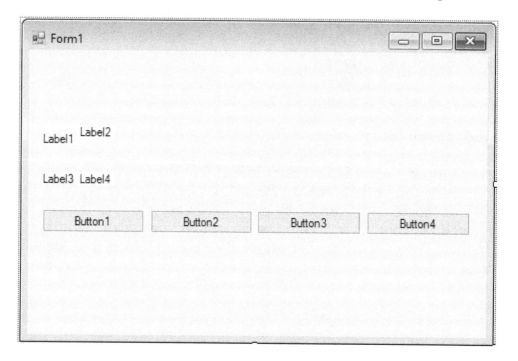

2. Use the **Data Source Configuration Wizard** to connect to the **books.accdb** database and form a DataSet (**booksDataSet**) that contains the **Title** and **ISBN** fields from the **Titles** table. Here, you simply repeat the steps just covered in the course notes. We use the default names for all components – you may change them if you like.

3. Set the following properties the form and each control

Form1:

Name	frmBooks
FormBorderStyle	FixedSingle
StartPosition	CenterScreen
Text	Books Database

label1:

Text	Title

label2:

Name	lblTitle
AutoSize	False
BackColor	White
BorderStyle	Fixed3D
DataBindings	Text: BooksDataSet – Titles.Title
Text	[Blank]
TextAlign	MiddleLeft

label3:

Text	ISBN

label4:

Name	lblISBN
AutoSize	False
BackColor	White
BorderStyle	Fixed3D
DataBindings	Text: titlesBindingSource.ISBN (this object will be added following binding of lblTitle)
Text	[Blank]
TextAlign	MiddleLeft

button1:
>   Name   btnFirst
>   Text   First Record

button2:
>   Name   btnPrevious
>   Text   Previous Record

button3:
>   Name   btnNext
>   Text   Next Record

button4:
>   Name   btnLast
>   Text   Last Record

When done, the form will look something like this (try to space your controls as shown; we'll use all the blank space as we continue with this example):

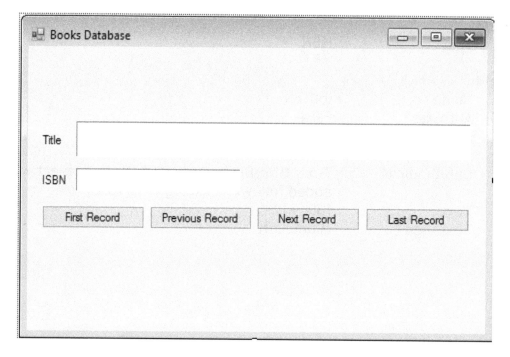

Other controls in tray:

BooksDataSet   TitlesBindingSource   TitlesTableAdapter

4. Add the shaded line to the **frmBooks Load** method:

```csharp
private void FrmBooks_Load(object sender, EventArgs e)
{
    // TODO: This line of code loads data into the
'booksDataSet.Titles' table. You can move, or remove it,
as needed.
    this.titlesTableAdapter.Fill(this.booksDataSet.Titles);
    btnFirst.PerformClick();
}
```

5. Add this general method (**UpdateTitle**) to display the **Text** property of the Form:

```csharp
private void UpdateTitle()
{
    this.Text = "Books Database - Record " +
(titlesBindingSource.Position + 1).ToString() + " of " +
titlesBindingSource.Count.ToString();
}
```

6. Use these four methods for the navigation buttons:

```csharp
private void BtnFirst_Click(object sender, EventArgs e)
{
    btnFirst.Enabled = false;
    btnPrevious.Enabled = false;
    btnNext.Enabled = true;
    btnLast.Enabled = true;
    titlesBindingSource.MoveFirst();
    UpdateTitle();
}
```

```csharp
    private void BtnPrevious_Click(object sender, EventArgs e)
    {
      btnNext.Enabled = true;
      btnLast.Enabled = true;
      titlesBindingSource.MovePrevious();
      if (titlesBindingSource.Position == 0)
      {
btnFirst.Enabled = false;
btnPrevious.Enabled = false;
      }
      else
      {
btnFirst.Enabled = true;
btnPrevious.Enabled = true;
      }
      UpdateTitle();
    }

    private void BtnNext_Click(object sender, EventArgs e)
    {
      btnFirst.Enabled = true;
      btnPrevious.Enabled = true;
      titlesBindingSource.MoveNext();
      if (titlesBindingSource.Position ==
titlesBindingSource.Count - 1)
      {
btnNext.Enabled = false;
btnLast.Enabled = false;
      }
      else
      {
btnNext.Enabled = true;
btnLast.Enabled = true;
      }
      UpdateTitle();
    }
```

```
private void BtnLast_Click(object sender, EventArgs e)
{
  btnFirst.Enabled = true;
  btnPrevious.Enabled = true;
  btnNext.Enabled = false;
  btnLast.Enabled = false;
  titlesBindingSource.MoveLast();
  UpdateTitle();
}
```

These methods increment/decrement the Position value, keeping track of beginning and end of records and enabling/disabling buttons when needed.

Save the application. (This application is saved in the **Example 11-1** folder in the **LearnVCS\VCS Code\Class 11** folder.) Run the application. You should see the first record:

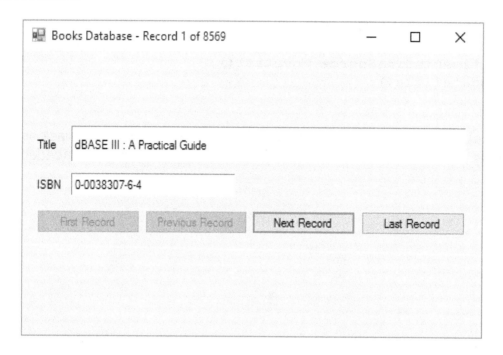

If you load and try to execute this project from the class notes, the books database must be located in the **LearnVCS\VCS Code\Class 11** folder or the application will not run. This will also be the case for other database examples and problems in this class. If you have the database in another folder, you need to go through the steps to configure the data source to point to your database's location. You may have to delete the **DataSet**, **DataAdapter** and **BindingSource** objects first. And, you might have to rebind the controls.

Cycle through the various book titles using the navigation buttons. Notice how the different buttons are enabled and disabled as you reach the beginning and end of the data table. This is part of good interface design.

Creating a Virtual Table

Many times, a database table has more information than we want to display. Or, perhaps a table does not have all the information we want to display. For instance, in Example 11-1, seeing the Title and ISBN of a book is not real informative - we would also like to see the Author, but the Titles table does not provide that information. In these cases, we can build our own **virtual table**, displaying only the information we want the user to see.

We need to form a SQL statement for the data adapter component to process. This will form a new data set containing the desired information. The steps to do this for our books database are covered in Example 11-2.

Example 11-2

Creating a Virtual Table

1. We will modify Example 11-1 so it will display an Author listing along with the Title and ISBN. To do this, we need to form a virtual table with three fields: Author (from the Authors table), Title and ISBN (from the Titles table). This will require a new dataset, a new data adapter and a SQL statement. Let's create the new dataset. Open Example 11-1. Choose the **Data** menu item, then **Add New Data Source**. Click **Next** on the first two screens until you see:

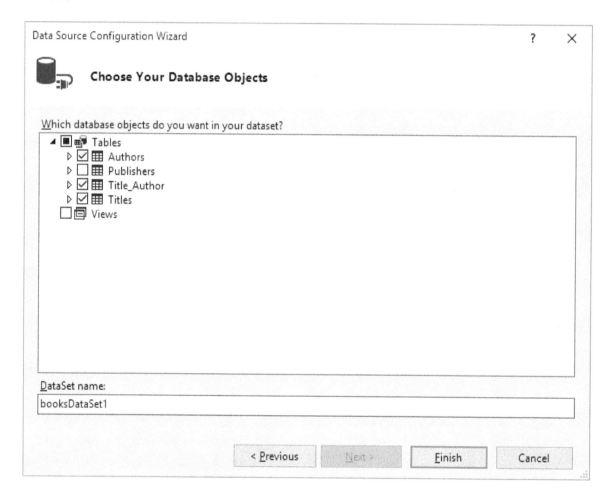

We need three tables in our dataset. Check **Authors**, **Title Author** and **Titles**. Then, click **Finish**.

A new dataset (**booksDataSet1**) will appear in the Data Sources window:

2. We now need to add a table adapter to generate the needed fields from the three tables to form another table. Right-click the **booksDataSet1** in the **Data Sources** window and choose **Edit DataSet with Designer**. This window, displaying the three individual tables, will appear:

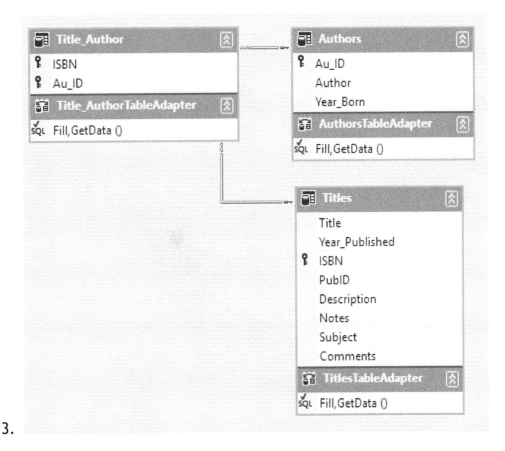

3.

Our virtual table will include the **Author**, **Title**, and **ISBN** fields. To build this table, we need a new **TableAdapter**. Right-click the display window, and choose **Add**, then **TableAdapter**.

A new adapter will added and the **TableAdapter Configuration Wizard** will start up. Click **Next** on the **Choose Your Data Connection** window and the subsequent **Choose a Command Type Window** (where we tell the adapter we are using SQL). The **Enter a SQL Statement** window will appear:

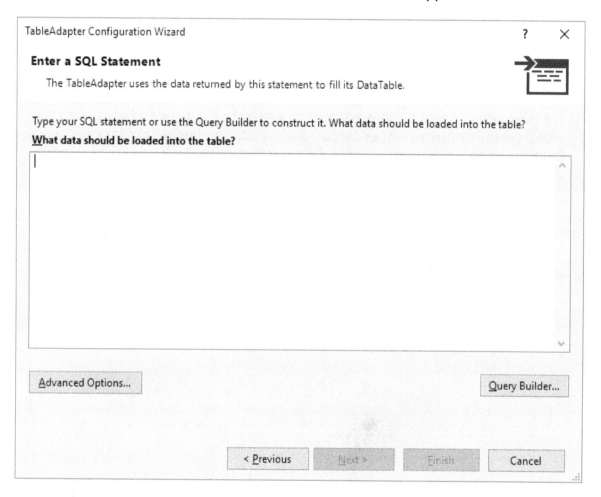

We can enter the SQL statement to build the table here or have Visual C# build it for us. We'll let Visual C# do the work.

Click **Query Builder** to see:

Select the **Authors, Title Author** and **Titles** tables and click **Add**.

Click **Close**. You will see:

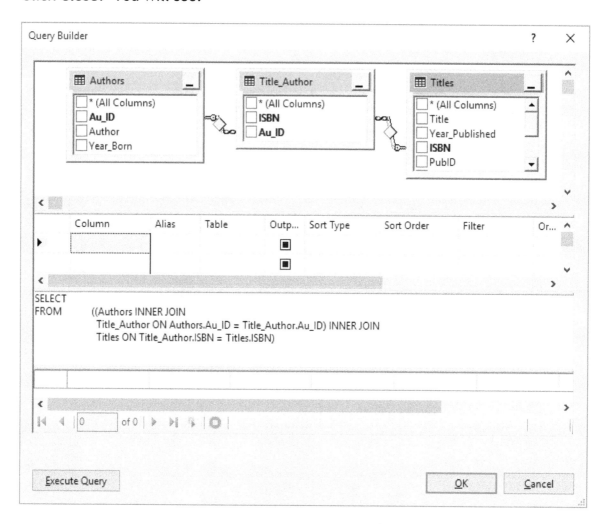

The Query Builder is showing the relationships among the three tables (i.e. how the **ISBN** value connects **Titles** with **Title Author** and how **Au_ID** connects **Title Author** with **Authors**). Select **Title** and **ISBN** in the **Titles** table. Then, select **Author** in the **Authors** table. Once added, select a sort type of **Ascending** in the table below. This will sort the table according to Author name.

Once your selections are complete, click **OK** and the window will appear as:

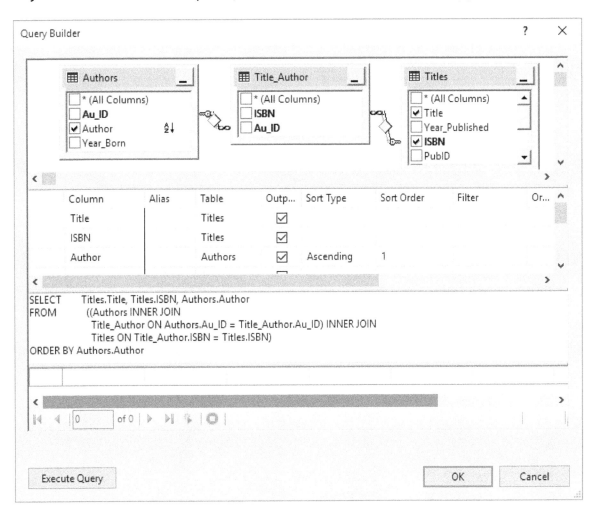

The following SQL statement is generated:

```
SELECT Titles.Title, Titles.ISBN, Authors.Author
FROM ((Authors INNER JOIN
 [Title Author] ON Authors.Au_ID = [Title Author].Au_ID)
INNER JOIN
 Titles ON [Title Author].ISBN = Titles.ISBN)
ORDER BY Authors.Author
```

Even without knowing SQL, you should be able to see what's going on here. The three desired fields are selected by 'joining' the Titles, Title Author and Authors tables using rules that match ISBN and Au_ID values. The results are ordered by the Author field. Click **OK**. Then, click **Finish** to complete specification of the table adapter.

A new data table (**DataTable1**, if you used the default name) will appear in the designer window and in the **Data Sources** window under **booksDataSet1**:

This table holds the virtual table including the Author, Title, and ISBN files for the books database. Admittedly, there were lots of steps needed to form this table. Once you've built a few tables though, these steps become second nature. Now, let's continue the example.

4. Add two new label controls to the form. Set these properties:

   label5:
Text	Author
TextAlign	MiddleLeft

   label6:
Name	lblAuthor
BackColor	White
BorderStyle	Fixed3D
DataBindings	Text: booksDataSet1 – DataTable1.Author
Text	[Blank]
TextAlign	MiddleLeft

The modified form looks like this:

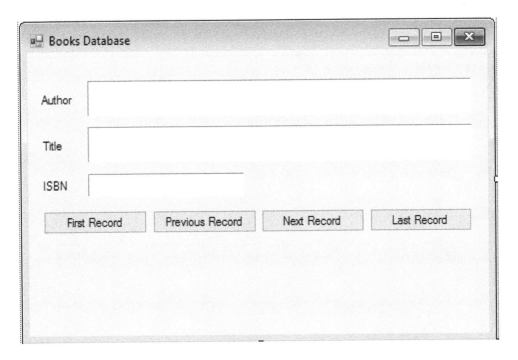

with three new objects added associated with the new virtual table:

5. Modify the data bindings on **lblTitle** and **lblISBN** so they are bound to the correct fields in the newly added **dataTable1BindingSource**. This will insure matching sets of Author, Title and ISBN as we move through the rows of the table. Correspondingly, change all references to the **titlesBindingSource** in code to refer to the new **dataTable1BindingSource**. I made such 9 such changes.

6. Save your work (saved in **Example 11-2** folder in **LearnVCS\VCS Code\Class 11** folder). Run the application and now you'll see the author information has been added:

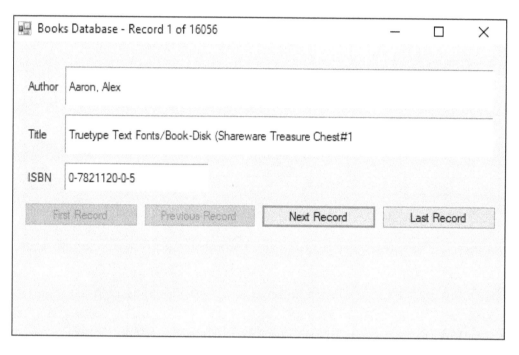

Notice how the books are now ordered based on an alphabetical listing of authors' last names.

DataView Objects

In many cases, we would like to see an alternate view of tables established by the data set object. Perhaps, we want the data sorted in a different manner or filtered based on some criteria. The **DataView** object allows us to do just that. The data view object is used to form a 'subset' of the records in the data set object. Like the data set object, controls can be bound to the data view object and navigation from one record to the next is possible.

The **DataView** object is selected from the **Data** tab of the Visual C# toolbox. The default configuration for this tab may not have this object. For example, my default tab shows:

To add the **DataView** object to the toolbox, right-click the toolbox and select **Choose Items**. When the **Choose Toolbox Items** window appears, click the **.NET Framework Components** tab and place a check next to **DataView**, then click **OK**:

The **DataView** object should now be in the toolbox (it may be in the **General** tab):

Once in the toolbox, the **DataView** object is added to a project like any other object. To use the **DataView** object, you first must have established a table in a data set. Once added, the **Table** property should be set to the table it will "view."

Once the **DataView** object is connected with a table, you can do many things to that table. We will look at how to sort and how to filter the table. To sort the records in a DataView object (named **myDataViewExample**):

```
myDataViewExample.Sort = "FieldName";
```

This will resort the table in ascending order using the specified **FieldName** as key. If you wish to sort in descending order, use:

```
myDataViewExample.Sort = "FieldName DESC";
```

To filter the data (obtain an alternate view of the table), use:

```
myDataView.RowFilter = criteria;
```

where **criteria** is a string data type indicating the 'rule' to use in filtering. The criteria is much like a WHERE clause in SQL. To form a criteria, specify the name of a column (field) followed by an operator and a value to filter on. The value must be in single quotes. For example:

```
"LastName = 'Smith'"
```

would return all rows (records) where the **LastName** field was **Smith**. The number of records returned by the **RowFilter** property is provided by the **Count** property of the data view object.

The **DataRowView** object allows us to examine (or establish) fields in each row of a data view. To see all values of a field (**myField**) in a DataView (**myDataView**), you could use this code snippet:

```
DataRowView myRow;
   .
   .
for (int i = 0; i < myDataView.Count; i++)
{
  myRow = myDataView[i];
   .
   .
  // Field is available as an Object type
  // in variable myRow[myField]
   .
}
```

In this snippet, **myField** is a string data type identifying the desired database field.

Navigation among records in a **DataView** object is analogous to navigation within a data set object. Add a **BindingSource** object to the project and set its **DataSource** property to the **DataView** object (unlike the data set, a binding source is <u>not</u> automatically added for us). Then, for a **BindingSource** named **myBindingSource**, the number of records in the corresponding dataview (table) is given by:

```
myBindingSource.Count
```

The 'record number' for the same binding source is given by:

```
myBindingSource.Position
```

This **Position** property is modified using one of four **BindingSource** methods: **MoveFirst** (move to the first record), **MoveNext** (increment Position by one), **MovePrevious** (decrement Position by one), **MoveLast** (move to the last record). When changed, all controls bound to the data view will be updated with the current values.

To see values generated in a **DataView** object, controls should be bound to fields in the data view's **BindingSource**. Simple binding is done using a method analogous to that of binding to a data set object. For the control to be bound, select the **DataBindings** property and point to the desired field in the listed **BindingSource** object.

Example 11-3

'Rolodex' Searching of the Books Database

1. We will modify Example 11-2 to allow searching for author names that begin with a selected letter of the alphabet. To implement the search, we'll use a 'rolodex' approach (borrowing code from Example 10-5). A **DataView** object will contain the resulting records. Open Example 11-2. Add a **DataView** object and set the **Table** property to **booksDataSet1.DataTable1** (the DataTable1 table of the data set). We leave the default name set to **dataView1**; you may change it if you like.

2. Add a **BindingSource** (default name **bindingSource1**) object and set the **DataSource** property to **dataView1** (look under **Other Data Sources**, then **frmBooks List Instances**). This will give us navigation capabilities for the data view.

3. Since the displayed data will now be taken from the binding source for the data view object (rather than the data set object), we need to change the data bindings on the label controls:

   lblAuthor:
       DataBindings   Text: bindingSource1.Author

   lblTitle:
       DataBindings   Text: bindingSource1.Title

   lblISBN:
       DataBindings   Text: bindingSource1.ISBN

4. In the code window, change all instances of **dataTable1BindingSource** to the new binding source, **bindingSource1**. I found 9 places where this change needs to be made.

5. Modify the code in the **frmBooks Load** procedure (new and/or modified code is shaded). The new code sets up the rolodex buttons (two rows with 13 buttons each - see Example 10-5:

```
private void FrmBooks_Load(object sender, EventArgs e)
{
    int w, 1, 1Start, t;
    int buttonHeight = 35;
    Button[] rolodex = new Button[26];
    // determine button width (do not round up)
    w = (int)(this.ClientRectangle.Width / 14);
    // center the resulting buttons
    1Start = (int)(0.5 * (this.ClientSize.Width - 13 * w));
    1 = 1Start;
    t = this.ClientSize.Height - 3 * buttonHeight;
    // create and position 26 buttons
    for (int i = 0; i < 26; i++)
    {
        // create and position new button
        rolodex[i] = new Button();
        rolodex[i].TabStop = false;
        rolodex[i].Text = ((char)(65 + i)).ToString();
        rolodex[i].Width = w;
        rolodex[i].Height = buttonHeight;
        rolodex[i].Left = 1;
        rolodex[i].Top = t;
        // give cool colors
        rolodex[i].BackColor = Color.Blue;
        rolodex[i].ForeColor = Color.Yellow;
        // add button to form
        this.Controls.Add(rolodex[i]);
        // add event handler
rolodex[i].Click += new
System.EventHandler(this.Rolodex_Click);
        // next left
        1 += w;
        if (i == 12)
        {
            // move to next row
            1 = 1Start;
            t += buttonHeight;
        }
    }
    // TODO: This line of code loads data into the
    'booksDataSet1.DataTable1' table. You can move, or remove
    it, as needed.
```

```
this.dataTable1TableAdapter.Fill(this.booksDataSet1.DataTa
ble1);
  // TODO: This line of code loads data into the
'booksDataSet.Titles' table. You can move, or remove it,
as needed.
   this.titlesTableAdapter.Fill(this.booksDataSet.Titles);
   btnFirst.PerformClick();
}
```

6. Use this code in the **Rolodex_Click** procedure (all new code). In this procedure, we use a **RowFilter** criteria that finds the first occurrence of an author name that begins with the selected letter button

```
private void Rolodex_Click(object sender, EventArgs e)
{
  Button buttonClicked = (Button)sender;
  if (buttonClicked.Text != "Z")
  {
    dataView1.RowFilter = "Author >= '" +
buttonClicked.Text + "' and Author < '" +
((char)((int)Convert.ToChar(buttonClicked.Text) +
1)).ToString() + "'";
  }
  else
  {
    dataView1.RowFilter = "Author >= 'Z'";
  }
  bindingSource1.MoveFirst();
  UpdateTitle();
}
```

Let's look at this code a little closer. The **buttonClicked** is determined, then a **RowFilter** value established based on that button's **Text** property (notice all letters are surrounded by single quotes). As an example, if B is pressed, the **RowFilter** is:

```
dataView1.RowFilter = "Author >= 'B' And Author < 'C'";
```

The resulting data view will only have books with authors whose last name begins with the letter B. Notice the letter Z requires its own filter value since there is no letter after Z.

7. Save your application (saved in **Example 11-3** folder in the **LearnVCS\VCS Code\Class 11** folder). Test its operation. It appears as:

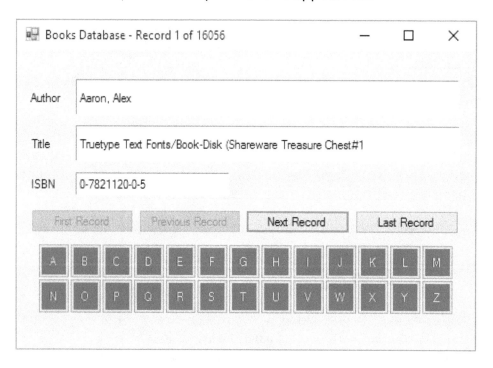

Note, once the program finds the first occurrence of an author name beginning with a selected letter, you can use the navigation buttons to move among the filtered records in the data view. If I click on '**L**', I see:

Complex Data Binding

In previous examples, we have bound a single field value to a single property in a control. This process is known as simple data binding. We can also bind an entire data source (table in a data set or data view) to a control. This process is known as **complex data binding**. We will look briefly at two controls that support complex data binding: the **list box** control and the **data grid view** control.

We have seen the **list box** control before:

In Toolbox:

On Form (Default Properties):

This control provides a list of items a user can choose from. The listed items are part of an **Items** collection.

With complex data binding, the list box **Items** collection can be bound to a particular field in a database table. To do this, follow these steps:

> ➤ Establish a data set or data view object using the procedures outlined in this chapter.
> ➤ Set the list box control **DataSource** property to the appropriate data object.
> ➤ Set the list box control **DisplayMember** property to the desired field to populate the **Items** collection.

As an example, say we have a **DataSet** object (**myDataSet**) for the **Titles** table in **books.accdb**. By setting a list box control's **DataSource** property to **myDataSet** and the **DisplayMember** property to **Titles.Title** (the **Title** field), the list box would the title of every book in the database. Here's what you would see:

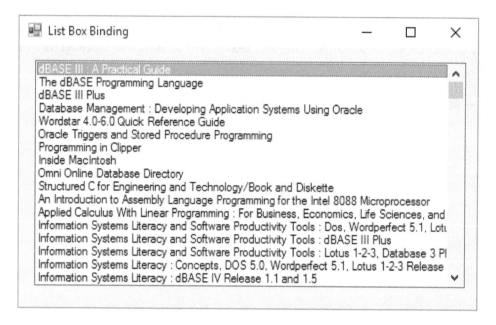

The **data grid view** control is even more powerful. It is found on the **Data** tab in the toolbox:

In Toolbox:

On Form (Default Properties):

This control can display an entire database table (or even a data set generated in code). The table can then be edited as desired.

The **DataGridView** control is in a class by itself, when considering its capabilities. It is essentially a separate, highly functional program. We'll just look at how to use it to display data. Refer to the Visual C# reference material and other sources for complete details on using the **DataGridView** control. To display data in the grid view control, follow these steps:

> ➤ Establish a data set or data view object using the procedures outlined in this chapter.
> ➤ Set the data grid control **DataSource** property to the appropriate data object.
> ➤ Set the data grid control **DataMember** property to the desired table to display.

As an example, say we have a **DataSet** object (**myDataSet**) for the **Titles** table in **books.accdb**. By setting a data grid control's **DataSource** property to **myDataSet** and the **DataMember** property to **Titles**, the data grid will show the entire **Titles** table. Here's what you would see:

Title	Year_Published	ISBN	PubID	Description
dBASE III : A Pra...	1985	0-0038307-6-4	469	22.5
The dBASE Prog...	1986	0-0038326-7-8	469	29.5
dBASE III Plus	1987	0-0038337-8-X	469	29.5
Database Manag...	1989	0-0131985-2-1	715	54
Wordstar 4.0-6.0 ...	1990	0-0133656-1-4	460	14.95
Oracle Triggers a...	1996	0-0134436-3-1	715	0
Programming in C...	1988	0-0201145-8-3	9	0
Inside MacIntosh	1994	0-0201406-7-3	9	99.01
Omni Online Data...	1983	0-0207992-0-9	156	0
Structured C for ...	1995	0-0230081-2-1	715	54

Data Grid View Binding

Web Applications

We all know the Internet has become part of everyday life. A great feature of Visual C# is the idea of web forms. With web forms, we can build applications that run on the Internet – **web applications**. Web applications differ from the Windows applications we have been building. A user (**client**) makes a request of a **server** computer. The server generates a web page (in HTML) and returns it to the client computer so it can be viewed with browser software.

Web applications are built in Visual C# using something called **ASP .NET** (**Active Server Pages .NET**). ASP .NET is an improved version of previous technologies used to build web applications. In the past, to build a dynamic web application, you needed to use a mishmash of programming technologies. Web pages were generated with HTML (yes, the same HTML used in Chapter 10 to write help files) and programming was done with ASP (Active Server Pages) and VB Script (a scripting language based on Visual Basic).

With ASP .NET, the process for building **web applications** is the same process used to build Windows applications. To build a web application, we start with a form, add web controls and write code for web control events. There is a visual project component that shows the controls and a code component with event procedures and general procedures and functions.

Like database applications studied earlier, learning about web applications is a course in itself. In these notes, we introduce the idea of web applications. You can use your new programming skills to delve into more advanced references on ASP .NET and web applications. Here, we cover a few web applications topics:

> ➤ Address the approaches used to build web applications using **web forms**.
> ➤ Discuss the **web form controls** and how they differ from their Windows counterparts.
> ➤ Demonstrate the process of building web applications with some examples.

Before beginning, you may be asking yourself is: if it's so easy to build a Visual C# Windows application and it is easily deployed to a user base, why would I need web applications? That's a good question and the answer is you may never need to build web applications. Let's briefly compare **web applications** and **Windows applications**.

The biggest advantage to a web application is related to deployment and maintenance. A web application can be used by thousands (even millions) of users at once. They merely access your application via their web browser and use it to perform the programmed tasks. When you need to modify or change your application, you only need to change the application on your server and your entire user base will immediately be using the upgraded version. E-commerce systems, on-line reservation systems and on-line data retrieval systems are obvious web applications.

Some browsers limit the performance of web applications. Some web pages may appear differently to different users. This can cause user confusion. Web application performance can be slow depending on network connections. Web applications are not amenable to power graphical programs such as games or CAD (computer-aided design).

If you use Windows applications and need to upgrade your software, a new copy must be sent to each individual user. This means you need to know where all your users are. If you are selling your software as an individual product or need to control who uses your application, this is the route you must take. Fortunately, though, the upgrade procedure can usually be done on the Internet via e-mail or software downloads.

Windows applications will run faster because there is no network connection. Windows applications are great for games. Windows applications can integrate easily with other applications such as word processors, spreadsheets and database management systems.

You need to decide if your planned application is better suited for desktop (Windows) or web deployment. Now, let's look at how to build a web application using Visual C#.

Starting a New Web Application

To start the process of building a web application, you select the **File** menu option in Visual C#. Then, click **New,** then **Project.** This window appears:

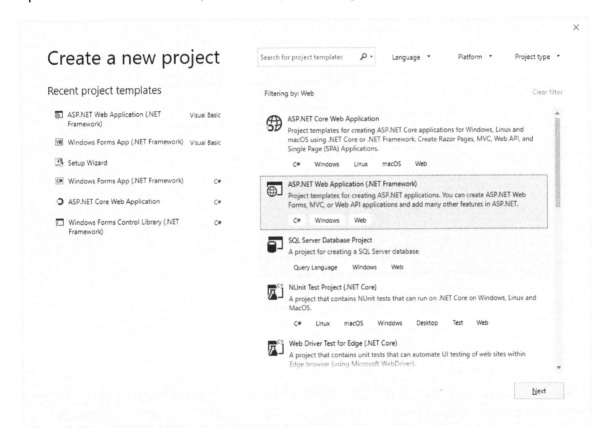

Select **ASP .NET Web Application.** Click **Next.**

This window appears:

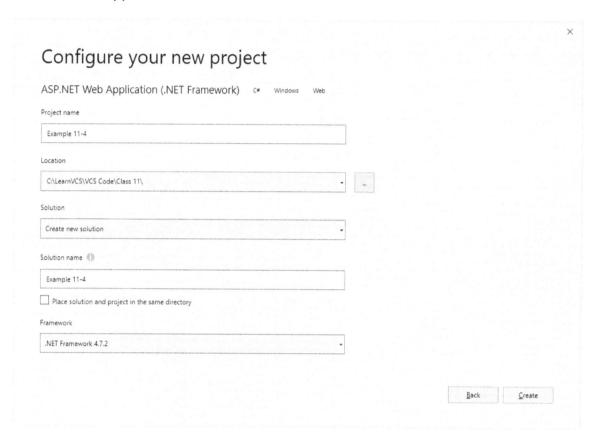

In the drop-down box to the left of the **Browse** button, either select or type the name of a folder to hold your new web site. Make sure the selected **Language** is **Visual C#**. Click **Create** to create the application.

This window appears:

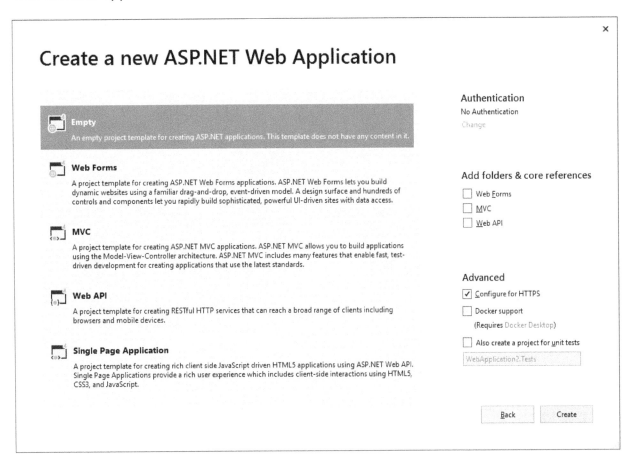

Choose **Empty** and click **Create.**

Once created, right-click the web site name in the **Solution Explorer** window and select **Add**, then **New Item**. Choose **Web**, then **Web Forms** and choose **Web Form**. Click **OK**.

A blank web form appears (with extension **aspx**).

Let's look at some of the files associated with the web site. Your web application is in the **.aspx** file. This is the file your user requests. When a browser requests a **.aspx** file, ASP .NET executes code and presents the web form. The code for a **.aspx** file is in a **.aspx.cs** file. A web application may also have a **Global.asax** and a **Web.config** file. The first has code for event handlers to start and begin the application. The **.config** file stores various configuration settings.

At this point, we can start building our first web application by placing controls on the web form and writing code for various events. A blank form will appear in the design window:

There are two views of the form: **Design** (the graphical display) and **Source** (the HTML code behind the form). Let's look at the controls available and how to place them on the form:

Web Form Controls

When a web form is being edited, the controls available for placing on a web form are found in the Visual C# toolbox. A view showing some of the resulting controls is:

The names in this menu should be familiar. The controls are similar to the Windows form controls we've used throughout this course. There are differences, however. The major differences are in the names of some properties (for example, the **ID** property is used in place of a **Name** property) and web form controls usually have far fewer events than their Windows counterparts. Let's look at some of the controls – feel free to study other controls for your particular needs.

Label Control:

A Label

The label control allows placement of formatted text information on a form (**Text** property). Font is established with the **Font** property.

TextBox Control:

abl TextBox

The text box controls allows placement of text information on a form (**Text** property). This is probably the most commonly used web form control. There is **no** **KeyPress** event for key trapping. Validation with web controls can be done using **validator** controls.

Button Control:

ab Button

The button control is nearly identical to the Windows counterpart. Code is written in the **Click** event.

LinkButton Control:

ab LinkButton

The link button control is clicked to follow a web page hyperlink (set with **Text** property). This is usually used to move to another web page. Code is added to the **Click** event.

ImageButton Control:

ImageButton

This control works like a button control – the user clicks it and code in the **Click** event is executed. The difference is the button displays an image (**ImageURL** property) rather than text.

HyperLink Control:

A HyperLink

The control works like the link button control except there is no Click event. Clicking this control moves the user to the link in the **Text** property.

DropDownList Control:

DropDownList

Drop down list controls are very common in web applications. Users can choose from a list of items (states, countries, product). The listed items are established using an **Items** collection and code is usually written in the **SelectedIndexChanged** event (like the Windows counterpart).

ListBox Control:

ListBox

A list box control is like a drop down list with the list portion always visible. Multiple selections can be made with a list box control.

GridView Control:

GridView

The grid view control is used to list a table of data (whether a data set from a database or data generated in your web application).

CheckBox Control:

CheckBox

The check box control is used to provide a yes or no answer to a question. The **Checked** property indicates its state. Code is usually added to the **CheckedChanged** event.

CheckBoxList Control:

The check box list control contains a series of independent check box controls. It is a useful control for quickly adding a number of check boxes to a form. It can be used in place of a list box control for a small (less than 10) number of items. The individual controls are defined in an **Items** collection (**Text** property specifies the caption, **Selected** specifies its status).

RadioButton Control:

The radio button control is identical to the Windows radio button control. It is used to select from a mutually exclusive group of options. The **Checked** property indicates its state. Code is usually added to the **CheckedChanged** event.

RadioButtonList Control:

The radio button list control provides an easy way to place a group of dependent radio buttons in a web application. The individual controls are defined in an **Items** collection (**Text** property specifies the caption, **Selected** specifies its status).

Image Control:

Images are useful in web applications. They give your application a polished look. The image control holds graphics. The image (set with **ImageURL** property) is usually a gif or jpg file.

By default, web controls are placed on the form in **flow mode**. This means each element is placed to the right of the previous element. This is different than the technique used in building Windows forms. We want to mimic the Windows forms behavior. To do this, choose the **Tools** menu option in the development environment and choose **Options.**

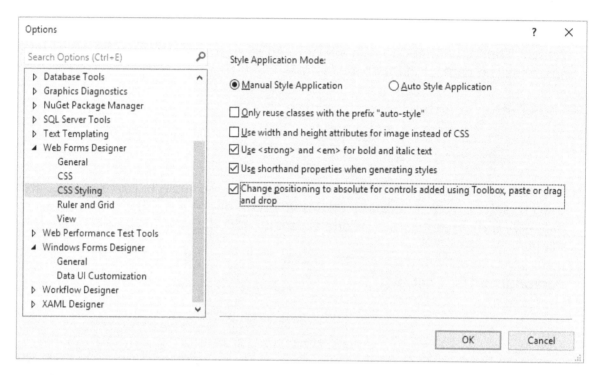

Choose the **HTML Designer** and **CSS Styling**. Place check next to "**Change position to absolute for controls …**". Then click **OK.**

With this change, there are two ways to move a web control from the toolbox to the web form:

Click the tool in the toolbox and hold the mouse button down. Drag the selected tool over the form. When the mouse button is released, the default size control will appear in the upper left corner of the form. This is the classic "drag and drop" operation. For a button control, we would see:

Double-click the tool in the toolbox and it is created with a default size on the form. It will be in the upper left corner of the form. You can then move it or resize it. Here is a button control placed on the form using this method:

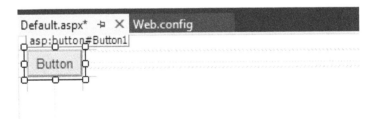

To **move** a control you have drawn, click the object in the form (a cross with arrows will appear). Now, drag the control to the new location. Release the mouse button.

To **resize** a control, click the control so that it is selected (active) and sizing handles appear. Use these handles to resize the object.

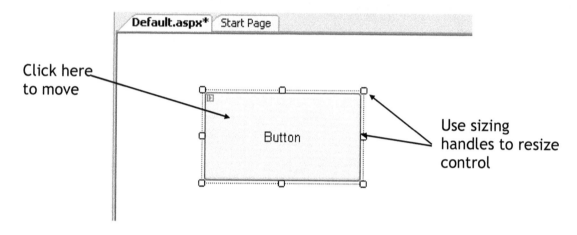

To delete a control, select that control so it is active (sizing handles will appear). Then, press **<Delete>** on the keyboard. Or, right-click the control. A menu will appear. Choose the **Delete** option. You can change your mind immediately after deleting a control by choosing the **Undo** option under the **Edit** menu.

Building a Web Application

To build a web application, we follow the same three steps used in building a Windows application:

1. **Draw** the user **interface** by placing controls on a web form
2. **Assign properties** to controls
3. **Write code** for control events (and perhaps write other procedures)

We've seen the web controls and how to place them on the web form. Let's see how to write code. You'll see the process is analogous to the approach we use for Windows applications.

Code is placed in the **Code Window**. Typing code in the code window is just like using any word processor. You can cut, copy, paste and delete text (use the **Edit** menu or the toolbar). You access the code window using the menu (**View**), toolbar, or by pressing <**F7**> (and there are still other ways – try double clicking a control) while the form is active. Here is the Code window for a 'blank' web application:

```
Default.aspx.cs  ╤ ✕  Default.aspx
⊕ Junk3                        ▾  ⁴⃰ _Default                   ▾  ⊕. Page_Load(object :
   1 ⃰  ⊟using System;
   2    │ using System.Collections.Generic;
   3    │ using System.Linq;
   4    │ using System.Web;
   5    │ using System.Web.UI;
   6    └ using System.Web.UI.WebControls;
   7
   8    ⊟public partial class _Default : System.Web.UI.Page
   9    │ {
  10    ⊟    protected void Page_Load(object sender, EventArgs e)
  11    │     {
  12    │
  13    │     }
  14    └ }
```

The header begins with **public partial class**. Any web form scope level declarations are placed after the bracket following this line. There is a **Page_Load** event. This is similar to the Windows form **Load** event where any needed initializations are placed.

Like in Windows applications, the box on the top, right of the code window is the **method list**, showing all methods in the code window. Double-clicking the control of interest will access default event methods. Or, events can be defined using the properties window. This is the same as we saw for Windows applications. That's the beauty of web forms – there is little new to learn about building an application.

One difference between web applications and Windows applications concerns form level variables. Such variables are declared in the same area (outside any method), but each variable declaration needs to be proceeded by the keyword static. This insures the variables maintain their values. Examples of such declarations are:

```
static int a;
static string myString;
static double[] myArray = new double[20];
```

Once your controls are in place and code is written, you can run your web application. Before running, it is a good idea to make sure your browser is up and running. Click the **Start** button in the Visual C# toolbar and your browser should display your application (the **aspx** file). You may see this window once started:

Special steps need to be taken to use the debugger with web applications. We will not take these steps. So, if this window appears, just select **Run without debugging** and click **OK**. Once running in the browser, select the **View** menu and choose **View Source** to see the actual HTML code used to produce the displayed web page.

We conclude this brief examination of web applications with a couple of examples. Study the examples for further tips on using the new ASP .NET paradigm.

Example 11-4

Loan Payments

1. The two lines of Visual C# code that compute the monthly payment on an installment loan are:

```
multiplier = (double) (Math.Pow((1 + interest / 1200),
months));
payment = loan * interest * multiplier / (1200 *
(multiplier - 1));
```

where (all **double** types):

interest   Yearly interest percentage
months   Number of months of payments
loan   Loan amount
multiplier   Interest multiplier
payment   Computed monthly payment

(The 1200 value in these equations converts yearly interest to a monthly rate.) Use this code to build a general method that computes **payment**, given the other three variables. Yes, this is like **Problem 10-3**!

2. Start a new web application. Place four label controls, four text box controls and a button control on the web form. It should look like this:

3. Set the following properties:

Label1:

Font Name	Arial
Font Size	Small
Text	Loan Amount

Label2:

Font Name	Arial
Font Size	Small
Text	Yearly Interest

Label3:

Font Name	Arial
Font Size	Small
Text	Number of Months

Label4:

Font Name	Arial
Font Size	Small
Text	Monthly Payment

TextBox1:

ID	txtLoan
Font Name	Arial
Font Size	Small

TextBox2:

ID	txtInterest
Font Name	Arial
Font Size	Small

TextBox3:

ID	txtMonths
Font Name	Arial
Font Size	Small

TextBox4:

ID	txtPayment
Font Name	Arial
Font Size	Small
ReadOnly	True

Button1:

ID	btnCompute
Text	Compute Payment

My finished web form looks like this:

4. Use this code in the **btnCompute Click** event:

```csharp
private void BtnCompute_Click(object sender, EventArgs e)
{
  // Define 4 major variables
  double loanAmount;
  double interest;
  int months;
  double paymentAmount;
  // Read text box inputs
  loanAmount = Convert.ToDouble(txtLoan.Text);
  interest = Convert.ToDouble(txtInterest.Text);
  months = Convert.ToInt32(txtMonths.Text);
  paymentAmount = LoanPayment(loanAmount, interest,
months);
  if (paymentAmount < 0)
  {
    return;
  }
  // Display payment
  txtPayment.Text = String.Format("{0:f2}",
paymentAmount);
  // Redefine payment to two decimals
  paymentAmount = Convert.ToDouble(txtPayment.Text);
}
```

5. Add this **LoanPayment** general method to compute the payment given the other parameters:

```csharp
private double LoanPayment(double loan, double interest,
int months)
{
  // Compute loan payment function
  double multiplier;
  if (months == 0)
  {
    return (-1); // set negative value for error flag
  }
  if (interest != 0)
  {
    multiplier = (double) (Math.Pow((1 + interest / 1200),
months));
    return (loan * interest * multiplier / (1200 *
(multiplier - 1)));
  }
  else
  {
    return (loan / months);
  }
}
```

6. Save your web application. (This application is saved in the **Example 11-4** folder in the **LearnVCS\VCS Code\Class 11** folder). At this point, if things all work well, you can click the **Start** button (remember to run without debugging) and see your first web application appear in your default browser. Input some values and click **Compute Payment**. Here's a sample from my browser:

Pretty neat, huh?

<u>Example 11-5</u>

Loan Repayment Schedule

1. In this example, we will modify the **Loan Payment** example. After a payment is computed, we will display a repayment schedule for the loan. The display will show a month-by-month accounting of the declining balance, as the loan is paid. We will show how much of each payment goes toward principal and how much toward interest. The repayment schedule will be displayed in a data grid control (briefly mentioned when discussing database applications). Open **Example 11-4** and add a GridView control at the bottom of the form. Set these properties:

GridView1:
```
     ID              grdPayment
     Visible         False
```

My finished web form now looks like this:

2. Modify the **btnCompute Click** method to fill the grid (new code is shaded):

```
private void BtnCompute_Click(object sender, EventArgs e)
{
  // Define 4 major variables
  double loanAmount;
  double interest;
  int months;
  double paymentAmount;
  // Read text box inputs
  loanAmount = Convert.ToDouble(txtLoan.Text);
  interest = Convert.ToDouble(txtInterest.Text);
  months = Convert.ToInt32(txtMonths.Text);
  paymentAmount = LoanPayment(loanAmount, interest,
months);
  if (paymentAmount < 0)
  {
    return;
  }
  // Display payment
  txtPayment.Text = String.Format("{0:f2}",
paymentAmount);
  // Redefine payment to two decimals
  paymentAmount = Convert.ToDouble(txtPayment.Text);
  FillGrid(loanAmount, interest, months, paymentAmount);
}
```

3. Create a general method named **FillGrid** to place data in the grid control. Use this code:

```csharp
private void FillGrid(double loanAmount, double interest,
int months, double paymentAmount)
{
  int monthNumber;
  double balance, p, i;
  // create data table and row objects
  System.Data.DataTable myPayments;
  System.Data.DataRow myRow;
  // Create  data table
  myPayments = new System.Data.DataTable();
  // create columns
  myPayments.Columns.Add(new
System.Data.DataColumn("Month",
System.Type.GetType("System.String")));
  myPayments.Columns.Add(new
System.Data.DataColumn("Payment",
System.Type.GetType("System.String")));
  myPayments.Columns.Add(new
System.Data.DataColumn("Principal",
System.Type.GetType("System.String")));
  myPayments.Columns.Add(new
System.Data.DataColumn("Interest",
System.Type.GetType("System.String")));
  myPayments.Columns.Add(new
System.Data.DataColumn("Balance",
System.Type.GetType("System.String")));
  // This assumes payment has been computed
  monthNumber = 1; // month number
  balance = loanAmount;
  do
  {
    // Find interest
    i = interest * balance / 1200;
    // Round to two decimals
    i = Convert.ToDouble(String.Format("{0:f2}", i));
    // Compute principal and balance
    if (monthNumber != months)
    {
      p = paymentAmount - i;
      balance -= p;
    }
    else
    {
      // Adjust last payment to payoff balance
```

```
      paymentAmount = balance + i;
      p = balance;
      balance = 0;
    }
    // Create new row
    myRow = myPayments.NewRow();
    myRow[0] = monthNumber;
    myRow[1] = String.Format("{0:f2}", paymentAmount);
    myRow[2] = String.Format("{0:f2}", p);
    myRow[3] = String.Format("{0:f2}", i);
    myRow[4] = String.Format("{0:f2}", balance);
    myPayments.Rows.Add(myRow);
    monthNumber++;
  }
  while (monthNumber <= months);
  // bind data table to grid
  grdPayment.Visible = true;
  grdPayment.DataSource = new
System.Data.DataView(myPayments);
  grdPayment.DataBind();
}
```

4. Save and run the application. (This application is saved in the **Example 11-5** folder in the **LearnVCS\VCS Code\Class 11** folder). Input some values and click **Compute Payment**. The data grid should be filled with the repayment information. With the example numbers from before, my browser shows:

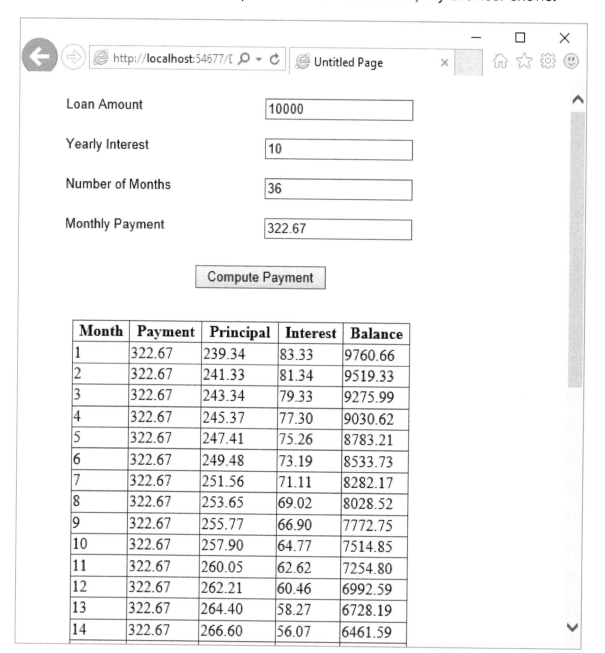

Month	Payment	Principal	Interest	Balance
1	322.67	239.34	83.33	9760.66
2	322.67	241.33	81.34	9519.33
3	322.67	243.34	79.33	9275.99
4	322.67	245.37	77.30	9030.62
5	322.67	247.41	75.26	8783.21
6	322.67	249.48	73.19	8533.73
7	322.67	251.56	71.11	8282.17
8	322.67	253.65	69.02	8028.52
9	322.67	255.77	66.90	7772.75
10	322.67	257.90	64.77	7514.85
11	322.67	260.05	62.62	7254.80
12	322.67	262.21	60.46	6992.59
13	322.67	264.40	58.27	6728.19
14	322.67	266.60	56.07	6461.59

In the browser window above the table:

Loan Amount: 10000
Yearly Interest: 10
Number of Months: 36
Monthly Payment: 322.67
Compute Payment

Class Review

After completing this class, you should understand:

> - The basic structure of a relational database
> - How to use the DataSet object to connect to an Access type database
> - How to form simple SQL statements to view database tables
> - The concepts of simple and complex data binding
> - How to use the DataView object to obtain a filtered view of a DataSet object
> - The basics of Web applications
> - The three steps to build a web application using a web form
> - How to use the web form controls

Course Summary

That's all I know about Visual C#. But, I'm still learning, as is every Visual C# programmer out there. The new environment is vast! You should now have a good breadth of knowledge concerning the Visual C# environment and language, especially regarding Windows applications. This breadth should serve as a springboard into learning more as you develop your own applications. Feel free to email us at feedback@kidwaresoftware.com and let us know what you liked or disliked about the course. We are always looking for ways to improve this course so your feedback is always welcome.

Where do you go from here? In this course, we only took brief glimpses at web applications and database applications. If the Internet is your world, you should definitely extend your knowledge regarding Web applications. And, if you're into databases, study more on how to build database management systems (look for our **Visual C# and Databases** course in the future).

Other suggestions for further study (note that each of these topics could be a complete book by itself):

> Advanced graphics methods (including game type graphics)
> Creating and deployment of your own Windows form controls
> Creating and deployment of your own objects
> Understanding and using object-oriented concepts of overloading, inheritance, multithreading
> Advanced data access concepts, including XML (extended markup language) usage
> Creating and deployment of your own web form controls
> Database access with web applications

And, the last example:

Practice Problems 11

Problem 11-1. New DataView Problem. Modify the books database example (Example 11-3) to allow searching by title (you'll need to resort the data view object on title, as well as author).

Problem 11-2. Multiple Authors Problem. Modify the books database example (Example 11-3) such that when an author search is performed, all authors with names beginning with the searched letter are placed in a separate list box control. When the user clicks on a listed author, have the corresponding record appear.

Problem 11-3. Stopwatch Problem. Build a web application that functions as a stopwatch. Refer way back to Example 1-3.

Exercise 11

The Ultimate Application

Design a Windows or Web application using Visual C# that everyone on the planet wants to buy. Place controls, assign properties, and write code. Thoroughly debug and test your application. Create a distribution and deployment package. Find a distributor or distribute it yourself through your newly created company. Become fabulously wealthy. Remember those who made it all possible by rewarding them with jobs and stock options.

More Self-Study or Instructor-Led Computer Programming Tutorials by Kidware Software

ORACLE JAVA PROGRAMMING TUTORIALS

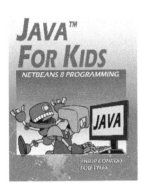

Java™ For Kids is a beginning programming tutorial consisting of 10 chapters explaining (in simple, easy-to-follow terms) how to build a Java application. Students learn about project design, object-oriented programming, console applications, graphics applications and many elements of the Java language. Numerous examples are used to demonstrate every step in the building process. The projects include a number guessing game, a card game, an allowance calculator, a state capitals game, Tic-Tac-Toe, a simple drawing program, and even a basic video game. Designed for kids ages 12 and up.

Beginning Java™ is a semester long "beginning" programming tutorial consisting of 10 chapters explaining (in simple, easy-to-follow terms) how to build a Java application. The tutorial includes several detailed computer projects for students to build and try. These projects include a number guessing game, card game, allowance calculator, drawing program, state capitals game, and a couple of video games like Pong. We also include several college prep bonus projects including a loan calculator, portfolio manager, and checkbook balancer. Designed for students age 15 and up.

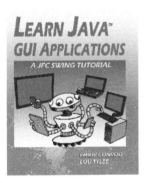

Learn Java™ GUI Applications is a 9 lesson Tutorial covering object-oriented programming concepts, using an integrated development environment to create and test Java projects, building and distributing GUI applications, understanding and using the Swing control library, exception handling, sequential file access, graphics, multimedia, advanced topics such as printing, and help system authoring. Our Beginning Java or Java For Kids tutorial is a pre-requisite for this tutorial

Programming Games with Java™ is a semester long "intermediate" programming tutorial consisting of 10 chapters explaining (in simple, easy-to-follow terms) how to build a Visual C# Video Games. The games built are non-violent, family-friendly and teach logical thinking skills. Students will learn how to program the following Visual C# video games: Safecracker, Tic Tac Toe, Match Game, Pizza Delivery, and Moon Landing. This intermediate level self-paced tutorial can be used at home or school. The tutorial is simple enough for kids yet engaging enough for beginning adults. Our Learn Java GUI Applications tutorial is a required pre-requisite for this tutorial.

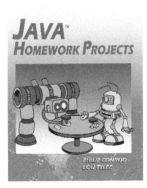

Java™ Homework Projects is a Java GUI Swing tutorial covering object-oriented programming concepts. It explains (in simple, easy-to-follow terms) how to build Java GUI project to use around the home. Students learn about project design, the Java Swing controls, many elements of the Java language, and how to distribute finished projects. The projects built include a Dual-Mode Stopwatch, Flash Card Math Quiz, Multiple Choice Exam, Blackjack Card Game, Weight Monitor, Home Inventory Manager and a Snowball Toss Game. Our Learn Java GUI Applications tutorial is a pre-requisite for this tutorial

MICROSOFT SMALL BASIC PROGRAMMING TUTORIALS

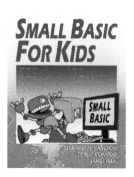

Small Basic For Kids is an illustrated introduction to computer programming that provides an interactive, self-paced tutorial to the new Small Basic programming environment. The book consists of 30 short lessons that explain how to create and run a Small Basic program. Elementary students learn about program design and many elements of the Small Basic language. Numerous examples are used to demonstrate every step in the building process. The tutorial also includes two complete games (Hangman and Pizza Zapper) for students to build and try. Designed for kids ages 8+.

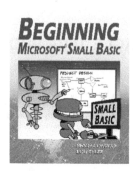

The Beginning Microsoft Small Basic Programming Tutorial is a self-study first semester "beginner" programming tutorial consisting of 11 chapters explaining (in simple, easy-to-follow terms) how to write Microsoft Small Basic programs. Numerous examples are used to demonstrate every step in the building process. The last chapter of this tutorial shows you how four different Small Basic games could port to Visual Basic, Visual C# and Java. This beginning level self-paced tutorial can be used at home or at school. The tutorial is simple enough for kids ages 10+ yet engaging enough for adults.

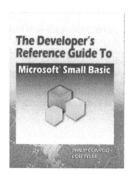

Basic Computer Games - Small Basic Edition is a re-make of the classic BASIC COMPUTER GAMES book originally edited by David H. Ahl. It contains 100 of the original text based BASIC games that inspired a whole generation of programmers. Now these classic BASIC games have been re-written in Microsoft Small Basic for a new generation to enjoy! The new Small Basic games look and act like the original text based games. The book includes all the original spaghetti code and GOTO commands!

Programming Home Projects with Microsoft Small Basic is a self-paced programming tutorial explains (in simple, easy-to-follow terms) how to build Small Basic Windows applications. Students learn about program design, Small Basic objects, many elements of the Small Basic language, and how to debug and distribute finished programs. Sequential file input and output is also introduced. The projects built include a Dual-Mode Stopwatch, Flash Card Math Quiz, Multiple Choice Exam, Blackjack Card Game, Weight Monitor, Home Inventory Manager and a Snowball Toss Game.

The Developer's Reference Guide to Microsoft Small Basic While developing all the different Microsoft Small Basic tutorials we found it necessary to write The Developer's Reference Guide to Microsoft Small Basic. The Developer's Reference Guide to Microsoft Small Basic is over 500 pages long and includes over 100 Small Basic programming examples for you to learn from and include in your own Microsoft Small Basic programs. It is a detailed reference guide for new developers.

David Ahl's Small Basic Computer Adventures is a Microsoft Small Basic re-make of the classic Basic Computer Games programming book originally written by David H. Ahl. This new book includes the following classic adventure simulations; Marco Polo, Westward Ho!, The Longest Automobile Race, The Orient Express, Amelia Earhart: Around the World Flight, Tour de France, Subway Scavenger, Hong Kong Hustle, and Voyage to Neptune. Learn how to program these classic computer simulations in Microsoft Small Basic.

MICROSOFT VISUAL BASIC & VISUAL C# PROGRAMMING TUTORIALS

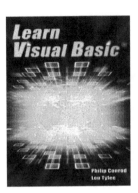

LEARN VISUAL BASIC is a comprehensive college level programming tutorial covering object-oriented programming, the Visual Basic integrated development environment, building and distributing Windows applications using the Windows Installer, exception handling, sequential file access, graphics, multimedia, advanced topics such as web access, printing, and HTML help system authoring. The tutorial also introduces database applications (using ADO .NET) and web applications (using ASP.NET).

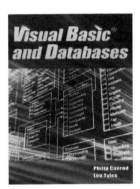

VISUAL BASIC AND DATABASES is a tutorial that provides a detailed introduction to using Visual Basic for accessing and maintaining databases for desktop applications. Topics covered include: database structure, database design, Visual Basic project building, ADO .NET data objects (connection, data adapter, command, data table), data bound controls, proper interface design, structured query language (SQL), creating databases using Access, SQL Server and ADOX, and database reports. Actual projects developed include a book tracking system, a sales invoicing program, a home inventory system and a daily weather monitor.

LEARN VISUAL C# is a comprehensive college level computer programming tutorial covering object-oriented programming, the Visual C# integrated development environment and toolbox, building and distributing Windows applications (using the Windows Installer), exception handling, sequential file input and output, graphics, multimedia effects (animation and sounds), advanced topics such as web access, printing, and HTML help system authoring. The tutorial also introduces database applications (using ADO .NET) and web applications (using ASP.NET).

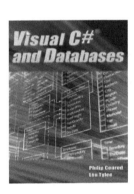

VISUAL C# AND DATABASES is a tutorial that provides a detailed introduction to using Visual C# for accessing and maintaining databases for desktop applications. Topics covered include: database structure, database design, Visual C# project building, ADO .NET data objects (connection, data adapter, command, data table), data bound controls, proper interface design, structured query language (SQL), creating databases using Access, SQL Server and ADOX, and database reports. Actual projects developed include a book tracking system, a sales invoicing program, a home inventory system and a daily weather monitor.

CPSIA information can be obtained
at www.ICGtesting.com
Printed in the USA
LVHW011020040921
696369LV00005B/24

9 781951 07